Dedication

To Antoinette with all my love always and all ways. You are everyone and everything to me.

Precis

Strange things continue to happen in the Coleman household. If anything unusual can happen then it will. The sixth volume of Vernon Coleman's diary contains an unbelievable but true saga of what happened when V&A tried to sell their Parisian apartment and (thanks to the absurd laws which control French property sales) were forced to accept a buyer who couldn't afford to buy it and didn't even have the money for the deposit. You'll read why Vernon paid £2,500 to have the grass cut and sold a car for very little more than half price. Plus Vernon explains why we should declare war on the EU and precisely why we would win in a matter of days. He also explains how and why he thinks everyone would benefit if the McCanns were taken to court. All predictions made in the book have been left as they were written on the day – even if they now look stupid.

The Author

Although he has a medical degree, Vernon Coleman has earned his living solely with his pen for 40 years. The pen has now worn out and the author isn't in much better condition.

Coleman has been described as the king of conspiracy theorists (*Talk Radio*), the king of media docs (*Independent*) and the king of the self-publishers (*Daily Telegraph*). That makes him three kings, but he isn't stuck up about it.

On the other hand, he was described by a despairing (and former) literary agent as a prophet crying in the wilderness but he doesn't talk much about that.

'All progress depends upon the unreasonable man,' wrote George Bernard Shaw. And so, once again, the curmudgeon awakes.

Note

All the errors, literals, grammatical cock-ups, blots, crumpled pages, misspellings, msitakes, scruffy covers, weak bindings and remains of little sticky labels disfiguring the cover are entirely my fault and my responsibility. (There are 183.5 of them altogether. The half is arguable.)

Antoinette, who understands the magic of these things, removes the most egregious errors and turns these books into kindle-friendly volumes but I insist on leaving errors scattered around in order to give the diary a natural flavour, a freshness and matchless literary verisimilitude. A garden without weeds has as much soul and spirit as a municipal clock or one of those traffic islands covered in bushes. These little idiosyncrasies are not unique. James Agate managed to refer to Johnson's Boswell and to the Wimpoles of Barratt Street. And the book *Dew on the Grass* by Eiluned Lewis, went through eight editions containing a reference to the Twelve Commandments. In January 1935, *The Times* court pages carried an advance notice of an upper class entertainment which read: 'Miss X will sin and a number of well-known young girls will take part'. And Agate himself once wrote a review of an actress's performance which included the words 'she was mistress of herself, the situation and everybody in the audience'.

If you find any of the questionable artefacts within my insubstantial pageant, you can give yourself a pat on the back. The more you find the prouder you should feel. (Though, if you find things like crumpled pages I am very impressed since this book is only available as an ebook.)

But please do not share your secret discoveries with anyone else. These secrets are best kept tucked away in some deep, dark, special place.

Foreword

Why write a diary? Well, I'm a writer. It's what I do and the stuff all builds up inside my head if I don't write it down. After a while, the inside of my skull gets clogged and feels uncomfortable. I feel better when the gubbins and the flapdoodle are all out in the open. Plus, writing down the bad stuff is truly cathartic. I feel better when I have written about some of the awful things that happen. I'm absolutely certain other people have worse things happen to them – and doubtless funnier things too. But I have to work with the things that have happened to us. To be honest, it's a joy to share the stuff that has happened in the past year – you're welcome to it. Much of it may be no more than adscititious persiflage. But it's my adscititious persiflage. (And the rest is shamelessly wanton and picayune.)

Of course, some people will object that there are bits and pieces about politics, news and medicine in the diary.

'A diary should be all about where you go and the people you meet,' they will say snootily. 'What did you order for lunch? Who was at the next table? Did you see anyone famous?'

'Well, bugger all that,' I will say in response.

I have no interest in writing (or reading) a diary which sounds like an appointments book. I'm not interested in recording what I had for breakfast or who I met for lunch (unless they said or did something exceptionally interesting). Someone else can hear all about Mr Cowell, Mr Morgan and the rest of them. Someone else can write about solemn stillness.

I include stuff about politics et al because these are things which affect me physically, mentally and spiritually. The book would be a lot shorter (and take far less time to put together) if I left these entries out but it wouldn't really be my diary of the year. (It would probably also receive much better reviews.)

Most of this diary is, like the five which preceded it, a record of things that happened in one particular year, how those things appeared to me and how they affected Antoinette and me. I cannot explain how things affect other people as well as I can explain how they affect my wife and me. Readers who have seen the previous five diaries will doubtless notice certain themes developing in my life.

Some people will doubtless object that there is too much about me in the book. Ah, well, that's a bit of a problem. It's my diary. And it must, therefore, be largely about me. I'm sorry about that. The truth is that I am not someone who enjoys being centre stage. (If I were, then I would still be appearing on television and radio and I would have accounts with Facebook, Twitter and other aspects of social media.) But I would find it difficult to write a diary about someone else – unless it was fictional. (Funnily enough, I did help one of my cats write two diaries. There is no

6

little irony in the fact that Alice's diaries have sold far, far more copies than this series of diaries; probably a hundred times as many. There's a lesson there somewhere but I'm not sure I'm brave enough to look for it.)

I also know some people take a peep at one of my diaries and become incensed at the fact that I have dared to say frankly what I feel.

Others complain that publishing a diary is self-indulgent. Well, maybe it is. And maybe, just maybe, it's a useful record of the days we are living through. There are not, after all, all that many honest diaries published these days. Most of the ones I've seen seem designed to glorify the writer or his mates.

And maybe, just maybe, our experiences of life might help some readers deal with their own bizarre and unwelcome experiences.

And, as I have already pointed out, writing is what I do for a living. I worked out this morning that I have, over the years, written over 21 million words which have been published. (It may be a little more and it may be a little less. It's within 5% of the 21 million. I'm not going to spend the next year counting every word I've written just to get it exactly right.) That total doesn't include television and radio scripts or web articles or articles or books which haven't been published. (Though to be honest, like all professional writers, most of the stuff I have written has ended up in print because anything which doesn't get used gets recycled.) Books take up just under half of that total – the rest is made up of newspaper and magazine articles and columns. I've written weekly columns for six national newspapers, several syndicated columns for local newspapers and columns for numerous magazines.

This probably explains why my fingers and brain are tired.

I try not to think too much about editing out the stuff that will probably result in one of those one star reviews which will kill a book. And I always put down what I really think about something rather than what I think I should think, or what other people might prefer me to think. Some of the entries are quite short. Some are longer. That's just the way things worked out. Some come at a tangent, because that is how my brain worked that day.

And (this is perhaps a little grandiose) I think that I am probably not alone in thinking some of the stuff in this book. Moreover, the chances are that if I don't put it down then no one else will. Editors everywhere are terrified of being accused of being politically incorrect. One result is that *Fortune* magazine is for ever running lists of powerful women (is there anything more patronising, demeaning and sexist than a list of the world's most powerful women?) and British television programmes now include *Loose Women* and *Women's Hour* when any suggestion of broadcasting *Loose Men* or *Men's Hour* would result in a mass attack of the vapours. (I would love to hack into the *Fortune* website and announce that they were producing a list of the 'Top 100 Businesswomen Who Look Really Good in Short Skirts and Low Cut Tops'. No more patronising than any of their own silly lists.)

There are many subjects which are now pretty well forbidden for writers and broadcasters. It is impossible to debate climate change, vaccination, the significance of iatrogenesis, racism against the English, ageism and the cultural threat posed by unlimited immigration. No one dares write about the EU being a Nazi plot. These are subjects which are considered too scary and too threatening and so they are suppressed. Fake news in the classroom is a major problem and the trouble is that most of the fake news is official (relating to the EU, vaccination, climate change and so on).

And so, when it comes down to it, that is another reason for this series of diaries: to tell the truth about things which no one else will talk about; to put those truths on the record so that those who share my views won't feel quite so alone.

I have also included pieces describing my almost daily battles with bureaucracy, banks and so on, in the hope that readers, who have probably been exposed to the same annoyances, can share my frustration. You know what they ought to say: a frustration shared is a frustration laughed about. Reading through the diary, I see, once again, that I am overly independent, stubborn, impatient and sensitive to the point of touchiness. I hate bullies and oppressors of all kinds. And I hate being taken for a fool. Hey-ho. It's probably too late to change.

To me a personal diary should include more than just a series of 'On Tuesday I had lunch with Nubar Gulbenkian', 'On Wednesday I had dinner with Basil Zacharov' and; 'On Thursday I stayed in and washed my hair.'

Would I write this if no one ever read it?

Samuel Pepys never intended his diary to be read by anyone. Would an actor still act if there were no audience? Some painters certainly paint without any intention of showing their work. People make sand sculptures knowing that the next tide will wash them away. Poets write on cigarette papers and then burn them or throw them to the wind. Would I write this if it wasn't intended for publication? Honestly? I don't know.

So, without further ado, this is my history of the world for 2017: complete with violations, exploitations, regrets, indignities, betrayals, humiliations, boredom, abuses, insecurities, fears, joys, hopes, failures annoyances and frustrations. Oh, my heaven, the annoyances and the frustrations. Bad people of all kinds (Nazis, eurocrats, Blair, almost everyone working for the BBC, *The Guardian* or the *Financial Times*,) have always endeavoured to manipulate public opinion through fear, rumours, terrifying incidents, scandals, lies and propaganda (described by Eric Ambler, the first and still the best real spy writer, as political sabotage). Today all this is dismissed as spin, as though it were harmless. But it is more important than that.

I know I cannot compete with the propagandists, such as the BBC. They have the big audiences, the money and therefore the power. But I can try. I do what I can. And, as they say, the truth will set you free. Not yet, maybe. But eventually, perhaps.

It has, it seems, been another bloody year. The French tried to fuck us over. No, that's wrong. They did fuck us over. I am convinced they hate the English more than ever now that we have voted to leave the European Union. (Many ignorant French people still believe that the EU was their idea.) We had numerous battles with large organisations (the phone company, a bank, etc.). Oh and I nearly died.

Finally, I do apologise if anything herein is offensive. That is not my intention. There are probably more than a thousand viewpoints in this book and none is included as gratuitously offensive. They're just there because they explain how I feel about things. It is, I know, the fashion these days for readers to condemn a book if they find one thing with which they disagree. Indeed, it is now illegal to hold and express certain ideas and beliefs. However, those readers who have survived this series of diaries are, I know, patient and broad-minded enough to accept that the world would be a strange place if we all agreed with everything someone else said or wrote. And my apologies to the kind, patient and ever-supportive American readers who stick with me despite the inevitably parochial aspect of many of these entries which deal with British and European matters.

And, finally, finally, I would like to thank the kind readers, mostly from the UK and America, who have reviewed the previous diaries so generously. In a way, I think of the reviews, both good and bad, as being part of the book. I once saw a television programme in which the artist David Hockney was describing how his joiner photographs worked. Sadly, a chemist who was developing one of the rolls of film Hockney had taken, made some sort of mistake in the laboratory and when Hockney received his pictures there was also a note from the chemist, apologising and explaining what had happened. Instead of getting excited, Hockney merely pinned the note into the sequence of photographs, taking its place where the missing pictures should have been. The note became part of the work of art. Similarly, maybe the reviews should become part of the book.

Vernon Coleman
Devon, Gloucestershire and Paris

January

1

It is fashionable to make lists of things one hopes to do with the rest of one's life. Jack Nicholson and Morgan Freeman made an excellent film called *The Bucket List*. I've turned the premise on its head. Here is a bucket list of things I don't want to do or, in the case of the ones I've done, don't want to do again:

Take an examination
Go to a funeral
Go anywhere in an aeroplane
Go on a cruise that lasts more than an hour
Eat in a restaurant where there is a wine list
Play any team sport
Take any drug stronger than aspirin
Eat anything derived from an animal
Go to London
Sleep in a tent
Drive a car with a manual gearbox
Move house

2

When I was four or five-years-old my parents used to visit an elderly relative who lived in one of a row of Alms Houses in Aldridge, then in Staffordshire. (It is probably now in Romania or Western France.) Naturally, I went with them. I knew her as Aunt Hannah but she was actually my great, great aunt and at the time she was in her mid 80s. (The Alms Houses, which had been there for donkeys' years seem to have disappeared without trace and have probably been knocked down and turned into a supermarket and mobile phone mast repository.)

I remember being puzzled by the fact that my parents had to give Aunt Hannah at least two weeks' notice of any intended visit. She had no telephone, of course, and so the arrangements would be fixed through the mail.

At the time, I could not understand why everything had to be planned beforehand. Aunt Hannah didn't ever go anywhere except to church on Sunday mornings. Why, I wondered, couldn't we just turn up and surprise her.

Now, thinking about it, I understand.

As Antoinette pointed out, she wanted to be properly prepared for our visit. She had respect for us and for herself. She wanted to bake a cake and make sure that she had in stocks of tea for my parents and lemon barley water for me. She wanted to make sure that her home was immaculate and that she had on a nice frock and had had time to brush her hair.

And she did not want to find herself being rushed and hurried. She did not like alarms, surprises or sudden excitements.

In all these respects I have become my great, great aunt.

3

The Liverpool Care Pathway (a murderers' charter, which allows doctors and nurses to withhold food, water and essential treatment from patients who are over 65 and who are, therefore, regarded as an expensive nuisance) is being replaced by something called Sustainable Development Goals (which originated with the United Nations).

Sustainable Development Goals allows the NHS to discriminate against anyone over the age of 70 on the grounds that people who die when they are over 70 cannot be said to have died 'prematurely' and so will not count when the nation's healthcare is being assessed.

The Government loves this new rule because it gives the State permission to get rid of citizens who are of pensionable age and, therefore, regarded by society's accountants as a 'burden'.

It is hardly surprising, I suppose, that this officially sponsored disdain for the elderly has trickled through into our courts. If you mug a 40-year-old you are likely to go to prison for a good length of time. But if you mug and kill an 80-year-old you will be unlucky if you go to prison for more than a few months. The lives of the elderly do not count for much. Indeed, you could be forgiven for assuming that the killing of the elderly was regarded as a socially responsible thing to do. How much longer before those who kill old folk are given a knighthood and a free flat in Kensington? This is particularly surprising since most of our judges are not exactly in the bloom of life.

Politicians are forever making decisions which directly affect people's lives. If you push up the spending on benefits then taxes have to rise. And if taxes rise then growth falls and the Government has less income to spend on hospitals. If you spend more on policing, then there is less money to spend on making roads safer. But if you spend less on policing, then people are more likely to be mugged or murdered.

And there have to be priorities within the health service. There isn't enough money for everything. Personally, I find it wrong that the NHS finds the money to pay for infertility treatment, cosmetic surgery and sex change operations but doesn't find the money for diagnosing and treating cancer and heart disease. I think it is wrong that there is no money for drugs which will treat macular degeneration and prevent old people from going blind, and no money for removing benign but unsightly and worrying growths, but that there seems to be plenty of money for gender reassignment programmes.

But what I find particularly distressing is the fact that governments everywhere (but particularly successive British governments) seem to have decided that the elderly are surplus to requirements.

There are clear policies designed to get rid of everyone who reaches the age of 60 or older. Pensions are kept pitifully small. (The UK's State pension is the worst in any developed economy.) Energy prices are allowed to soar so that subsidies can be given to wind and solar energy programmes (satisfying the 'green' lobbyists who care nothing about the elderly). The result is that tens of thousands of older people die of the cold because they can't afford to eat and to keep warm. (How long will it be before energy prices are subject to postcode pricing – whereby people who live in more expensive houses pay more for their energy?)

The Sustainable Development Goals are just another example of the anti-old people policy which is prevalent these days.

4

I was cutting some overhanging branches outside in the lane when one of our Devon neighbours came out to say hello. The folk in Devon are much friendlier than the folk in the Gloucestershire 'Clotswolds' where we have our other house.

We don't have any near neighbours but this fellow lives close enough for us to hear his lawnmower. I'd met him a couple of months earlier but hadn't seen him since. He waved and smiled. 'I never forget a name,' he said, when we'd shaken hands. He pointed at me and then held up a hand to stop me from saying anything. 'I'll get it in a moment,' he said. 'Got it! Your name is Eugene isn't it?'

'Er, actually, no, it isn't,' I admitted, rather shamefacedly. He had looked so pleased with himself that I had genuinely thought of saying my name was indeed Eugene.

'No? Are you sure?'

I said I was pretty sure it wasn't Eugene.

'I was sure it was Eugene,' he said, shaking his head and walking away. He turned back and looked at me quizzically. 'Are you positive it isn't?'

'I'm afraid it isn't.'

'Then who is Eugene?' he asked me, genuinely puzzled.

'I'm afraid I don't know,' I had to admit. 'I don't know anyone called Eugene.'

He tottered off, looking very bewildered.

Do these things happen to everyone? Or is it just me?

5

A friend of mine visited his brother and sister- in- law and broke a mug. Knowing that his sister-in-law takes such things seriously, he didn't say anything but took the mug away with him, hoping to be able to mend it. When he realised that there was a small piece missing and that the mug was entirely irreparable, he spent half a day wandering around the shops looking for a replacement.

Eventually, he managed to find one. It was, inevitably, the most expensive mug in the shop.

When he next visited his brother and sister-in-law, he put the replacement mug on the kitchen table, when no one was looking, hoping that it would just be recycled into household life.

'What on earth is this doing here?' demanded his sister-in-law when she saw it. 'This is one of those awful old mugs I used to give to workmen. I thought I'd taken them all to the charity shop yesterday.'

6

I purchased some wing nuts on eBay and made the classic mistake of not looking at the measurements. When they arrived, they were so small that they were utterly useless for anything other than maintenance work inside a dolls' house.

Careless suckers like me are, it seems, still getting conned by the oldest trick on eBay.

I have been told repeatedly, by the way, that I should only buy from websites which are decorated with a little padlock. The implication is that this somehow means they are 'safe'. Do the people who say this genuinely believe that hackers and scammers are incapable of faking a little padlock to put on their websites?

7

Cyclists cause lots of accidents and delay traffic.

In cities they ride along on racing cycles, heads down, arrogant dismissing the rights of other road users and of pedestrians. They seem to think they are entitled to priority everywhere.

Because of the traffic jams they create, cyclists have much bigger carbon footprints than motorists. It seems absurd that only drivers of motorised vehicles pay a tax to use the roads. Cyclists are, ipso facto, there by the generosity of paying road users.

In a genuine attempt to improve safety on the road and to enhance the relationship between motorists and cyclists, I have created some new rules.

When coming up to pass a cyclist, a motorist should give a long beep on the vehicle's horn.

When a cyclist hears a car approaching from either direction, he or she must dismount from his or her machine and stand to attention beside it on the pavement.

When passing a cyclist, the motorist should wave two fingers in recognition of the fact that the cyclist is operating a machine with two wheels.

Cyclists must not re-join the highway until they are satisfied that there are no vehicles approaching from either direction.

In towns and cities, all cyclists must walk alongside their machines. Riding a bicycle in a built up area is an offence under the 'Don't Annoy Motorists Because They Pay For The Roads Act'.

It is an offence for any cyclist to wear tight fitting Lycra. Research conducted at great expense has shown that many motorists find Lycra particularly offensive.

It is an offence for any cyclist to have a camera fitted to his person or machine.

Cyclists who fall off their machines should remove themselves and their machines to the side of the road with all haste in order to avoid inconveniencing motorists.

If a cyclist and a motorist are in dispute then the motorist is always right.

Cyclists must carry a large flashing light on their heads at all times to ensure that they are clearly visible to proper road users.

8

On the beach, a mother was having trouble with a petulant child. She gently slapped him on the thigh. He was wearing trousers. The slap couldn't have hurt. He probably hardly felt it. He sniffled a bit, but he stopped shouting and stamping. He snuffled for a moment. Then mother and son had a hug and all was forgotten. But, inevitably, the camera phones came out and the interfering fusspots started tutting.

Smacking is now firmly out of fashion – I suspect it is now probably somewhere between paedophilia and hatred of the EU on the Lineker-Allen Official Scale of Political Incorrectness.

Parents who read *The Guardian*, live in Islington and still have faith in the BBC, prefer to punish their children by depriving them of their Facebook and Twitter accounts for a week or by refusing to allow them access to the family guacamole dish for a month. A modest infraction of family rules will result in a week without television or a weekend's forced confinement to the home.

The truth is that punishments, by virtue of the fact that they tend to continue long after the cause of the punishment has been forgotten, are cruel and unusual and likely to do lasting damage to the punishee and to the child-parent relationship.

A gentle, smack on the bottom is, when applied rarely and judiciously, still the fairest and healthiest way to punish children. There's a lot of sense in the old saying 'spare the rod and spoil the child'. Dr Benjamin Spock, author of the most successful childcare book of all time, eventually concluded that mild physical punishment was the best way to admonish an erring child.

It is, after all, what animals do with their young.

I once watched an older cat trying to teach a pair of kittens how to hunt. When the cat wasn't looking, the kittens would fool around, not paying attention. Spotting this, the cat tutor bopped the kittens firmly but with love. The kittens, duly chastised, then paid attention to their lesson.

Punishments work best when they are over quickly – and when they are clearly related in time to the sin involved.

Stretching out a punishment over time is more likely to lead to anger and resentment.

The essence of the smack is the fact that it shows disapproval. It is a clear expression of parental criticism and dissatisfaction.

It definitely isn't about pain.

The advantage for all concerned is that a timely applied smack is over quickly.

Of course, there are now officious social workers, policemen and even doctors who will regard an occasional smack as something irredeemably wicked. Parents who dare to punish their children this way are likely to find themselves arrested, humiliated or demonised. Parents who smack in public are likely to find themselves starring on YouTube.

So, sadly, it can't be done.

Smacking, the best way to punish naughty children, is a definite no-no.

But, to balance the debate, I would just point out that we should all bear in mind that those individuals who prefer the long, drawn out punishment, the week-long ban from television or mobile phone use, and who may like to consider themselves to be on the high moral side of every equation, politically correct and beyond reproach, are deliberately extending the punishment they choose to give.

And that, let us all remember, is one of the definitive qualities of sadism.

9

Antoinette was quite ill today. She gets a lot of oedema (affecting her ankles and her hands) and frequently suffers from heart arrhythmias. As a result, she gets very tired on bad days. She has all the symptoms of a leaky heart valve and when I listened to her heart, I was sure I could hear a valve problem. Her systolic blood pressure rarely rises above 100 mm Hg and her diastolic is often down to 60 mm Hg. The trouble is it is a long time since I listened to hearts and I am no longer very good at defining the type of problem or the nature of the valve abnormality.

And Antoinette refuses point blank to see a hospital specialist and has a real and understandable phobia about hospitals. Some years ago she had extensive neurological investigations done at Frenchay Hospital near Bristol and she has lost all faith in the medical profession. Despite numerous visits and investigations, and visits to a variety of doctors, I don't think anyone actually bothered to listen to her heart. They did a scan and so on but didn't pick up anything relating to her heart. The polite way to describe the whole investigative process was that it was a shambles. (I wrote about it in a previous diary.) She was treated appallingly by a bunch of neurologists who seemed to me to be both uncaring and incompetent.

Through a variety of incompetences, doctors were responsible for the deaths of my mother and my father (both of whom Antoinette adored). It is not impossible that these factors may have also influenced her refusal to seek medical advice.

I am ashamed of my own former profession and I understand entirely why she is now reluctant to see any healthcare professional.

10

At breakfast I was reading a small book called *Battlefields in Britain* by C.V.Wedgewood. The book is in the Britain in Pictures series (I managed to complete my collection of the set a few years ago) and Wedgewood, of course, is an excellent biographer and historian. (Her books on Florence Nightingale and the Charge of the Light Brigade are classics.)

But I couldn't help feeling that she'd rather missed an opportunity in this book. Or maybe it is just that I have a tabloid sort of brain. All those years working for *The Daily Star*, *The Sun*, the *Mirror* and the *Sunday People* probably did something to my neuronal networks.

Here's a paragraph I found:

'A false alarm caused by an accidental fire in Northumberland set the beacons leaping across the lowlands of Scotland in Napoleon's time. The borderers sprang to arms and marched to defend the coasts.'

That's it. That's all she gave us.

I know that in those days lookouts kept watch and in case of invasion used to arouse other citizens by using beacons. Throughout the years, when there were threats from the Spanish Armada and Napoleon, brushwood was piled up around the coasts and inland too and watchers stood ready with the flints – waiting to start their beacon the moment they spotted a ship approaching. Once one beacon was blazing, other watchers along the coast and inland would light their fires. And the defence armies would be warned and ready.

So, how the hell do you set fire to a brushwood beacon by mistake? Who did it? Did they try to put out the fire? Were they drunk? Did they get severely bollocked afterwards? You'd think so, wouldn't you?

The watchers didn't have Zippo lighters or Bryant and May matches in those days. They had to rely on a couple of bits of flint, some dry straw and a lot of patience.

19

Incidentally, Wedgewood also pointed out that whereas the English were considered to be excellent shots with bows and muskets, the same could not be said of the Scots. It occurred to me that no historian writing a similar book today would dare make this point. Our history is being rewritten for us by teenage reviewers with racist tendencies.

11

A friend of mine who is trying to give up smoking is chewing nicotine gum.

I can't understand why this stuff is still sold.

Nicotine gum contains the same sort of nicotine which is a vital ingredient of tobacco. What most people probably don't realise is that smoking cigarettes causes more deaths from heart disease than from lung cancer. And it is the nicotine in the tobacco which causes the problem.

So taking your nicotine fix as gum rather than as a cigarette, a cigar or a pipe may help your lungs but it won't do anything to protect your heart.

In fact, chewing nicotine gum to help yourself give up smoking is like stopping hitting yourself on the head with a brick and, instead, hitting yourself on the head with a plank of wood. Not much sense to it.

12

Less than a fifth of children now walk to school. Most of the rest are driven by car. And many of the car journeys are for less than half a mile.

When Antoinette and I lived in Weston-super-Mare, we lived not far from a school and every morning hordes of parents would arrive, bringing their offspring. The parents would park their cars across driveways, double park and often block the road completely. Worst of all, the moronic parents would leave their cars running for ten or fifteen minutes at a time. By half past nine every morning, the air in the locality was poisonous. And it would have just about become breathable by the time all the cars returned to pick up the children and pump out some more lung destroying pollution. These were probably the same parents who complain bitterly about air pollution. (There were numerous mobile phone masts right by the school. I complained because there's a real risk they could harm young children. But the parents thought the masts were brilliant because they ensured good reception for their phones.)

It is hardly surprising that a fifth of all children are obese by the age of 10.

Naturally, however, most of the parents of these fat kids insist that their children are 'just right' or 'perhaps a tiny bit chubby but who wants a skinny child?'.

The British are now the fattest and laziest people in Europe (and, outside the US, that means in the world). Nearly 10% of the NHS budget is spent on looking after people who suffer from the type of diabetes which is caused by eating too much and being overweight. Astonishingly, around 700,000 NHS employees are overweight or obese and half of our policemen and policewomen are either overweight or overtly obese.

We tend to blame the hypocrisy of the food companies who, obeying EU nonsenses, make their chocolate bars smaller so that people buy two and eat two. But parents are just as responsible. You don't see kids running around in the parks during the school holidays these days. They're all indoors bent over their computers, their game consoles and their bloody mobile telephones. A bag of crisps and a bottle of soda to keep them stocked up with calories.

13

When Nubar Gulbenkian, the Armenian millionaire, was getting old, he chose a burial site above the village of Grasse in southern France. He chose his final resting place solely for the view but when he made an inspection of his chosen site a year or two later, he found that the view from his grave was egregiously impeded by a new Shell petrol station.

Gulbenkian wrote to the oil company and complained, suggesting that they might like to consider moving the petrol station to another site.

An executive from the company wrote back hoping that Mr Gulbenkian, who was famous for having made a vast fortune out of trading oil, would perhaps agree that of all men he had little cause for complaint should a petrol station diminish the view from his grave.

Mr Gulbenkian, after some thought, agreed that this was a fair appraisal of the situation, and withdrew his opposition.

14

A woman who lives in Lewisham has been threatened with unspeakable consequences for putting up posters in the windows of her own home. The posters advise passers-by to support Brexit and vote Conservative, and officious officials from the council have written to her demanding that she remove her posters immediately or they will 'take action'.

I wonder if councils anywhere are threatening citizens with 'action' for putting up posters or flags supporting the European Union. I suspect not.

Do the people responsible for this attempted infringement of freedom not realise that the vote to leave the EU was the largest vote for or against anything in British history. A substantial majority of the people voted to leave the EU. And yet numerous little Hitlers (including a good many of them paid by taxpayers and working at the BBC, the Bank of England and the Treasury) conspire still to thwart the will of the people. To hear them talk you would imagine that Britons will starve if we leave the EU. Do they not know that just over 7% of London's economy relies on trade with the EU? Looked at another way, nearly 93% of London's trade is with non-EU countries. If they don't know this then they should all be shot for ignorance. If they do know then they should be shot for being stupid. This makes a complete nonsense of the absurd and entirely impractical claims by some half-wits that London should remain within the EU when the rest of England leaves.

In another age there would be heads on pikes. That there are not is a tribute to the good manners of those who understood the history and purpose of the EU and therefore wanted Britain to leave and to regain its freedom.

15

There is a house nearby in Gloucestershire which Antoinette and I refer to as the roundabout house because the garden looks like a traffic island.

The people who live there seem to insist on having their grass cut twice a week in the summer and their bushes and trees trimmed and shaped and cosmetically enhanced at very regular intervals. The sound of machinery whining is incessant.

Today, I suggested to the owner that they would be better off if they concreted the entire garden and then painted the concrete green.

'That's a very good idea,' he said, quite seriously. 'Or maybe I could look at laying down artificial grass. They make very good artificial grass these days.'

He is not a man who jokes.

Crumbs, what have I done?

16

Greedy lawyers (and unhappy patients) are destroying what is left of the NHS.

The NHS is now spending almost half its entire budget on compensation payments and legal costs. This means that the NHS spends far more on lawyers than on doctors and nurses.

Over the last year or two the money spent on compensation has rocketed.

Just two years ago, the NHS spent £31 billion on legal fees and costs. (That was a mere one third of the NHS budget).

But the figure has now risen dramatically.

Who is to blame?

It's easy to blame greedy lawyers.

But the NHS loses 76% of all the cases which are taken to court. And it pays out billions in compensation without even trying to provide a legal defence.

So it is clear that it isn't just greedy lawyers who are to blame.

The real problem is incompetence.

Doctors and nurses working for the NHS are providing a rotten service.

Errors are made so often that anyone who sees a GP or ventures into an NHS hospital is taking their life in their hands.

The main reason for the huge rise in the amount of damages which are paid out is that the NHS does not appear to have learned that what wronged patients want more than anything else is an admission that something went wrong, an apology and an assurance that it won't happen again. Patients who sue the NHS often do so in anger as much as in the need for compensation. I still feel aggrieved that although doctors killed both of my parents I never received even the flimsiest of apologies.

It is absurd to have one person in charge of the NHS. It is absurd to pretend that it is a 'national' health service. And the real absurdity is that the wrong people are making all the big decisions.

The result is an organisation which is intrinsically corrupt, incompetent and uncaring and which encourages the suppression of debate or criticism. The NHS has, for years, been failing, over-spending and over-performing.

The organisation survives not because the staff believes in it but because people have become addicted to the fact that it appears to be 'free' (in the same way that the internet appears to be free) and because the occasional innocent and naïve customer boasts about how pleased they were with the service they received.

Could it be, I wonder, that one of many problems is the fact that the NHS is now dominated by women. Nine out of ten nurses are women. The majority of doctors are women. Most social workers, ancillary workers and admin workers are women. And the problem is that a huge number of women employees want to work part time.

The time has come to put the NHS out of its misery.

The nation would save money – and the citizens would be healthier – if everyone in Britain was given free, private medical insurance.

The NHS has been a disaster for years. It was always doomed because it is all about rights and authority. Responsibility has been forgotten. Patients' wants (which aren't necessarily the same as their needs) are endless and impossible to satisfy because everything is free. All power has been handed over to administrators. No one accepts responsibility any more. When things go wrong, the lawyers negotiate another fat settlement and no one ever gets punished. A jumped up traffic warden and a former journalist at the General Medical Council destroyed general practice with their utterly absurd revalidation programme.

The latest figures, which show that the NHS now spends more on lawyers than on doctors, proves that the time has come to close it down.

17

Two immigrants, a woman from British Guiana (who seems to me to be the smuggest, most self-satisfied woman I have seen in my life and who, it has been said, has an even bigger ego than Richard Branson, though this seems unlikely bordering on the impossible) and a hairdresser from Brazil, have used the law to defeat the will of the British electorate in the battle for democracy and freedom from Nazi born tyranny.

The Supreme Court, which sounds very ancient and grand but which dates back to the dark and distant days of 2009, was set up so that the British would satisfy the demands of the European Convention on Human Rights (the ECHR).

And the ECHR is, surprise, surprise, so closely linked to the European Union that both have the same silly flag and Teutonic anthem. Surprisingly, this is not something that the British media have made clear.

So, to summarise:

The British Parliament gave the British people a Referendum. It was agreed by Parliament that the Government would act according to the wishes of the British people.

The British people voted clearly to leave the European Union.

The Supreme Court, which was set up to satisfy the EU, has agreed with two immigrants that the will of the British people must be ignored. As, indeed, must the will of Parliament which, don't forget, gave the British people the right to determine whether or not we stayed in the EU or left. So much for democracy EU style. Thanks to their arrogance, the pound will slide and investment in Britain will falter. And EU officials (who now hate Britain with a vengeance) will laugh themselves silly. The Immigrant Two and the Supreme Court have not only stuck two fingers up at the British people, they have also made Britain a laughing stock; they have unsettled the nation and they have weakened Britain for generations to come.

Meanwhile, the Remainers continue to lie and deceive the British people.

They say that we will be leaving the world's most successful economic bloc but that is a lie. Since the euro was formed, the euro-zone has grown by 27% while the UK has grown by 40%.

They say that we will be leaving our biggest market. But that is nonsense. We will still be able to sell to other European countries (just as they will want to sell to us).

They say that we will not be able to trade unless we have a trade deal with the EU but we trade with the US and we don't have a trade deal with them.

They say that studies have shown that the UK will be worse off outside the EU. But that isn't true. Because we won't be paying billions to the EU, and supporting the absurd Common Agricultural Policy, we will be much better off. And our food will be a good deal cheaper.

And they say we have to be members of the Single Market if we are going to trade with it. But that's yet another lie. America and China aren't in the Single Market but they trade with the EU. Of course, the less intelligent young Remainers have good reason to believe in the EU. They have been indoctrinated and most are so poorly educated that they have no idea how to set about finding the truth. They rely on the internet, which is a considerably less reliable source of information than the toxic old witch who lives at No 23.

The older Remainers, (Cable, Heseltine, Clarke et al) have no such excuse and I can only put their perfidious behaviour down to a woeful lack of patriotism.

My oh my, we have become so terribly flabby as a nation. We are so damned weak and masochistic.

18
Lefty liberal luvvies (most of whom who don't actually do any work or pay any tax) frequently argue that Britain should welcome everyone who wants to take advantage of the NHS.

We should, they say, be happy to provide cosmetic surgery, AIDS treatment, infertility treatment and obstetrics care for everyone who wants to come.

This is lunacy.

Nowhere else in Europe offers free State paid for health care, and so the UK is a magnet for health tourists who have no interest in Britain other than as a source of free treatment.

Consequently, the NHS is besieged by thousands of foreigners arriving in Britain for free health care.

Many want to have their babies on the NHS.

Some want cosmetic surgery or sex change operations.

A good many want treatment for AIDS.

The cost of providing treatment runs into billions.

And it is one of the reasons Britons have to wait months or years for essential investigations, treatment or surgery. It is the reason expensive treatments are often withdrawn.

Those who believe that foreigners are entitled to use the NHS probably don't have friends or relatives who have suffered or died because of NHS shortages. And they probably don't realise that NHS resources are finite.

When thousands of pounds are spent treating a foreign patient then another patient, usually a British patient, must be denied treatment they need.

The fact is that every time our NHS resources are used to treat a foreigner, a British patient will die because he or she has had to wait months for an essential X-ray or because the NHS can't afford to provide vital treatment.

The bottom line is that the lefty luvvies who insist that the NHS should provide free care for everyone in the world are directly responsible for thousands of British deaths. But maybe they're happy about that.

19

Someone called Guy Verhofstadt, who is apparently the Brexit negotiator for the European Parliament, has claimed that Sir Winston Churchill would have voted Remain – to stay in the European Union.

This is, to put it mildly, pie in the sky: yet another piece of wishful thinking from a representative of Adolf Hitler's Nazi theme park dreamland.

Here are two genuine Churchill quotes which relate to the EU (both taken from my book *OFPIS*):

'Britain could not be an ordinary member of a federal union limited to Europe in any period which can be…foreseen.' – Winston Churchill

'If you ask me to choose between Europe and the open sea, I choose the open sea.' – Winston Churchill.

So let's have no more nonsense from the desperadoes at the European Union.

Sir Winston Churchill, who knew that the EU was Hitler's dream, would have hated the European Union, would have recognised it for what it is, and would have fought against our membership with all his heart.

20

In order to please the EU, Britain is closing down its old-fashioned, traditional coal fired power stations. China and India are, on the other hand, planning to build 800 new coal fired power stations.

Britain is reducing its carbon emissions faster than any other major country.

By pushing up the price of heating our homes, the EU's mad policies have endangered the health of millions. Thousands of elderly Britons have been killed as a direct result of the EU's crazy policies.

We haven't replaced our old coal stations with anything else. Green campaigners won't allow the Government to build nuclear power stations. Wind, solar and wave power generation is inefficient and expensive. America's solar industry employs nearly 400,000 people and provides only 1% of America's electricity production. Global subsidies for the fashionable renewables, cost taxpayers and energy users $100 billion a year and yet the renewable industry still hasn't worked out how to cope with peak demand hours. The renewables have been subsidised for nearly half a century, and you'd have thought that if they were going to prove viable they'd be viable by now.

Other countries with low carbon electricity have long established electricity production methods which we cannot possibly emulate. Norway and Sweden use vast amounts of hydroelectricity and France relies mainly on nuclear power.

It takes more electricity to produce and run those huge windmills which scar the countryside and the sea than the ugly things ever produce. (Our ancestors, particularly the Victorians, produced great buildings, beautiful bridges and so on. We have built ugly windmills and solar farms. We sneer at the Victorians but without their creative skills we would not have any infrastructure.)

Moreover, even if we covered the country with solar panels and wind farms, there still wouldn't be enough electricity to keep us all warm.

Thanks to the EU and a bunch of hypocritical pseudo-environmentalists (celebrity pseudo-environmentalists are the ones who tell the rest of us what we should and should not do while they themselves own private jets which enable them to fly around the world without coming into painful contact with the hoi polloi), England, the most overcrowded country in Europe, will soon be the only country in the world without any electricity!

And the selfish many who drive electric cars are making things worse.

Selfish greens and sanctimonious and hypocritical electric car drivers will result in thousands of deaths when the electricity runs out – which it soon will.

Where do these folk who drive electric cars think the electricity comes from? Britain has had to introduce special diesel powered generators to provide enough electricity to keep electric cars on the move. It has been proved that the sad and sanctimonious, self-satisfied fools who buy electric cars are doing far more harm to the environment than people who drive diesel and petrol driven vehicles. (As an aside, driverless cars are an even more stupid idea. They may work on the wide, open roads of America but on English country lanes they will be a disaster. What happens when two driverless cars meet on a single track Devon lane? The two cars will never move and the passengers will starve to death waiting for one car to back up.)

Hospitals and factories have been asked to install back up diesel generators because Britain now has just 0.1% of spare electricity. As I have warned many, many times over the last decade and a half, our electricity generating system is about to collapse.

Every motorist who buys an electric car is making things worse.

The chances are that electricity will soon have to be rationed.

Shops, factories and homes will have to go back to the three day week.

Energy prices will rise rapidly.

The cuts in electricity supply will endanger the health of millions.

And it will be the EU, the Greens and the electric car owners who must share the blame.

Here, in summary, are some good reasons why you should blame the Greens when the electricity runs out.

Many Greens ride bicycles on public roads. But bike riders invariably produce queues of cars driving along at 10 or 15 miles an hour. At those speeds, motor vehicles are very inefficient and use far more fuel than when travelling three or four times as fast.

Greens are madly enthusiastic about wind power – and they pressurise governments to give subsidies to wind power installations. (These subsidies have distorted energy prices and mean that the poor and the elderly pay most of the cost of wind power.) But windmills are not just ugly and dangerous to birds – they are also horrendously inefficient. They require vast amounts of energy to build. And they are never energy efficient.

Greens campaign to stop governments building coal or nuclear power stations. Without those power stations, the electricity will soon run out.

Greens are enthusiastic about solar power. But solar power is, like wind power, inefficient and expensive. And it won't ever produce enough electricity to keep us warm and fed with hot food.

The Greens are forever flying around the world to attend conferences on global warming. All that pointless travel uses up vast amounts of valuable energy. Internet banking and Bitcoin also use up huge amounts of electricity. (And what will happen to all those internet accounts when there isn't any electricity? It hardly bears thinking about.)

Greens seem convinced that renewables can be used for all our energy needs. Someone should point out to them that renewables only produce electricity and electricity provides less than a fifth of the world's energy needs. Imagine a world without 80% of our energy supplies and you will have a vision of the sort of world the Greens would like us to inhabit.

21

The Mayor of London, Sadiq Khan, has supported a ban on smoking in pub gardens.

I've been campaigning against smoking since the 1950s (which is probably longer than the Mayor has been interested in the health problems of smoking) and, as a doctor, I've probably treated more patients suffering from the effects of smoking than he has.

But banning smoking in pub gardens is daft.

There is now clear evidence that banning smoking in pubs has simply pushed smokers into smoking (and drinking) at home.

And since booze is cheaper when you buy it at the supermarket, the exiled smokers drink far more than they did when they drank and smoked in pubs.

Publicans have made it clear that if smoking in pubs is banned completely then more of them will go bust.

We have now reached the point where I am prepared to argue that, for the sake of the nation's health, we should have 'smoking pubs' where patrons are allowed to smoke indoors. Non-smokers who objected to cigarette smoke would be invited to do their drinking elsewhere.

Of course, the issue of passive smoking is also important.

And once again I have considerably more experience of this problem than the Mayor. Decades ago, I was the first doctor to write about the hazard of passive smoking and the opposition was vociferous for many years.

But if pubs which allow smoking in their beer gardens ban children, and make it clear to patrons that entrance to their beer garden is voluntary and not compulsory, then the risks are ameliorated.

The only potential victims are the smokers themselves.

So, why is the Mayor of London so determined to stop smoking in pub gardens when he must know that if he succeeds then many more pubs will close?

Could it be possible that the Mayor is supporting this proposed ban, in part at least, because he is a devout Muslim – and Muslims are fiercely opposed to the consumption of alcohol?

When their customers are banned from smoking outside, as well as inside, a good many pubs will go bust and close.

22

In Britain, it is now against the law to let a dog be dangerously out of control anywhere, including in public places, in private places and even in the owner's own home.

According to the law, a dog is considered to be dangerously out of control if it injures someone or makes someone worried that it might injure them.

The second part of that sentence is the crucial one.

The dog doesn't have to bite to be dangerous.

All the law requires is that someone FEARS that the dog might do them harm.

The penalties are severe.

A dog owner can get an unlimited fine or be sent to prison for up to six months (or both) if their dog is dangerously out of control. And the dog owner convicted may not be able to own a dog in the future. The dog may be destroyed.

Astonishingly, very few dog owners know the law.

This morning an out of control dog ran up to me and pinned me against the side of my car. When I politely pointed out to the owner that she was breaking the law, and liable to severe punishment, she called me a liar and insisted that there is no such law.

Well, she was wrong.

I suggest that all dog owners in the UK visit the British Government's website and look for the heading 'Controlling your dog in public'.

Or simply key the words 'Controlling your dog in public' into a search engine.

Those who are nervous of dogs might also like to take a look at the details of the new law. It is well worth knowing.

And it might also be a good idea if a few police officers updated their knowledge of the law relating to dogs.

Sadly, a surprising number of police officers don't seem to understand the importance of the new law.

I suggest that anyone who has difficulty in persuading the police to take a complaint seriously might consider making a formal complaint against the police officers concerned, reporting the incident to the press and threatening legal action against the police and the owner of the errant dog. (Complaining, by the way, is very good for you. It provides exercise for the brain and it's much better for you to find a target for your anger than to allow it to fester inside.)

There are far too many dangerous, unstable and ill-controlled dogs in Britain. And every year, thousands of people are injured (some of them fatally) by out of control dogs. My credentials as an animal lover are beyond question but I believe that the full force of the law (now that it is available) must be used to force owners and the police to take the situation seriously.

There are many wonderful parts of Britain where I used to walk or cycle but which are now so dominated by uncontrolled dogs that they are effectively no go areas. I used to walk along the cliffs near Mortehoe in North Devon but no more. I loved walking along the river to Watersmeet at Lynmouth but no more. And I have ridden the cycle path between Bideford and Barnstaple hundreds of times. But I haven't done that for years. In each case, the uncontrolled dogs, many of which seem dangerous, own the areas.

In 2016, a record number of 7,673 people were admitted to hospital as a result of dog bites.

23

The tax authorities are clamping down on everything that could possibly be described as tax avoidance.

Tax avoidance used to be entirely legal.

It was tax evasion that led to trouble.

But the Government and HMRC are now desperate to raise more money (to pay for wars, foreign aid, interest on the nation's massive debts and Ministers' expense accounts) that they are clamping down on everything that could possibly be described as tax avoidance.

And accountants are now worried that anyone who gives up smoking or drinking alcohol could face the wrath of HMRC.

Cigarettes and tobacco carry a huge amount of tax.

As does alcohol.

Anyone who gives up either will save a good deal of money.

And the Government will lose tax income.

So what will happen?

Accounting experts say that there is a real risk that the tax authorities will charge those who give up smoking or boozing with the new crime of tax avoidance.

I love it.

Welcome to the mad, mad world we now live in.

24

The Food Standards Agency (FSA) has issued a warning about a chemical called acrylamide which, it says, may cause cancer.

But their warning is rubbish and is NOT based on scientific evidence.

Acrylamide is, says the FSA, produced when starchy foods (such as bread and potatoes) are roasted, fried or grilled for too long at high temperatures.

And so the FSA has issued a standard nanny state warning that people shouldn't eat nicely browned toast or, presumably, the nice crispy bits you get in the bottom of a bag of chips.

But the evidence upon which the FSA has based its warning is a result of research on animals.

The idiots at the FSA have assumed that what happens in animals also happens in humans.

But this is not true.

And the FSA should know that the animal research evidence they're using is utterly valueless.

You don't have to just take my word for this.

Drug safety agencies around the world now ignore scientific evidence showing that drugs cause cancer and other serious health problems when given to animals – because they know that research on animals is utterly without value.

As proof, I have published on my website (www.vernoncoleman.com) a list of several dozen widely prescribed drugs which are known to cause serious health problems when given to animals but which are considered safe for human use.

If the FSA really wanted to cut the incidence of cancer, they would warn people not to eat meat.

Meat is known to cause cancer. There's a ton of research involving humans which proves this beyond a doubt. (My book *Food for Thought* contains a list of 26 scientific papers providing proof that meat causes cancer in humans.)

But the FSA won't dare take on the powerful meat industry. And they won't dare upset the burger eating millions. They prefer to believe that several million lemmings cannot possibly be wrong.

So they're cowards as well as idiots.

Any why does the FSA hand over huge amounts of taxpayers' money to 'celebrities'?

For example, a retired athlete called Denise Lewis received £10,000 earlier this year from the FSA for supporting this campaign.

I wonder if this is the same athlete called Denise Lewis who at one stage in her career hired a coach who was the former head of East German's drug assisted athletics team.

Good role model for giving out health advice?

Incidentally, I am always shocked to see 'celebrities' charging fees for public service works. A great many also charge exorbitant fees for charity appearances – slamming in huge invoices for turning on Christmas lights or opening fetes.

25

It has been reported that the McCanns (the parents of missing Madeleine) are threatening to sue Goncalo Amaral, if the Portuguese policeman's book *The Truth of the Lie* is published in the UK. This is odd because an English translation of Goncalo Amaral's book has been freely available on the internet for some time. I know because I've read it. The UK libel laws are, however, still the most stringent in the world.

But do the McCanns really want to go to court?

Do they really want a UK libel trial – where they would be on trial as much as the defendant? A lot of people could tell them just how dangerous it is to bring a libel action in the UK. Oscar Wilde was ruined after he brought a libel action. So was Jonathan Aitken. Bringing a legal action for libel didn't ruin Jeffrey Archer but it put him in prison. Music hall star Maud Allan was ruined by a libel case which she lost. An MP called Neil Hamilton was damned near ruined by a libel case he brought.

And if there is going to be a court case about the McCann case, maybe the McCanns themselves should be the defendants.

The McCanns are, of course, famous (or should that be infamous?) for having left three small children in their holiday apartment while they went out for dinner with friends. One of the children, a little girl called Madeleine, disappeared.

It is, of course, inconceivable that the McCanns could be in any way responsible for the death of their daughter. It would have been the most heinous family crime in history. (Although they did, of course, leave her unattended and so have to accept some of the responsibility for whatever happened.)

But there still seem to be many unanswered questions and puzzles about this enormously high profile case.

Isn't it about time a relatively small amount of money was spent taking the McCanns to court so that their story could be properly investigated?

I suspect that some parents might welcome an opportunity to put all the available evidence in the public domain and to have witnesses and critics properly and publicly questioned.

Some might think that discussions about the case have in the past been limited by the McCanns' alleged reluctance to answer some of the questions which have been asked, and by their perhaps understandable willingness to take legal action against critics.

Would not everyone – especially Madeleine – benefit if all the confusions and contradictions could be cleared away by a clear cut, forensic examination of all those involved and a proper analysis of the available facts?

Much taxpayers' money has been spent on looking for Madeleine. Surely, there could be no complaint if a little more public money were spent on a proper investigation in a court of law. Indeed, would the McCanns themselves not benefit from an opportunity to put all the facts before a court? Would not an analysis of the evidence help in finding a conclusion to this tragic case?

There are, it seems to me, a vast number of questions which could usefully be asked in a courtroom – questions for which very few answers have been forthcoming. I am sure that the McCanns have reasonable explanations for them all. Given all the circumstances, the questions do not seem to me to be intrusive or unfair. And surely the answers to them might, just might, help the police. Might not the answers also help members of the public understand the background to Madeleine's disappearance a little more clearly? Might not lessons be learned which could help other parents? And aren't those things which everyone wants?

There are few couples in Britain who are better known than the McCanns. And yet the paradox is that there are few public couples about whom less seems to be known. They are surrounded by mystery, confusion, controversy and contradictions. Has any couple ever sought publicity quite so determinedly and yet managed to remain quite so enigmatic? Has there been a crime in British history so well publicised and yet so full of unanswered questions? Has there ever been a crime where the truth has become quite so lost amidst rumour and what seems to me to be a lot of spin – some of it apparently organised by professionals rather than a pair of doctors on a holiday.

Whatever the truth, we should not forget that the McCanns left their daughter unattended and so have to accept a good part of the responsibility for whatever crime occurred. And in February 2017, a judge in Portugal's highest court pointed out that the McCanns had not been ruled innocent.

The questions below are all genuine questions. I do not know the answers to any of them. (If I did I would write them as statements.) But I think it is in the public interest that the questions are asked. And I hope that one day they will all be answered.

Surely a trial would help the couple by enabling them to answer many of the often asked questions? Otherwise, the suspicions will never go away. Indeed, I fear that the suspicions and doubts and rumours will grow stronger as the years go by. It is almost certain that whatever any of the Tapas Nine do with their lives, the first sentence of their obituaries has already been written.

It seems to me that the McCanns, the police and the politicians (how they became involved is a mystery in itself) have made things worse by what appears to be an endless publicity circus, which it seems to me was to some extent made worse by them or their associates. Precisely, what did Tony Blair and Oprah have to do with helping to find a small girl? What on earth made Prince Charles think he needed to get involved? It has, I understand, been claimed that in such cases too much publicity can actually be harmful and can frighten abductors into doing something which they might not have planned. I suspect that is true.

Would not everyone – especially Madeleine – benefit if all the confusions and contradictions could be cleared away by a clear cut, forensic examination of all those involved and a proper analysis of the available facts? Would not questions asked, and answers given, under oath, help clear away the rumours and the fabrications – whatever their source?

Why am I constantly reminded of the confusion after the extremely mysterious death of Dr David Kelly?

Over £12 million of taxpayers' money has, it is said, been largely spent on looking for the alleged paedophile ring that the British police apparently believe is responsible for abducting Madeleine. To some, the police seem to be following the McCanns' strong assertion, right from the start, that Madeleine had been abducted rather than following the possibility that she might have wandered or been killed in the locality.

The police will, of course, know that 70% of child murders are committed by people who know, or who are in some way close to, the child who is the victim.

(In reality, if Madeleine had wandered off then surely she would have been far more likely to have encountered someone who would have taken her home than that she would have happened to meet a wandering paedophile or paedophile gang?)

Is it true, as Kate McCann is reported to have claimed, that the shutters to the window of Madeleine's room had been forced up?

Or is it true, as others have suggested, that they might not have been forced? This is a simple and crucial question.

And here's another mystery.

The loss of any human being is a tragedy.

But £12 million and more on an investigation into one missing child seems a good deal when untold thousands of other children go missing without any notable expenditure of public funds, when the police do virtually nothing to stop slavery in Britain, when rape gangs rampage unhindered and when enforced prostitution is commonplace.

To put this in perspective, the current official 'value of a prevented fatality' in the UK is £1.83 million. In other words, that is how much the Government thinks it is reasonable to spend to prevent a single death. Every year, thousands of people die because the Government doesn't think it is worth spending taxpayers' money on drugs or surgery that would save their lives. This same figure must be used to justify road safety improvements. The NHS would not spend a fraction of the money which has been spent on the search for a possibly imaginary paedophile gang even if it knew for certain that a life could be saved. This is of significance because the nation's financial resources are inevitably finite. David Cameron, when Prime Minister, authorised the spending of this huge sum in this seemingly quixotic way.

Why was that?

Why are the McCanns apparently considered so very, very special and more worthy than thousands of other parents, grieving in similar circumstances? A growing number of people seem to feel that this is one of many mysteries that ought to be aired. It isn't entirely absurd to say that anyone whose child goes missing abroad and who doesn't have at least a bus load of Government employees fawning over them within a week should now feel cheated. And anyone who doesn't have at least three cabinet ministers on the phone might also feel hard done by. Is it true that special branch officers escorted the McCanns back from Portugal? If so, is this now normal practice for all parents in such circumstances?

Here are just a few of the obvious questions which might usefully be asked in a courtroom and which would help remove for ever any undoubtedly unjust fears and suspicions some people might still have about Madeleine's disappearance:

Is it true that the McCanns left their children at a crèche or play area in the mornings and the afternoons, and then left them unattended on at least some of the evenings while they were in Portugal? This seems odd to me because I would have thought that most people would, when taking their children on a family holiday, want to spend most of their time in their company. What was the relationship like between the McCanns and Madeleine before the trip to Portugal? Was Madeleine seen at the crèche or play area on the afternoon of the day she disappeared? And if so, by whom?

Is it really true that when the McCanns left their children unattended in the apartment, one of the doors was unlocked? I suspect that some people wouldn't leave their camera or mobile telephone in an unlocked, rented apartment in a holiday area. Doesn't it seem strange to leave three small children in such a situation? Have the McCanns ever taken public responsibility for their behaviour? Have they ever apologised for their behaviour? Is it true that Gerry McCann was playing tennis within days of Madeleine's disappearance?

There is some confusion about how far away the McCanns were when they were dining. It has been said by Kate McCann that dining at the restaurant was akin to having a meal in the garden with the children upstairs in a nearby bedroom. ('We were sitting outside and could just as easily have been eating on a fine spring evening in a friend's garden, with the kids asleep upstairs in the house,' she writes in her book.) But there seems to be evidence that the dining table was between 70 and 150 yards away from the apartment (different reports give different figures) and it seems to me unlikely that anyone dining there could see or hear what was happening in the apartment. (I have seen it claimed that Gerry McCann has suggested that they were 'essentially performing (their) own baby listening service', though I find it difficult to understand this claim.) It has been claimed that the couple could see the apartment but this has been disputed. What is the truth? And even if they could see one outside wall of the apartment then, unless they are claiming to have X-ray vision, they wouldn't be able to see what was happening inside.

The law in Britain is that if parents leave a child alone, and in such a way that the child might be at risk, then the parents can be prosecuted. Hundreds of parents are arrested every year for leaving their children (sometimes much older than the McCann children and sometimes for much shorter periods of time) without adult supervision. One father was arrested for leaving his child alone for just two minutes. Why was the behaviour of the McCanns considered acceptable? Since the McCanns claim that Madeleine was abducted (and this theory seems to be accepted by the British police) and that she must, therefore, have been left at risk, why have the McCanns not been charged by the British police? I believe the McCanns claim that their actions were 'within the bounds of responsible parenting' but is it not also the law in Portugal that it is an offence to leave children unattended? Why did social workers not take action over the fact that three small children had been left 'at risk'? Would a single mother living in a council flat have been treated with such leniency if she had left three young children alone in an unlocked apartment? (In her book, Kate McCann writes: '...we had a meeting with a social services manager and a local child protection officer. They went through various formalities with us and, while they took care to keep everything on a totally professional footing, I could tell they felt uncomfortable about having to subject us to this sort of scrutiny. But we'd resigned ourselves to it. We'd expected it, accepted it and we had nothing to hide.') Whatever happened to Madeleine, there are doubtless many who find it difficult to avoid the feeling that her parents were at least partly responsible and that the authorities have behaved very strangely in taking no action. Am I alone in thinking that the McCanns should have been charged with child neglect? And should they have been allowed to remain in charge of their two remaining children? Indeed, should the two McCanns have been allowed to retain their medical certificates? These are surely serious questions.

It has been alleged that Madeleine was a poor sleeper who occasionally walked in her sleep. Is this true? If so, was not it particularly risky for two doctors to leave her unattended in a strange, unlocked apartment in a foreign country? Did it not occur to either of them that a young child who was a poor sleeper and possibly a sleep walker might wander off through the unlocked door and then come to some harm? Is it not true that a babysitter could have been hired?

Prior to the holiday, was Madeleine ever given any form of medicine to help her sleep? Is it true that none of the McCann children was given anything at all by the McCanns to help them sleep during a holiday where their restlessness or failure to sleep might prove particularly inconvenient? Were any of the children given medication by anyone else?

How much alcohol did the McCanns consume while dining with their friends? Precisely how often did they check on their children? Are there no independent witnesses who can provide precise answers?

It is alleged that after Madeleine's disappearance, the McCanns received telephone calls and/or support from Cherie Blair (the Prime Minister's wife), Gordon Brown (the Chancellor of the Exchequer, due to become Prime Minister within weeks), Margaret Beckett (the foreign secretary) and the Pope. The local Ambassador is reported to have been involved. Is there any explanation for all this high profile support? The official figures in the UK show that another child goes missing every three minutes – well over 100,000 children a year. Do Cabinet Ministers telephone the parents of all these missing children? According to these figures, it is reasonable to estimate that several hundred children went missing on the same day that the McCanns lost their child. Did all those parents receive the same level of official support? If not, why not? Did Blair and Brown really provide the McCanns with a public relations representative? Who paid the bill? Can it conceivably be true (as has been alleged) that the British Government threatened to use the McCann investigation as a reason not to sign the Lisbon Treaty? Were SIS (MI5 and/or MI6) officers involved? Was it just a coincidence that alleged paedophile Sir Clement Freud had a holiday home close to the McCanns' apartment? Is or was Gerry McCann a member of the Freemasons or any other private body? Has he signed the Scottish Bill of Rights?

Is it true that the McCanns continued to take their remaining children to the children's play area after they had lost Madeleine?

What is the truth about the trained sniffer dogs which allegedly picked up the scent of a dead body in the McCanns' apartment and in their hire car – as well as on Madeleine's toy? Were these findings of any value? Were the dogs reliable? Was blood really found in the McCanns' holiday apartment? If so, is it true that the blood was identified as Madeleine's? If not, whose was it? There seems to be confusion about all these issues.

Is it true that Kate McCann refused to answer some of the questions posed by the Portuguese police? If so, why was this? Were any or all of the McCanns' children conceived using IVF? Was Gerald McCann the father of them all?

Is it true that the McCanns have appointed a number of PR experts and high-powered lawyers (including extradition specialists and libel lawyers)?

Is it true that the McCanns' friends had a 'pact of silence'? If so, what was the reason for this?

Is it true that the McCanns refused to take a lie detector test? If so, what was the reason? Even if the test had not been admissible in court, it might have silenced some critics.

Is it true that the McCanns deleted some mobile phone records and that the Portuguese police were refused permission to examine medical, financial and credit card records? If so, why was this? Were the Portuguese police helped in every way possible by the British authorities?

Why did the McCanns form a fund raising company within less than a month of Madeleine's disappearance? How did their limited company manage to spend £141,747 on administrative expenses in less than the first year? And was it really necessary to spend £26,113 on media monitoring? Precisely how has all the money donated to the Madeleine fund been spent? It has been claimed that the McCanns did not receive any remuneration from the fund but is it true that some of the money was used to help to pay the McCanns' mortgage? If so, was that really what donors expected their money to be used for? Exactly how much of the money donated has been spent on legal fees on behalf of the McCanns? What was the McCanns' financial situation before Madeleine's disappearance? Why did directors of the fund resign? Why did last year's accounts for Madeleine's Fund: Leaving No Stone Unturned Limited (as published on the 'beta.companieshouse.gov.uk' website) show that Madeleine's Fund had £490,839 in 'investments'? What were the 'investments'?

As mentioned above, the British police are alleged to have spent £12 million of taxpayers' money on investigating one particular possibility – the abduction by a gang. Have they spent any effort (and any of our money) on investigating other possible scenarios – such as, for example, the one which appears to be favoured by the Portuguese police chief who investigated Madeleine's disappearance? If not, why not. Are not taxpayers entitled to know exactly how their money has been spent? What was the police reaction to the fact that a number of people thought that one of the photo fit suspects looked remarkably like Gerry McCann? (As an aside, the Portuguese police investigation seems to me to have been extremely thorough and professional.)

Why, within months of Madeleine's disappearance, did Gerry McCann go to the United States of America to appear on television and visit the White House? Was there ever any suggestion that Americans might have been involved in the alleged abduction? Was there a theory that Madeleine might have been taken to the USA? Might it not seem odd to some that a parent should fly across the Atlantic when their daughter had gone missing in Portugal?

Have all the friends with whom the McCanns were dining been thoroughly investigated and cleared by the British police?

The chief of police who was initially responsible for the search for Madeleine has made some serious allegations. Have any or all of these allegations been investigated by the British police?

Is it true, as has been claimed by a former British Ambassador (though not to Portugal), that British diplomatic staff were under instructions to put pressure on the Portuguese authorities? Is it true, as has been alleged, that British authorities were ordered to be present at every contact between the McCanns and the Portuguese police? If so, who initiated these orders? And why?

These are all simple and straightforward questions and to most of them there should, surely, be some simple and straightforward answers. There are, of course, many more questions. How many photographs of Madeleine did the McCanns take with them to Portugal? What happened to Gerry McCann's sports bag? Were the contents also missing?

Given all the circumstances, the questions do not seem to me to be intrusive or unfair and they are not intended to be.

44

And surely the answers to them might, just might, help the police. It seems to me hardly believable that after ten years there is still so much mystery over some of the answers.

Might not the answers also help members of the public understand the background to Madeleine's disappearance a little more clearly? And might not some of the answers help counteract some of the remarkable rumours, insinuations and assertions which now surround this case?

The McCanns seem to have been protected by some very powerful individuals. Inevitably, there are questions being asked. Why did three Prime Ministers, a Foreign Secretary, a Pope, much of the Foreign Service, a Prince, the police and most of the mainstream media put so much effort into protecting a fairly ordinary pair of middle class doctors from the sort of natural suspicion which would, in any normal circumstances, be considered perfectly proper and reasonable? Why was the abduction claim (made so immediately and without much if any serious evidential support) be regarded as the only real explanation for Madeleine's disappearance?

Might not lessons be learned which could help other parents and help prevent something similar happening in the future?

Every few minutes a British child disappears. The problem of missing children is a huge one.

Surely every step should be taken to safeguard all other children.

Isn't that what everyone wants?

26

There are some subjects which can no longer be discussed in public.

No one is allowed to question the existence or extent of Hitler's concentration camps. To do so is likely to lead not to a contemptuous dismissal but to arrest and imprisonment.

Anyone who publicly questions the popular myth of climate change will be barred from BBC programmes and university lecture halls. (The BBC will occasionally allow an honest discussion but the station is required to ensure that controversial subjects are treated with 'due impartiality' and this it clearly does not do.) Those who dare to question the commercially and politically convenient myth of climate change will have to be prepared to be demonised by the Climate Change Industry and its media apologists.

Climate change is, in almost every respect, the 21st century equivalent to AIDS in the 1990s. I know for a fact that the AIDS crisis was blown up by homosexuals as a ruthless public relations campaign designed to gather attention, sympathy and support. Aggressive homosexuals spread misinformation widely.

Today, lobbyists and vested interests and crooked scientists have again hyped and spun a modest problem into a money-spinning apocalyptic threat. It changed its name from global warming because too many people wanted to know when the warming was going to start because it didn't seem to be getting any warmer and their heating bills were quite definitely going up. They changed the threat from Global Warming to the considerably more 'wishy washy' Climate Change when it became abundantly clear that the world wasn't getting warmer. The global warming moniker didn't do well since people who were looking forward to the chance to wear their shorts and skimpy tops more frequently, were inevitably disappointed.

Every unusual weather event is blamed on climate change. Scientists are supposed to declare conflicts of interest and to present evidence accurately and honestly. Sadly, according to those criteria, most of the scientists who are quoted these days are not entitled to call themselves 'scientists'.

(The simple truth, of course, is that there have been unusual weather events since the beginning of records. For example, back in 1709, Europe froze for several months. It was so cold that people skated on the canals in Venice. Church bells shattered when they were rung. It was possible to ride across the Baltic Sea on horseback. Was this due to man-made climate change?)

During the 1980s, it was not considered acceptable to question the widely held (but unsustainable) belief that AIDS was about to kill us all. I was repeatedly banned from television and radio programmes because the scientific truths I wished to share were considered politically unacceptable. I seem to remember listening agog as the British Medical Association and the Royal College of

Nursing both forecast, quite seriously that we would all be affected by AIDS by the year 2000. These organisations created panic, mass fear and hysteria and were responsible for many suicides. More people were killing themselves because they were frightened of AIDS than were dying because they had AIDS. Representatives of both organisations attacked me frequently and robustly when I disagreed.

The enthusiasm for the climate change myth reminds me very much of the enthusiasm for the AIDS myth. In both cases, the facts have been ignored by ignoramuses who do not realise that science is, or should be, about facts and that facts demand scientific integrity and accuracy. And in both cases, the promoters of the myth have a good deal to gain and the whole thing smacks of good old-fashioned lobbying.

Even though many eminent Victorians did so with immense effectiveness it has never been thought acceptable to question vivisection. The medical establishment (sponsored and controlled by the pharmaceutical industry) says that animal experiments are valuable, indeed essential, and so anyone who says otherwise, however much evidence they may be able to produce on behalf of their point of view, will be regarded by the media as, at best, an oddball and at worst a dangerous lunatic. (To be fair, several hundred A-list celebrities signed my anti-vivisection campaign and although they received libellous letters from the pro-vivisection lobby most remained steadfast and loyal.)

And the same is true of vaccination.

For some years now, there has been no public debate about vaccination. No debate is allowed. The subject is closed. Decades ago, I debated the issue many times and never lost – not because I am good at debating but because the facts are all on my side. Today, no television or radio station in Britain would dream of organising an interview or a debate on the subject because to do so would risk exposing their innuendo, bigotry, prejudice and evasions against the harsh light of unwelcome scientific evidence. They would as soon organise a debate questioning the truth of the holocaust. On the other hand, all media outlets will happily promote scares designed to increase vaccine uptake figures. (Just before the annual flu vaccine jab bonanza, there are always scares

47

about the flu. Similarly, when measles vaccinations are due there will be false, scare stories about measles epidemics.)

I have been campaigning about vaccination for nearly half a century, and many years ago I wrote a book collecting together the scientific evidence which proves conclusively that vaccination does not work and is not safe. We sent out 600 review copies. Not one review appeared. If I had proof that vaccination programmes were deliberately designed to kill people, I really don't think anyone in the media would be interested.

I wonder how many parents realise that vaccination programmes for children are designed to protect the health of the community, at the possible expense of the health of the individual child. No one ever tells parents this because the establishment fears that if parents knew then they would not allow their children to be used. Vaccination is fascism in action.

A year or two ago I offered $1,000,000 to anyone who could produce incontrovertible clinical evidence which satisfies me that all vaccines are completely safe and effective. I sent details of the challenge to the national press.

The result?

Silence.

You would have thought, would you not, that a journalist somewhere would consider such an offer newsworthy?

But no.

I am a doctor and I know the facts about vaccines and vaccination and I am considered too dangerous to be allowed to air my challenge outside my website.

The pro-vaccine industry (consisting of drug companies and doctors – all of whom make a huge amount of money out of vaccines) has been so effective in brain washing the media that no one will even report the existence of the challenge.

And so the vaccination myth must remain unchallenged.

Meanwhile, millions of men, women, children and infants continue to be vaccinated, injured and killed. Vaccines are never tested to see if they work long term or if they are safe long term. No one ever tests to see how well (or badly) vaccines react with other vaccines. And no one deliberately looks for or measures the side effects – however deadly those side effects might be.

And the scandal continues unchecked.

History will show that vaccination is a bad thing.

In a few decades time our descendants will look back upon vaccination and find it difficult to believe that doctors actually injected children with such dangerous and ineffective substances.

And when vaccination has finally been banned, as far too dangerous to allow, the tide will turn and anyone proposing or defending vaccination will be banned from the airwaves and the media.

The funny thing is that if I am still around by then I will not support such a ban.

I'll be happy to debate the issue of vaccination with anyone.

Because freedom of speech is crucial.

And I know the facts are on my side.

'All great truths begin as blasphemies', said George Bernard Shaw, who was an opponent of vaccination.

It's just a matter of trying to make a difference.

27

The eurocrats are demanding that we hand over huge amounts of money to leave the European Union? Some call it the price of a divorce. Others call it a punishment (to deter other countries which might be toying with the same idea). But why should we pay a penny to quit?

EU staffers want us to give them £60 billion to leave Hitler's one remaining concentration camp.

Stuff that.

We don't need to give them one penny in severance.

Indeed, if money is going to change hands then the EU should pay us for all the damage the wretched organisation has done to our economy and our culture.

Looking after immigrants forced upon us by the EU will cost us at least £100 billion in NHS bills alone.

Providing benefit payments for immigrants who don't want to work will cost us another £100 billion. One in five unemployed in Britain is an immigrant.

And sorting out the legal mess their daft rules has created will cost another £50 billion.

So, even if we don't charge them damages for the chaos caused by stupid EU laws about light bulbs and cucumbers they are still on the hook for at least £250 billion. (And we'll have that in sterling, please: a proper currency. Not their toy town euro stuff

If they make a fuss about paying our bill then we'll bill them for cultural losses. And we'll charge them for the stress of EU membership.

That'll be at least another £250 billion.

That's the bottom line.

We aren't paying the EU to leave the damned club.

We will demand that they pay us at least £250 billion in the divorce settlement.

And since the euro is a rather dodgy currency we'll take it in cash, please.

Real money: sterling.

28

I heard today from a friend who lives in Northern Ireland. He tells me that he waited in all week for a new fridge to be delivered. Each day he telephoned the company from which he had bought the fridge. Each day they told him that the fridge was on its way. Each day he stayed in. Each day there was no fridge delivered: five wasted days and still no fridge.

As I have got older I worry more because I know just how many things that can go wrong with everything we do but particularly with everything where some corporate or business entity is crucial to the success of the endeavour. The amount of time we all waste waiting for stuff to be delivered or for workmen to turn up is phenomenal.

Thinking of workmen: why don't they ever make notes?

You walk round the house or garden with them, telling them exactly what you want them to do. You explain in detail. They make no notes whatsoever. 'Do you want to write this down?' you ask. 'Oh no,' they say, clearly insulted. And then when they turn up they have forgotten everything. 'What was it you wanted me to do?' they ask. 'You wanted a stone arch building over here didn't you?' 'No, I wanted you to sort out the blocked drains.' 'You wanted the hall painting?' 'No, I wanted you to repair the woodwork on the conservatory roof.'

29

A pal who smokes has written to me pointing out that Parkinson's Disease and Alzheimer's are both less common among smokers. I don't know whether or not to point out to him that these are both diseases which tend to affect older citizens. And many smokers simply don't live long enough to suffer from disorders of old age.

30

In Devon I saw our nearest neighbour again today. He is a nice fellow who always has a cheery smile.

'Good morning, Eugene!' he said brightly, holding out his hand. We shook.

'I never forget a name,' he said proudly. 'You're Eugene, aren't you?'

I smiled and sort of nodded.

I think I will become Eugene for him. It is an insignificant price to pay to please a fellow man.

31

There are, we are told, far more EU citizens living in the UK than there are Britons living in other European countries. They've got three million living here and we have one million living there.

Why could this be?

I have come up with four possible explanations:

They love our climate.

They want to be here so that they can stand outside Buckingham Palace and watch the changing of the guard.

They love our food and prefer our cooking to anything available in their home land.

They love the fact that Britain is the only country to hand out free money to EU citizens.

February

1

Every time you wash out a jam jar, three small African children die of thirst.

I can't prove that, of course.

It might be five small African children who die. It might be ten.

But my headline is more accurate than anything the local council, the Government or the European Union will tell you about recycling.

The simple truth is that water is in desperately short supply.

That's why pure drinking water often costs more than oil products such as gas and petrol.

Local councils in the UK insist that citizens wash out bottles, jars and tins. They are obeying absurd recycling rules introduced by the EU. (There is no little irony in the fact that local councils everywhere spend a fortune printing and distributing expensively designed and produced leaflets, booklets and newspapers describing the true Joy of Recycling.)

But anyone who washes out tins or bottles with fresh, drinking water is wasting the planet's most valuable natural resource.

And that is a crime against humanity.

If local councils really cared one jot about the environment and about people they would abandon their absurd recycling programmes and spend the money they saved trying to persuade more people to turn vegetarian. That would dramatically reduce global starvation and do infinitely more good for the environment than all the recycling programmes on the planet. It won't happen, of course. The meat industry is far too powerful and would never allow it. Bottom line is that you cannot be 'green' or claim to care about the environment or be a logical recycling fan if you continue to eat meat. Keeping of cattle is the biggest single cause of starvation, environmental damage and water shortage on the planet. Millions of people die so that the rich can eat steaks and hamburgers. And if global warming ever turns out to have been anything other than a marketing strategy to sell peak oil then it will have been because of our affection for eating meat.

Incidentally, I read today that the biggest use of plastics is now for making recycling boxes. It would be much better for hygiene and the environment if all rubbish was collected in black plastic bags and used as landfill. There would be less expenditure on sorting, washing, putting into lots of different plastic boxes and sending round lots of different trucks.

Throw the black bags into the crusher and bob's your uncle (or, these days, quite possibly your aunty).

2

While standing in a queue in the bank I heard a man admit to a friend that he had started to dye his hair. His companion, who was quite bald, smiled at him and replied: 'My hair died all by itself.'

3

We were expecting a parcel today but it didn't come.

I later discovered that the delivery driver who was supposed to bring the parcel was a woman who refused to bring it because it weighed too much. I am told I have to collect the parcel myself.

The parcel weighs 1.5 lb and is smaller than a shoebox.

I was told by a representative of the delivery company that they couldn't do anything about this nonsense because if they reprimanded the woman they would be accused of sexism.

This is the second time this has happened to us – and I think this was a different driver.

4

The correct relationship between society and the individual is conflict, because society forces people to do things they don't want to do and charges them money for the doubtful privilege of doing it.

That's how things have always been – until now.

But in our 21st century society things have changed, and for millions the relationship with society contains no conflict because they are in debt to society; they have become its slaves, because they are totally reliant on the hand-outs they receive.

5

Re-reading 'Leave it to Psmith' by the immortal P.G.Wodehouse I found this sentence: 'Even head-gardener Angus McAllister was as happy as a Scotsman can ever be.'

If Wodehouse had been writing this today, his editor would have encouraged him to remove the sentence simply because some readers today are raddled with political correctness. And if 1,000 people read a book it only takes a few to be offended for the book to be trashed and destroyed.

And that's the frightening thought.

Writers of all kinds, of fiction and of non-fiction, are removing anything contentious from their work lest they upset a tiny minority of over-sensitive and snappy readers.

Not for the first time I am glad I am not a young writer, just setting out on my journey. The road was always rocky but these days there are many more hazards and the cautious will doubtless be inclined to stay on the safe and well-trodden paths. Books are gilded or gelded on whims.

Writing about reviewers reminds me that the other day I saw a review of a book by C.S.Forester. The writer of the review damned the book simply because it wasn't another in his famous Hornblower series.

(Forester, who was a doctor, wrote a good many other marvellous books including African Queen and The Gun, both of which were filmed).

To give a bad review of a book because it isn't something else (which no one ever said it was) is mean and spiteful.

Oddly enough, however, the biggest problem with reviewers isn't with amateur reviewers but with the professionals. Many reviewers work for big publishers (usually as 'readers') and there is far too much back scratching going on. ('If I give good reviews to the books published by Scrumpley and McHair they'll give me more work.')

The whole business reaches a nadir when it comes to authors reviewing books. Then there is an obscene amount of back scratching. ('I'll give your book a good review if you'll write a good review of my book.').

Finally, there is the fact that the few professional reviewers around tend to be people who want to be creative artists but don't have the talent, the temperament or the imagination. And they are probably the worst because they hate authors who can make a living out of their books.

6

I amused myself this morning by making a list of twelve things the EU has given us. Here it is:

1) Giant rats: Because of the EU's absurd and scientifically unsound obsession with climate change local councils are not allowed to collect rubbish in the sensible, old-fashioned way. Councils are heavily fined if they do not force householders to put their rubbish into recycling containers. Residents in some areas are told that their rubbish must be out on the pavement before 7.00 a.m. and they will be fined if they put out their bins and boxes before midnight. No one cares that the carefully sorted recycling rubbish is then sent to China to be dumped. Not collecting rubbish regularly means that the rat population in Europe is soaring. And rats are getting healthier and bigger. Rats have up to 14 babies in a single litter and the young rats are themselves reproducing within five weeks. The increase in the rat population is pretty well entirely dependent upon the amount of available food and so it's a fair bet that the total rat population of Britain will be rising fairly dramatically in the coming years. Local councils don't seem to understand that rats are perfectly capable of eating their way into those disgusting plastic food containers which householders are encouraged to put outside their homes. Indeed, in towns and cities the rats are now probably big enough to carry the containers away with them. There are other problems in addition to the rats. Councils are increasing their income by fining local residents who

make mistakes. Last year councils in Britain fined seven million people for failing to put their bins out at the right time, for not washing their yoghurt cartons properly or for mistakenly putting the right piece of recycling into the wrong container. The new system dramatically increases the spread of infection with bin men transferring bugs from one container to all the others they touch. And, of course, strict rules about when bins are put out and brought in cause chaos and confusion (particularly among the elderly). I firmly believe that the EU bin policies are spreading dangerous bugs. How many people wash their hands thoroughly when they have collected their variety of bins and plastic boxes from the pavement outside their home? (Wherein the tidiest of passers-by will have doubtless deposited their unwanted cans and wrappers). The bin men who empty these bins and boxes will have spread bugs from everyone else's bins and boxes onto yours and, unless you wear disposable gloves when handling the bin, or wash your hands very thoroughly after doing so, you will have contaminated yourself and your home with every possibly lethal bug in the neighbourhood.

2) Short-term contracts and insecurity for low paid workers. The EU's employment legislation has forced employers to put many low paid workers on short-term contracts. The result is a loss of security for millions of workers. Eurocrats who created this daft legislation have no understanding of the real world because their own working lives are so protected and undemanding.

3) Rising unemployment among young women. EU legislation on maternity benefits means that employers are now unwilling to hire young women who might become pregnant. The whole damned benefits programme has destroyed generations. Providing benefits with such freedom has enabled the idle and created the entitlement generation. The system has gone so mad that politicians are now demanding that unemployed parents must be given extra money to pay for child care. I am mystified by the claim that parents who don't go out to work need child care more than parents who have jobs.

4) Soaring food prices. The Common Agricultural Policy which rewards farmers with vast profits has pushed up food prices throughout Europe. British citizens pay thousands more because of the EU farming subsidies. The poorest suffer most – and either go hungry or eat cheap, rubbishy food.

5) Massive queues in shops. The lack of staff in shops is a direct result of EU employment legislation. More and more shops are introducing self-pay tills but there often isn't enough space and so there are queues at these too.

6) Poor GP service. If you have to wait a month to see your GP, you can blame the EU. Once again, employment legislation forced upon us by the EU has resulted in GPs working a 35 hour week. At nights and at weekends there is no GP availability because of the EU. It is this absence of out of hours GP services which has forced Accident and Emergency Departments to break down under the strain of too much work. (Why, incidentally, was the name changed from 'Casualty' to 'Accident and Emergency Department'?)

7) Rotten hospital services. Hospitals are now punished by the EU if doctors work more than 40 hour weeks. And so there are often no doctors in hospitals at night or at weekends.

8) Rising cancer rates. EU laws have resulted in cancer rates soaring. Food sold within the EU is often packed with approved carcinogens, toxins, hormones and antibiotics. And no one yet knows what damage will be done by the EU allowing food manufacturers to sell genetically engineered food. It was the EU which pushed diesel cars onto our roads – now known to be a major cause of pollution.

9) Buggered up pensions. Finance laws and policies introduced by the EU have helped to destroy private pensions. EU employees , however, have massive, inflation-linked pensions which are unaffected by EU legislation.

10) Disappearing bees. Genetically engineered crops packed with insecticides mean that the bees are dying in their millions. Many people don't think that this matters much but without bees, crops are not pollinated. And this is another reason why food prices are soaring.

11) Red tape affecting profits. Small businesses have been hit hard by red tape introduced by the EU. When small businesses are damaged, they cannot grow or hire extra employees. Large businesses are not affected by red tape because they can employ specialist departments to deal with the bureaucracy. Indeed, most EU red tape was introduced in response to requests from big corporations. That is a perfect example of practical fascism. The people who make any country great are the people who start businesses, not the people who run businesses which were started by someone else. The people who create wealth are the ones who have ideas, visions and take risks, work nights and weekends and mortgage their homes to raise the capital they need. They are the sort of people who wade through acres of rules and regulations and deal with all the EU inspired problems of starting a business and hiring employees.

12) Electricity shortages. Britain is about to run out of electricity because nutty EU laws have forced us to close many of our existing power stations. And electric cars, which use vast amounts of electricity, are making things worse. Unsightly windmills and solar panels are grossly inefficient and rely on massive taxpayer subsidies. (Biofuels, which led to increasing starvation around the world, were another EU enthusiasm.)

7

We are beginning to toy seriously with the idea of selling our apartment in Paris.

The fact is that we will both be glad to sell up.

The tragedy is that for us Paris has stopped being fun. It has also become (whisper it softly) very ugly. I have been travelling to Paris for over 60 years but I now dread going there.

The process of travel (moving from one country to another) has become unbearable. Motorway travel in the UK is slow and tiresome. Border guards have become rude and aggressive. Eurostar has lost all its charm and has become as much fun as the 8.15 to Wapping. Eurostar used to have comfortable seats, good lighting and old-fashioned lamps. The attentive staff wore smart uniforms. There was champagne before a three-course lunch and hot towels and chocolates afterwards. Eurostar has cut so many corners that I can see them expecting customers to pedal in a couple of years' time. I always thought trains were much more exciting than planes because they were far more comfortable and they made the journey slower and therefore an adventure.

The Parisians are ruder than ever. And Paris itself has given in to the terrorists and is awash with armed police, concrete blocks and barbed wire. In every conceivable way, Paris has become uglier. The city is full of pickpockets and confidence tricksters.

Our home in Paris has lost its charm too. Since the electricity people dug out the foundations last year the whole building has acquired serious cracks. It wouldn't surprise me if all the buildings in the street were showing signs of subsidence. In fact, it is only the fact that the buildings are attached that stops them all falling down. The electricity company dug a deep trench underneath the front part of the entire street. They actually dug out the rock and stone from underneath the front few feet of the building and then, when they'd finished, they replaced the rock and stone with sandy soil. So, now our building has developed huge cracks as a result of the inevitable subsidence.

The other residents of our building are now young millennial renters who don't care about the building or about anyone else. They make too much noise, they throw their rubbish about and they leave the front door and the cellar gate wide open. The building used to be occupied by older residents who were polite, quiet and respectful. Those residents have either died or moved away.

The owners of a building next to ours allowed someone to build a metalwork workshop in their courtyard. Amazingly, the French planning people didn't seem to object. So now we can hear nothing all day but the sound of grinding and hammering. The owner of the workshop must live nearby for he works weekends too. There is always someone doing something noisy – usually involving drills. The floor below in our apartment building is occupied by three apartments and the people in one of the apartments have been noisily renovating their apartment for six months. Their apartment has two rooms. What can you do to a two room apartment that takes six months?

My advice to travellers is simple. If you have already been to Paris: don't go back. If you have never been to Paris: stay away.

8

If you spend more than an hour in Paris then, sooner or later, you will need to abuse a Frenchman (or woman). This is just the way things are and it is no shame on you or the French person you will be abusing.

When this happens there is one very important thing to remember: however well you speak French you should revert to English.

English friends of ours who are quite fluent in French admit that they always revert to English when they need to berate a workman, traffic warden or difficult concierge. (If you feel you must speak French to the natives then the trick, I am told, is to speak quickly, firmly, confidently and loudly. Allow no dissent, interruption and definitely no corrections. Once you allow a French person to correct your French you are lost for ever.)

'I always freeze and forget what I want to say if I try to shout in French,' admits the husband, who, to our ear, speaks French like a native. 'You are at a huge disadvantage if you try to have a row in their language,' he says. 'Their invective will always be better than yours. Your only chance of getting the upper hand is to shout in English – and speak very quickly. You will know better words and there is a good chance that, if you show sufficient imagination, they won't have the faintest idea what you are saying. If you should lose your temper and say something quite unforgivable you will get away with it because they won't know what you've said.'

The important thing to remember is that although nearly all French folk speak English it is a sad fact that no Frenchman has ever learned to speak English properly although, of course, they always think they speak it fluently. They think they speak perfect, idiomatic English but in reality they speak atrocious English and we don't say anything to them because we are far too polite. But that's part of the fun. I never correct them. Indeed, I always encourage their mistakes and the worse they speak French the more I praise them. (The French do not suffer from self-doubt or regret. And since these are the two big causes of heart disease this is why the French who smoke a good deal and drink even more, suffer surprisingly little from heart disease).

The other thing which is important to remember is that although the French think they have a great and sophisticated sense of humour – they don't. And they don't have any sense of irony. So, if you say to a Frenchman : 'My word, your English is very good' (even if it isn't) they will purr with self-satisfaction because they will accept the compliment at face value.

Usually, the English are far too polite to tell the French that they're making zillions of mistakes every time they open their mouths.

But if you want to annoy one just correct his grammar, choice of vocabulary or, best of all, his pronunciation.

Don't feel in the slightest bit bad about doing this because all French citizens, but particularly the ones in Paris, absolutely delight in correcting foreigners who try to speak their language. (It is strange, I know, but to the French we are 'foreigners'. Quite absurd.) Anyone who gets a tense or a conjugation wrong will be subjected to a deep sigh and a French lesson.

And every foreigner always pronounces French words incorrectly.

So, go to it! Enjoy yourself! Abuse a Frenchman – but do it in English.

9

We are still in Paris, trying to decide when and how to sell our apartment.

Here are some of the things we have discovered:

There is a 21% tax on any capital gains.

There is another 15.5% social charge on any capital gains. This is not officially a tax and so it cannot be put against the capital gains tax which will be charged by the British authorities. The EU seems to have ruled that taking the social charge from foreigners is illegal but the French never take any notice of EU rulings which they do not like.

There is an additional 5% tax on any capital gains if the property being sold is worth more than about ninepence.

The estate agent must be paid between 5% and 10% commission on the sale price. They will not produce a brochure though they may put up a snap in their window and on their website. (With this sort of commission, why isn't everyone in France an estate agent? I can't imagine why anyone does anything else for a living. Indeed, I am told that every ambitious French boy and girl grows up wanting to be an estate agent, it pays better than medicine, lawyering or anything else.)

Huge fees must be paid to the notaire so that he can make sure that all the necessary taxes are all paid.

Special tests must be done to ensure that the property satisfies EU regulations about energy use, the presence of asbestos, the suitability of the gas and electricity supplies, the presence or absence of termites and/or aliens in the cellar. A fairly standard report on a small property will run to 100 pages, not be as useful as a survey, and be incomprehensible to anyone who hasn't been trained to read EU technical reports. Absolutely wrong.

There is a currency charge of 5% or more to convert euros back to sterling.

A cruel and quite incomprehensible wealth tax will be charged on any savings or properties which suggest that the owner has earned more than a low level bureaucrat.

A good deal of paperwork will be involved in the actual sale – which will be protracted. A simple proxy or power of attorney will be at least six pages long. The French bureaucrats have a simple rule: 'Never limit yourself to one page of waffle when you can produce six.'

10

I was reading July 10th 1954 issue of *The Cricketer* magazine at breakfast time and spotted a full page advertisement headed 'What's Jeff got that I haven't got?' The advertisement, presented as a cartoon strip, showed the 'hero' looking on wistfully as another chap (Jeff) stands surrounded by lovely young ladies.

'Looks! Personality! If that's what it is, I just can't compete. Or maybe it's physique,' thinks our hero.

In the next frame he is in the gym, struggling to lift some weights. 'Must be a better way than this. Gosh, yes! Always drinks Guinness Jeff does.'

And then there is our hero, with a glass of Guinness in his hand and a big smile on his face. In the background, a waitress looks at him approvingly.

And in the final frame there's a simple message from our hero: 'No, I can't say I get any more dates, but I enjoy everything much more than I used to.'

So that was how alcohol was promoted in the 1950s.

11

A man who lives in our building in Paris told us that his aunt occasionally used to dance naked on the table at dinner parties.

No one ever knew when she would do this but eventually someone noticed that it only happened when she ate shellfish.

It had not, apparently, occurred to anyone until I mentioned it that when she ate oysters she always drank copious amounts of champagne to wash them down.

12

We watched a documentary called *Citizenfour* – a film about Edward Snowden, the American who leaked valuable information about how we are all spied upon by our Governments.

What Snowden did was vital but the film seemed to me to show that Snowden's motive was at least partly inspired by vanity. He talked beforehand about allowing himself to be nailed to the cross and when expecting to be photographed by the world's press, he spent ages putting gel onto his hair and making sure it looked pretty. The journalists who were involved in the release of the information he stole also seemed to be more interested in the media than in the message. And did *The Guardian* newspaper (which published the leaked information) pay Snowden for the information he leaked?

I found the film one of the most boring and badly made I've ever seen. It apparently won the Best Documentary Oscar in 2015 but it could have done with a bit more planning and editing. I fell asleep after an hour or so of interminable smug, self-congratulatory nonsense but naturally, however, *The Guardian* gave the film a plump five star rating. (They would do though, wouldn't they?)

I found, some time ago, that the quickest way to find out if a film is worth watching is to see if it has been reviewed by *The Guardian*. If it has, and *The Guardian* liked it, then the film will be dull and unwatchable. We use this as an easy, quick rule of thumb guide when finding new movies. The mistake *The Guardian* writers always seem to make is in assuming that incomprehensible, unintelligible, badly made and dull combine to mean highbrow and superior. The corollary, of course, is that they also assume that anything which is readable, and which gives pleasure to people or, heaven forbid, makes them think, is lowbrow and worthless. In addition, anything which is popular, must by their definition be worthless. This is intellectual snobbishness at its worst.

The tragedy, of course, is that *The Guardian's* strange, upside down philosophies have contaminated many other sections of our world because, for example, it is pretty well impossible to obtain a job working for the BBC unless you are an avid *Guardian* reader.

13

We spent a pleasant afternoon in the little park near to Les Invalides.

While we sat in winter sunshine, Antoinette studied her Russian grammar. I read a small volume of essays by E.V. Lucas. It is strange, is it not, how authors can go out of fashion. In his day, Lucas was one of the most popular and prolific of authors. Many of his books consist of essays which first appeared as newspaper articles. They are erudite, humorous and delicate. I would rate him alongside Hazlitt as one of the greatest of English novelists. Alas, he is now pretty well forgotten and his books can be picked up very cheaply in second hand bookshops or, I assume, from

Amazon or eBay. Most of his volumes are small and pocket sized and therefore extremely handy for travellers.

Of course, Lucas isn't the only author to have fallen out of fashion. Who reads Arnold Bennett these days? I worked my way through some of his forgotten novels recently and found a number of delights. *Riceyman Steps* is one of his best. I've also managed to obtain a copy of his Journals, which I thought I had read half a century or so ago but which I don't remember at all and so cannot possibly have done. They are wonderful. I bet no one alive when he was in his pomp thought that Bennett's oeuvre would be largely out of print less than a century after his death. Sic transit and all that.

The full edition of the Bennett journals is over a million words long and runs to four volumes but the copy I have is the Penguin edition, edited by Frank Swinnerton and published in 1954. It consists of selected bits and pieces and runs to 493 pages. There is a selection of Bennett's handwriting on the cover of my Penguin and it is more illegible than mine. I pity whoever had the job of turning the stuff into print. Bennett was not a doctor but maybe he had aspirations.

14

One of our squirrels in Devon has carefully removed the Perspex front from the feeder box I fill with nuts and seeds. He hasn't just removed the front, however. He has taken it and hidden it somewhere. Squirrels always do this. If a feeder is in some way troublesome or a challenge, they will alter it or adapt it to better suit their requirements.

I now put food in the feeder and the squirrel no longer has to lift the lid to get at it.

The unexpected beneficiary is our robin who can now hop into the box and help himself to nuts and seeds.

15

I have always found things to worry about but there is so much to fear these days that on some days my capacity for fear is so overladen that it breaks down and I don't fear anything.

Never in my lifetime have there been so many things to worry about.

The media live on creating fear.

Politicians thrive and survive according to the fear they have created.

Central bankers create fear whenever they open their mouths.

Social media fanatics spread fear as though their lives depended upon it: fear about health, fear about legal hazards, fear about terrorism, fear about muggers and murderers, fear about the roads, fear about the food we eat. And on and on and on ad infinitum.

Governments, armies, police and spies depend entirely upon a sense of fear and impending doom among the public. It is in their interest to promote fear in order to exploit its consequences. Without impending disaster and doom, governments can do nothing.

When the iron curtain fell, security services targeted animal rights campaigners as the big threat, not because they were but because there was a fear vacuum. Today, the security services never bother with animal rights because they don't need them.

16

The mad greens and other proponents of the myth of climate change (nee global warming) say that the oil in the ground (or under the sea) will have to stay there as their campaign gains more power. They are wrong, of course, for several reasons.

First, the climate change silliness has been developing for well over a century. The campaigners like to think they invented it but pseudo-scientists have, since the 19th century, been putting forward the theory that greenhouse gases could change the climate. Only the converts think the evidence is convincing.

Second, the alternatives to fossil fuels are frighteningly inefficient. For example, it takes more energy to make a windmill than the windmill will ever produce. So, the more windmills we produce the more energy we waste.

Third, the clever alternatives to oil and the internal combustion engine are also silly. Using food to make fuel (the biofuels nonsense) exacerbated the starvation problem and the Greens have condemned hundreds of thousands to death by campaigning for yet more food to be turned into fuel for rich people.

Fourth, the whole idea of electric cars is daft. Making them requires massive amounts of polluting energy. And running them requires vast quantities of electricity – most of which is produced inefficiently using oil or coal. Then there is the problem of what to do with all the batteries when they need to be thrown away. And how big will the batteries need to be to power lorries, let alone aeroplanes? And because electric cars are inefficient they use more fossil fuel than traditional cars running on oil. I wonder how many fans of Tesla (the electric car company) know that the company deliberately stunts its batteries – reducing the range that drivers can travel between charges. If you own a Tesla motor car and want it to travel further, you have to pay the company an extra fee to have your battery upgraded. Nice. And I wonder if any Tesla fans realise that some petrol fuelled cars are allegedly 'greener' than Tesla's electric cars. How can that possibly be? Well, the answer is simple. Some electric cars have higher lifecycle greenhouse gas emissions than petrol driven vehicles. Sanctimonious enthusiasts point out that electric vehicles have no exhaust pipes. But they conveniently forget that making electric cars requires massive amounts of energy and that quantities of rare earth metals such as lithium and cobalt required for the batteries have to be dug out of the ground. (Much of it is apparently dug out of the mines by children as young as seven so it is nice to know that the Greens are providing work for so many under 12s.) An electric car can require 10 kg of cobalt and 60 kg of lithium. Recycling the parts of an electric car (and its batteries) requires more energy. And, of course, the electricity to fuel an electric car has to be produced (usually by burning coal or diesel). It is a plain, old-fashioned lie to claim that electric cars are 'zero emission vehicles'. Tesla is the most over-rated, over promoted company on the planet. I suspect that the shares are due for a massive collapse in the next year or two.

The media, which is as potty over electric cars as they were over the equally daft enthusiasm for biofuels are busy telling us all that electric cars are going to save the planet and that the big car manufacturers are going to stop making diesel or petrol driven cars.

How long will it be before we are forced to buy and drive the damned things either because there isn't any alternative or because we will be punished so severely if we dare disobey?

Has anyone realised that, as Antoinette has pointed out, because electric cars are silent there will doubtless be a good many accidents involving pedestrians?

The fact is that electric cars have been around for 100 years and they don't have a future (unless we are all forced to buy them) because they are a crap idea.

Fifth, if we stop using fossil fuels then the greens will have to give up using their beloved laptops and mobile phones and they will have to walk everywhere. All those lovely climate change conferences in wonderful locations will have to stop. And no electricity means that there won't be any Skype or video conferencing either. It is one of the strange ironies that greens are among the world's most enthusiastic travellers (and, therefore, users of fossil fuels). It apparently does not occur to them that until someone invents a solar powered aeroplane they will be using up vast amounts of the world's depleting supply of natural energy.

The real truth is that the oil is running out and the recent enthusiasm for the ancient climate change theory was created by politicians who wanted to introduce a whole raft of new laws restricting our use of energy so that there would be plenty of oil left for tanks and jet fighters.

The final irony is the fact that if more of the greens would give up eating meat then the world's environmental problems would disappear pretty well immediately. And there would be no more starving people in Africa, or anywhere else.

But the greens want to be self-righteous and to keep their hamburgers and their social media accounts.

17

Tidying a stationery cupboard in my study, I realised today that I have accumulated a four year supply of notebooks. I use an average of two notebooks a week and they must have good plain paper, stout covers, a marker ribbon and some sort of elastic band to use when closing the notebook. Oh, and they must be pocket sized. (I keep larger notebooks for use in and around the house.)

The Moleskin notebooks are perfect and even have a small expanding pocket inside the back cover wherein can be stored small pieces of loose paper upon which scribbled notes have been written.

But a four year supply of notebooks seems a trifle over the top and so I think I must stop buying them for a while.

18

I am delighted to see that the Government is planning to give people marks according to behaviour.

The Government will measure people's behaviour in order to decide what services they are entitled to.

Anyone who incurs black marks for traffic offences, fare dodging or jay working will find that they are no longer entitled to the full range of public services and rights.

Moreover, internet activity will also be used to assess behaviour.

Individuals who do bad things on the internet (or whose searches are considered questionable) will find themselves 'black marked'.

Individuals who have 'responsible' jobs will be subjected to enhanced scrutiny.

At the moment, it is only the Chinese Government who is planning to give its citizens a 'social credit score'.

But who wants to bet that Western Governments won't soon follow suit?

19

Scientists have (again) proved what most of us have known ever since we were old enough to use a knife and fork: that if you think of nice things, good memories, happy places, then you will feel better.

I'm waiting for news that scientists have done research showing that eating food is good for us.

20

Juncker and the bunch of thugs and crooks at the EU are cross with Britain because we dared to say 'No' and to mean it.

We are the only country brave enough to stand up to the EU's brand of Nazi fascism.

The EU has, in the past, always succeeded in overturning national votes which it found inconvenient or threatening. When the Irish voted 'No' to the Nice treaty, the EU forced through a reversal.

Again when the Irish voted 'No' to the Lisbon treaty, the EU managed to fiddle a reversal.

When the Danes voted 'No' to the Maastricht treaty, the EU forced a change of heart.

When the Dutch and the French both voted 'No' to the European Constitution, they merely renamed the European Constitution the Lisbon Treaty and that was that for the Dutch and the French voters.

When the Greeks voted 'No' in 2015, the EU just ignored the inconvenience of a democratic vote they did not like.

The EU has always opposed democracy. The EU has always been crooked and incompetent and run by bullies and thugs. And as Brexit continues, it will be increasingly clear to anyone who wants to look, that the EU has not matured or softened its attitudes but that it has hardened its approach. The plan, it is clear to see, is to do away with democracy completely, to form the United States of Europe which was Hitler's dream and for a small group of unelected, overpaid eurocrats to make all the rules and take all the decisions.

In addition to being the genuine home of fascism, the European Union is the ultimate home of cronyism, jobs for the boys (and girls), crookedness, greed and self-interest. It will be interesting for Britons to sit and watch the whole crooked edifice crumble. Incidentally, those who think the EU is a 'good idea' should read Stanley Adams's book *Roche v Adams*. It is one of the earliest and most terrifying accounts of EU wickedness and it will make your blood run cold. Anyone who reads it and still believes in the EU has to be a psychopath.

I wrote a letter to Juncker of the European Union:

'Dear Juncker,

First let me say, on behalf of all the British people (except Lily Allen whose dad was an actor and Gary Linker who was a footballer) that I think the EU stinks and you are an uppity twat.

We have decided to leave the EU without more ado and we will be off next Monday as soon as we've had breakfast.

Here's the deal.

And, by the way, you can take it because there is no option.

We leave the EU and all your stupid rules.

We will not pay one penny more to the EU.

We will not buy any more German cars, French cheeses or anything else made within the EU.

We will not sell anything to EU countries.

All EU citizens currently living in the British Isles must piss off immediately. They will not be allowed back.

In future, all our trade will be done with the Commonwealth, the United States of America and Asia. That should be quite sufficient for all our needs.

Travellers from other EU countries will in future need visas. Only short-term two week visas will be issued for the purposes of tourism.

And if you want a war that's fine with us.

We're already two nil up against the Krauts and the Eyeties. The Frogs all keep a white flag in their knapsacks and they'll roll over in an instant. The only way the French will win a war will be if they declare war on themselves.

Finally, let us suggest that you ignore all those morons (such as George Soros) who have suggested that Britain will one day rejoin the European Union.

Soros once made a bundle betting against sterling and has, ever since, liked to think of himself as some sort of genius. He is, in fact, just another twat who is completely out of touch with the public mood in England. There is absolutely no chance that the British people will ever vote to rejoin Hitler's gloomy band of fascists. We will enjoy watching Hitler's dream collapse and fail.

Just don't ask us to bail you out.

Vernon Coleman'

Meanwhile, the British Government seems to misunderstand the meaning and purpose of Brexit.

Our politicians are, it seems, consumed by fear of everything. The whole thing is quite simple. We are divorcing the EU. We don't want to live together. There has to be a deal. A bloke I know suggests that it's really very simple: we should invite the EU to take Northern Ireland to the zoo every alternate Saturdays. And if we want a hard Brexit let's just fill the Channel Tunnel with stuff we don't want. In the absence of anything more suitably sized. we could fill it and block it permanently with Gary Lineker's head.

There's a couplet that Theresa May and her Ministers should remember:
'Whatever you can do, or dream you can, begin it
Boldness has genius, power and magic in it.'
Under the circumstances, the irony is that it was written by Germany's solitary literary giant: Goethe.

I fear that our Prime Minister does not seem to be bold in any way. She seems rather woeful and beaten. The EU negotiators will eat her up and spit out the bones. We desperately need a Prime Minister (male or female) who has balls. And it would be good to have a cabinet which did not consist almost entirely of cryptorchid eunuchs. Where, among our political leaders, is the passion, the defiance, the pride, the strength or the brains? Where, indeed, is the leadership.

21

I have two parcels to send off to a friend who has decided to have a birthday. I have scales and all the appropriate measuring devices produced by Royal Mail at home but after some minutes, I gave up. I was hoping to be able to weigh and stamp the parcels and then slip them into a nice wide Post Box mouth. But now I will have to stand and queue for an hour. The rules and regulations produced by Royal Mail are incomprehensible and require anyone doing the posting to be able to measure weight, height, width, depth and then decide whether the object for posting is a letter, a large letter a small parcel or a medium sized parcel.

I am quite sure that Royal Mail makes the rules so complex in the knowledge that it will receive huge additional payments in fines and penalties.

22

I found an old T-shirt today. It was one of thousands printed by the *Sunday Mirror* when the paper serialised my book *Bodypower*. The next time someone complains that I don't do social media, I must point out that I have been a T-shirt.

And you really can't get much more multi-media than that.

23

The leaders of nationalists in Scotland, Wales and Northern Ireland all want their countries to leave home and fend for themselves in the outside world. There is, say the Scottish Nationalists, going to be another referendum on the issue of independence. And then another referendum. And another, until the Scottish voters get the answer right. The Welsh nationalists also want a referendum.

Why am I reminded of a trio of parasitic, grown up children threatening to leave home?

Just what the unhappy trio plan to do for money is a mystery.

Obviously, of these three, only Scotland needs to be taken seriously.

Scottish nationalists want independence so that they can spend English money the way they want to spend it – without the English having any say. But the nationalists haven't yet realised that when Scotland is independent it will have to find its own money. England will cut the purse strings. The Sturgeon must have great faith that the sale of kilts and sporrans can be boosted and that Americans, Greeks and Arabs can all be persuaded to buy armfuls of Tam o'Shanter hats.

Fat chance.

Truth is that the majority of the English are cheering the SNP's demand for a second referendum.

They know they can look forward to an independent England with joy in their hearts and oodles of extra cash in their pockets.

So why shouldn't England have a vote in whether or not Scotland leaves the Union?

The departure of Scotland will have a big impact on England. We are entitled to vote on whether or not Scotland leaves.

Actually, if they had any sense, the Scottish Nationalists would campaign to allow England to vote on whether Scotland leaves the Union for there is no doubt that the majority of English voters would enthusiastically support the SNP and vote for Scotland to leave.

Without having to support Scotland, the Chancellor should be able to knock at least 10p to 20p off the basic rate of income tax in England.

Surely, the English are entitled to a vote on whether or not they want their income tax to be reduced so dramatically.

Here are ten other things we can look forward to if the Sturgeon woman ever gets her way and is allowed the Second Referendum she seemed to have promised but has now discovered that she can't have.

If Scotland votes for independence:

Everyone in England will be much richer. The UK spends more than £3,000 a year each more on the Scots than it spends on the English. Everyone agrees this is completely unfair but the Scots whinge so much that no one dares suggest sharing out the loot more equitably. If Scotland leaves the Union, the English will enjoy a massive fiscal boost to their wallets.

We can make bagpipes illegal in England. Bagpipes are, in any case, a recent invention. If Scots were true to their own history, they would play the harp – which was the instrument of choice for their ancestors.

The Sturgeon woman will disappear from our lives forever. She will get no more airtime or print inches than the Prime Minister of Ruritania. Can you name the Ministers of Ireland, Northern Ireland or Wales? No, I thought not. Sturgeon, who has the sour, disappointed look of someone who has been given a dead cat for Christmas, will disappear from our consciousness and we will be all the better for it.

The SNP will disappear from our Parliament.

Thousands of minor but intensely annoying Scottish celebrities will have to go back to Glasgow. They obviously won't want to remain in England as foreigners.

We won't have to pretend to support Andy Murray. (Or his ever present mother.)

The Scots can have their banks back. The Royal Bank of Scotland and HBOS were the cause of our economic collapse in 2008. They have cost English taxpayers billions. And hundreds of thousands of jobs were lost as a result of Scottish banking ineptitude. The Royal Bank of Scotland is still losing money at an indecent rate. We will all be richer without it though quite what the Scots will do with it I cannot imagine. They certainly won't be able to afford to keep it. Incidentally, I find it strange that the RBS is allowed to issue its own banknotes. And stranger still that its new £5, £10 and £20 notes will all contain pictures of women no one outside Scottish universities has ever heard of. Actually, I rather think that these were done as a joke. The woman on one note, Catherine Cranston, is described as a 'leading figure in the development of tea rooms'. Actually, I suppose it is rather sweet that the world's most incompetent bank should celebrate Scottish history with a picture of a woman who ran a chain of tea rooms.

There will be more jobs in England because English companies will bring their call centres back home. And there is a chance we may understand what the people on the other end of the phone are saying.

We will be freed from all that whingeing and ingratitude.

The BBC will have to sack all those Scottish employees whose accents we cannot understand. We cannot have foreigners on our national stations.

We won't have to change our clocks twice a year. (Summer Time was originally introduced so that Scottish farmers wouldn't have to go out in the dark. It has resulted in thousands of unnecessary deaths.)

We can pass another law to ban the kilt. The kilt, incidentally, was invented by a kindly Englishman called Thomas Rawlinson in the early 18th century. Rawlinson, who was an industrialist, invented the kilt because it was cheaper to make than a pair of trousers – and the Scots were poor. However, about two decades later, in 1746, the British Parliament banned the kilt (in the 1746 Dress Act) because it was considered an embarrassment and too different to be an acceptable form of attire. We can pass another Dress Act.

It will be fascinating to watch how Scotland survives without immensely generous hand-outs from the English.

Scotland has very little industry and the little remaining oil in the North Sea is now worse than worthless because closing down the drilling platforms will cost more than the remaining oil will earn. (Why don't they just leave the oil rigs where they are? They will stand there like the forts which are scattered around off the British coast. The sea will slowly claim them. Any dangerous materials could be removed. And permanent lights could be put aboard to warn shipping. It would save a fortune and avoid the problem of what to do with them when they are brought ashore.) A reliable industry estimate is that Scotland's share of the oil industry is now worth minus £50 billion. I find it mind boggling that there are people in Scotland who still believe that their country can survive as an independent nation. If they do leave the Union, they will be living on bread and dripping without the dripping.

Never in a million years will the EU allow Scotland to become a member. The eurocrats know that Scotland would be a drain on the remaining EU resources. And countries such as Spain will block Scotland's membership.

The new Scotland will have to invent its own currency. Called 'The Sporran' perhaps? They could have 100 'kilts' to the 'sporran'. (The New Scotland will not be allowed to use the pound. The name 'Bank of England' should give a clue as to why.)

But England will be rich and free. And so, the English should now start campaigning ferociously for Scotland to leave the Union. And they should demand a chance to vote in the Scottish independence referendum. The campaign to aid the Scots should, perhaps, be titled: 'Bugger off Scotland'.

24

The phrase 'bed blocking' is once again being bandied about in discussions about the National Health Service.

'Bed blocking' is a phrase which is used exclusively when an elderly patient occupies a hospital bed and is too ill to go home.

The phrase 'bed blocking' is never used about patients under the age of 60 or so, however long they need to stay in hospital.

It is clear, therefore, that the phrase is ageist.

25

I had to telephone the company which provides the server for my website. (It is, quite possibly, the most incompetent company in the history of companies.) The man to whom I spoke, needed to look at the website.

'Is this the one?' he asked. 'There's a picture of an old bloke in a hat on the front page. He's wearing a mac.'

'That's the one,' I said. 'I'm the old bloke in the hat and the mac.'

The photograph, incidentally, was taken at a corner of first floor cloisters of Les Invalides in Paris. Antoinette took the picture.

26

Britain is rich enough to spend £50 billion on a new rail link (widely regarded as unnecessary) between London and wherever you can reach with the amount of railway line you can buy for £50 billion. (My bet is that the total cost will be well in excess of £100 billion. Politicians and civil servants are 'careful' with their own money and greedy when claiming expenses but they are always profligate when dealing with public money.)

I wonder how many people know, incidentally, that the spending per capita on transport infrastructure in London is £1,000 whereas the spending per capita on transport infrastructure in other parts of the country is as low as £200 per capita. London has excellent infrastructure, excellent broadband and massive mobile phone coverage. Much of England has rotten roads, very slow broadband and absolutely no mobile phone coverage.

Britain is rich enough to waste billions every year on foreign aid (most of it is creamed off by greedy consultants and self-serving charities).

And, apparently, we are, as a nation, rich enough to pay £350 million a week for membership of the European Union.

And yet 40,000 to 60,000 elderly citizens die of cold every winter in the United Kingdom. (The number varies according to the extent of the cold).

Surely this is proof, if proof be needed, that we do not live in a civilised country?

How can we possibly call ourselves civilised when 40,000 of our citizens can't afford to keep warm in cold weather?

If 40,000 asylum seekers died of the cold, the liberal lefty luvvies would be twittering as fast as their fingers could fly. They would be appalled. They would demand action.

But they don't give a toss about elderly Britons.

Liberal lefty luvvies make a huge fuss about foreigners who want to come to Britain to grab some of our free money.

But you don't often hear them worrying about the plight of the elderly, do you?

The truth is that the elderly are our oppressed and forgotten people.

More than a million old people who have trouble with basic activities receive no help whatsoever. Nothing.

A contact working in an English hospital tells me that elderly patients are deliberately put onto a ward where MRSA is endemic in order to get rid of them as quickly as possible.

(Could this be one of the reasons hospitals seem apparently reluctant to take the simple steps that would eradicate killer, antibiotic resistant bugs?)

In every conceivable way, the elderly are poorer today than ever before.

And things seem about to get worse.

Politicians are now talking about taking the State pension away from people who have savings on which they can live. State pensions are a not a luxury or a favour. They are an entitlement. They are paid for. But I suspect that within a decade or so those who have savings or pensions of their own will find that they no longer receive the State pension. (The State pension in the UK is lower than it is anywhere else in the developed world. Nowhere in any industrialised country are old people so destitute; so likely to starve to death or freeze to death.)

What is going to be next?

Are insurance companies going to refuse to pay out because they think you've got enough money? Are the slightly better off elderly going to be banned from using the roads or calling the fire brigade?

This is ageism and it stinks. This is as much ageism as calling 70-year-olds 'Pops', 'Grandpa' 'Old Man' or 'Grandma'.

And yet our politicians don't give a stuff. As far as they are concerned, the elderly are merely a nuisance – and an expensive nuisance at that. Worse still, they tend to be patriotic, remember Hitler, understand German ambition and want to leave the EU.

Modern politicians (particularly Labour ones) use politics as a stepping stone to self-enrichment. Politicians have proved themselves to be more incompetent, more stupid and more crooked than almost any section of society. National policies which waste tens of billions of pounds of taxpayers' money are launched for whimsical, personal reasons and then abandoned as quickly as they had been introduced. Look at the number of politicians who are in, or have been to, prison and who then generally assume they can simply continue their political and public careers. Let us never forget the expenses scandal which showed that virtually every national politician in Britain was a chiselling crook. I described some of the idiocies of one leading politician in my book *Gordon is a Moron* in which I described how Gordon Brown, a former Chancellor of the Exchequer and later one time Prime Minister, had damned near destroyed the country he was supposed to be helping to govern. The Royal Bank of Scotland, which Scot Brown rescued with our money, has cost taxpayers nearly £30 billion.

And the Entitlement Generation are too busy thinking of themselves to give a toss about the elderly or, indeed, about anyone else in need. There are, I fear, too many people now who want to milk the system, grab their entitlements and take full advantage of everything they can grab. That is the pinnacle of their ambition.

This is not a new thing, of course. Since the Welfare State was born, there have been people who think like this. But there are more, far more of them now than ever before. The spirit of entitlement and expectation has become endemic.

What the politicians and the Entitlement Generation forget is that one day they too will be old.

By then they will have helped build a society in which anyone over the age of 60 will be regarded as worthless and disposable.

Incidentally, I have discovered that one trick to surviving increasing old age is to expect the number and variety of small frailties to increase and to be prepared to put up with them. I have friends, sadly both dead now, who were both investigated, treated and medicated to death. They were long-term members of a health insurance scheme and I sometimes felt that they were forever eager to get their money's worth.

And Antoinette and I know an octogenarian who went to her doctor demanding to have her varicose veins dealt with 'because they looked unsightly in the summer'.

For heaven's sake! Don't people realise that every surgical procedure is risky. And that the risks increase with age.

27

The latest news from the 'entitlement generation' (aka millennials, aka snowflakes) is that 20-30 year olds are now again complaining that they are so hard done by that they need their parents to re-mortgage their homes and give them the money. They presumably intend to spend it on coffees made with hand-crushed beans and served in sun-dried avocado skins. They insist that they must buy their expensive, little treats, and to pay the price they think nothing of selling their souls, their dignity, their integrity, their honour and their parents' dignity and honour too. They are like cuckoos, forever demanding, never satisfied.

This is the way the millennials deal with their own sense of unbridled expectation. A whole generation of people has turned into beggars.

Members of the entitlement generation claim that they cannot afford to buy a house of their own because they don't have enough money. They claim that their parents should keep them indefinitely or should, at the very least, provide them bags full of free money.

Millennials are divas without the talent and they live in cloud cuckooland. They appear to have no comprehension of the concept of 'consequences'. They do, however, exhibit the same assumption of all-knowing infallibility that used to be common among young teenagers; they are bumptious and chock full of 'it' but don't yet realise that for everyone else there are two letters missing from the front of the word 'it'. The millennials are afflicted with the teenage affliction of false omniscience; convinced that they know all and that, therefore, their opinions are more valuable than everyone else's. They learn only what they are taught in school and, tragically, they never learn how to learn or even that they need to keep learning.

Not all millennials are still in their 20s. There are millennials in their 60s and beyond. Stand up Jeremy Corbyn. A world run by millennials is going to be totally unbearable. My only consolation is that it is going to be totally unbearable for them too.

Am I the only person to have noticed that millennials in general, and the generation which follows them, are not only mostly spoilt, snotty, smug, self-absorbed, self-satisfied, self-important whingers but all look small, weedy and very young? The millennials all behave like school prefects (the junior equivalent of prison trustees); fussing around and oozing condescension. If they achieve a modicum of success in their chosen field, they expect to have a retinue, a team of 'people' headed by a Chief of Staff. (As in 'my people' will be in contact with 'your people'.) And they practise grievance or insult politics. They find a sore, scratch it until it bleeds and then blame someone, anyone, everyone, and build a career out of the vengeance.

And there is something else odd: the males look rather effeminate and the females are confused.

There are good reasons for all this, of course.

First, I have been pointing out for 30 years that our drinking water is enriched with female hormones (the reasons are explained on my website). It is clear that those hormones are now having a dramatic effect on the human race.

Second, no generation in the history of mankind has been more spoilt than the entitlement generation. A toxic mixture of reality television and social media has created life goals that are far removed from reality. It is salutary that social media users don't have 'friends' or 'contacts': they have 'followers' and 'fans'. There is little proper debate on social media for disagreement invariably leads to abuse and a sense of outrage that someone should hold another point of view. I wonder how many millennials know that the personality traits which trigger heart disease (and which are just as potent as smoking and fatty food) are hostility, cynicism, isolation and extreme self-involvement. There is going to be a veritable epidemic of heart disease in another decade's

81

time, and thousands of men and women in their 40s will be demanding instant heart transplants.

Here are some basic facts about millennials:

1) They cannot empathise, don't understand the concept even.

2) They are strangely puritanical in some respects (but only when it suits them).

3) They can't adapt at all well.

4) They say that all they want are experiences. All new generations say that but the millennials are lying a lot. They want experiences plus a home, a washing machine and a laptop and a printer and at least two telephones. They are painfully materialistic. These are people who spend £1000 each going to Glastonbury Festival and then complain they can't afford to pay the rent.

5) They want to isolate themselves from real contact with people but to spread their opinions as widely as possible. Their meaningless self-serving chitchat is nothing but self-aggrandisement.

6) They are proud collectors of prejudices.

7) They whinge. All the time. About everything. They want all the good things that the previous generation enjoyed but they don't want any of the bad stuff. And they want to enjoy a pleasant work-life balance. They don't want 24% interest rates. They object to paying university fees and would presumably rather go back to the days when interest rates were between 15 and 20% if you were lucky and 24% was not uncommon and the basic rate of income tax was 33%.

8) They are confused about what is 'stressful' and what isn't. They appear generally unmarked by life's vicissitudes but decorated with superficial signs of anxiety as deep as their tattoos. I was the first writer to draw attention to the significance of stress on human health and I have to say that worrying about whether to have a

tattoo of a pirate ship on your left buttock or a tattoo of a wolf disappearing into a closely situated orifice is not stressful. Not being able to have your latte served in an avocado skin is not a stressful experience. Millennials despairing of stress because of keeping up with the demands of Twitter and Facebook. Why not just keep off social media? Maybe they should study John Milton's *Paradise Lost*: 'The mind is its own place in itself, can create a Heaven of Hell, a Hell of Heaven. What matter where, if I be still the same.' There is very little awareness of the fact that millions are now addicted to social media. They get a 'pleasure hit' every time they receive a 'like' and do not realise that they are being exploited. The social media sites are providing short-term joy and creating long-term problems. Millions of social media users are addicted but do not realise just how much they are harming themselves. This is a problem which will bubble away quietly and become an obvious crisis in a generation's time.

9) They cannot cope with bad days. People have always had bad days. They would face them, deal with them, get through them and go on to the next day. But millennials don't get through them. They become incensed that all is not perfect for them; angry, resentful and endlessly demanding. 'Make it right!' 'It's not fair'. 'How can this be allowed to happen to us?' Millennials always blame someone else for what goes wrong. They are never willing to take any responsibility. When things go wrong they want someone else to solve the problem for them so that things go their way. Like spoilt children. They lead mean and carping lives of dissatisfaction and complaint.

10) They are supercilious and painfully hypocritical; and not as rebellious as they like to pretend they are.

11) They want reforms but only as long as the reforms pander to their own, largely financial, needs. Other than that they don't really seem to know what they want.

12) They are afraid of independence and freedom and so they tend to be keen supporters of the European Union; millions of millennials have been institutionalised; and they are as afraid to

live outside the stultifying embrace of the EU as lunatics are afraid to live outside the asylum.

13) They refuse to accept defeat not in an old-fashioned, healthy way (we will fight on) but in a delusional 'it didn't happen because we didn't want it to happen' sort of way. They have all the arrogance which used to be associated with thirteen-year-olds who didn't yet know that they didn't know everything and weren't the only clever people in the world.

14) They have blessings previous generations never even dreamt about but all they see are grievances. Never satisfied, they whinge like wheezy red-faced old men in the members stand at a cricket club but they complain not about what is happening but about what has happened. The saddest thing is that millennials, who are already soaked in resentment, are being constantly encouraged to hate the elderly. The result, of course, will be that euthanasia will become compulsory. It won't be long before anyone over 70 who dares to keep on living will be put to sleep to keep the millennials happy. Aristotle liked the young because he felt their innocence was attractive. 'They are not cynical but guileless, because they have not seen much wickedness; credulous because they have not often been deceived; and optimistic, because they have not often experienced failure.' And all that makes the young easy to deceive, of course. And that is what Corbyn has been doing, taking advantage of their inexperience to Pied Pipering them into a never-never land where their parents are responsible for everything that is bad in the world and where the impossible can easily be promised. What is surprising, of course, is that Aristotle was talking about children. But today those children are in their 20s and 30s. They never grew up and maybe they never will.

15) They are too naïve, too protected from reality by an education system which is designed to ensure that everyone wins a prize and no one ever fails.

16) They claim to be without fear but they mistake fearlessness for bravery. In fact, you cannot be brave if you are fearless. They are attention seeking because they have been taught that they are

invincible. They are intolerant and unquestioning because they have been taught that their hubris is justified. They are uncaring, demanding and selfish as that is how they have been brought up to be. And if they work, they favour non-jobs such as 'influencer' on the internet. Or 'life coach'. The fastest growing profession in America is now that of 'life coach'. There are millions of them and their industry is worth $2 billion a year. Who are these 20-year-olds who deign to tell other people how to run their lives? And who the hell hires them? (These people have joined the elite, alongside charity executives, quango directors, fundraising professionals, lobbyists and spin doctors. These are all people who earn vast salaries but do nothing of any value.)

17) They refuse to accept responsibility for their actions and seem unable to deal with defeat of any kind – result of no such sports or prizes for everyone.

18) They adore the idea of socialism because it offers them the hope of not working but living on the State and not paying any student fees or taxes. They want to be able to continue to buy stuff they don't need and don't particularly like, with money they haven't got so that they can impress people they don't know and whose opinions are of no practical consequence. Why else would so many millennials spend good money buying 1970s ripped jeans?

19) Modern socialism is not about caring, it is about greed, resentment, selfishness and a sullen reluctance to accept any responsibility married to an equally sullen grandiose expectation that all will be provided by someone else, at their expense (it doesn't matter if the someone else is the state, a relative or an elderly, hard done by taxpayer – anyone's money will do nicely) it is about a self-righteous sense of moral outrage and, when things go well, some good old-fashioned tax avoidance since, after all, it is the State's responsibility to pay for everything and only the little people who don't work for the BBC should contribute.

20) Millennials say they want experiences not things but they don't realise that is what every generation says. Then as they get older,

they realise that bungee jumping and sleeping on trains isn't as much fun as it used to be. The millennials think they are being original, of course.

21) They don't understand that there are always Consequences.

22) Millennials are sometimes known as snowflakes because they are so bloody sensitive. It's odd that they should be both mega critical and also mega sensitive because you don't have to be particularly intelligent or insightful to realise that these are pretty incompatible, and today's snowflakes are creating for themselves a world of unending misery in which they do little but criticise, whinge and sulk, criticise, whinge and sulk, criticise whinge and sulk. The constant sharing of opinions goes to their heads. (It is this fact which explains why millennials, who are forever giving out opinions on social media, are so unbearably full of themselves.)

23) Their role model is Jordan, famous for her ability to breathe and for her breast enlargement operations, has built an industry on thin air, which was fine and good for her but is hardly a sustainable role model. Girls in the 1970s and 1980s used to dream of becoming actresses or singers or ballet dancers and though occasionally they would work towards those goals they would mostly recognise them as dreams and their real hopes would be simpler and more realisable: a faithful, sober husband, a nice home, a television set that worked and a couple of kids who didn't get into trouble with the police. Today, girls simply know that they will become stars if they disguise their imperfections and enhance marketable body parts with plastic surgery, cover themselves in tattoos, turn themselves into blowsy Barbies and publish enough trivia on social media. Ambition and hope have been replaced by expectations, driven by a sense of entitlement, which are invariably followed by the disappointment and resentment which fuel their anger and their rage at the world.

24) Millennials have not yet worked out that their only true destiny is old age. So why do they hate old people so much?

25) Millennials don't want a fair society. They all want to be as famous like Jordan, the woman with the inflated boobs, and vastly overpaid like Gary Lineker. They have been brought up to whinge every time they don't get their own way or their feelings are hurt. TV reality shows which offer a brief taste of fame and a little money are inundated with applications. Over 80,000 people applied to appear on an edition of a British programme called 'Love Island'. I suspect that they know they will be used, abused and spat out when the programme makers have finished with them but their desperation for fame is greater than their common sense fears.

The entitlement generation will not, of course, have read Lao Tzu's *Tao Te Ching*. It was written over 4,000 years BG (before Gates) and is therefore undoubtedly considered out of date by millennials weaned on mobile telephones and Twitter wisdom. Indeed, in our universities it has probably been stigmatised and categorised as unsuitable.

But here's a quote from the *Tao Te Ching* that all millennials might benefit from reading:

Fill your bowl to the brim
And it will spill
Keep sharpening your knife
And it will blunt
Chase after money and security
And your heart will never unclench
Care about people's approval
And you will be their prisoner
Do your work, then step back
The only path to serenity

None of this, of course, is how we live now. Today we live in a world of constant criticisms, judgements, approvals offered or withheld, YouTube videos and raw, cold, ruthless ambition. The millennials are doomed because they are always wanting and waiting for something better, never satisfied. And all this is because they have had things too easy. They had examinations which everyone could pass. No school sports because someone might lose.

The more we feel the need to succeed, and the more our happiness and contentment depend upon our succeeding, the more stressed we become and the more disappointed and frustrated we feel. And this eternal dissatisfaction and discontent is the curse of the millennials bred to think of themselves as entitled to success, fame, glory and riches without the annoyance of having to do anything to earn those things.

And all that explains why today's young movers and shakers are such a pathetic, bigoted, hypocritical pain in the butt.

28

I had so much to do I didn't know where to start so I sat outside in a bout of unexpected sunshine.

After a while I took out a notebook and made a list of my favourite 12 medical people of all time. It was going to be doctors but I had to include Florence Nightingale.

Here is the list I made – in no particular order. (I confess I looked up the dates when I went indoors):

1) Dr John Snow (1813-1858) was an English physician who proved the relationship between cholera and contaminated water supplies. He was also one of the first anaesthetists.

2) Dr Ignaz Semmelweiss (1815-1865) was a Hungarian obstetrician who worked in Austria and whose views on infection and puerperal fever brought him ridicule. Depressed by the criticism he became insane and died early.

3) Dr Ernesto 'Che' Guevera (1928-1967) was an Argentinian physician, military theorist, politician, revolutionary and guerrilla leader.

4) Edwin Chadwick (1800-1890) was an English civil servant, lawyer and journalist whose work to improve sanitation around the world probably saved more lives than any practising physician.

5) Rhazes aka Muhammad Ibn Zakariya al-Razi (c 850-c 932) was a Persian physician who was also a mathematician, philosopher, astronomer, chemist and musician.

6) Roger Bacon (1214-1294) was born in England but worked in Paris. Known as Doctor Mirabilis he was a physician but also a mathematician, physicist, chemist, astronomer, geographer, philosopher and comparative philologist.

7) Dr William Harvey 1578-1657) was an English physician and anatomist who was the first to describe the circulation of the blood.

8) Dr John Hunter (1728-1793) was an English surgeon and anatomist.

9) Dr Oliver Wendell Holmes (1809-1894) was an American physician, anatomist and author of the Breakfast Table series of books. (Not to be confused with his son who became a justice of the US Supreme Court.)

10) Dr Joseph Lister (1827-1912) was the English doctor who (while working in Scotland) introduced the principle of asepsis into the operating theatre.

11) Paracelsus aka Aureolus Philippus Theophrastus Bombastus von Hohenheim (1493-1541) was something of a showman but helped turn medicine into a science.

12) Dr William Thomas Green Morton (1819-1868) was an American dentist and honorary MD who played an important role in introducing anaesthesia into medical practice.

13) Florence Nightingale (1820-1910) was an Englishwoman who revolutionised nursing.

And here is a list of my favourite authors who were medically qualified: Dr Arthur Conan Doyle, Dr W.Somerset Maugham, Dr C.S.Forester, Dr James Bridie and Dr Anton Chekov.

March

1

In 1975, I wrote a book called *The Medicine Men*. It was the first book to draw attention to the oh-so-friendly relationship between the medical profession and the drug industry.

In 1977, I wrote a book called *Paper Doctors* in which I explained how and why researchers waste money and effort on doing research (and writing scientific papers) which are of little or no value.

Those two books began a small revolution and spawned scores of copycat books.

Suddenly it was acceptable to criticise doctors, scientists and drug companies.

But the medical establishment never forgave me for shining light on some of the profession's most corrupt practices.

And with drug company money backing them, doctors have done everything possible to suppress my books and to ensure that people cannot hear my warnings or follow my advice. (It is important to remember that drug companies could not do 'bad' things without the support of doctors.)

Anyone who upsets the establishment must be portrayed as a dangerous and ill-informed lunatic and the lobbyists do that with great enthusiasm, aided and abetted by quangos, committees and lobby groups which exist to defend the establishment's right to rule without question, opposition or discussion.

As a result of those early books, I have been threatened, spied upon and burgled. I have been lied about and banned in many different but effective ways. I've been threatened with legal action and my books have been suppressed. My website has been hacked and taken down more times than I can remember. And within the medical profession my name has been muddied and the mud has stuck. (When my father was in his 80s, he told me that his GP in Budleigh Salterton had instructed him to ignore any medical advice I gave because I was not practising and therefore out-of-date. That GP subsequently managed to help kill my mother by failing ever to make the diagnosis of normal pressure hydrocephalus, and his colleague managed to kill my father by prescribing a drug he should not have been given.)

But I'm still here.

Now here are 50 biggest, fattest lies which doctors commonly tell.

(If you want to find more information about these lies (and the truth) you will find everything you need to know in books such as *Coleman's Laws*, *How to Stop Your Doctor Killing You*, *Anyone who tells you Vaccines are safe and effective is lying*, *Power over Cancer* and *Doctors Kill More People than Cancer*. All these are available as ebooks on Amazon. I'm not pushing these books, you understand, but merely making their availability known.)

Lie no 1: Doctors say it is important to reduce cholesterol levels (the truth is that evidence suggests that reducing cholesterol levels can be dangerous – and make no difference to a patient's health)

Lie no 2: Doctors say statins are safe (the truth is that there are horrendous side effects with these drugs – which are commonly prescribed for healthy individuals)

Lie no 3: Doctors say vaccines are safe (the truth is that there is no evidence proving that vaccines are safe – but there is plenty of evidence showing that they can be dangerous)

Lie no 4: Doctors say vaccines are effective (the truth is that there is no evidence proving that vaccines are effective – but there is plenty of evidence showing that they are often not effective)

Lie no 5: Doctors say prostate screening is valuable (the truth is that the standard prostate screening test is useless and does more harm than good)

Lie no 6: Doctors say high blood pressure cannot be cured (the truth is that thousands of patients who have dealt with the problem which has caused their high blood pressure have been cured – stress and overweight are common causes of high blood pressure)

Lie no 7: Doctors say you can't catch flu from the flu vaccine (the truth is that the nasal flu vaccine is attenuated but it can help spread the flu)

Lie no 8: Doctors say breast screening is safe and effective (the truth is that X-ray screening programmes actually cause cancer of the breast)

Lie no 9: Doctors say vegetarian diets are dangerous (the truth is that research shows that a vegetarian diet is by far the healthiest human diet, meat is a major cause of cancer and death but contains nothing that cannot be obtained in healthier foods)

Lie no 10: Doctors say hospital infections are under control (the truth is that, as a result of poor hygiene, killer infections caught in hospital are totally out of control and are now spreading into the community)

Lie no 11: Doctors say aspirin is too dangerous to use (the truth is that aspirin taken in soluble form is probably the safest effective painkiller available over the counter)

Lie no 12: Doctors say dementia and Alzheimer's disease are the same thing (the truth is that only just over half of patients with dementia have Alzheimer's disease)

Lie no 13: Doctors say tests and investigations are important but harmless (the truth is that routine investigations help doctors make a diagnosis in only 1 in 100 patients – and many tests are so hazardous that patients can be killed)

Lie no 14: Doctors say chemotherapy is the best way to treat cancer (the truth is that chemotherapy has been shown to do more harm than good in most patients who take it; it often doesn't do any good but it frequently does a great deal of harm to the body and to the patient's quality of life). Chemotherapy is favoured by drug companies (who make big money out of it) and the charities which earn huge sums by working with drug companies.

Lie no 15: Doctors say depression can be safely and effectively treated with drugs (the truth is that most cases of depression cannot be helped with drugs – when doctors say 'let's try this' then you know that they are guessing because they don't have the faintest what to do)

Lie no 16: Doctors say drug side effects are uncommon (the truth is that drug side effects are very common and dangerous side effects are frequent; it is also a fact that prescribing is a very hit and miss affair and (as above) it is no coincidence that doctors often say 'I will try you on this drug' – the word 'try' is very significant)

Lie no 17: Doctors say drugs are tested on thousands of guinea-pig patients before being prescribed (the truth is that drugs are often tested on very few patients before being made available to GPs for mass prescribing – side effects then only appear months or years later)

Lie no 18: Doctors say dementia cannot be cured (the truth is that many cases of dementia can be cured – for example, thousands of dementia patients have a condition called normal pressure hydrocephalus which can be cured with a small operation – but GPs and hospital doctors admit they don't bother to test for this because 'old people aren't worth the trouble')

Lie no 19: Doctors say experiments on animals help doctors find new cures (the truth is that evidence shows clearly that animal experiments are entirely worthless but that they help drug companies put useless and dangerous drugs onto the market)

Lie no 20: Doctors say radiotherapy is safe and effective (the truth is that it is often dangerous and ineffective)

Lie no 21: Doctors say tobacco is the biggest cause of cancer (the truth is that the biggest cause of cancer in humans is meat – but the meat industry is powerful and has suppressed the truth very effectively)

Lie no 22: Doctors say medical screening is worthwhile (the truth is that evidence shows that medical screening is wonderful for doctors and screening clinics but not very good for patients)

Lie no 23: Doctors say drugs prescribed for children have been properly tested (the truth is that most of the drugs given to babies and children have never been tested on babies or children but have only ever been tested on adults)

Lie no 24: Doctors say that alternative remedies are ineffective and dangerous (many alternative remedies are safer and more effective than orthodox treatments)

Lie no 25: Doctors say psychiatry is a science (the truth is that psychiatry is a pseudo-science, more akin to black magic than anything else)

Lie no 26: Doctors say heart surgery is the only way to deal with heart disease (the truth is that many patients with serious heart disease can be cured by losing weight, adopting a vegetarian diet and controlling their exposure to stress)

Lie no 27: Doctors say antibiotic resistance is caused by patients not completing the course of drugs they have been prescribed (the truth is that antibiotic resistance is partly a result of wild and careless overprescribing by doctors and partly a result of the fact that farmers frequently give antibiotics to their animals)

Lie no 28: Doctors say hormone replacement therapy is a safe and effective way of dealing with the menopause (the truth is that it is dangerous and usually quite unnecessary)

Lie no 29: Osteoporosis occurs only in menopausal women (the truth is that osteoporosis occurs in adult men and women of all ages)

Lie no 30: Doctors say that thanks to doctors and drug companies, we are all living longer than ever before (the truth is, life expectancy has hardly changed for adults – it is the reduction in infant mortality rates, resulting from better sanitation and drinking water, that has made the difference in average life expectation)

Lie no 31: Doctors say that cow's milk is good for children (the truth is that it causes allergy problems, is very unhealthy and should be avoided)

Lie no 32: Doctors say that women naturally live longer than men (the truth is that they don't; now that women are drinking and smoking as much as men, and living stressful lives, male and female life expectancy are equalising.)

Lie no 33: Doctors say that asthma is a common disease (the truth is that it is commonly diagnosed but it isn't particularly common – only around one in ten of the people diagnosed as having asthma actually have the condition)

Lie no 34: Doctors say that neurosurgery can help patients with a variety of psychiatric problems (the truth is that in these circumstances brain surgery is about as much use as being run over by a bus)

Lie no 35: Doctors say that women who have a genetic susceptibility to breast cancer should have their breasts removed (the truth is that surgery is brutal and unnecessary; women who have a genetic susceptibility to breast cancer should simply adapt their lifestyle – and give up eating meat – to normalise the risk)

Lie no 36: Doctors say that tamoxifen is a safe drug which will prevent breast cancer (the truth is that tamoxifen causes cancer of the uterus – so it might prevent one cancer but cause another)

Lie no 37: Doctors say that drugs and surgery are the only two ways to deal illness (the truth is that in nine out of ten illnesses the body will heal itself)

Lie no 38: Doctors say that X-rays are harmless (the truth is that they aren't – X-rays are a major cause of cancer)

Lie no 39: Doctors say that as a result of vaccine programmes and antibiotics, infectious diseases are under control (the truth is that infectious diseases are coming back with a vengeance; vaccine programmes have failed miserably and many bugs are now immune to antibiotics)

Lie no 40: Doctors say that repeat prescribing is a safe way to supply patients with essential drugs (the truth is that repeat prescribing saves doctors time and money but helps boost drug company profits at the expense of patient safety – thousands of patients regularly take potentially damaging drugs which they don't need)

Lie no 41: Doctors say that psychotherapy is a powerful way of dealing with mental health problems (the truth is that chatting to a hairdresser or barman probably does more good than talking to a psychotherapist)

Lie no 42: Doctors say that eczema and dermatitis always need to be treated with powerful creams and ointments (the truth is that most skin conditions of this type are caused by some sort of allergy problem – and the best way to cure them is to remove the cause of the allergy)

Lie no 43: Doctors say that medicines bought over the counter are always safe (the truth is that the medicines sold in pharmacies can cause serious side effects and can mask symptoms and signs which indicate serious illness)

Lie no 44: Doctors say that maturity onset (type II) diabetes always needs treatment with drugs (the truth is that type II diabetes can best be treated by diet – without any drugs at all)

Lie no 45: Doctors say that gallstones always need surgery (the truth is that many patients with gallstones need no treatment at all – except cutting down on their consumption of fatty foods)

Lie no 46: Doctors say that tap water is just as good for you as bottled water (the truth is that much tap water contains drug residues which can cause serious and permanent health problems)

Lie no 47: Doctors say that they can be trusted to keep secrets (the truth is that doctors are no longer allowed to respect patient confidentiality)

Lie no 48: Doctors say that patients who ask too many questions are likely to be unpopular with doctors (the truth is that patients who take an active interest in their own health, and who regularly ask questions, are more likely to survive than patients who merely allow themselves to be treated as objects)

Lie no 49: Doctors say that they can be trusted to give you all the options (the truth is that you cannot because surgeons tend to operate and physicians tend to prescribe drugs – it's what they do)

Lie no 50: Doctors say that they can always be trusted to give you good, impartial advice (the truth is that these doctors do what they are told to do by their government and by drug companies – very few bother to do their own critical reading or research)

All this may sound a little depressing.

Indeed, the more you know about the quality of care currently provided by GPs, the more depressed you are likely to become – especially if you are over the age of 60. For example, research involving over 28,000 patients and more than 5,000 GP surgeries recently showed that GPs miss two out of every three cases of pneumonia because they are (to put it bluntly) lazy and incompetent.

There are four easy checks a GP can do to find out if a patient has pneumonia. The first is to check the pulse rate. (It's a bad sign if it is unusually high.) The second is to check the temperature. (High is not good). The third is to check oxygen levels in the blood. (You can buy a device to do this at the local pharmacy.) The fourth is to listen to the chest to see if the patient's breathing sounds rough and crackly. (Any GP with a stethoscope should be able to do this – or should retrain as a car mechanic.)

Once pneumonia has been diagnosed, it can usually be treated with antibiotics. But when GPs don't do those simple checks, the diagnosis is missed and treatment starts too late and the patient often dies 'of pneumonia'. It is, of course, the over 60s who are more likely to die this way.

But there is an answer: we all need to learn to take control of own bodies and our own health.

When you are well, take the time and the effort to learn how your body works and what signs and symptoms to look out for. And if you are unfortunate enough to fall ill, then spend time doing your own research into your illness. Within a surprisingly short time, you will probably know more about your illness than your doctor.

Moreover, don't be afraid to nag your doctors. Patients who sit (or lie) quietly and wait for treatment are too often dead before they get it.

2

I recently unearthed an old copy of *Horizon* magazine which included an article by Beverley Nichols, writing about the time he met Oscar Wilde. The Great Man with the Green Carnation (Wilde not Nichols) was speaking in Leeds and had been invited to stay for one night at the Nichols home.

It was 1883 and the ever strapped for cash Wilde was probably happy to save the cost of a hotel.

For breakfast, Beverley Nichols's grandmother had prepared a feast that appeared 'almost ostentatious'. She was clearly eager to impress her guest. There was a chafing dish filled with kedgeree, Georgian silver platters piled with sliced ham, a Regency sauceboat full of picked cranberries, Sheffield plate well stocked with cold grouse and a cumbersome Victorian device, sitting on top of a spirit lamp, which contained eggs, bacon and sausages.

This was no ordinary breakfast in the Nichols household. This was a very special breakfast for a very special guest. No trouble or expense had been spared.

Eventually, Oscar arrived for breakfast. He was wearing his famous fur coat.

'What would you like to begin with?' asked Beverley's grandmother, confident that she could supply any requirement the Great Man might have.

Oscar studied the sideboard and stood in silence. Then he walked to the window and looked out at a cheerless, snow-laden winter landscape.

'I should,' he said, speaking softly, 'like some raspberries'.

'I beg your pardon, Mr Wilde?' said the grandmother, feeling that she could not have heard correctly.

'Some pale yellow raspberries,' said Oscar.

3

A man in a car park swerved in front of me causing me to brake suddenly. Responding to some primeval driving force I yelled, 'Wanker!' through the open window.

When the driver got out of his car, I could see that this might have been unwise. He was about seven foot tall, five feet wide and as solid as a pyramid. He also looked belligerent.

'What did you say?' he demanded gruffly.

'I said 'danke',' I lied. 'It's German for Thank you,' I said in my best German accent.

'Thank you for what?'

'Just 'thank you',' I said.

He looked puzzled, but he went away and did not kill me so I count it as a win.

4

I wonder how many people who support the EU know that it is now planning something called Bail-ins if banks look like collapsing.

They did it in Cyprus of course but the future plans are much tougher.

It will mean that if one or more banks look dodgy then all bank deposits will be controlled by the EU – and effectively owned by the EU.

There will be an outcry when it happens. Even the Remainers will be upset to have lost all their money.

But it will then be too late.

5

I am reading a brilliant biography of James Agate, the diarist and dramatic critic. Written by James Harding it is without a doubt one of the best biographies I have ever read. And although Harding clearly respects, admires and enjoys his subject's peccadilloes, he does not spare the rod. So, for example, he quotes Hugh Walpole (now forgotten but at the time a major novelist whose books sold by the truckload) complaining about the fact that Agate would often review books without reading them properly (or sometimes at all). 'Now, you may be right in your attitude to current literature, but as you know, a book is a book to the author of it. One has been a year or more living with it, caring for it, cursing it. Why should one deliver it over to someone who will certainly mock it without reading it?'

6

The NHS, designed as a health care service to provide good health care for everyone is now run by administrators and is controlled by a potent mix of vested interests and lobby groups. The vested interests include drug companies and trade unions representing medical professionals such as doctors and nurses. There is little or no concern for the needs or rights of patients and the majority of those who work for the NHS take out private health care insurance because they would never entrust their own health (or that of their relatives) to the service which employs them.

All the important decisions, including vital decisions relating to the allocation of resources, are made by people who know absolutely nothing about medicine, patients or illness.

Today, so much money is spent on the wrong things that before long our ambulance service will consist of a bloke on a pushbike with a box of plasters and a bottle of aspirin in his saddle bag.

7

I am beginning to feel sorry for Lance Armstrong, the disgraced cyclist and seven times Tour de France winner. Just about every cyclist who was convicted of using drugs has been forgiven. Alberto Contador is a hero in Spain. David Millar is a respected television commentator.

And so on and on.

But Armstrong is still the black sheep.

Why?

Could it be simply because he cheated better and more effectively than the rest when putting himself on level terms with those who were born with a clear physiological advantage?

8

Something called 'The Wildlife Trust' has announced plans to recruit 5,000 volunteers for a 'Squirrel Crushing' campaign. Recruits will be trained how to bludgeon grey squirrels to death; to crush squirrels' skulls with rocks, hammers or whatever else useful comes to hand. Seriously, someone called Dr Cathleen Thomas, representing the Wildlife Trust and programme manager of 'Red Squirrels United' wants volunteers to trap and kill grey squirrels by putting them into a bag and knocking them over the head. Their ultimate aim is to kill grey squirrels so that there will, they hope, be more red squirrels. This is, of course, the animal equivalent of racism based on colour and it is utterly unacceptable.

My guess is that the Wildlife Trust, which complains that the grey squirrels are immigrants, wants to kill grey squirrels for cosmetic reasons: maybe Dr Thomas and her little chums think the red ones look prettier and will attract more customers to their bits of sanitised woodland. 'Oh, look, there's a pretty red one, Doris! Take a selfie.'

Inevitably, the Wildlife Trust has created some arguments in favour of its brutal form of ethnic cleansing. They seem to believe that if the grey squirrels are eradicated then the red squirrels will come bouncing back and they presumably want the squirrels which they think are 'prettier' posing daintily in their domesticated bits of woodland. In my view, this is nothing more than a murderous fashion statement and is entirely inappropriate for an organisation which claims to be a friend of animals.

There are, I believe, some serious errors in the thinking of all those who believe that grey squirrels are foreign invaders who do much damage, while red squirrels are charming, home grown and harmless.

First, the red squirrel does every bit as much damage as the grey squirrel and was itself, not long ago, regarded as a pest.

Second, the red squirrel does not help trees by planting their seeds. The red squirrel piles up its stored nuts and this is of no value whatsoever to trees. In contrast, the grey squirrel buries nuts and forgets where they are – with the result that thousands of trees are inadvertently planted. (The grey squirrel plants nuts with great care and precision, digging a hole just the right depth and then covering the buried nut with soil and leaves.)

Third, because of its habit of planting nuts and then forgetting about them, the grey squirrel has been shown to do a vital service for oak, walnut and beech trees. And woodland experts believe that if the grey squirrel is driven out then our forests will suffer enormously. In our garden, grey squirrels have damaged just two branches of a beech tree by ring barking them (and the tree thrives without those branches) and they have (to my knowledge) planted at the very least 50 hazel and beech trees – a dozen or so of which I have dug up, moved and replanted in more convenient positions.

Fourth, the sort of evil discrimination being planned by the Wildlife Trust isn't new, of course. But it is strangely reminiscent of a cull that took place a century or so ago. The irony is that the last time there was a cull it was red squirrels which were targeted. Red squirrels were once considered a real menace in this country; so much so, that in response to the damage they had caused to woodlands, the Highland Squirrel Club was formed in 1903 with the aim of exterminating as many red squirrels as possible. The members of the Club set about doing this with great gusto. In the first 30 years of its existence, the Highland Squirrel Club managed to kill 82,000 red squirrels.

Fifth, the Wildlife Trust doesn't like grey squirrels because they came from America. They seem to regard them as unwanted immigrants. If they'd done their research properly they would know that many of the red squirrels are immigrants too. Back in 1844, someone called Lady Lovat imported a good many red squirrels from Sweden. It is not the greys' fault that they were introduced into this country. They have been in Britain for over 100 years; how long do they have to live here before they are considered native? There is even some debate as to whether or not the red squirrel was ever native to this country, but this is not something that the anti-grey squirrel brigade likes to discuss openly.

Sixth, the Wildlife Trust seems to think that the grey squirrel can be blamed for the decline in the number of red squirrels. But they're wrong about that too. The main culprit for the massive decline in the red squirrel population in Britain is the loss of habitat. Greys are far better suited to deciduous woodlands or mixed woodlands and are able to eat a wider variety of foods; much of the food that makes up the diet of the grey squirrel is indigestible for the red squirrels. The red squirrels thrive best in coniferous woodlands, which is why they do well in Scotland where many of the pine forests are. It seems obvious, therefore, that for red squirrels to flourish in this country then they need more of their right sort of habitat: coniferous woodlands. So, if the Wildlife Trust really wants more red squirrels they should just plant a few more trees.

Seventh, the Wildlife Trust also claims that the grey squirrels are passing the squirrelpox onto the red squirrels. However, research has shown that the red squirrels had this deadly disease before the greys were even introduced into this country. And if their numbers had not been so badly decimated in the early part of the 20th century, then they too would have probably acquired immunity to the disease by now – just as the greys have done. In fact, there have been recent reports that red squirrels have shown signs of acquiring immunity to the virus. So the squirrelpox argument is hollow.

The bottom line is that red squirrels, being prettier and not so ubiquitous, are boosting tourism in the areas where they have been artificially reintroduced. Grey squirrels are suffering from commercial expediency and a bad press. And I suspect that it is for commercial reasons that 'Squirrel Coshing' is being encouraged.

The Wildlife Trust has received millions from Heritage Lottery and EU Life Funding for this foul work. I know that anyone working for the EU must be a mad fascist with a strong streak of racism running through their cold veins. But is the same true for those at the Heritage Lottery?

The Wildlife Trust's ultimate aim is to kill grey squirrels in the hope that there will, in due course, be more red squirrels. But the Wildlife Trust's desire to get rid of grey squirrels is neither logical nor scientific.

There is much wrong with the Wildlife Trust's bit of blatant colour prejudice.

But there is another problem.

I am especially worried about the effect this bizarre squirrel bashing policy will have on the people recruited to do the squirrel bashing – and on their friends, relatives and neighbours.

The Wildlife Trust staff are encouraging people to stuff living creatures into a bag and to then hit them on the head with something – presumably a handy rock.

Amazingly, this is legal.

But in my professional view (as a doctor) anyone who can do this must either be a psychopath or have psychopathic tendencies.

Serial killers and mass murderers usually start their evil work by killing animals.

And that is the truly scary thing: The Wildlife Trust is not just recruiting psychopaths. (Who else is going to volunteer to stuff squirrels into bags and then hit them on the head?) It is turning the psychopaths who volunteer into potential murderers.

Does the Wildlife Trust not realise that killing small animals will appeal to psychopaths? Do they think sweet, little, old ladies are going to volunteer for this evil work? Of course not. The Wildlife Trust will be recruiting its own small army of thugs. Are they incredibly naïve or incredibly stupid or both?

Do they not know that psychopaths who kill small animals may then progress to killing humans? Nearly all serial killers started their 'careers' by killing animals.

In my opinion, the 'Crush a Squirrel' campaign is nothing more nor less than an officially approved apprenticeship scheme which will train thousands of potential murderers, wife beaters and child abusers.

It is important to understand that the Wildlife Trust is organising a scheme which will be more barbaric and more harmful to mankind than fox hunting, bear baiting or cock fighting.

How can I make such a claim?

Simple.

In fox hunting, dog fighting and cock fighting, the humans involved are at a distance to the actual killing. In fox hunting, it is the dogs which do the killing. In dog and cock fighting, the killing is done by animals – not humans.

But the Wildlife Trust's scheme demands that human beings do the killing themselves. It's a hands-on killing programme which is, I believe, pretty well guaranteed to create thousands of bullies, thugs, muggers and murderers.

There is, of course, a mass of evidence available showing that people who are cruel to animals may progress to being cruel to people.

Cruelty to small animals is, indeed, regarded by criminologists as an important stepping stone in the development of dangerous criminals, wife beaters or child abusers.

The Wildlife Trust's members may start off by bashing the skulls of squirrels but some of them will enjoy what they are doing so much that they could end up doing the same thing to humans. There is clear evidence showing a relationship between those who are cruel to animals and those who are cruel to humans. The sort of people who abuse animals (whether by killing dogs or cats, or by putting squirrels into a sack and then bashing them on the head) are the sort of people who end up abusing humans.

Here are some facts to back up my claim:

The police in the UK have been urged to keep records of people who have been cruel to animals. Members of the Wildlife Trust will presumably have to be included in those records.

'Violent behaviour towards animals is often a pointer to violent behaviour towards humans,' said one police spokesman.

A spokesman for the probation officers' union has stated: 'There is a clear link between the torture and abuse of animals and violence against the person.'

A study performed in New Jersey, US found animal abuse in nine out of ten households where there was violence against children. Frighteningly, a third of child victims of violence aged between four and twelve, had physically or sexually abused animals.

Research in the US has shown that animal cruelty is a common factor among serial killers and so-called spree murderers.

A survey of 57 families guilty of child neglect or abuse, conducted by child protection teams around Newcastle, found examples of animal cruelty in 80% of cases.

Robert Thompson, who murdered toddler James Bulger, had a long history of cruelty and boasted of tying fireworks to the tails of dogs.

Railway rapist and multiple killer David Mulcahy bludgeoned a hedgehog to death in his school yard when he was 13-years-old.

Ian Kay, who killed a Woolworth manager in a raid (and later stabbed Yorkshire Ripper Peter Sutcliffe in Broadmoor) once fed a stray kitten to his dog.

Boston Strangler Albert de Salvo killed cats and dogs.

Cannibal Jeffrey Dahmer killed 17 men and many animals and impaled the heads of dogs on sticks.

Peter Kurten, known as the Dusseldorf Monster, who murdered more than 50 people, practised bestiality on dogs as he tortured and killed them.

Luke Woodham set fire to his own dog and also stabbed his mother and killed two teenage girls.

David Berkowitz, who killed six people, also shot his neighbour's dog and poisoned his mother's parakeet.

Patrick Sherrill murdered 14 people and stole local pets for his dog to attack.

Jack Bassenti, a murderer and rapist, buried puppies alive.

Randy Roth who killed two wives, used an industrial sander on a frog and taped a cat to a car engine.

Edward Kemperer chopped up cats and killed his grandparents, mother and seven other women.

Henry Lee Lucas killed animals and had sex with their corpses and also killed his mother and his wife.

Michael Cartier, a murderer, threw a kitten through a closed window and pulled a rabbit's legs out of their sockets.

Opponents of animal cruelty included Lord Shaftesbury, George Bernard Shaw, Abraham Lincoln, Gandhi, Mark Twain, Voltaire, Sir Isaac Newton, C.S.Lewis, Robert Browning, Buddha, Charles Darwin, Leonard da Vinci, Albert Einstein, John Locke and Dr Albert Schweitzer. Most also campaigned against vivisection.

Those are the facts. There is a painfully strong link between cruelty to animals and cruelty to people. The link is well substantiated.

So, how dare the Wildlife Trust organise such a terrible scheme.

What makes the red squirrel so special that the Wildlife Trust wants to encourage us to go out into the woods and beat grey squirrels to death with bricks and clubs?

I'll tell you.

The only discernible difference is their colour. And their colour (and relative rarity in some parts of the country) makes the red squirrel more attractive to tourists and, therefore, to hoteliers.

The Wildlife Trust is a charity which claims to be 'dedicated to the protection of nature'.

Huh?

Did they forget to mention in their mission statement that the bits of nature being protected must be both pretty and commercially attractive?

It seems to me that the raison d'etre of the Wildlife Trust is fraudulent; a downright lie.

What the hell difference does it make whether a squirrel is red or grey?

It's like suggesting that a man (or woman) who is white (or black) is better than a man (or woman) who is black (or white).

It's plain, unvarnished colour prejudice.

Try getting a Heritage Lottery grant for that!

Are we now going to kill people because they're the wrong colour?

If the Wildlife Trust ever rules the world, will volunteers be recruited to kill all the whites because they stand in the way of the black people? Will the Wildlife Trust want to kill black people so that there will be more food for white people?

That's the bottom line; that's what the Wildlife Trust's policy is really all about. It's animal racism taken to the ultimate, blood curdling conclusion.

This is the most ill-conceived, nauseatingly indefensible scheme ever devised by a charity which claims it exists to protect 'nature'.

I've studied squirrels for years and they are intelligent creatures. They have complex social lives. They have families. They are no threat to human life. They don't attack babies. All they really want

107

to do is to eat some nuts, bury some nuts ready for the winter, play games, enjoy an energetic courtship ritual and have some babies. They are intelligent enough to organise the nuts they store by quality and variety. Some squirrels can stockpile up to 10,000 nuts a year and can separate their caches according to the types of nuts they are storing. So, they store one sort of nut in one place and another sort of nut in another place – in just the same way that humans will store different groceries on different shelves.

Criminals, eh?

And the liberal luvvies (who I suspect were the ones who thought up this disgusting scheme) can be comforted by the knowledge that squirrels have never been known to vote Brexit or wave an England flag.

The people who support this wretched scheme, the ones who cheerfully endorse this unprovoked mass slaughter, probably think of themselves as environmentalists.

But though I suspect they are stupid enough and ignorant enough to drive electric cars, I bet they're the sort of superficial environmentalists who aren't quite prepared to go as far as giving up eating meat. The supporters of the 'Squirrel Slaughter' are, I bet, the sort of morons who favour a view of the world which is dominated by superficial, *Guardian*-style environmentalism; city-driven sentimentality devoid of understanding or genuine caring.

(The more extreme environmentalists are, in my experience, not nice people. They are humourless, spiteful and vindictive and rather toxic. 'Trash him and his books' was the advice given online by one Totnes green environmentalist who knew nothing about me or my work except that her leader had published a book on the oil shortage and that she wanted to kill the sales of my book on the same subject. The trashing, still visible was inspired by nothing more than old-fashioned jealousy and it was very effective. I suspect the average mad Green Party supporter doesn't work but spends their time washing out yoghurt pots and putting their recycling neatly into the boxes and bags duly provided by the State Apparatus. Any time left over is utilised taking and distributing photographs of their recycling on Facebook and Twitter to like-minded friends. (I recently had what I think is a great idea. The best way to run the country would be to find out what the Green

Party proposes and then do the exact opposite. The result would be happiness and wealth all round.)

The BBC will, I have no doubt, support this squirrel slaughter scheme.

The damnable Springwatch programme endorsed and promoted a similar scheme when it was launched in a smaller way by a bunch of animal racists on the Isle of Anglesey.

In my view, the people behind this scheme have completely lost touch with reality and have been consumed by a twitter-like superficiality.

They have forgotten that we share our planet with animals. We don't own planet earth. Grey squirrels aren't visitors. They live here. They aren't a threat to us in any way. Killing them is as absurd and as indecent as would be a scheme to kill horses because they aren't striped like zebras.

The Wildlife Trust has forgotten that our superiority gives us massive responsibilities.

The Wildlife Trust has ridden roughshod over the notion that animals have rights and has come up with a grotesque idea which values grey squirrels as fashion accessories and regards grey squirrels as a commercial and aesthetic nuisance.

The bottom line is that people who can support a scheme like this cannot really give a stuff about animals – other than the cute cats seen on YouTube.

Anyone who believes in decency, morality and the rights of animals to be left alone whenever possible must object strongly to the policy now espoused, endorsed and promoted by the Wildlife Trust.

One thing is for sure: I bet the Wildlife Trust visitors wouldn't like to be put into a sack and hit on the head.

Let's hope the Trust's psychopath training programme doesn't result in too many mass murderers wandering their woodland glades.

I hope no one ever gives any more money or help to the Wildlife Trust. It is a disgusting organisation which deserves to be culled. This is an organisation which needs to be put into a bag and hit on the head with a big rock.

9

Worries come along en masse these days.

Every day seems to bring news, by mail or email, that will necessitate changing something that really doesn't need to be changed, complicating something that once was simple and efficient and which has, as a result of the change, become complex and unworkable and which in future will doubtless be incomprehensible and intolerable.

10

I have noticed that sellers on eBay do some funny things with their prices.

I was looking for a biography of Arthur Henry Sarsfield Ward, better known as Sax Rohmer (the creator of the *Fu Manchu* novels) and found one on eBay priced at £12.95. I thought this a trifle high so I didn't buy it. A few days later, I changed my mind and decided to buy it. The price had then risen to £42.50. Once again, I decided not to buy it. A week later, out of curiosity, I looked to see what the price had become. It had fallen to £2.96 including postage and packing. I bought the book.

11

I read that a woman in Kansas who is on the FBI's most wanted list had complained about the fact that the police used an unflattering mugshot.

12

I read today that a couple preparing for their wedding are charging their 60 guests £150 each to cover the costs of hiring a posh venue.

13

Here's a rather jolly quote from Arthur Schopenhauer, the great philosopher: 'One need only look at a woman's shape to discover that she is not intended for either too much mental or too much physical work.'

I offer that as probably the most sexist remark ever made by a great philosopher

Or, quite possibly, anyone else.

Oh, no, it can't be.

Noel Coward once wrote that 'women should be beaten regularly, like gongs'.

I think Schopenhauer actually meant what he said (and that's what makes it wonderfully, absurdly hysterical) but Noel was simply being Noel and he got away with it because he recognised that he was a genius.

14

We drove through Chard and saw an advertisement for the local hospital which apparently has a Minor Injury Unit only. How do you know if your injury is 'minor'? What is a 'minor injury'? Is a broken arm a minor injury? A sprained ankle? A two inch cut? A four inch cut? A six inch cut? I ask because I am honestly curious.

The sign also says 'Not 24 hours'. But it doesn't say what the opening hours are. So, presumably, there is a constant stream of wounded individuals being turned away because their injuries aren't considered 'minor' enough or because they don't arrive in bandaging hours.

15

Here are the ten fundamental building blocks upon which the EU has been erected:

1) Lie
2) Steal
3) Threaten
4) Bribe
5) Cheat
6) Bully
7) Deceive
8) Misinform
9) Blackmail
10) Suppress

16

In most decent lives the regrets of omission (the things we didn't do) far outweigh the regrets of commission (the things we did but shouldn't have done).

And that's because in any civilised group, our sensitivities, our feelings, our guilts, our fears, hold us back.

The politically correct won't like me saying this but in some cultures and societies people think differently. This isn't opinion; it's fact.

So, to take an extreme example, cannibals don't feel bad about eating human flesh. We would be filled with remorse. But the cannibals just wonder whether this nice piece of thigh needed another 15 minutes and a little more horseradish sauce.

It's just cultural.

Cultures are different. And pretending that they're not is infantile, dangerous and self-destructive.

It seems to me that this is an important thought and one that is either overlooked or suppressed by the folk who believe that we are all the same, that globalisation is a Good Thing and that forcing people of different cultures to live together in a multicultural melting pot is also a Good Thing.

What the liberals don't realise, perhaps, is that when you force different cultures to live together, the different groups will not meld together to form a sort of human soup. Instead, the strongest and most ruthless group will win out and will overpower (physically and culturally) the weaker groups.

And that is exactly what is happening in Britain these days.

To take just one example: the police in many parts of the country have refused to take action against Muslims accused of raping white girls on the grounds that to do so might upset the Muslim community. Our weakness (which we like to describe as broad-mindedness) has resulted in our society being demeaned.

17

Antoinette bought me three wonderful CDs – The Squadronaires (the Royal Air Force Dance Orchestra playing music from 1941-

1953), Glorious Victory (the best of military bands playing such standards as '633 Squadron') and Wartime Memories which includes a wonderful track in which George Formby sings 'Mr Wu's an Air Raid Warden Now'. The song includes the line: 'If you've got a chink in your window you'll have another one at your door' (suggesting, in the nicest possible manner that a defect in your blackout could result in the oriental Air Raid Warden becoming frisky). I can't understand why no one has done a modern version of the song.

Listening, I am reminded that the British charts were often dominated by what were called novelty records: I remember Benny Hill and the 'Fastest Milkman in the West', Rolf Harris and 'Two Little Boys' and Ken Dodd with 'Tears' and 'Happiness'.

If you compile a list of the ten biggest selling singles in British chart history, those four should be in there. But the compilers never put them in of course because they are considered too embarrassing. (The Rolf Harris record wouldn't be there anyway, of course. It would be in the locked box in the cellar, together with the Gary Glitter records and a bucketful of radioactive waste.)

There was even a group called the Rockin' Berries which specialised in novelty records for the Christmas market.

The music industry takes itself far too seriously these days.

Where are the fun, novelty records of today?

18

Thinking again about the Wildlife Trust, I dug out a poem about squirrels which I wrote and published in a book called *Animal Miscellany* which Antoinette and I wrote together a few years ago:

Who stole my nuts?
The squirrel demanded
When I capture the culprit
I'll see he's remanded

There were acorns and beech nuts
And cob nuts galore
When I find out who stole them
I'll start a small war

I know where I put them
It was just about here
I tell you quite firmly
Of that I am clear

They were under the oak tree
Two steps to the left
And now that they're gone
I feel quite bereft

Or could it just be
Now here's a strange thought
That the tree that they're under
Is not the same sort

And ten minute later
There's a glorious screech
As the squirrel declares
They're under this beech!

19

Whenever I switch on an internet related computer, I receive tons of adverts for stuff I've already bought. The advertisers buy my name from companies who have sold me stuff which I no longer need because I've already bought it.

However, I learned today that some of these marketing companies have managed to put together mailing lists of gambling addicts.

And, naturally, when the gambling addicts turn on their computers they see nothing but attractive adverts from gambling sites.

Nice, eh?

20

In just six years, as a direct result of EU legislation, the sum of £900 million has been spent by Britain on shipping carefully collected rubbish over to continental Europe.

And what did the EU do with all those yoghurt cartons, etc. which it had insisted that kind-hearted, well-meaning citizens spend time and water washing out so carefully? (To save the planet.)

They burnt them.

And turned them into smoke and hot air.

Meanwhile, the fastest growing industry in Britain today is the small, local private collecting of rubbish.

Councils everywhere have become increasingly unreasonable and unwilling to provide the services (such as refuse collection) which they are paid to provide. Councils can blame the EU for all this of course. It is EU laws which have forced them to institute utterly pointless recycling regulations which result in ship loads of carefully sorted waste being shipped abroad, to China or the European mainland, to be burnt or buried. (Heaven knows what will happen when China stops taking our rubbish. My guess is that it will be quietly burnt.)

It is EU regulations which have forced upon us a system of recycling which does far more harm than good. It is EU regulations which have resulted in time and energy being wasted on pointless sorting, washing and collecting. It is EU regulations which have resulted in the manufacture of millions of plastic containers and specially designed collection lorries. The whole recycling nonsense wastes far more energy than it saves and has wrecked our society in numerous ways.

But councils are forced by a system of EU punishment fines to accept the nonsensical legislation designed in Brussels and they have leapt on laws which help them avoid spending money on useful services.

And so now small private contractors are filling in the gaps and will take away your rubbish if you can afford their services.

21

Back in the days when *Private Eye* used to be funny, pertinent and dependably intrusive they used to hammer me a good deal but much of the jolly nonsense was so inaccurate that I never minded much. (At least one high-powered libel lawyer wrote inviting me to sue the magazine. I didn't bother.) Other scrofulous publications, such as *The Independent on Sunday*, also published nasty stuff.

I probably should have minded (and sued) because some of the garbage that was printed so carelessly in a variety of publications has settled onto the wastelands of the internet like dandruff on the shoulders of a car salesman's cheap suit.

Instead of suing, I invariably merely accepted a published apology. It seemed the sensible thing to do at the time.

And today the original articles still exist on the internet. But the apologies have long since disappeared.

And there the harmful nonsense will doubtless remain until the Greens ensure that the electricity runs out and the internet dies an un-mourned death.

22

For the umpteenth time, we watched the first of the Jason Bourne films. It is, I think, the best of the series. The quality steadily deteriorated and the fourth film in the series is so bad that after watching it we threw the DVD straight into our charity bag.

The most unbelievable bit in the first film is the fact that Bourne always seems to be able to find a parking space in central Paris.

23

I picked up a copy of one of the Toff novels by John Creasey in a junk shop. Creasey wrote over 600 novels using 28 different pen names, and I am ashamed to say that I don't think I've read any of them – though I have seen some of the films made about his Gideon character. I have no idea how he kept up with what he was doing and what he'd done. I have a job keeping up with my miniscule output.

After receiving hundreds of rejections, Creasey wrote crime thrillers, romantic novels, science fiction and westerns and was, like Leslie Charteris, pretty well ignored by the critics. (I read most of the Saint books when I was 12, interspersing them with

Dickens, Tolstoy et al and enjoying them all in their very different ways).

Creasey's long running characters include The Baron, Gideon of Scotland Yard and The Toff. And, boy, did he write! In 1937 alone, he published 29 novels. I don't think even Dame Barbara Cartland managed that sort of output. Creasey founded the Crime Writers Association in 1953 and his total sales are measured in tens of millions.

Creasey knew how to write a damned good book. And I'm always prepared to keep learning my craft so I'll read a few of Mr Creasey's.

24

We received a council tax bill today. The council tell me that if I pay by credit card there will be a surcharge of £40 for the privilege.

Naturally, I sent the bastards a cheque.

25

Today I found myself absent-mindedly saying 'thank you' to a recorded voice which had told me how important my call was and that an agent would be with me shortly.

I was so cross with myself that I put the receiver down, lost my place in the queue and afterwards couldn't remember who I'd been calling or why.

26

A man whose dog was attacked by cows has written to the papers complaining and demanding that farmers should not be allowed to keep cows in fields where there are footpaths or where people walk their dogs.

It apparently did not occur to the idiot that he should not take his dog into fields where cows were grazing.

Or that he should keep his dog on a lead.

27

I changed some euros for sterling at a Post Office (where the rate is awful but slightly better than the bank). I pushed the euros across the counter and asked the clerk if she would be kind enough to give me some proper money in return.

She looked at me very sternly and said: 'That's a xenophobic remark.'

I think she will probably report me to the authorities.

I don't care.

28

A fellow came round to our home in Gloucestershire. He was wearing one of those fluorescent jackets which people wear when they are out of the office so that passers-by realise they are especially important and must not be run over.

I didn't open the door but found a coloured leaflet, expensively printed, about our not having put out our proper assortment of waste boxes.

We have obviously been dobbed in by someone.

If they come back, I will tell them that I eat all our rubbish.

Or maybe I will tell them that I am a member of a religious group and not allowed to touch or sort rubbish. I will say that we are 'Humanitarian Theoperceptualists' and associated with the 'Brother and Sisterhood of Humanitarian Muslims and United Semites' and that any attempt to force me to put out our recycling rubbish will be regarded as a racist assault.

Or maybe I will just be very old and slightly senile when the council's recycling specialist calls. It's not a stretch, as they say.

'What did you say? You want to know if I'm interested in going cycling with you? Oh dear, no thank you. I used to be very keen but I'm a bit wobbly these days. It's nice of you to ask though. Just wait a moment and I'll find you a shilling to buy yourself some new tyres.'

29

Friends of friends of friends were burgled a few months ago and the burglar was caught. Today he was sentenced. The police caught him because the burglar left behind his torch. He wore gloves but didn't wear gloves when putting new batteries into the torch and the police caught him from the fingerprints on the batteries.

Wonderful!

Worthy of S.Holmes Esq.

30

It is often forgotten that schools were originally designed to keep children occupied while their parents worked. That was the aim – nothing more and nothing less. The idea of educating children while they were being minded came along later.

Today, however, the basic, original purpose seems to have been subverted by teachers who, unsatisfied with holidays which seem to stretch forever, are now choosing to close their schools on Fridays at lunchtime.

This may be jolly nice for teachers, who can have a long weekend every weekend, but it's a bit glum for parents, who have to take time off work or else leave their offspring wandering around snorting coke and having sex in the street.

31

I am fed up with rich celebrities sharing their 'liberal' views on immigration. I'm also fed up with them demonising patriotism and talking up the benefits of globalisation, world government and the glories of Adolf Hitler's European Union.

(The strange thing about patriotism is that the politically correct, metropolitan, elite, liberal democratic establishment has a two-faced view of patriotism. The members of the establishment, the Blairs et al, expect us to be patriotic when they want us to support one of the many wars they promote. They want us to love and respect our country, and to feel a strong sense of duty, when they want us to fight and die or pay for the bullets and bombs. But they want us to forget all about patriotism when they are promoting the United States of Europe. They are so unpatriotic themselves that they think that patriotism is something that can be switched on and off at will.)

I really loathe wealthy, liberal luvvies.

They never have to wait a year for hospital treatment. They go straight into a private hospital or, better still, a private ward in an NHS hospital. They never have to watch their kids struggle at a school where no one else speaks English. They unblushingly send their children to private school or they cherry pick a 'good' school where there are no foreign pupils holding everyone back. They don't have to worry about rising taxes (because they know how to take full advantage of the available tax avoidance schemes). And they don't have to sort their own rubbish and put it into nine separate plastic containers because, thanks to the EU's immigration policies, they have their cheap immigrant labour to do that for them.

It's normal and healthy for immature 18-year-olds to believe in socialism. But sensible grown-ups usually grow out of this nonsense as they learn a little about the real world.

Socialism and communism never ever provide the good times they promise. There was mass starvation in the Soviet Union and in China. And more recently there has been mass starvation in Korea too. When China allowed a little capitalism to temper the communism, the people suddenly started to eat regularly.

In all countries where socialism has leant towards towards communism (in the way favoured by the Corbynistas), people have been killed or imprisoned (or both) without trial and political opponents have disappeared.

That, sadly, is a real fact of life.

But the rich liberal luvvies don't know much about those facts of life.

April

1

I put this April Fool gag on my website as a news item: 'BBC is to celebrate men and is planning a regular 'Men's Hour' programme. The new programme will be launched on International Men's Day and will deal exclusively with male issues. The presenters and contributors will all be male.'

Unfortunately, everyone who saw it knew immediately that it was a joke.

Antoinette's idea was much better.

She wrote a piece reporting that an American company was planning an electric car which would be powered by lightning. The car would have a large battery which would store energy taken into the vehicle through a specially adapted lightning conductor.

More seriously, it has been confirmed (again) that in recent years alone, the BBC has received millions of pounds from the European Union. I first revealed this in my book *England Our England* in 2002.

So now no one need wonder why the BBC is biased in favour of the European Union and why its news and documentary programmes are bent. It is, of course, also why the BBC was biased in favour of the Remain vote during the run up to the Referendum.

2

It is my honest opinion that Tony Blair is a war criminal who should be locked up for the rest of his life. His lies and deceit and personal ambitions took us into an unjust and unjustifiable war. He is responsible for far more deaths than Harold Shipman, Ian Brady and all the other infamous murderers of the 20th century.

I firmly believe that Blair has become rich because of his support for that illegal war.

But I'm now pretty certain that Blair (who, remember, used to be a critic of the EU) has also gone stark raving mad.

Blair led us into war in the Middle East. British armed forces killed many innocent people.

He is surely one of the main reasons that so many Muslims hate Britain.

Now Blair, a fanatical supporter of the EU and its immigration policy, wants the people he bombed and made homeless – including Muslim extremists who hate us and our culture – to come and live in Britain through the ever-generous auspices of Hitler's European Union. It's as though Churchill had invited Nazis to come and live in Britain in 1940 and then been surprised at the outcome. We bomb Muslims and seem surprised so many hate us. We then invite them into the country in their millions, allow them to live under their rules, and then surprised when we get attacked and bombed.

It is important to remember that a well-established Muslim target is the takeover of a nation without the effort and expense of going to war. And they are doing very well. There are already a number of Muslim mayors in English cities (including London, of course). There are over 3,000 mosques in England and over 130 Muslim Sharia courts. There are areas of England which are no-go areas for whites and where pubs and off-licences are unwelcome. More than three quarters of Muslim women are unemployed and accepting free benefits and free housing. The incidence of unemployment among Muslim men is almost as high. Muslims often have half a dozen children or more – all paid for by British taxpayers. And British schools now serve halal meat to all children – despite the fact that this method of killing animals is unbelievably cruel and regarded as uncivilised by most Britons. Not long ago, 100,000 Muslim men met in a park and everyone seemed to think this entirely acceptable. If 100,000 BNP members met, they would be arrested and vilified in the press.

3
The number of council staff in England and Wales earning over £100,000 a year soared by 53% last year. There are now 2,314 council workers earning over £100,000. And there are 539 council

workers earning over £150,000. And these aren't just bosses with big responsibilities.

For example, one London council has 44 members of staff earning over £100,000. They can't all be running things.

The people who do the real work (dig holes and file bits of paper) are subjected to a pay freeze. But council bosses have stuck their noses deep into the trough.

Making it worse, far worse, is the fact that these overpaid council bosses have massive and wildly over-generous pension plans.

And they can retire in their 50s or early 60s.

The result is that councils are now spending a huge proportion of their income on salaries and pensions for council workers who sit around in big offices doing very little. Or sit around in the golf club bar.

The average big company boss now receives 300 times the pay of lower paid workers. That's a disgrace. They are stealing money from other workers and from shareholders.

But council workers who are earning these massive salaries (rather, that should be 'receiving' rather than 'earning') are an even bigger disgrace.

Their greed is destroying local services and putting a huge financial burden on the elderly for whom council rates are a massive proportion of their unavoidable expenditure.

There is no excuse for any council worker to be paid over £100,000.

They will all claim that they deserve these huge salaries.

But cut them down to £50,000 a year (with lower pensions) and see how many quit to take their chances in the real world.

Of course, the chances of this happening are as great as the chances of the BBC planning a regular 'Men's Hour' programme to celebrate International Men's Day.

In other words, no chance at all.

4

Would you let a bunch of strangers put their unwashed fingers into your mouth?

I thought not.

You know as well as I do that this would be a great way to pick up all sorts of nasty bugs and, at the very least, end up with a two day bout of vomiting and diarrhoea.

So, why on earth would anyone buy a huge bag of crisps designed to be shared among a lot of people with grubby fingers?

I mention this because I see that Gary Lineker, a former footballer and now the unthinking person's liberal luvvie crisp salesman, is flogging very big bags of crisps designed to be shared.

This is utter lunacy. Crisps are not good food because they tend to contain far too much fat. And in my view, the crisps which Lineker promotes (Walkers) are, like all similar products, likely to lead to obesity, heart disease and an early death.

(It is a salutary thought that children die because of the product which is helping to make Lineker rich.)

Now, the 'sharing bags' are likely to add a variety of nasty infections to that list of illnesses.

Incidentally, am I the only person who is offended when this damned crisp salesman tries to take the high moral ground on political issues such as Brexit and on immigration and opening our doors to endless refugees?

I respectfully suggest that in my opinion, Lineker possibly knows less about the EU than he knows about nutrition and child obesity.

Lineker has been reported to have very good advisors who help him minimise the amount of tax he pays. Don't you just love these people? Bono is the King of these tax avoiding hypocrites but Lineker appears to come a close second.

I am quite prepared to accept that Lineker may not have done anything illegal – in the sense of going to prison illegal – but the sort of crafty tax avoidance of which he has been accused is certainly morally questionable.

And for a multi-millionaire who pontificates about how the Government should spend taxpayers' money, it is definitely, quite definitely, grotesquely hypocritical.

5

Contrary to the claims being made by the Greens and Liberal Democrats who are closet fascists and who adore Hitler's plans for

Europe, the vast majority of Britons who oppose the EU and unlimited immigration are not racists.

The patriots who voted for Brexit, partly because of the problems created by immigration, didn't do it because they are racists but because they are wise enough to realise that a substantial number of immigrants who come to Britain, through the auspices of the EU, are not coming because they admire our culture, our history or our way of life but for other, largely mercenary, reasons.

Many older Brexit voters, now being unjustly abused and reviled, fought for Britain against fascism.

Many are voting to leave the EU because they understand that the next generations will be better off if Britain is outside the EU.

'If we want things to stay as they are then things will have to change,' wrote Giuseppe Tomasi di Lampedusa in *The Leopard*.

The wise folk who voted Brexit realise that many immigrants do not intend to merge into our society, to be part of our nation. On the contrary, they want to retain their own culture; an attitude which is ungenerous and discourteous in itself.

Amazingly, 1.3 million children in England do not speak English as their first language and English is no longer the first language for the majority of pupils in more than 2,000 primary and secondary schools. In more than 200 schools, English is not the native language for nine out of ten pupils.

It is hardly surprising that schools are now struggling to teach pupils how to read and write and it is hardly surprising that the incidence of illiteracy and innumeracy in Britain is increasing at an alarming rate.

Many immigrants insist on us adopting their culture and way of life because they believe it to be superior, and to them the only acceptable way of life. A good number continue to wear their native dress although it is hardly appropriate for our climate. (One reader asked me why Arab men wear white robes whereas Arab women wear black. The answer is simple: white clothing reflects the desert heat and keeps the wearer nice and cool on hot days and black clothing, on the other hand, absorbs heat and keeps the wearer uncomfortably hot. Feminists may see some significance in this.)

Many even want to discredit our history by, for example, tearing down statues of great English heroes.

That is where the racism comes in; for that is a racist attitude.

And it isn't immigration in the way that many Britons emigrated to Australia and became Australians.

Or the way that the Irish emigrated to America and became Americans.

In both cases, these emigrants took to their new countries with enthusiasm. They embraced their new nations and the way of life they found. They became proud Australians and proud Americans.

But Britain is now suffering an invasion; a subtle but deliberate and significant act of war. Immigrants who enter the country with a passion and a ruthlessness and a belief in their own culture (and who believe that their culture is better than anyone else's) will overcome the weak who do not have enough pride in themselves and do not have the mental strength to defend themselves, their culture, their history and their future.

I don't know why the Remainers don't understand any of this.

I suspect that many of the older Remainers have been bought with money and promises.

And they have persuaded younger Remainers to support the EU with lies and false threats.

6

A year or so ago, I bought a couple of hundred copies of *Punch* magazine from the early 1950s. They are a joy to read. I enjoy them as a substitute for modern periodicals. P.G.Wodehouse and John Steinbeck were among an impressive list of regular contributors.

There doesn't appear to be much of a market for old magazines and these cost me £1 each which was a snip. (Especially when you consider that the issues containing pieces by authors such as Wodehouse have a considerably enhanced value for collectors.)

You can even buy old magazines from the mid 19th century for little more than pennies. Many, such as *Punch*, are much sharper than modern magazines such as *Private Eye* and *Viz*.

And they contain some surprising news features.

In the *Punch* issue dated June 22nd 1955, there is an article by Lord Kinross in which he describes a scheme devised by the brothers Bernstein who were apparently aiming to make shopping 'a more alluring experience for housewives'.

The brothers had hired a small army of housewives whose job it was to shop all day long. They were paid ten shillings for each purchase they made and at every shop they visited, they filled in a form, giving marks for Sales Efficiency, Customer Contact, General Appearance of sales assistant and even what the assistant said at the end of the sale. The form also contained a place for the shopper to make remarks about the whole shopping experience.

And it wasn't just shops which were the target of this survey.

Cafés and pubs were also being investigated, with marks being given for cleanliness and the demeanour of the waitress or barmaid.

So the review system now so popular on the internet isn't new after all.

7

I was, for a while, almost a little bit famous. I was on television several times a week, on the wireless even more frequently (through the miracle that is provided by pre-recording programmes) and my picture was printed in the national press several times a week. I was a T-shirt, and posters advertising my books and columns appeared in bus shelters and on television. People occasionally recognised me in the street, in shops and on railway platforms.

(In those days, it was perfectly acceptable for a publisher to advertise an author. It was not, however, acceptable, for a self-published author to advertise his own books. The rules have now changed and I don't have the foggiest idea what the rules are. I'm not even sure if there are any rules.)

I never much liked being a little bit famous.

But I have met people who would do anything, only just short of dying, to be famous.

A friend of mine once admitted to me that his only ambition in life was to be recognised in the supermarket where he did his weekly shopping. He confessed that he would do anything to achieve this aim. Sadly, it never happened. He touched the hem but at the last moment it was always whisked away from him. Someone else always got the plum part in a television advertisement. Someone else got the TV presenting job. Someone else got the show on national radio. It must have been excrutiating, tantalising and endlessly frustrating. No one could have tried harder.

He was yet another example of why I always get cross when I hear people who have been successful crediting their glory on 'hard work' and ignoring the two other essentials: talent and, most important of all, good luck. It's intensely depressing to those who work hard without great success.

Success comes from talent, timing, work and luck. My pal had plenty of talent and he worked hard.

But he didn't have the luck. He was never in the right place at the right time.

He got enough work to live but I very much doubt if anyone ever recognised him at the cheese counter or at the cooked meats counter.

He went recently to the Great Studio in the sky.

I hope lots of people recognised him when he got there.

8

I needed to print something today. We have three printers in the house and I cannot make any of them work. One of them requires a disk but the laptop I am using has no disk drive. The other two printers require me to connect my computer to the internet and I refuse point blank to do this.

Fortunately, Antoinette remembered that we keep a 'dirty' laptop which we do connect to the internet. So I moved the stuff I wanted to print to the 'dirty' laptop and printed it out.

In the bad old days, twenty years ago, I had a printer which I had attached to my laptop without any outside assistance. I just connected a lead from the printer to the computer. And plugged the printer into the wall socket.

It worked and did everything you can ask of a printer.

Now everything is just too complicated.

9

There aren't many great English eccentrics about these days. Most have been crushed by the need to conform.

No one would have crushed Lt Col Jack Churchill.

In France, early in the Second World War, he was the last soldier in history to kill an enemy soldier with a longbow.

In a raid on a Nazi post in Norway in 1940, he stood on one of the landing boats playing his bagpipes. When he landed, he swapped the bagpipes for a claymore sword. I bet the Germans were terrified. I would have been. He then threw a grenade before charging at the enemy.

In 1944, he was captured but a year later he escaped and walked over the Alps to rejoin the Allied forces.

Can't see many millennials doing any of that stuff can you?

10

Hackers are taking over the world and the frightening thing is that the big computer companies and banks seem to be just as vulnerable as the rest of us. Tens of millions of pounds have been stolen through the SWIFT banking network. More than a billion Yahoo accounts were compromised. That's a billion with a 'b' and not a million with a 'm'. Hackers have stolen credit card details from Home Depot and Neiman Marcus and they have managed to wriggle inside banks such as JP Morgan Chase. Google and Facebook were conned by a hacker who took them for $100 million. A company called OneLogin, which promoted itself as a secure password management service, lost some of its customer data to hackers. Linkedin said that 6.5 million accounts had been hacked but later it turned out that they had slightly underestimated, since 117 million names and passwords had been put up for sale by the hacker. Over 9,000 bank accounts at Tesco were emptied by hackers. It appears that Uber, the sort of taxi service, lost the personal details of 57 million people but kept quiet about it for a year (after paying the hackers $100,000 to keep silent and to destroy the stolen material).

An American credit rating company called Equifax which promises its customers that it 'help protect you against fraud' has admitted that data from between 143 million and 145.5 million customers may have been compromised in a security breach. The company's job, its reason for existing, is 'to collect, securely store and aggregate information'. They didn't do it very well. The information stolen included: names, social security numbers, birth dates, addresses, driving license numbers and credit card details. And the company, which promises to protect its customers (that, after all, is part of its raison d'etre), didn't get round to telling them that their personal information had been stolen for 40 days. That makes the whole thing a real scandal because if people had been warned they could have been more careful. The company initially claimed that less than 400,000 customers in the UK had been affected. A couple of months later, they admitted that actually they'd got that slightly wrong too because the hack wasn't limited to 400,000 but affected 15,200,000 customers. An easy mistake to make if you are a complete idiot, I suppose.

Why aren't these companies ever brought to book? Why is no one ever arrested for incompetence? Why hasn't Equifax been shut down and all its executives fed to the lions? With companies like this looking after our security we might as well have all personal details tattooed in some visible part of our bodies for all to see. Most of us could have our details on our foreheads and starlet, reality TV types could have their bank numbers, passport details and so on emblazoned on their bosoms. There would be more room there and the details would be seen by more people.

Incidentally, by one of those odd, little coincidences which seem to happen so often to overpaid individuals working in large, powerful companies, three executives of the company, including the finance chief, sold some shares (worth $1.8 million) just after the theft was discovered. What a surprise they must have had when they realised what they had done, for according to the company, the three had no idea about what had happened. You'd think, wouldn't you, that senior executives in a company, senior enough to hold loads of shares, would know what was going on and would have an inkling when 143,000,000 of their customers had had their personal details stolen and are now at risk of having their identities stolen. (I've had a small taste of that and it is no fun at all. Last year Americans lost $16 billion as a result of identity theft. And they will have also lost a great deal of time and suffered an enormous amount of stress.) But hey-ho we are told that the three executives who flogged their shares knew nothing of the hack.

(The company, by the way, referred to the theft as an 'intrusion' which we can add to all those other mealy mouthed misnaming words which are so popular with executives these days.)

And what lucky folk the three were for the shares they had so fortuitously sold went clunk and lost 35% when the theft was finally revealed.

The chief executive of Equifax earned almost $15 million last year. (Mind you, Tim Cook, the chief executive of Apple, received a total of over $150 million in salary and bonuses and vested shares so the boundaries and expectations for company bosses these days seem limitless.)

Still, justice has been done. After the hacking debacle, the chief executive retired in disgrace and had to leave with only $70 million in benefits and bonuses. I bet that was a lesson for all chief executives.

There are, it seems, few if any penalties for such egregious incompetence.

Indeed, it seems likely that Equifax will make money out of the fiasco. If just one in ten victims buys its credit monitoring services as a result of what happened then Equifax will double its annual income and the company's remaining executives will be in line for even bigger bonuses.

I do not believe anyone who ever tells me that their system is immune to fraudulent hacking. Children in their bedrooms are forever hacking into the personal computers of CIA and FBI bosses. (They are, of course, always autistic since this ensures that they cannot be extradited). I really don't understand why the authorities don't simply hire the child hackers instead of wasting money prosecuting them.

My pension company is still trying to force me to go online by claiming that their website cannot possibly be hacked. I am punished for refusing to do so not just because I have to pay more to do anything but because they won't send me any paperwork if I deal in shares on the telephone. And nor will they let me know what cash I have available for investing. The result is that I don't change anything and so they don't earn any commissions at all.

All companies can be hacked (whatever their assurances) and none can be trusted to tell you when your personal details have been stolen. This is Coleman's First Law of Privacy.

And yet no one seems to take online fraud seriously.

Four out of five IT managers admit that their company has released computer code before testing it for bugs or resolving security issues.

11

There is no political party standing up for the English. (Although I realise that UKIP gets close it isn't a party for England).

There is no one asking who will pay for the asylum seekers. There is no one pointing out that the NHS cannot cope with an endless series of foreign patients demanding treatment for their AIDS or providing them with free obstetrics care or heart surgery. There is no one explaining that the NHS has collapsed and that English taxpayers (the least well looked after citizens in the British Isles and yet the ones who pay for just about everything) are dying because of long waiting lists. There is no political party wondering if women should be allowed to breast feed in restaurants. There is no political party wondering whether or not homosexuals should be allowed to marry and adopt children from far off countries. There is no political party promoting the virtues of a Christian life (with or without the formal church). There is no political party brave enough to question the myth of climate change.

England is definitely, completely, permanently stuffed.

12

I think I first noticed the end beginning around 25 years ago.

I used to make regular appearances on a late night live television show which came from studios in Birmingham. At the end of one programme, I said goodnight to the director and producer and announced my intention of walking back to my hotel. The director and the producer looked at me as if I were completely mad. 'You can't do that!' they said. 'You'll never get there!'

132

I stared at them in astonishment.

I went to medical school in Birmingham. Even though the city centre has been turned inside out several times, I still know my way around. Besides, I could see my hotel. I could see my room window. It was no more than a few hundred yards away. I could walk there in five or ten minutes at the most.

'We'll get you a taxi,' said the producer. He sent someone off to order a taxi. Television companies always have someone ready to go off and order a taxi.

And they stood in the doorway to prevent me going outside by myself.

Thanks to Birmingham's traffic system, it took three times as long to get to the hotel by cab as it would have taken me to walk there.

Today, there isn't a city in England where I would feel able to take a walk after ten or so at night. In many parts of many cities, I wouldn't feel comfortable going out after dark.

The sad thing is that most English cities are not just unsafe, but they have also lost their identity. Treasured landmarks are being demolished without hesitation. Traditions are abandoned. Bits and pieces of Victoriana are smashed away with enthusiasm.

And though it is undoubtedly considered racist to say this, this is because the immigrants the EU has forced us to accept have taken over our nation. They have absolutely no interest in our culture or our history.

It is not fashionable, and probably not even legal, to say this but large numbers of immigrants came to England not because they admire our culture, our approach to civilisation, our interpretation of democracy, our history of generosity to those in need, our inventiveness or our attempt at a judicial system but because they want our money and, when they've got it, they want to replace our world with their world.

Immigrants don't come to London because they like our London. They come to London because they want to use our money to turn it into their London.

And they are doing well.

In the last 12 months for which figures are available, 93,000 Britons moved out of London. That figure is 80% higher than the figure five years ago and the total is rising at a massive rate. Just about every home born citizen who can afford to leave is quitting – selling their overpriced home and buggering off. Most are going abroad. Some are simply heading out into the countryside.

But the population figures do not reflect this.

London's population is now 8.8 million and rising fast as more and more immigrants pour in – ensuring that there will never again be a white English mayor in charge of England's capital.

Does it matter? Of course it bloody well does.

Ancient Rome ended up with slaves doing all the work and the ordinary citizens living on hand-outs. The toga-wearing bosses just had a good time.

That didn't turn out too well for them did it?

It is not a bit like London today. It is exactly like London today. The slaves are the immigrants who work for sub-minimum wages. The citizens living on hand-outs are the remaining Britons. The few happy middle and upper class Britons remaining in London are the liberal luvvies who enjoy having immigrants to do their menial work: the cleaning, the gardening, driving the Uber car, digging out the basement, caring for the children.

It is because of the liberal luvvies that the immigrants are paid wages which keep them in poverty and turn huge areas of London into slums and ghettoes.

London is a lost city. The rest of England should, perhaps, just build a wall around it and abandon it.

London has become a city where terrorists are acclaimed as long as they are foreign born, hating Britain.

It is a city where brain-dead liberal luvvies and millennials offer the incomers everything we have left – on a platter.

London is a city of political correctness, gender awareness, action days, grinding poverty, blatant racism, violence and ageism (if you are English and elderly). London is now more crime ridden and dangerous than New York City with rape, robbery and violent offences far higher in London. London is a city of rage and noise and bowls of cornflakes sold to the millennials for a fiver. It is a city of vigils and crocodile tears and clichéd nonsenses. It is a city where Islamic terrorists are reared. It is a city where immigrants take endless advantage of our generosity, our welcome, our everything.

Our security bosses will eventually realise that the terrorism risk, now being home grown and home sustained, will soon be a permanent part of British life. When a white man, probably mentally disturbed, made a pretty half-hearted attack on Muslims, it was instantly branded a terrorist attack. But when Muslims attack Britons, which they do with rather more consistency and determination, no one likes to call it terrorism. It's dismissed as just an isolated instance of extremism. But it is yet another isolated instance of extremism.

London is filling up with the dregs from other countries while many of the best and hardest working home-grown citizens are emigrating.

Most young professionals now say that if they had the opportunity to do so they would quit Britain, which they see as having no present and no future. Most of those who are quitting say they are leaving because Britain has been changed too much by immigration. Some, of course, leave for more lenient tax regimes. (You can be resident in Malta, which is an EU country, without spending a single day there.)

But it is a politically motivated nonsense to say that Britons are leaving because they want to live in sunnier countries or because they are attracted by lower tax rates. Britons, and especially Londoners, are merely abandoning a half sunken ship.

London may now be a city of diversity. But it is no longer a city of tolerance.

In London today there is more religious and cultural intolerance than ever before. London is a city which even Dr Johnson would be tired of.

In the days of Daniel Defoe, around 11% of the English population lived in London. Today, that figure is falling dramatically as the English sell their overpriced flats and buy country homes with a few acres and a barn.

London an international city? Don't make me laugh.

We now do everything we can to avoid it.

Britons will continue to leave and within ten years there won't be a Brit left in the damned place and you'll be unlikely to meet a native English speaker anywhere within Mr Khan's sheikdom.

I used to love London.

I loved walking up from Whitehall, through Trafalgar Square (which used to be full of tourists photographing the pigeons but which is now full of tourists looking lost), up Charing Cross Road (which used to be packed with bookshops), into Shaftsbury Avenue (where there are still some theatres), to Leicester Square, then cut down along Jermyn Street (where the tailors and hatters which remain are usually offering massive sale offers), back up to the Burlington Arcade (which now sells only overpriced tat to the richest tourists) then up Bond Street. We would take a taxi to Paddington from the top end of Bond Street.

It was a walk best done on a misty, drizzly night.

I doubt if I will ever enjoy that walk again.

London is now too dirty and too unsafe.

It isn't just London, of course.

Despite the fact that disillusioned, saddened Britons are leaving their country in huge numbers, the population is rising rapidly as immigrants continue to pour in.

The inevitable result is that the nature of our country has changed.

Even our prison service has been bloated by immigrants who now make up 14% of the UK's jail population.

It's madness.

13

I read today that Britain's sandwich industry now employs more people than work in agriculture. The sandwich industry is far larger and far more advanced than anywhere else in Europe. Around four billion sandwiches are produced and packed in Britain each year.

Why?

The obvious answer is that people are too busy to sit down to a meal and far, far too busy to make their own sandwiches. Most of those sandwiches, by the way, are infected with potentially unpleasant bugs such as Escherichia coli.

We all spend too much of our lives rushing around. My list of things to do before I die includes a lot of sitting around in the garden with a good book.

14

Drug companies are spending big money on looking for drugs that will boost the body's immune system so that it can tackle cancer.

They're all in it now.

What a pity they waited so long.

And what a pity that the *Daily Mirror* (encouraged and aided and abetted by a major cancer charity linked with the drug industry) chose to help shut down my website 20 years ago when I first suggested that strengthening the human body's immune system was the way to fight cancer most affectively.

15

People used to say that things were better 'then' and when the 'then' was 100 years ago everyone knew it was bollocks. Things were only better if you were rich.

Now, I'm not so sure.

Thinking about it as objectively as is possible, I do think things were better 'then' if then was just half a century ago.

Back in the 1950s and 1960s we had antibiotics which worked, anaesthesia, antiseptics (with no hospital acquired resistant bugs) and roads you could drive on with a reasonable expectation of getting where you were going before the seasons changed. Women wore frocks and dresses and skirts and men wore hats and took them off when greeting women. On buses, men would offer their seats to women without being abused. Obesity was far less common and infant mortality rates had fallen dramatically. Life expectancy for adults was much the same as it is now.

16

I have for some years been collecting evidence which shows clearly that the framework for the EU was built in the 1940s by Adolf Hitler and other Nazis.

Everyone who now supports or defends the EU is ipso facto a Nazi sympathiser. There is no doubt that the truth makes uncomfortable reading for the EU's many supporters – most of whom stick their fingers in their ears and shout a lot if I ever try to tell them about it.

Liberal Democrats and liberal lefty luvvies don't like to be told that in supporting the EU they are helping to promote the work of Adolf Hitler and other Nazis. But the facts show that they are. Anyone who claims otherwise is either ignorant or in denial. The EU, an undemocratic, truly fascist and much reviled organisation, was created exactly as Hitler and his Nazi colleagues said it should be. Even the euro was planned by the Nazis.

(There is much irony in the fact that the EU's critics are often denounced as 'fascists'. Fascism was invented by Mussolini and it is perfectly clear to anyone who has studied the subject that the EU is the most perfectly fascist organisation ever invented.)

The EU was designed by Nazis, and, moreover, was designed to make Germany stronger. It is no coincidence that Germany is the one country to have benefited from the EU's formation.

Ignorant members of the Entitlement Generation do not realise that the European Union was designed by Adolf Hitler and his Nazi chums and that the EU as it exists is designed to promote Germany's interests.

You only have to look at how the euro has advanced Germany's economic position in the world to see just how this happened in practice. Thanks to the way the euro was structured, Germany makes a huge financial surplus each year and is destroying the economies of other euro-zone countries. The Germans are getting rapidly richer and the citizens of other countries are becoming poorer. It is no exaggeration to say that the EU has killed Europe in order to enrich Germany.

And that, of course, was the plan. It is why the EU was founded.

It is nonsense to claim, as some Remainers still do, that the EU is a modern creation, founded by Kohl of Germany and Mitterand of France. We have heard it suggested on the BBC that these two politicians were so scarred by their memories of World War II that they decided to build a new Europe 'where there would be peace, happiness and prosperity for all'.

This is patently untrue, and yet there are many credulous citizens who believe it.

The truth is that the history of the EU goes back much, much further than its proponents will usually admit. I have exposed the

Nazi background to the EU before but much of the important material below is new.

It was back in the 1930's, in Hitler's Germany, that the European Union was invented and designed. Hitler wanted to destroy national identities and create a united Europe, consisting of new regions to be ruled from Berlin. In 1936, Hitler told the Reichstag: 'It is not very intelligent to imagine that in such a cramped house like that of Europe, a community of peoples can maintain different legal systems and different concepts of law for long.' Even before that, in Italy, the founding father of fascism, Mussolini, said in 1933 that: 'Europe may once again grasp the helm of world civilisation if it can develop a modicum of political unity.'

Adolf Hitler wanted to get rid of the plethora of nations in Europe. His advisor, Funk, agreed that 'there must be a readiness to subordinate one's own interests…to that of the European Community'.

In 1940, Herr Arthur Seyss-Inquart called for a new European community which would be above the concept of the nation state. Seyss-Inquart was, at the time, the Nazi in charge of the occupied Netherlands. He predicted that once national barriers had been removed there would be increased prosperity in Europe.

Hitler was the man who gave bones to the dreams first expressed by Charlemagne and Napoleon but the finishing touches to the EU as we know it were put in place during World War II by a man called Walther Funk, who was President of the Reichsbank and a director of the Bank for International Settlements (BIS). It was Funk who laid the foundations for European economic unity – and the euro. Funk was also Adolf Hitler's key economics advisor.

The European Union was designed by Nazis and it has been carefully created according to the original design. It is not, you will note, a 'group' or an 'association'. It was always a union. And in a union the members are not affiliated, they are joined. 'What good fortune for governments that the people do not think,' said Adolf Hitler.

The BIS was then and still is the world's most powerful and secret global financial institution. During the Second World War, the BIS accepted looted Nazi gold (handling 21.5 metric tons of Nazi gold) and supported the development and launch of what would, in 2002, become the euro. The Bank for International Settlements (BIS) was set up by the governors of the Reichsbank and the Bank of England in 1930. It still exists and no one controls it and yet it is, to a large extent, in charge of the world's finances.

During WWII, the BIS was used by the Nazis and the Allies as a point of contact. Walther Funk's deputy, Emil Puhl, described the BIS as the 'foreign branch' of the Reichsbank. At the end of WWII, the Reichsbank became the Bank deutscher Lander and the Bundesbank. The BIS helped these to ensure that Germany continued to dominate Europe – despite its having come a poor second in the Second World War.

There were many connections between the BIS and the German banks. For example, Karl Blessing worked at the BIS during the 1930s before transferring to the Reichsbank. While at the Reichsbank, Blessing oversaw slave labourers in Germany. He later became president of the Bundesbank.

It was Hitler and Funk, working with the BIS, who designed the EU as it exists today. The Nazis wanted to get rid of the clutter of small nations which made up Europe and their plan was quite simple. The EU was Hitler's dream but it was Funk who outlined the practical work which needed to be done.

In 1940, Funk prepared a lengthy memo called 'Economic Reorganisation of Europe' which was passed to the President of the BIS (who was an American called Thomas McKittrick) on July 26th 1940. (A copy of this historic document is stored at the BIS in Basel.)

'The new European economy will result from close economic collaboration between German and European countries,' wrote Funk. It is important to note that even then the EU was seen as a union between Germany, on the one hand, and the rest of Europe, on the other. There was never any doubt which nation would be in charge of the new United States of Europe. (The phrase United States of Europe was devised by Adolf Hitler himself).

There are commentators and economists today who note Germany's control of today's EU with surprise, and who seem puzzled by the fact that Germany is booming and has by far the largest and most dominant economy in the EU. No one should be surprised because the EU was always planned that way. Germany is benefitting enormously from the euro crisis but Funk knew that would be the case. Back in 1940, Funk had the idea for the euro but warned that even after monetary union it would be impossible to have one standard of living throughout Europe. He knew that the euro would be flawed but he also knew that Germany would come out on top. He would not be in the slightest bit surprised by the fact that modern Germany is by far the largest and most dominant economy in the European Union. That was always the Plan. In reality, of course, the euro was bound to cause chaos and massive unemployment throughout many parts of the European Union because of policies which German politicians set in process after the unification of West and East Germany and before the foundation of the euro. The policies, which were designed to enable a unified Germany to control the EU, involved Germany entering the euro at an advantageously low exchange rate, thereby giving it a huge competitive advantage over other euro countries. The aim was that Germany would get richer while other countries got poorer and that is exactly what is happening. (The French stupidly and short-sightedly chose to join the euro with a strong franc because it meant that they could enjoy cheap holidays in the rest of Europe.)

Because the euro is undervalued relative to the German economy, Germany exports far more than it imports and grows ever richer and stronger at the expense of its other euro 'partners'. Germany currently runs the world's biggest trade surplus – and has been running big surpluses for a decade. German politicians have refused to spend the money they have been accumulating and so other countries in Europe, struggling to cope with a euro artificially strengthened by a rich Germany, have slumped further and further into depression and their unemployment rates have soared.

The Germans are fighting hard to protect and preserve the euro, and will continue to pay money to preserve the status quo, because if the European currency breaks up, two things will happen: first, Hitler's plan for a German dominated United States of Europe will be in tatters and second, the Germany mark will suddenly be as strong as the Swiss franc, and cars and refrigerators made in Germany will be priced out of many markets.

If the Germans can keep the euro alive then in due course, the inevitable will happen: Germany will control the European Union and Hitler will have a posthumous victory.

Economists, who tend to have a limited understanding of the world, are constantly producing articles expressing surprise at the fact that the euro was created at all and dismay that, despite all the evidence showing that it has caused enormous damage to countries and individuals, it is being kept alive. If they understood how and why the European Union was created (and who created it) they would, perhaps, have a better understanding of why it exists and why those who support it will fight to the death to preserve it.

Remember all this the next time you see a British politician claiming that our enormously expensive membership of the EU is vital for Britain. And remember too that many of the EU's loudest and most persistent supporters have received massive financial support from the EU; sometimes in the form of grants and sometimes as fees. The EU spends billions every year on keeping its supporters happy. The BBC, a renowned supporter of the European Union and an organisation which has confessed to being biased in the EU's favour, has received millions of pounds from the EU. The money is invariably described as being given as a 'grant' but the word 'bribe' might be more appropriate. The BBC seems to repay this financial support by opposing Brexit, by defending unpopular EU policies (such as those on immigration), by insisting that all measurements referred to in its programmes are in EU friendly metric units rather than proper British imperial measurements and by taking every opportunity to disparage England and the English. The BBC, like most organisations which depend upon the State, has a powerful liberal-socialist bias and I doubt if you could find more than a handful of Tories in any such institution. Why should you? All these organisations depend upon the benevolence of the State and will therefore support it to the hilt. Plus the BBC recruits pretty well exclusively from the readers of *The Guardian*; the house journal of lefty liberal heads in the sand luvvies who like lots of immigration because the immigrants make excellent, cheap domestic staff.

Joseph Goebbels, the Minister of Propaganda in the Third Reich, would have been proud of the BBC which is now an essential part of the Fourth Reich. Goebbels would have probably also been proud of the fact that scores of universities have professors funded by the EU. The professors are paid to teach students the value of European integration. And, naturally, the EU has, over the years, spent many large fortunes producing literature and teaching aids for teachers to use in European schools. (A recent survey showed that 80% of university lecturers in the UK are left wingers; which, assuming they are adults, means they are immature, ill-informed and far too stupid to be teaching anyone.)

On the rare occasions when voters in European countries have been invited to vote on EU issues, the EU has been the main financial contributor to 'Vote Yes' campaigns. That's another example of the way the EU views democracy. (And European politicians have the nerve to point the finger at Russia's President Putin!)

In 1941, Walther Funk was still planning the new European Union. He launched the Europaische Wirtschafts Gemeinschaft (European Economic Community) to integrate the European economy into a single market and to establish his idea for a single European currency. It was Funk who helped plan the European Union Community although when it was established he was still labelled a war criminal and still a resident of Spandau Prison in Berlin and it wasn't considered a terribly good idea to give him medals or to organise a thank you 'roast'. All subsequent suggestions that Funk be recognised as the founding father of the European Union have been rejected on the grounds that it is too soon to put up a statue to the man to whom Hitler handed the responsibility of ensuring the good health of the Fourth Reich. Funk planned the EU in precise detail. It was Funk who planned a Europe free of trade and currency restrictions.

In June 1942, German officials prepared a document entitled *Basic Elements of a Plan for the New Europe* which called, among other things, for a European clearing centre to stabilise currency rates with the aim of removing foreign exchange restrictions, securing European monetary union and 'the harmonisation of labour conditions and social welfare'.

The original plan was for the Reichsmark to be the new European currency but Funk, a far sighted pragmatist, never saw this as crucial, or being as important as Germany having economic leadership of Europe. The far-sighted Funk saw Germany as central to the planned EU, and argued that it would result in 'better outlets for German goods on European markets'. Back in 1940, it was Funk who planned to introduce a United States of Europe via a common currency. Today, it is clear that Walther Funk, economist, banker and war criminal, is the true father of the modern European Union and is one of the most influential figures in European history.

Hitler and the rest of the Nazi leadership welcomed Funk's plans and in 1942, the German Foreign Ministry made detailed plans for a European confederation to be dominated by Germany. In the same year, a group of German businessmen held a conference in Berlin entitled 'European Economic Community'. (The phrase 'European Economic Community' had been first used by Hermann Goering in 1940.)

In 1942, Reinhard Heydrich, who was head of the Reich Security Central Office and renowned for his ruthlessness against enemies of the State, published *The Reich Plan for the Domination of Europe* – a document which is notable for its remarkable similarity to the EU's Treaty of Rome.

In March 1943, 13 countries (including France and Italy) were invited to join a new European federation which would be under German military control.

When the Nazis realised that they were losing the war they knew that they had to make a deal in order to preserve German domination in Europe. Thomas McKittrick, the president of the BIS, acted as go between and helped set up the negotiations. The underlying plan was to ensure that Germany dominated post-war Europe and Funk and his colleagues decided to talk about European spirit, liberty, equality, fraternity and worldwide cooperation as the basis for their planned European Union. They decided to agree to share power, and even to allow other countries to take charge for a while. The Nazis knew that all they needed to do was retain men in power in crucial posts. And this they succeeded in doing.

In 1943, Heinz Pol, a former newspaper editor from Berlin, who had fled to the US, published a book entitled *The Hidden Enemy* in which he explained that Germany realised that the war was lost and was planning to preserve its domination over Europe. Pol explained that the BIS was playing a vital part in the Nazi plan.

Here is how Pol predicted that post war German leaders would trick the rest of the world into accepting that they had abandoned Nazi ideals: 'To obtain a peace, which would leave them in power, they will suddenly flaunt 'European spirit' and offer worldwide 'cooperation'. They will chatter about liberty, equality and fraternity. They will, all of a sudden, make up to the Jews. They will swear to live up to the demands of the Atlantic Charter and any other charter. They will share power with everybody and they will even let others rule for a while. They will do all this and more, if only they are allowed to keep some positions of power and control, that is, the only positions that count: in the army – were it even reduced to a few thousand men; in the key economic organisations; in the courts; in the universities; in the schools.'

This is precisely what happened. Pol had predicted with startling accuracy just how the Nazis would win the peace.

In 1944, a secret conference was held in Berlin entitled 'How Will Germany Dominate The Peace When It Loses The War'. Rich and powerful Germans decided to move a huge amount of money out of Germany and to take it to America. (The money stayed there until after the Nurnberg Trials when it came back to Europe.)

In August 1944, the heads of the Nazi Government and a group of leading German industrialists, met at a hotel in Strasbourg and decided to hide more large sums of money in order to pay for the fight for a German dominated Europe to continue if their country lost the war. The Nazis realised that their back-up plan for European domination would take years to reach fruition but they believed that if their military tactics failed then their subtle economic and political tactics would prove successful.

Today, of course, Strasbourg is the seat of the Council of Europe and the European Parliament. (Strasbourg was occupied by Germany and the Nazis during World War II but became French again after that war.)

The technical preparations for Funk's 'European Large Unit Economy' (now better known as the Eurozone) began in 1947 when the Paris accord on multilateral payments was signed, were strengthened in 1951 when the European Coal and Steel Community was created as the first step towards the development of a new European nation to be run by Germany, and continued in

1964 when the Committee of European Central Banks (made up of Bank Governors) met at the BIS to coordinate monetary policy.

In 1961, US President Kennedy told British Prime Minister Harold Macmillan that the White House would only support Britain's application to join the Common Market if Britain accepted that the true goal of the Common Market was political integration – Hitler's famous United States of Europe.

In 1966, American President Johnson encouraged Britain's membership of the developing European Economic Community and so Foreign Office civil servants in London decided that the 'special relationship' with the USA would be enhanced if Britain joined the Common Market. In 1968, the Foreign Office warned that 'if we fail to become part of a more united Europe, Britain's links with the USA will not be enough to prevent us becoming increasingly peripheral to USA concerns'.

The European Central Bank (ECB), (which today has so much power over European citizens) was designed and set up by the German Bundesbank which was Germany's post war central bank. The Bundesbank was the son of the Reichsbank which was the name of Germany's central bank before and during World War II. The President of the Reichsbank before and during World War II was, of course, Walther Funk.

The ECB would probably have a Walther Funk Founder's Day if they thought they could get away with it and the only surprise that Funk hasn't yet found himself portrayed on euro coins and notes. He has more of a right to appear on them than anyone else because they were his idea.

Today, thanks to the Maastricht Treaty, each EU member's gold reserves belong to the EU and are effectively controlled by the ECB. As planned, the ECB (grandson of Hitler's Reichsbank) is not democratically accountable to anyone. It is actually prohibited from taking advice from Eurozone Governments and the European Parliament has no authority over it. No one knows how the ECB makes decisions because everything is done in great secrecy.

There are some supporters of the EU who claim that the absence of democracy within the organisation was never the original intention. They are wrong. The EU was always designed to be an undemocratic organisation: it is the Anti-Democracy.

Way back in 1950, Clement Attlee, Britain's Labour Prime Minister recognised the problems associated with the planned European unity. He said, when responding to the Schuman plan for the European Coal and Steel Community (the initial version of the EU): 'It (is) impossible for Britain to accept the principle that the economic forces of this country should be handed over to an authority that is utterly undemocratic and is responsible to nobody.'

The unwritten, unspoken aims of the European Union are to regulate every activity and to ensure that everything which every citizen does will be controlled by the State. The plan is to eliminate small businesses, small hospitals and small everything else. As far as the EU is concerned 'small is bad'. It is much easier for the State to control production and tax gathering if it only has to deal with large international companies.

(It is hardly surprising that the executives of large companies are among the most vocal of the EU's supporters. In the UK, for example, they will often threaten to close down factories if citizens vote to leave the EU.)

By licensing every occupation, and insisting that individuals pay annual licensing fees, the EU can control citizens and take in more taxes. Individuals who speak out or protest can be controlled by having their licenses withdrawn.

On January 1st 1999, eleven countries launched the euro and in January 2002, Funk's dream currency finally replaced national currencies. The secretive BIS was crucial in helping to force through the euro – the first step towards the new European state. The truth is that the introduction of the euro was nothing more than the final instalment of World War II – the realisation of the Nazi dream shared by Adolf Hitler and Walther Funk. Herr Funk had predicted that uniting countries with different cultures and economic policies would be disastrous. But he knew Germany would come out on top.

Members of the British press were massively enthusiastic about the euro but got so excited that they forgot to give due credit to Herr Funk and his boss. Commentators drew attention to the fact that travellers could now use the same currency over much of Europe and could buy ice creams in Italy with money they'd taken out of the bank in France. No attention was paid to the fact that when countries decide to share a currency they are making a significant political decision. No one seemed to care that the majority of people in all the countries which gave up their currencies were opposed to the euro. (The EU has never pretended to be a democratic organisation. Hitler and Funk believed in federalism and centralisation but they weren't desperately enthusiastic about democracy which they regarded as a sign of weak leadership.)

'It was a very peculiar thing to have a central bank without a Government,' said Paul Volcker, chairman of the Federal Reserve in the USA. French politicians believed that the single currency meant that Germany would not be able to start any more wars. They also believed (quite wrongly, of course) that Germany would no longer be able to dominate the European economy.

Everyone involved with the creation of the euro knew that the new currency was fatally flawed. The aim was to use the euro to force through a political union, against the will of the European people and in spite of the massive, inevitable cost in terms of unemployment and hardship. Millions of people now face a lifetime of poverty and unemployment because of the hasty introduction of a new currency which no one needed and no one wanted.

Economists recognised from the start that the euro would be problematic and would create huge social difficulties (including terrible levels of unemployment) but politicians ignored all the warnings. They knew that introducing the euro would make the creation of a federal Europe inevitable and unstoppable.

In 1945, Hitler's Masterplan was captured by the Allies. The Plan included details of his scheme to create an economic integration of Europe and to found a European Union on a federal basis. The Nazi plan for a federal Europe was based on Lenin's belief that 'federation is a transitional form towards complete union of all nations'.

It is impossible to find any difference between Hitler's plan for a new United States of Europe, dominated by Germany, and the European Union we have today.

The EU was never wanted by the people of Europe and it has been built on years of deceit, corruption and hidden agendas. A group of fanatics, inspired by Hitler's dream of a United States of Europe, realised that their dream could only be turned into reality if they moved one small step at a time, set limited objectives, ignored public opinion and prepared treaties which required individual countries to relinquish only a little of their sovereignty in any one agreement.

And so a relatively innocuous Coal and Steel Community was slowly transformed into Hitler's dream: the European Union.

The Remainers who are so vocal in their support of the EU are nothing more nor less than Nazi sympathisers; fighting to sustain the Nazi plan for Europe.

You won't hear any of this on the BBC.

And no one else will publish it.

Which is why I've included it here.

At least you and I know the truth.

17

It is widely acknowledged that people benefit enormously from sharing their lives with a pet of some sort – a cat, an aardvark, a dog, a goldfish or a giraffe will all produce significant improvements in physical and mental health. If you have a dog you can take it for a walk and talk to it. If you have a goldfish you can take it for a swim.

But I suspect that there are also benefits to be gained by having a stuffed toy in your life. Stuffed toys require no feeding. They produce no mess. You can cuddle them. If you have to leave them then you can do so easily – knowing that they will be there when you return. You can take them on holiday with you.

18

We are back in Paris. Having spent much of the last 20 years in Paris, the most important thing I have learned is that one should never admit to speaking French. Not a word. None. Nothing. Not even 'mercy buckets'.

Here's why:

If you speak French, the locals (especially in Paris) will criticise everything you say. They will delight in picking holes in your grammar and they will constantly correct your pronunciation.

If you speak French to a Frenchman (or German to a German), you will always be searching for the appropriate word. You will be forever on the back foot, struggling to make sure that you aren't making a mistake which will result in your listener collapsing onto the floor and holding his stomach as he struggles to contain his laughter. If he's trying to speak your language you can chuckle merrily and raise eyebrows occasionally.

If you insist on having all your conversations in English, the French person will be on the back foot. They will have to put a lot of effort into struggling to cope with a foreign language and they will have less brain available to deal with the problem at hand. And you can help to destabilise them by constantly correcting their English. (All native French speakers, however cocky they may be about their language skills, make terrible mistakes when they speak English.) When correcting a foreigner who is speaking English I always try to be understanding and patronising. I tell them they are doing really well and I ask them if they learned their English at school. If they seem fluent, I ask them how many weeks they have been learning English. This drives most of them almost insane.

If you need time to decide what to say or do, you can pretend not to understand what they are saying. If they say 'I am unhappy with clause 17 in our contract', you reply 'I'm sorry, did you say you are having trouble with your carburettor?'

If a foreigner is forced to speak English they will feel inferior and intimidated. This is always a Good Thing.

Acquire a good knowledge of English idioms and distribute them at random. Also, try using unusual words. So, for example, when saying goodbye, I always say 'Toodle-pip' or 'Pip pip'. This leaves foreigners who profess to speak perfect English blank-faced and rather bewildered. 'Tinkerty tonk' is, I find, also quite extraordinarily effective and firmly to be recommended when dealing with those unfortunate enough to have originated somewhere on continental Europe.

19

There is much talk about class distinction in Britain. But the truth is that the real distinction is between those who work for the Government and those who do not.

Those who have worked for the Government receive massive, inflation-proofed pensions. Those who have never worked for the Government struggle by on derisory pensions.

Those who survive on universal tax credits must wait weeks for the money, starving and shivering but those who manage the system are egregiously overpaid.

I read today that civil servants at the Department for Work and Pensions have been receiving massive bonuses despite the fact that the nation's key welfare system, the Universal Credit, is woefully mismanaged. The permanent secretary, the director general of digital technology and the director general of Universal Credit all of whom seemed to be about as much use as elastic tape measures received bonuses of up to £20,000 a piece last year – on top of salaries of around £200,000 a year.

And, of course, there will doubtless be a knighthood in due course.

Civil servants are punished rather than rewarded when they make egregious mistakes.

20

Reading a book about English wars, I read today that in the hands of a skilful archer a longbow can be a remarkably deadly weapon.

Back in the 13th century, it was known for an iron tipped arrow to pin an armoured knight to his horse, piercing chain mail, human thigh and wooden saddle.

Ouch.

21

French people demanded the other day that I provide evidence that I am English. I was, at the time, wearing a worn tweed sports jacket, a pair of rather ropey corduroy trousers, a checked shirt, an MCC tie and brown brogues.

'What the hell do I look like?' I demanded back. 'I'm certainly not a frog, am I?'

22

The Paris police have been busy taking the blankets from homeless tramps in the city. I assume that someone in the Police department (or the Mayor's office) thinks that if the tramps just lay on the pavement without blankets they would look neater. They would, of course, die sooner and it would therefore, be permissible to take them away and cremate them.

The Mayor and the Police Chief might like to reflect on the fact that the clochards of Paris are something of a tourist attraction.

On the other, the tons of concrete bollards, miles of wire fencing and presence of armed policemen make the city distinctly unattractive.

The gutless, lily-livered bosses of Paris have handed the city over to the terrorists. They might just as well let the clochards have a bit of it too.

23

Around £645 million worth of stuff is confiscated at security gates at British airports each year.

Where does the stuff go?

Who helps themselves to all those expensive penknives?

24

I heard a young woman of 16 going on 36 (or maybe that should be the other way round) quoting Nietzsche today. Naturally, she quoted that silly remark about 'that which does not kill us makes us stronger'. It is just about the only thing that is widely remembered about Nietzsche's work.

But even Nietzsche must have realised that what he wrote was absolute garbage – especially since he later went mad when he saw a horse being mistreated in the street. That didn't make him stronger did it?

Nietzsche was, as I'm afraid he often was, talking absolute bollocks.

The truth is that the crap that doesn't kill you just makes you weaker and more wary. Only psychopaths are made stronger by adversity.

Over the years, both Antoinette and I have been through some troublesome times. And we both agree that although the troubles, worries and anxieties have not killed us they have certainly not made us stronger. On the contrary, they have doubtless weakened us and made us far more vulnerable.

25

A day or two ago, I was wondering why writers today produce so few words compared to their predecessors. Frank Richards, for example, used to write 10,000 words day in day out on an old sit up and beg typewriter. Heaven knows how many words Mark Twain produced even before he discovered the typewriter.

But when you stop and think about it there is no real mystery.

We all waste hours every day dealing with the unavoidable crap and the endless stream of emails, trashy advertisements and so on. (I used to try to deal with the crap before doing fun things. In olden times, this was possible. But today there is so much crap that I have changed my attitude to the crap. It now takes second place. Annoying emails and letters are deleted or burnt. Most of the time I don't even bother to check that our utility companies aren't over-charging by putting us on a high tariff programme.)

This afternoon my Windows programme suddenly stole my work. I always, always save my stuff every few minutes but I had been so engrossed in what I was doing that I worked for three quarters of an hour without saving.

And then one of those bloody irritating anti-virus ads popped up and in the confusion of trying to get rid of it, I exited my programme and lost my work.

It is no wonder that I sometimes write my stuff with a pen on pieces of paper or in a notebook.

The computer and the internet have made life more complicated than it was and have, I suspect, done great damage to our personal productivity. The average person now looks at their phone between

150 and 200 times a day. Millions are constantly distracted by their internet connected gadgets and forever shopping or checking their social media status. All this matters because it takes around half an hour for an individual to recover from each interruption and to settle down to what they are supposed to be doing. A rush of emails is so deadening that it reduces an individual's IQ by around 10 points.

26

I parked the car close to a charity shop so that we could take in several boxes of books without having to carry them too far. (I don't know why I do this. When we closed Publishing House, we gave 30-40,000 books to three big charities for them to sell in their shops. The books ended up online, wrecking my income for years.) The car was parked legally and off the road. I had just lifted the final box from the boot when a motorist turned up. Antoinette was in the shop dropping off several bags of stuff and I couldn't move the car without putting down the box so I hurried and was back in less than a minute. The driver of the vehicle and his passenger could see exactly what I was doing but when I returned they shouted abuse at me. (The driver could have driven around my car but that would have meant turning the steering wheel which is, of course, against health and safety regulations.) The merry pair also pulled out the inevitable and ubiquitous mobile phones and filmed me, shouting that they would report me to the police and put the film on YouTube. Though the pair of them were several decades younger than I am I snarled, 'piss off you old farts'. I was cross with myself afterwards: if I'd been quick enough I'd have shouted the title of my latest book and got a free advertisement on YouTube.

I assume I will now be issued with one of those ASBO things. What a treat.

27

I overheard this today in the local newsagents.

'I've just come past your cottage. I noticed that you had left the key in the front door.'

'Oh, it's OK I locked the door.'

'But the key…'

'If I take it with me I might lose it. If I leave it in the door then I always know where it is and I know that it will be safe.'

Pure Bilbury.

28

I spent the afternoon making walking sticks. If you have as many hazel bushes as we have it is easy to find very suitable straight pieces of wood. And I managed to buy a collection of suitable ferrules and ornate handle ornaments through the internet last year. I'm particularly proud of a five foot high thumb stick which is both stout and as straight as an arrow. God grew it. But I picked it out. So we share the credit.

29

I noticed today that a number of commercial vans now have dash cams fitted front and aft.

It seems that everything is filmed these days.

I'm thinking of having advertising slogans painted on the bonnet and boot of the Bentley to take advantage of these outstanding commercial opportunities.

30

I realised today that I have been looking at my emails four or five times a day. I have also found myself checking the news several times a day and looking at the stock market and currency markets just as often. I have even been checking to see how well my books are selling.

This is just plain silly.

There is really no need to look at emails more than once a day. And nor is there any need to look at the news or the markets more than once a day.

Most of the emails I get can be deleted without reading. The interesting ones (which are pretty few and far between) can always wait. No one is going to change their minds about buying Estonian rights in a book I wrote in 1983 if I make them wait a day.

I don't trade shares on the markets and so I don't need to look at prices more than once or twice a week at most. (Share trading is the quickest way to lose all your money because the trading costs will ruin you. Proper investing requires making a macroeconomic geopolitical decision and then sticking to it for a decent time interval.)

The news largely is depressing (and deliberately made so by news providers who are desperate to gain more readers) and I subscribe to a free service which sends me news updates, I am not going to miss some important event if I don't look at the news every day.

May

1

American doctors have noticed that an increasing number of elderly citizens are falling. No one seems able to understand this phenomenon. They're really genuinely puzzled. The same thing is happening in Britain. More and more elderly patients are falling and breaking bones.

I'm standing at the back of the room waving my arms in the air but no one notices.

I know what the problem is.

And I know what the solution is.

Many of these elderly patients have a condition called 'normal pressure hydrocephalus'. Falling for no apparent reason is one of the early symptoms.

I believe that the Alzheimer industry is helping to suppress the truth because those involved want the words 'Alzheimer's' and 'dementia' to be synonymous.

(Many health problems have spawned industries. There is a cancer industry. And an AIDS industry.)

The fact is that NPH affects 1 in every 1,000 people. And that isn't rare. In fact, normal pressure hydrocephalus is, for example, commoner than Parkinson's disease. It is one of the commonest causes of dementia. And it is the only common cause of dementia which is curable. It's curable with a simple, cheap operation. And yet a huge proportion of all the patients treated in the UK for this disorder are seen by a single neurologist working in Bristol. Meanwhile, thousands of elderly folk who could be cured are falling and breaking bones. Falling is the first symptom of normal pressure hydrocephalus. Dementia comes next.

I have been exposing medical scandals for decades.

Believe me when I tell you that this is the biggest medical scandal of our time. And no one seems to give a damn. Why? That's simple. Because the people involved are elderly.

157

Oh, and today's medical journalists are so ignorant that they wouldn't recognise a real medical story if it sat on their head and hiccupped.

I will not be shocked when I see a headline reporting that 'People Who Stop Breathing are at Risk of Dying'.

2

I feel much, much better now that I have stopped looking at emails more than once a day. And avoiding the news has freed up much time for reading books, planning books, writing books and looking out of the window.

A few years ago, when I had an office with staff, I didn't look at emails at all. I had the important ones printed out and faxed to me. It seemed a civilised way to deal with them. I would then scribble my replies on the faxed message and sent them back to the office to be turned into emails.

Although I've had a website since websites were first invented, I didn't really look at the internet at all until relatively recently.

And I still prefer my small electronic Seiko device for doing simple, basic research. Antoinette bought it for me a few years ago, though the model I now use is a more modern version which she also bought for me. The Seiko contains the Oxford Dictionary, the Oxford Thesaurus, the Oxford Dictionary of Quotations, the Oxford Dictionary of Modern Slang and Abbreviations, Flower's Modern English Usage and the Britannica Concise Encyclopaedia.

There are no advertisements.

And, I have just re-discovered there is even a Game section.

I pressed the General Knowledge quiz and was asked the name describing 14 species of 'stout-bodied, diurnal, terrestrial squirrels'.

I typed in Marmot and was congratulated.

Brilliant.

Now I just have to forget the Game section is there or else I'm pretty much back where I started.

3

On the 23rd of February of this year, our telephone started to play up. The phone would sometimes work for a couple of minutes at a time. But the crackles made it nigh on impossible to hear anything the other person said. And our broadband and wifi had disappeared completely. Since we have no mobile telephone service where we live in Gloucestershire we were, to say the least, rather stuffed.

I rang our phone supplier, a company called Phone Coop. They seem to me to be expensive but they claim to be for the people and of the people.

They did tests on the phone line and found no problem.

They then told me to take the front plate off the incoming phone line box. To my surprise, I managed to do this. But it did no good.

They told us that we should buy some filters.

I bought these on the 27th February. It took me a day to find the darned things which seem to be somewhere between mare's nests and hen's teeth in rarity. I wandered around Cheltenham for hours (literally) trying to find a shop which sold telephone filters.

Eventually, I found some. I bought three in case the first two didn't work. I took them home. I fitted one, and then another and then the third.

None of them made a damn of difference.

I rang again. And explained once again what the problem was.

This time I was told that we probably needed a new router.

I ordered a router from Phone Coop. That was another £60.

For some reason which I don't understand ('it's the way we do things') we had to wait the best part of a week for that to arrive.

The new router made no more difference than if I'd attached a banana to the telephone.

Eventually, after more thinking and talking, Phone Coop agreed to call Open Reach to come and check our telephone line.

They warned me, with great solemnity, that if Open Reach didn't like the look of us and thought that the problem was in some way our fault they would charge huge fees which would be taken out of my bank account. How much would they charge? None of the Phone Coop employees I spoke to had any idea.

Would I be told how much it was costing?

No. But the fee would be taken out of my bank account so I'd find out when I got my bank statement in six weeks' time.

I was becoming accustomed to, and rather fed up with, the largely uncaring, unsympathetic attitude of the staff at Phone Coop.

By now we had been without a phone, broadband or email for weeks. The absence of any mobile telephone coverage meant that this was not funny. We were marooned.

'What do we do if we have an emergency?' asked Antoinette.

We moved down to the Devon house.

Eventually, we were told that we would have a visit from Open Reach. So we raced back up to Gloucestershire.

The guy they sent was very pleasant but he'd only been a phone engineer for six months and he had never seen a system like ours.

After several hours of messing around all over the house (including spending sometime in the loft) he decided that the problem lay in the wire which connected the house to the telegraph pole at the top of the garden. The pole, which seems quite a small one as telegraph poles go, supplies no one else and it is on our land, about 100 yards from the house.

The engineer rang his boss and got permission to put up a new wire.

But then he decided that he couldn't do that because he didn't think the telegraph pole was safe to climb.

He told us that they would have to send people round to take out the telegraph pole and put in a new one. And then, when they had replaced the pole, they would be able to replace the wire.

'How do they put in a new pole?' I asked.

'They use a crane.'

Neither he nor I had any idea how they would get the necessary crane to the house which is difficult to reach even for a car or small van.

He went away.

So did we.

While we were away, another Open Reach man visited the house. Phone Coop telephoned my mobile (which worked where we were) and told me that the problem had been sorted and that everything was working perfectly.

We went back to Gloucester.

Nothing had changed except that the phone line was worse than ever.

There was no sign that anyone had been except that whoever had called had left a garden gate wide open and dog walkers had, inevitably, allowed their dogs to roam around our lawns.

On 29th March, I rang again. And answered all the usual questions. And had the line tested by the Phone Coop people. They said there was nothing wrong at their end. I said I knew there was nothing wrong at their end but that there was a fault on the line near to the house. I asked when Open Reach would replace the pole and if they did would we have to pay to have it replaced. Phone coop didn't know. I asked if we would have to pay to have the line replaced. Phone coop didn't know that either. They told me that they would just take whatever they needed from my bank account and that I would know what they'd taken when I got my bank statement. I got the impression they didn't care much either.

I asked if Open Reach would come and have another look at the pole. I was told that they would fix up an appointment for a few days hence. I pointed out that we weren't living at the house because without a phone we did not feel safe. Phone Coop didn't seem to mind. They refused to ring Open Reach to ask them if they could come tomorrow. I asked if I could telephone Open Reach to try to fix an appointment. I was told that I was not allowed to ring Open Reach myself. I got the impression that Phone Coop was fed up with our broken telephone.

On 31st March, another Open Reach employee arrived.

He did all the usual stuff. He went into the loft and wandered around and came to the conclusion that the problem lay with the line or the pole. He couldn't go up it, he said. I asked what the previous engineer had done. He said he didn't know. He said they would have to send contractors with some scaffolding and another Open Reach man to do things to the wire.

I asked how long we would have to wait.

He said that he hoped something might happen within a week.

That would mean another week without a viable telephone service; another week without email; another week without internet access.

And this, remember, is a house in an area which has absolutely no mobile phone coverage. (Visiting workmen, including the Open Reach technicians, had to walk or drive to the nearest village in order to get any reception on their mobiles.) We couldn't order food, pay bills or ring for a taxi.

We locked up and left the house. The Open Reach guy said he would make a note that whoever came should go into the garden without us being there and do what needed to be done.

We went back to Devon.

On the 3rd April, I received an email telling me that Open Reach had decided that they needed to put up scaffolding before they could deal with the problem.

I then had another message to tell me that Open Reach had applied to the council for permission to close a road. Since the road concerned cannot be closed because it is the only access to half a dozen houses, I pointed out that this would mean that our telephone would never be repaired. I asked why they needed to close the road and was told that they needed to dig it up. I asked why they felt it necessary to dig a hole in order to deal with a problem at the top of a pole, and pointed out in addition that the pole is in our garden and not adjacent to a road of any description.

The woman at Phone Coop told me that Open Reach would not waste money doing something that was unnecessary. I am afraid that I laughed. I couldn't help it. Clearly offended by my laughter the Phone Coop woman put down the phone. Phone Coop describes itself as the 'ethical phone provider'.

By 20th April, Open Reach had visited four times. They had twice claimed (wrongly) to have mended the fault.

The fact is that it has become difficult, bordering on impossible, to survive without broadband. More and more companies now save money by pressurising customers to pay bills online. Some like Phone Coop itself, penalised customers who want to continue receiving paper bills. HMRC has announced that all citizens will soon have to submit their new quarterly returns online. (There is a suggestion, however, that they may excuse people who are not VAT registered from this regulation. If they do this then my bet is that they will reduce the VAT registration threshold to make sure that they catch everyone.)

My pension company refuses to post vital information. I even need internet access in order to find the date of our next rubbish collection.

Phone companies must be forced to take their responsibilities more seriously. They have an obligation to provide a useable broadband service since broadband is now as fundamental as an electricity supply.

But although we begged for help, we received none. And Phone Coop continued to take money for providing us with a telephone line.

A fourth Open Reach engineer came. He wouldn't go up the pole either. I compiled a list of reasons the engineers had given explaining why they would not climb up our pole and replace the damaged wire:

I'm not trained to climb a pole.

I'm not allowed to climb poles

The pole is too old to be climbed

The pole is not quite straight

The pole does not have a sign to show that it has been recently inspected

The pole is made of wood and might be rotten

I'm not sure how far down into the ground the pole goes

The pole is too close to a tree

There are no supporting stays holding up the pole

All this was offered in the name of health and safety. I'm surprised that Open Reach engineers are allowed to climb a doorstep without a helmet and a safety rail.

No one seemed to give a damn about our health and safety.

When the fifth arrived, I told him the problem was the pole

'That's what you think is it?' he said, rather snottily.

'No,' I replied. 'That's what the previous four OR engineers told me.

This engineer wasted an hour and a half repeating the checks the other engineers had done and then decided that the junction box hanging open on the pole might be the problem and buggered off. I assumed he was going to come back but he didn't.

We were given another date for another visit. We waited. No one came. That was another waste of a day and a good deal of petrol.

We decided that the Open Reach engineers didn't need us there. Indeed, our only function seemed to be to provide cups of coffee. All five engineers had agreed that the problem was in the wire or

163

the junction box at the top of the pole. None had done anything to repair the problem. We left the gate open and told Phone Coop that they could tell Open Reach that they had permission to mend the line without us being present.

Eventually, on 28th April, someone at Phone Coop contacted a manager at Open Reach (as I had repeatedly asked them to do) and reported the problem to someone in authority.

Within a couple of days Open Reach managed to replace the line without closing the road, putting up scaffolding or hiring a helicopter.

They sent a bloke with a ladder and enough courage to climb up a telegraph pole.

We had gone 47 days without a usable telephone or any reliable internet access.

Phone Coop offered to knock a few quid off our bill.

It seems to me that between them Phone Coop and Open Reach have mastered the art of making the simple as complicated as possible.

And in the case of Open Reach of putting the interests of their employees first second third and fourth and the interests of their customers absolutely nowhere.

When, I wonder, did 'The Customer is always Right' become 'The Customer is an idiot, always wrong and a wazoo to boot. We must scam and ignore the customer.'

4

Whatever happened to car bumpers? In the bad old days car manufacturers used to build cars with bumpers at both ends. Minor collisions resulted in dents to the chromium-plated bumper. If the bumper got badly damaged it could be removed and replaced. Today, I counted four cars which had dents in their back ends. All the dents were clearly a result of the owners backing into posts or trees. (I know from bitter experience that a car's sensors are useless if there is a single post or tree behind when you're reversing.) Repairing the dents costs a fortune, and often means replacing a huge chunk of bodywork.

I've probably answered my own question about why car manufacturers have stopped fitting bumpers.

I suspect that British drivers will soon adopt the French way of dealing with dents: ignore them or regard them with the same pride that the Heidelbergers used to regard duelling scars.

5

eSports is the fastest growing business in the world. Nearly 400 million people will watch eSports events in 2017 – mostly online, but also on television and at live events.

I couldn't believe this when I heard about it but it's true. The revenue from eSports is fast approaching $1 billion a year.

To my astonishment, people pay good money to watch other people play computer games. Some watch game players online. Some sit in a hall and watch big screens showing pictures of other people in the hall playing computer games against one another.

eSports are becoming so popular that some say they would soon be bigger than real sports. The best computer game players are becoming stars. They are paid huge sums and they have coaches and managers. Amazingly, the University of York, now teaches eSports. All around the world, it seems, you can now get a degree in playing computer games.

Why not?

What's next?

How about a B.A. in hopscotch?

Or maybe a B.Sc. in thumb twiddling?

Perhaps a Ph.D. in watching television?

It wouldn't surprise me at all. I have lived long enough to see it all and I am very tired of the 'it all'.

Most amazing of all is the fact that computer games seem set to be medal events at the 2022 Asian Games. There is lots of money involved so it seems inevitable that computer games will shortly be medal events at the Olympic Games as well.

But I suspect that the 'disruptors' will soon themselves be disrupted. eSports may be the future for sport and entertainment but where is the role for humans? Human players and commentators are easily replaced with computers which will be better and faster. Humans will have a role only as team owners and spectator management. The eSports industry will be disrupted and totally computerised within three to five years. It will be machine versus machine; all self-operating and self-programming.

There will be robots in other sports too.

For example, in motor racing, the drivers are utterly superfluous and virtually invisible and interchangeable at the moment. Most are so characterless that they are effectively no more than plug-in components like carburettors or batteries. So the whingeing, overpaid stars will be replaced by computers. And boxing will be far more fun when the combatants are a pair of robots who can fight to the death.

Sometimes I think that the world is changing too fast for the millennials but nowhere near fast enough for me.

6

Hackers from North Korea have done their best to close down my website and prevent my emails getting through.

They were moderately successful for several days and many emails were lost.

I have no idea why the North Koreans were so annoyed, though it is possible that the offenders were using a North Korean address in an attempt to disguise their identity.

7

Here are a few health facts which the BBC almost certainly forgot to tell its viewers and listeners:

In 2007, the Labour Government gave patients the right to choose to be treated in a nice, clean, private hospital (instead of a nasty, dirty NHS hospital) for non-urgent operations. For some inexplicable reason, the number choosing this option is soaring. But doctors rarely tell their patients that they have this choice.

More Britons are given flu vaccinations than the citizens of any other country. The flu vaccine doesn't work very well (especially in the over 65s in whom it certainly does more harm than good) and can be dangerous but British doctors receive huge fees for promoting it.

More British women are screened for cancer than women in any other country. It is now (at last) widely accepted that cancer screening programmes do more harm than good. But in Britain, cancer screening is big business.

More than half of all individuals over the age of 70 have at least two medical conditions. The drugs prescribed (often unnecessarily) for the two conditions often interact dangerously. Doctors spend next to no time studying the problem of drug interactions.

Research shows that an astonishing 48.7% of medical stories published in newspapers are utter rubbish. Most of the health stories published are a result of self-serving press releases issued by drug companies, charities or grant-seeking researchers. Since you probably don't know which stories are trustworthy and which are nonsense it is clearly wise to ignore all health stories published in newspapers (or in magazines or on television or radio). There seems to be nothing new these days. I can't remember seeing a worthwhile health story in any national newspaper that I hadn't first written 30 or more years ago. (Buy a copy of *How to Stop Your Doctor Killing You* and you don't need to buy a newspaper for the health stories.)

Local authorities in the UK have closed 214 playgrounds in the last two years. And they have immediate plans to close another 234 playgrounds. And then folk wonder why children are obese and spend all their days playing computer games.

A study published in an American medical journal showed that patients are far more likely to be treated well when the hospital is being inspected. Teaching hospitals are particularly likely to try harder when they are being assessed.

We now have so many laws that it is almost impossible to get through a day without committing a crime. This, inevitably, causes a constant and underlying quantity of toxic stress. Doctors treat this stress with vast quantities of addictive and harmful tranquillisers.

8

Today, Antoinette and I had a pleasant day out in Cheltenham.

Antoinette and I took coffee and ginger biscuits at the Café Nero within the House of Fraser store. The biscuits they serve are excellent for dunking. It isn't widely appreciated but dunking is both an art and a science. It is important not to dip too much of the biscuit into the liquid. Between half and three quarters of an inch at most. And the biscuit must be held in the liquid for just the right length of time. Antoinette reckons a count of 'one and two' should suffice for most biscuits, though double biscuits such as custard creams and bourbons would require longer if you were to consider them appropriate dunkers. I have it on the best authority that the Queen of England is a committed dunker. So too was Bill Hayden of the television series of 'Tinker, Tailor, Soldier, Sailor.' Incidentally, I have found that Café Nero is the only coffee house chain capable of producing drinkable coffee. Costa Coffee and Starbucks produce stuff which reminds me of British Rail coffee from the 1970s. Even Café Nero can't make coffee to compare with the stuff Antoinette makes with the aid of a Bialetti and a can of Illy Espresso coffee.

In Cheltenham town centre, I saw a man wearing a T-shirt which carried the following message: 'GCHQ: Always listening to our customers.' The man told me he worked at GCHQ. I got the impression he didn't think of the slogan as a joke. They clearly take their spying seriously in Cheltenham.

I noticed that the fashion of wearing jeans with holes at the knees has been resuscitated. This fashion was first popular two or three generations ago. It is, I assume, designed to suggest that the wearer spends her life alternately scrubbing floors and giving blow jobs

Attracted by the lovely carpets therein, I bought some books and magazines in the local branch of WH Smith. The till wouldn't work so I persuaded the cashier to write out a receipt using a pen and a piece of paper torn from a till roll. It took him quite a while to find a pen, though there were several hundred on sale just a few feet away. I shall cherish my hand-written receipt – possibly the last in Britain.

Later, I had my hair cut. I asked for a trim and settled down for a nap. When I woke up, I was shocked to discover that the demon barber had given me one of those haircuts which are favoured by men in their 30s who are hoping to hide the fact that they are going bald. I shall not be going out of the house again until my hair has grown back to a decent length. The barber was a trifle clumsy and managed to cut my neck with his clippers. This was my first ever hairdressing injury. A multi million pound lawsuit beckons and pictures of the wound will be published on my Snippy-Snappy social media account.

9

While clearing out an old filing cabinet, I found an old invitation to speak at a Birmingham Post literary luncheon. I seem to remember speaking at a few of these (though naturally they never ask me anymore). The one I remember, however, is the one I missed.

After I'd written my book *Mindpower* I was booked to go on a long author tour. Two days before the tour started, I went down with flu. I felt awful. But there was no way I could cancel scores of TV and radio interviews – particularly since the book was about the ability of the mind to heal the body. And so I told my body not to be silly and I got better and completed the tour without mishap. (Except that a journalist in Yorkshire wrote a lengthy article about the fact that I had developed cramp through sitting on a hard chair for an hour. She used this as an example that I was as susceptible to illness as people who didn't have *Mindpower*.)

However, a week after the tour finished, I was booked to appear at a *Birmingham Post* literary luncheon or dinner (I can't remember which it was) with American thriller writer Ed McBain (whom I was keen to meet).

And, inevitably, two days before the luncheon the flu came back.

My body had kept it away during the tour but when I got back home, I relaxed and the flu decided to reappear.

I had to cancel the damned luncheon/dinner – and was mortally embarrassed

10

The average millennial now spends five hours a day watching television and 5.6 hours a day messing around on digital media (posting and reading tweets, sending selfies and updating the holy Facebook page.

All this use of mobile phones, and the internet, has encouraged selfishness and self- obsession.

Evidence shows that when millennials use the internet they are usually ranting, complaining or reviewing.

Politically, the internet is controlled by loony lefties and Greens. They have the hubris, the conceit, to believe firmly not just that they are right but that no one who disagrees with them could possibly ever be entitled to hold an opinion or be heard. The one thing they aren't doing is learning or increasing their (or their employer's) productivity. UK productivity is way below that in Germany. I don't believe it is a coincidence that Britons use social media far more than Germans.

When will someone notice that there could be a link?

The internet is a great learning tool for the discerning who can use it to learn how to paint, speak Mandarin or grow azaleas.

But I find it terrifying that schoolteachers still regard the internet as a useful teaching tool and encourage their students to use it for research. The internet is so full of unreliable rubbish that it is really only useful for research when you are looking in an area in which you are already an expert.

Yesterday, I saw an online entry in which an innocent user had asked what caused 'chills on the kidney'.

The reply, provided by someone who called themselves a doctor but who must have had a doctorate in divinity or metallurgy, was that wearing clothes which didn't meet and which left an expanse of skin open to the air was a likely cause of kidney chills.

Everything that happens is fine, say the millennials, because things are now different.

'This is the 21st century. The world has changed forever.'

Nuts.

Nothing has changed except that people have become more stupid.

11

There's apparently another storm been generated on the internet by a cyclist. He has published a photograph of a driver whom, he claimed, upset him in some modest and fairly ill-defined sort of way. Cyclists do this a great deal these days. They have little cameras glued to their helmets and they ride around trying to annoy motorists so that they can put the resulting snaps and bits of film onto their Facebook or Twitter pages. I wonder how many cyclists realise that the helmets they wear probably make them more, not less, liable to serious injury.

Why don't cyclists pay a road tax? They use the roads, they demand special privileges (for which they pay nothing) and by impeding traffic flow they add enormously to congestion and delays.

By slowing motorised vehicles to a crawl they add massively to petrol and diesel consumption and therefore add to air pollution. (It is, of course, cyclists who suffer most from the pollution they create. Anyone who rides a bicycle on a busy road is committing slow suicide.)

Cars often collide when forced to overtake cyclists on narrow, busy roads.

The bottom line is that cyclists are a clear danger to motorists and pedestrians. They should pay the same level of road tax as small vans. The road tax on a Bentley Continental W12 is £500 a year and rising annually. Why should cyclists (who cause far more pollution) pay nothing?

I write as someone who has been a keen cyclist for 65 years – which is considerably longer than I have been a motorist and only slightly shorter than I have been a pedestrian.

And I write also as someone who is fed up with the fact that hardly a day goes by without a cyclist complaining online that he or she has been inconvenienced in some modest way by tax paying road traffic.

Every time I go out onto the roads in a car, I find that I am inconvenienced by discourteous, arrogant and often aggressive cyclists. There are so many cyclists around, and they are so aggressive, that pedestrians are now seriously at risk. The number being killed by cyclists is increasing at a rather frightening rate.

The other day we drove back from Cheltenham behind a pair of cyclists who were travelling at 10 mph and keeping to the middle of the road as they chatted away. Both were wearing black Lycra so it was impossible to see them in the gloaming. It was impossible to overtake safely. Within a mile or two, we had a massive queue behind us – all travelling at the same speed.

Internal combustion engines burn up far more fuel when travelling slowly and those smug and selfish cyclists doubtless did more harm to the environment than a thousand motorists.

Cyclists are almost as big a menace to road users and pedestrians as are dog walkers.

It seems good sense to me to ban cyclists from all roads and pavements. They should be allowed to ride their bicycles on cycle tracks only. Where there is no cycle track, the cyclist should carry his machine. Cycling is a good activity for children and a fine sporting endeavour but why would anyone want to risk life and limb cycling to work?

And cyclists should pay a road tax like every other road user.

12

We are in Gloucestershire today. Looking around I realised that all the local gardens now look like traffic islands.

There are plenty of neatly trimmed bushes and billiard table lawns but nothing that will bear any flowers. There's lots of nice, neat decking too. It is no wonder that there were no bees or butterflies around last summer. There won't be many around this summer, either. And people will doubtless wonder why.

13

The hysterical 'scientists', bureaucrats and commentators who insist that they are right about climate change, that there is nothing to debate and that those who dare to disagree must be crushed, have (as I seem to remember I pointed out a few months ago) been captured by the same irrational mood of intolerant enthusiasm as was apparent among those who, back in the 1980s, stated so vehemently that AIDS was going to kill us all within a decade.

The odd thing is that the climate change mythologists (who describe their opponents as 'deniers' in order to demonise them) never care to mention that if the world really were getting hotter, then it would benefit in almost every conceivable way if people stopped eating meat.

They don't mention this because to do so would risk annoying the meat industry which is one of the most powerful (and rich) lobby groups in the world.

The world is, it seems, full of people who are provably wrong but who 'know' they are right.

For example, in other areas, such as vaccination, the scientific evidence shows quite clearly that the proselytisers are wrong. I have no doubt that vaccination does more harm than good. But doctors and journalists have been bought or indoctrinated into believing that vaccines are essential and so that is the only story that people hear. Politicians and others are fond of using the phrase 'informed consent' when talking about vaccines but you can only have 'informed consent' when both sides of an argument are being aired. I have resounding evidence that attempts to question the validity of statements about vaccination are totally suppressed in the UK. Parents are constantly pressured by doctors, nurses and health visitors who offer no evidence to support their brazen insistence, merely conviction founded on Government exhortations, drug company propaganda and (in the case of the doctors) the prospect of healthy fees for doing something between nothing and very little.

And the same, of course, is true about the European Union. The evidence shows that the EU is a corrupt, incompetent, truly fascist organisation but none of the evidence is ever published or even discussed.

These days, experts are entirely unreliable because they have been corrupted and no one knows or cares about the corruption because newspaper proprietors and editors do not give a damn about publishing the truth. They know that all readers really care about is gossip. Moreover, they have been bought by industries and their lobbyists.

14

I have compiled a list of 10 countries which are members of the United Nations but have considerably smaller populations than, say, Manchester:

Grenada

Liechtenstein
Maldives
Malta
Marshall Islands
Monaco
Nauru
Saint Kitts
San Marino
Tuvalu

Tuvalu has a population of just over 11,000 and Nauru has around 13,000 citizens. If they were in Britain or America these would be classed as large villages. It seems odd to think that all these tiny countries have a say in world affairs. It is hardly surprising that some of these tiny countries can be 'bought' by large superpowers who want their votes.

15

Antoinette had another bad day with her heart. I believe she has a malfunctioning heart valve but she refuses to see what I would describe as a 'proper doctor'. She has a weak pulse and an incredibly low blood pressure and today her heart beat was all over the place. Her ankles and hands swell regularly – standard signs of a heart that isn't working properly. Exceptional stresses make things considerably worse.

I realise that most people would not believe this but I can steady and slightly improve Antoinette's heart rate simply by holding her hand and keeping my fingers on her pulse.

I have long been a believer in 'healing' and Antoinette has twice healed me of quite serious muscle and joint problems. She healed a bad shoulder and a bad knee – both of which were extremely painful. In neither case did I have any surgery or take any medication.

How does it work?

Love.

The person being treated doesn't need to do anything. The person doing the healing has to donate love.

16

I spent a pleasant evening fiddling with our central heating system.

I have to put more water into the system every few days.

This is not, as heating engineers would insist, because we have a leak but because our Edwardian pipes and radiators are so capacious that the system still contains vast amounts of air. Whenever the system is turned on, the rumbling of air through the pipes suggests that our system is a sufferer from a particularly bad case of irritable bowel syndrome.

As the air leaks out through a valve in the loft, so the system pressure falls and needs topping up with another 20 gallons of water.

17

The TV Licensing people have taken to sending us letters informing us when their door-to-door thugs will visit us to make sure that we aren't watching television. I think the letters are supposed to be frightening but in fact they are quite useful because they remind us to make sure that the big gate at the bottom of the drive is locked, bolted and very barred against intruders. We can't see the gate from the house and so they definitely can't see us. One of the many things which annoys me about the TV Licensing Gestapo is that they insist that we have two licences for two houses. Since we never rent out either house, just how do they think we can possibly watch television in two places at once?

I expect they'll soon revive their hoary old myth about TV licence detector vans.

(Has anyone ever been caught by one of these fictional vans? If they existed, we would know because someone would have leaked the story. The myth of the BBC having a fleet of vans equipped with special equipment which can tell who is watching television is as fictional as the idea of BBC impartiality.)

However, I have this week discovered that sending rude and vaguely threatening demands through the post, and inventing imaginary detector vans, is not enough for the TV Licensing thugs.

They have now taken to sending out spam emails inviting me to pay a fee online for watching television. They claim that loads of people already do this though why I cannot imagine. Since the BBC is an unpatriotic (bordering on treacherous), sexist and racist organisation, I would have thought it is our duty to make it as difficult as possible for their Shylocks to collect money to pay obscene salaries to thousands of bureaucrats. The BBC licence fee is a bizarre anachronism. I refuse to pay a BBC licence fee and support a corrupt, bigoted, sexist, ageist and racist organisation which pursues an agenda favoured by its fascist staff rather than the agenda favoured by the people who pay the bills. The price, not watching television, is well worth paying.

I've received two of these emails in the last two days, explaining to me the joy of paying for a TV licence by some sort of online system. Actually, the letters were sent to my email address but addressed to someone else.

I wrote to the TV Licensing thugs demanding that they stop sending me junk mail.

They didn't bother to reply and I doubt if they will take any notice.

I hate the TV Licensing thugs so much that I think I would vote for anyone (even Jeremiah Corbyn) who promised in blood that they would get rid of the BBC Licence fee (well, maybe not Jeremiah Corbyn).

The good thing is that in my experience, the Licence Thugs eventually give up and stop sending threatening letters. I always post back all the letters I receive. I'm tempted to wrap them around something heavy (like a house brick) so that the recipients have to pay huge amounts of postage but sending bricks through the mail is probably illegal these days.

Paying the BBC licence fee in order to watch or listen to anything broadcast, is as rational as having to pay a licence to consume food knowing that all the money will go to a State owned, State friendly supermarket chain which only sells you the food it wants you to buy.

The BBC resolutely sneers at and attacks Brexiteers, English nationalists, Christianity, proposed Government cuts, old, white men (unless they work for the BBC or are Labour MPs), American Presidents (unless they are black) and supports the EU, the NHS, pressure groups, subsidises, actresses who claim to have been propositioned, victims who claim racial or sexual abuse (unless the abuse has been perpetrated by a BBC employee) and scientific myths such as vaccination, vivisection and global warming.

18

It is my birthday so we stayed in, turned off all electronic devices and left the postbox unopened. (The post at both our houses goes into a box rather than onto the mat. Actually, the post in Paris also goes into a box.)

We like to protect our birthdays from the horrors of the real world.

19

Antoinette bought me a beautiful silver penknife. She has bought so many penknives from the same shop that they know her by name and they buy in stock especially for her. But the penknife she bought today is the second one she's bought from that shop which is faulty. This one (which was displayed with the blades open) doesn't close properly. The previous disappointment (which was displayed with the blades shut) had one blade which wouldn't open at all.

When you take advantage of your regular customers by cheating them, they stop being your regular customers.

Why do so many people feel it necessary to rip off their customers? I simply don't understand it.

I find it increasingly difficult to trust businesses, shopkeepers or workmen these days. Banks rip me off. Utility companies rip me off by making it difficult for me to work out which tariff I should be on. Telephone companies rip me off. It sometimes seems that no one offers a fair deal for a decent price.

20

In the last 20 years, nearly 40% of Britain's top paid chief executives have been sacked after presiding over disasters, incompetence or crookery.

This astonishing fact rather damages the claim that chief executives are worth their multi-million pound pay packages.

21

Someone called Richard Dawkins has got a lot of publicity for saying that he does not believe in God.

Well, I've never met this chap Dawkins and I've seen no evidence whatsoever that he really exists.

And, therefore, I do not believe he exists.

And since I do not believe that he exists he clearly does not exist.

Quod erat demonstrandum.

Seriously, I consider that Dawkins is a bad man. I think he has done a vast amount of damage. Indeed, I don't think it is any exaggeration to say that he and his ilk are responsible for causing much misery and probably some deaths.

I don't care whether or not he believes in God.

But what harm is done by personal belief in a superior being and an afterlife? It is undoubtedly possible to argue that religions have done much harm but there can also be no doubt that a good deal of good has been done not least in that religion has provided support, guidance and strength to millions – especially the bereaved. Any attempt to take away that comfort on what amounts to no more than an unsupportable and insignificant hunch is bordering on the criminal.

The biggest cause of mental illness (and much physical illness) is loneliness. And it's a deep, scalding loneliness which is not assuaged by the sort of relationships created and sustained by social media.

People today aren't just lonely – they are also isolated.

We are, as a race isolated from others, isolated from our inner selves and our real feelings and the prospect of anything resembling inner peace.

Of course, the problem isn't entirely down to Dawkins et al. The Christian Church must also take much responsibility for failing to stick up for Christians. In our society today, it is commonplace for Christians to be treated with contempt and disrespect that would never be tolerated in the treatment of Muslims. The habit of shutting churches during weekdays doesn't help. I realise that theft and vandalism are problems but what is the point of a closed church?

And, thanks to the failures of the Church, and to the efforts of people like Dawkins, we are isolated from the comfort of a higher force; the love and support which previous generations took from religion, in all its various forms.

Edgar Baerlein, thirteen times winner of the Amateur Tennis Championship, once said that he had worked out the odds against a future life and decided that they were 'a shade worse than five to two'.

22

We have just had a note from Sainsbury's which, for some bizarre reason which I still don't entirely understand, sells us our gas and electricity – though I am pleased to say that they send it along in pipes rather than bringing it round in orange, plastic bags. They tell us that our current tariff ends in June and that our prices will double unless we move to another tariff or take our business elsewhere.

Double! That is price gouging. It's the worst sort of Shylocking.

The bastards are talking of doubling the price of our gas and electricity!

That is inexcusable.

Sarwjit Sambhi, the Managing Director who wrote to tell me this jolly news, should be horse whipped in public.

We can, of course, do something about this deliberate and premeditated mugging.

But millions won't, don't or can't.

The elderly, the frail and the poor often don't have internet access. They still assume that energy costs are pretty well uniform. And so, largely out of trust and loyalty, they do nothing.

And Sainsbury's (and the other gas and electricity suppliers) take advantage of them.

Bastards.

Every year tens of thousands of elderly folk die of the cold because they can't afford to heat their homes properly.

Sarwjit Sambhi and Sainsbury's know this, of course.

And yet they have a price policy which results in thousands of deaths.

I find it difficult to see why that isn't manslaughter.

Sainsbury's will be responsible for many more deaths than the late and very unlamented Ian Brady.

This is, of course, also true of the other big energy suppliers.

23

John Adams, the second president of America and one of the nation's founders warned against two party systems: 'There is nothing which I dread so much as a division of the republic into two great parties, each arranged under its leader, and concerting measures in opposition to each other'.

But that is exactly what we have.

Politics today is an industry, designed not to improve, protect and defend the nation, but to provide well-paid employment to armies of politicians, advisors, researchers, spin doctors and hangers on. The only people who benefit from the two party system are the people who are directly involved in the world which has been created: the pollsters, consultants, fundraisers, think tanks, lobbyists and correspondents.

Added to this dross are the media representatives who have all aligned themselves with specific parties.

Our political system is designed to serve the interest of the big parties and their associates. The rules and regulations which exist are designed to enhance their power, defend themselves against intruders (at the last election UKIP received millions of votes and one seat in the Commons) and take power away from the electorate.

Political boundaries, and the structure of the House of Commons (and the ever-looming presence of the House of Lords) mean that there is now no point at all in voting in parliamentary or local elections. The number of union officials, PR people and ex-charity executives in the Commons has gone from virtually none to 11% and the number of spin doctors in the Commons has gone up to 17% – so at least a third of the House of Commons is made up of people who have no knowledge of or connection with the real world and whose previous training has been largely in learning how to deceive and lie. The House of Lords is full of failed and former MPs who have been given jobs for life simply because they know someone. The place is packed with former EU employees receiving EU pensions and doubtless under written or implicit instructions not to criticise their benefactors. There are at least eight former EU commissioners sitting in the House of Lords. It is no surprise that the wishes of the British people who pay their wages, and who voted for Brexit, are dismissed with ignorant disdain. As for MEPs! Well, they are just politicians who couldn't get on either of the UK gravy trains.

The same thing is happening everywhere in the western world – and it explains the worldwide revolt against the political system.

The Brexit Vote and the rise of Donald Trump were, in part, signs of the disconnect and the dissatisfaction.

This is an attitude with which I can readily sympathise.

I have, throughout my life, always voted against the status quo and the establishment.

When I am asked to vote I always vote against the Committee's recommendations or the Board's advice. This way the dissenters (who probably have a good case) will be guaranteed of a little support.

24

Here's a revolutionary thought: only people over the age of 30, who have paid taxes for at least five years, should be allowed to vote.

25

Today, we met our estate agent in Paris. I picked his firm because they have the biggest, smartest offices near to our apartment. I fixed up the appointment by email.

So we now have an estate agent in Paris. His name, though he may not know it, is Monsieur Pompadour de Snootsville.

His fee for selling our apartment will be 50,000 euros. So an estate agent in Paris only needs to sell one apartment a month to have an income of £500,000 a year.

And that, believe it or not, is a cut price rate in Paris.

Our agent is a 40 something Frenchman who wears a blue blazer with gold buttons, jeans and a scarf thrown negligently around his neck. You know he doesn't garden or put up shelves in those jeans. They probably cost more than an Armani suit. The scarf is tied in that negligent way the French own but which takes them ten minutes to tie and 30 years to learn. Whenever I try it, I look as though the scarf got there by mistake. He already seems to me to be patronising, precious, self-important and arrogant; though he is far too old to be within sneering distance of being a millennial. It is probably the fact that he is French which explains all this.

Blindly faithful, innocent and more full of hope than expectation, I trusted him and signed the documents I was given. It seemed reasonable to expect that for a fee of 50,000 euros for finding a buyer for our apartment I might get a little loyalty and honour and respect.

26

The EU is very, very bad for our health.

Many of its policies, dreamt up and imposed upon us by overpaid, unelected eurocrats in Brussels have resulted in death; a lot of deaths; tens of thousands of deaths.

It is worth remembering that in addition to the unelected eurocrats, the EU is run by a bunch of commissioners – many of whom are failed national politicians who ended up running Europe because they had pretty well messed up their domestic careers. British examples include His Highness Lord Mandelson of building society notoriety and the awful Kinnock of Sheffield election rally infamy. The rest were unelected bozos such as Jonathan Hill (a former PR person and lobbyist) and Catherine Ashton who had never been elected but seems to me to have skills which enabled her to be in the right place and to know the right people. Both were, for some reason, appointed to the House of Lords and given power over the rest of us.

Here are just a few specific examples of ways in which EU policies kill people.

The number of people smoking roll-up cigarettes is increasing rapidly. This is a direct result of EU laws. Instead of giving up cigarettes, smokers have merely turned to rolling their own cigarettes. The EU's well-meant but ill-thought out policy has pushed people into smoking much more dangerous products than they smoked before. How many cigarette smokers put filters onto their cigarettes when they roll their own? The real irony is that the EU has given millions of euros to farmers to help them grow cheap tobacco.

Laws on rubbish collecting are stressful and probably cause heart attacks and other stress related disorders. But the big health problem is the rise in the number of huge rats in towns and cities. Few cities employ dedicated rat catchers because the job is too dangerous. I know of one city where the last such employee had to retire after developing leptospirosis as a result of a rat bite. He has not been replaced. Rats can and do kill people and this is a growing health problem – caused entirely by EU policies.

The EU's daft energy policies mean that street lights are often switched off at night – or turned so dim that they are worse than useless. The result is that there are far more accidents – with far more pedestrians being injured or killed. Pedestrians are run over. And those who have been to the pub and are wandering home are more likely to trip and fall.

The EU's agriculture policy means that food prices have soared. Many poorer families, and elderly folk trying to live on pensions, can no longer afford to eat properly. This is entirely the fault of the EU's pro-French farmer policies. If we left the EU, the cost of food will fall dramatically and more people would be able to eat properly.

Domestic energy prices in the UK have soared to unprecedented levels entirely because of EU rules which have forced us to close down power stations and subsidise anything that the EU decides is a green source of energy. The result is that 40,000 old people die of the cold every year. The EU is responsible for most of those deaths.

EU legislation banning smoking in pubs has led to more and more people drinking at home with booze which they buy at the supermarket. It is, of course, well known that because the booze bought in shops is much cheaper than the booze bought in pubs, people who drink alone tend to drink more.

The new EU approved light bulbs are dim and take forever to work. The result is a massive increase in the incidence of accidents in the home. Thousands of old people have tripped and fallen because EU lights meant that they could not see properly. This massive rise in the number of accidents at home has added to the pressure on failing Accident and Emergency services. The light bulbs also contain large amounts of mercury – which is toxic.

EU employment legislation means that hospitals no longer provide 24 hour medical cover. Many small hospitals are closing because the new laws mean that they cannot hire enough doctors and nurses. (Even when they are sleeping but on call, doctors are deemed by the EU to be working.) It is now common for hospitals to have no doctors available at weekends. The same EU employment legislation means that GPs now work the same hours as librarians. It is almost impossible to find a GP at night, at weekends or on bank holidays. The result is increased pressure on hospital departments. The average wait in Accident and Emergency departments in British hospitals is now between four and nine hours. There is no point at all in the Government buying TV ads telling patients to get to hospital quickly if they have a stroke, when they may have to wait for nine hours when they get there. (The target waiting time in hospitals is just four hours. Can you imagine a member of the Cabinet waiting four hours to be treated? Do you think Prince William has to sit and wait for four hours if George has earache? Thanks to the EU, more and more people are dying, untreated in British hospitals.)

The immigration policies forced upon us by the EU have created a good deal of stress. And, of course, every country in the EU has shown increased levels of violence (particularly against women) as the number of immigrants against women has soared. EU immigration policies also have led to a fall in average wages (because those immigrants who are prepared to work are often happy to do so for lower wages)

EU laws mean that many shops now routinely fire workers who reach the age of 25 and hire younger ones who don't have to be paid so much. For customers this means poorer service in shops and restaurants. (It won't be long before cafés will have the automatic self-serve coffee machines which are already popular in petrol stations. Drinks will be served in waxed cardboard containers and customers will be asked to clear their own tables and put their rubbish into the bins provided.) But for the workers who are fired, it often means tragedy and poverty and an early death.

The EU's policy on diesel engines has resulted in considerable pollution in Europe. Americans who bought German diesel cars made by the appalling VW company are up to their knees in compensation. But in Britain, the unfortunate sods who bought VW cars will (thanks to the awful Merkel and the EU) have to pay for their mistake. In America, VW is paying out $30 billion but the company sold very few cars in the USA. In Europe in general, and the UK in particular, VW sold gazillions of vehicles and tens of thousands of EU citizens have been killed by the resulting air pollution. But VW, protected by Germany and the EU, will pay out approximately nine pence halfpenny. For example, in Europe last year, 257,000 people were listed as having died as a result of air pollution. What did the EU do about that? It made things worse by encouraging the manufacture of diesel cars to support the German automobile industry. Moreover, it seems that anyone who listened to the Labour Party and bought any sort of diesel-powered vehicle will be publicly whipped and humiliated. (There is some irony in the fact that the electric cars which are so fashionable run on electricity derived largely from burning diesel.) The EU's laws favoured diesel cars because that was what the German car industry wanted. Once again, the EU sold out to big industry. Another example of pure fascism in action.

The EU's attempts to create a single superstate, and to take away national identities, have predictably, led to extreme nationalism in many European countries. Many people have been killed or injured in the resultant demonstrations. This will only get worse.

Like all truly fascist organisations, the EU's laws are designed to help the rich (particularly big companies) and to punish the poor; it protects big industry and doesn't give a damn about people.

The EU, the organisation which imposed VAT upon us without so much as a by your leave and which now wants to eradicate nationalism, culture, independence and freedom is an organisation which is run by a mixture of unelected fools, drunks, crooks and freeloaders. (Not many people seem to remember that VAT was a Common Market invention. It began at 8% and has steadily worked its way up to 20%. When we leave the EU we will, if we wish, be able to say goodbye to value added tax.)

In the UK, the EU is supported most enthusiastically by those who have been employed by it and who are now comfortably ensconced in first class compartments on the EU gravy train – with magnificent pensions due to them. In this category, we can put the many malodorous buffoons who have previously worked for the EU (and are therefore entitled to massively generous pensions). These EU-lovers don't spend a lot of time reminding us all of their financial links with the EU.

The rest of the EU's support comes largely from tax avoiders, tax exiles, foreigners, traitors and the intellectually deprived.

27

In most parts of the world, queues are getting longer.

The British queue because it is the polite thing to do.

The Russians queue because they have grown up queuing and it is, for them, a sort of national sport. They enjoy it. A day without a good long four-hour queue to buy half a loaf of stale bread or a pair of second-hand shoelaces would be a wasted day. To them queuing is like breathing or walking.

But the French don't queue. In shops and at bus stops they just mill around. It is, I believe, a serious character flaw.

28

We are conditioned early on in our lives to accept certain values. Those values rarely change by much or for long. Indeed, we tend to become more committed to them with age. Only war changes them.

Our values are, however, being damaged, questioned and destroyed by massive, uncontrolled immigration.

And when our values suffer in this way we tend to feel uncomfortable and frightened – though we mostly don't know why we feel uncomfortable and frightened.

29

French pharmacies sell plenty of dental floss but they don't seem to sell interdental brushes. This is rather strange because many dentists now agree that dental floss does far more harm than good. The problem is that when you pull the floss downwards, it is very easy to cut into the gum and to push the food debris into the gum too. This inevitably causes infection. Interdental brushes which enable the user to remove bits of food from the spaces are far safer and much more effective.

Antoinette was, I believe, the first person to realise the problems with dental floss.

I wrote about her conclusions in my now defunct Health Letter and we included the advice in our (now out of print book) *Health Secrets Doctors Share With Their Families*.

The people making interdental brushes produce them in all sorts of different sizes and the trick is to find the biggest size you can use. I find that I need two brushes of two different sizes and I suspect this is the case for most people.

Talking of dentists reminds me of my other bugbear: why don't dental records travel with patients in the same way that medical records do? I realise that a new dentist can see which teeth are missing and which are filled but there is (or should be) much more to dentistry than simply removing and filling teeth. The fact that dental records do not move with patients means that much time is wasted. So, given that fact, I am confident in predicting that nothing will change.

30

We have a lot of stuff in our Paris apartment which we want to take to England now that we are selling up. Most important of all we have a good many books which we don't want to abandon. There isn't enough stuff to hire a removal company (which would, in any case, pose horrific logistical problems) so we have solved the problem in our own way.

Today we posted 22 parcels full of books to England. We carried them to a nearby Post Office a few parcels at a time – using suitcases to carry the parcels.

At the Post Office, there was much confusion and I paid different prices for all the parcels – even though they all fell within certain guideline weights. (The key, it seems, is simply to keep the parcel weight under 5 kilos.)

Three or four different counter clerks gave entirely different instructions and put different stickers on the parcels they handled. One said that we could have a cut price rate for sending books abroad. Another said that the cut price rate only applied if the books were printed in the French language.

Once again, I was reminded that posting stuff to Britain costs considerably less than posting stuff from Britain. Our parcels, all weighing around 5kg each, were posted air mail for between £5 and £10 a parcel (depending upon the mood of the counter clerk who took them in) and arrived at our home in England a couple of days later.

I dread to think what the parcels would have cost if they had been travelling in the other direction.

31

The people who believe most fervently in the EU want it to become a superstate, a United States of Europe.

The problem is that they know absolutely nothing of history.

Look at the mess the British and the Americans made of the Middle East by drawing up artificial boundaries and creating fake countries.

Look at the mess colonialists made of Africa.

Look how the USSR (an artificially created stew of different countries) ended.

Look at Yugoslavia.

Look at Czechoslovakia.

Look at Belgium, for heaven's sake. (An artificially constructed country which is being torn in two.)

How can anyone seriously believe that the EU (designed to give Germany the control of Europe which they weren't good enough to win through violence) could possibly survive?

June

1

We never used to think of Paris as being dangerous. The City of Light was always well lit and well policed. It was possible to walk just about anywhere at any time of night. No more. At night, Paris is now pitch black and the streets are too dangerous to walk about. Paris is now the city of concrete anti-tank blockades, automatic weapons and suspicion.

Clearing out some cupboards, ready for our possible sale of the apartment, I came across some old videotapes of me speaking to animal rights campaigners. I used to do a good deal of it in the 1980s and 1990s and travelled all over the country to attend and speak at rallies and protests.

I often used to meet up with a friend who ran the Animal Liberation Front (better known as ALF) and when we got together there would always be quite a crowd of us. Actually, he didn't tell anyone he ran the organisation but always called himself the Press Office which sounded and seemed perfectly proper. At the time, the animal rights movement was considered the nation's most serious terrorist threat. The security services had talked up the threat because there were then no other real dangers and they needed a reason to exist. My pal was always followed by a bunch of special branch detectives and MI5 agents and because I had a fairly high profile as an animal rights campaigner, I was also followed around by a similar band of security guys. The result was that when we met, his gang of policemen and my gang of policemen would bump into one another. We both had camera crews following us, equipped both with video cameras and still cameras, and to tease them we would hide our mouths and whisper to each other. The authorities took it all far more seriously than we did. What they did not know was that my pal was the ALF. There was no organisation and there was no membership. It was really just him. Special Branch and MI5 were devoting millions to a spectre.

I remember that some very strange things happened to us both but particularly to him.

He believed that the police had once put a gun into his car boot, which was rather silly of them since, as he pointed out, he knew they were following him and even if he had possessed a gun (unlikely since he was the most peaceful fellow I ever knew) he would be hardly likely to keep it in his car. He was arrested and taken to court but the case fell apart because the police forgot to put any bullets in with the gun. They also made another fundamental mistake. Armed policemen surrounded his car and waited for him to come back to it though they could never explain why they thought he had a firearm. Their worst mistake, however, was in not wearing any bulletproof vests. They knew he didn't have any bullets for the gun they'd planted so they didn't bother putting them on. Since they would have worn the vests if they'd really thought there was a risk, their case fell to pieces.

On another occasion he was arrested for being part of a conspiracy to do something or other but by the time the case got to court, the co-defendants had all fallen by the wayside (they had alibis and the police had abandoned the case against them). That case, which had cost something like £10 million to put together, fell apart when my pal's barrister pointed out to the judge that it is impossible to have a conspiracy when only one person is involved. The case never even got started and the red-faced prosecuting counsel had to go home with his tail dangling between his legs.

On one occasion, the police did manage to get my pal into a holding cell on some charge or other. Sitting in the cell with a pile of rough looking fellows, my rather small and very gentle pal protested when one of them was about to stamp on an insect.

'Who the hell are you?' demanded one of the toughs. 'What are you in here for?'

'The ALF,' explained my pal.

At the time, the ALF was considered to be the most dangerous terrorist organisation in the country. Police and gangsters quailed at the very mention.

The tough guys apologised and treated my pal as though the Kray Twins were his underlings.

2

A month ago, the Tories were a shoe-in to win the election. But slowly, deliberately and vote by vote they have thrown away every advantage they had.

Now, it seems possible that the Prime Minister could have a smaller majority than she had before she called the election!

Worse still, there could be a hung parliament.

Unimaginably, Diane Abbott could be Home Secretary and Jeremy Corbyn could be Prime Minister. The unbelievably awful Thornberry could be Foreign Secretary! I wouldn't trust any of them to mow the lawn or clean a pair of shoes.

What happened?

Complacency? Arrogance? Stupidity?

Those are possible explanations.

The Tories have certainly made one serious error after another. To describe the Tory campaign as 'lacklustre' is being generous.

Taking money from English pensioners and then taxing the same people so that Scottish pensioners wouldn't lose out was an electoral disaster (though pretty good for the SNP).

Introducing new laws designed to make life harder for small businesses wasn't exactly a vote winner.

Not even the EU would dare to suggest some of the daft legislation proposed by the Tories.

Theresa May chickening out of a TV debate made her look like a loser.

The dementia tax was madness.

Promises on immigration numbers have been wishy washy to the point of ineffectual.

There is another, more sinister explanation: what if the Tories have been paid to lose this election?

Sounds mad, I know.

But think about it.

If the Tories lose the election (or have a very slender majority) the EU will benefit enormously. A Labour Government (or a hung Parliament) would probably hand over the £100 billion the eurocrats want us to pay – and which Theresa May says she wouldn't pay.

The banks which didn't want us to leave the EU will be happy. Currency speculators will make huge profits if the Tories lose. A Conservative loss could be worth several hundred billion to banks and financiers. Is it really irrelevant that Theresa May's husband works in financial services?

A hung Parliament, with a Government controlled by the SNP, the Liberal Democrats and the Greens would destroy Britain's hopes for a decent exit from Hitler's dream organisation.

The members of these parties all think they are taking part in a revolution but in reality they are fascists, desperately supporting the establishment. The soft lefties and self-indulgent greens are nasty, spiteful, jealous, vindictive, hypocritical, selfish, self-important, self-centred, stupid and often wicked people.

Britain would be destroyed if Labour won the election or if there were a hung Parliament.

But the EU would benefit enormously. And so would the bankers and hedge fund operators.

(The bankers tend to make the rules these days. Bankers and hedge fund operators have taken over from big oil companies, drug companies and arms companies and now control the world. There are just under two million people working in financial services in England. Just think how rich the country would be if they all did something useful for a living instead.)

So, have the Tories been paid to lose this election?

Doesn't sound so mad, does it?

3

Selling an apartment in France has been designed by bureaucrats to be as incomprehensible, difficult and time consuming as possible.

I was told by our agent that I must first sign an Achat – which is, I was assured, a meaningless document drawn up by the estate agent. This, I was told is not a legally binding document but merely showed that the would-be buyer wanted to buy and the would-be seller wanted to sell.

Then, when all the paperwork has been done, there will be two contracts to sign. This will be when the notaires come into the whole affair.

But I am assured by our estate agent that the first signature is entirely meaningless; just another piece of pointless French bureaucracy. I am told that when I sign I am agreeing that I might sell the apartment if I decide that I will sell it and that if I do agree to sell it then I might possibly sell it to the person who has expressed an interest and the prospective buyer signs to say that he might possibly buy it at the price agreed if he decides to buy it and not to buy something else instead or decides not to buy anything but to move to Switzerland instead. It is as worthless a legal contract as it is possible to sign, and I'm surprised that those involved in printing these things do not die of shame and embarrassment every time they get one signed.

I asked if our would-be buyer had the cash for the purchase or if he needed to borrow money. I was assured that he was not signing the special document which implied taking out a loan.

I must say that the French seem to want to make the whole business of buying and selling a property as uncomfortable, as time consuming as expensive and as annoying as possible.

I thought that buying and selling property in Britain was difficult but the French have taken the whole business of contemptuous arrogance and lack of concern to new levels. The French have made it unattractive to buy, sell or hold property and so foreign owners cannot unload properties without a great deal of fuss and nonsense.

I don't wish to be cruel to our little Gallic friends but this quote from Hot Water by P.G.Wodehouse seems appropriate: 'If you ask me what's wrong with the world, there's too many Frenchmen in it. Never liked them and never shall.'

This was written by a man who spent several years living in France.

4

Our Devon garden robin has gone. Antoinette saw him perched on a bench singing his heart out. Then, in a flash, a sparrow hawk swooped and he was gone.

All robins are lovely little birds. They love people and wherever I work in the garden (even if I am not digging and therefore unlikely to unearth a quick meal or two) the robin turns up to say hello.

In Gloucestershire we have numerous bird feeders hanging on poles and branches (we daren't in Devon because of the seagulls) and whenever I put out food the resident robin is there within seconds, taking food out of the feeder as I put it in.

We miss our Devon robin terribly.

He used to sing all day long and spent much of his time on the back of a garden bench. When he saw our car coming off the driveway he would fly to a bush near the house to greet us. (He knew that I would brush crumbs off my trousers when I got out of the car. I don't know how the crumbs get there because I never eat while driving, of course.)

Another robin will take over the garden in a day or two.

And we will enjoy his company. And in due course he will doubtless learn about the crumbs. But we miss the one who has gone. I doubt we will see his like again.

5

Our ageing population and a consequently shrinking workforce are supposed to be major socio-economic problems and are certainly the excuse for encouraging mass immigration.

Governments everywhere claim that their nations need hordes of immigrants because they have ageing and dependant populations of pensioners.

This is an immensely stupid argument.

Many (though not all) pensioners would like to work. Most are perfectly capable of doing excellent work. Most have extremely marketable skills. Most need to work. Most have been forced to give up work solely because of their age.

The solution is simple enough even for politicians to understand: allow all pensioners to work if they want to and punish anyone who forces an over 65-year-old into retirement against their wishes.

And lo and behold!

The need for vast numbers of immigrant (and the massive cultural disruption they bring) will disappear overnight.

Or is that too simple for politicians to understand?

6

There is a local literary festival and a nearby town is full of would-be authors, members of the literary establishment (nothing to do with authors) and the metropolitan elite who buy books as display items rather than to read. These people are not authors. Authors, people who write books for a living and who struggle each day with the twin demons of an empty sheet of paper (or an empty screen) and a need to put words into the space in order to pay the bills, are shy, private people who, given a choice of root canal dental surgery or a Question and Answer session at a literary festival would, with no hesitation opt for the dentist's chair.

The people who appear at literary festivals are mostly folk who do something else for a living (television celebrities, politicians and so on) but who have written a book. Or more accurately written some captions to go with the illustrations in their book. Or, even more accurately, put their name on the front cover of a book for which someone else has written the captions to accompany the illustrations which were taken by yet someone else.

They are, these so-called authors, chefs and politicians, television presenters and people who are famous because they are loud mouthed enough to be selected to appear on one of those cheap to make reality television programmes.

7

I spent hours at the dentist's surgery.

My last dentist was awful. My six monthly examinations took about three seconds. He would look into my mouth, grunt and tell me to make another appointment. He never said or did anything.

When your new dentist says: 'All dentists do things differently. It doesn't mean that one is right and the other wrong' you know that your last dentist fucked up.

I had numerous fillings, an abscess cleared and the gums underneath my teeth scraped.

Oh, what fun that was.

8

I have been trying to work out why millennials (aka snowflakes) are the way they are and I have decided that it is also partly the fault of our educational system.

Education has failed us, and teachers are responsible for creating a generation of self-centred, ill-educated folk who, for no sensible reason, like to call themselves the 'millennials', though nearly all of them were born in the last millennium. I think a far more appropriate label would be 'the entitlement generation'.

It is because of bad teaching methods that vast numbers of young people are illiterate and innumerate. Maths and English appear to be optional subjects and have been replaced by gender studies, sex education and ethnic diversity training.

Bizarre new ways of teaching, designed so that teachers don't have to work as hard, haven't helped much.

It is because of naivety that millions now believe that the internet is a valuable and reliable source of information.

Incidentally, whenever I go into a card shop, I am astonished to see the number of cards, banners, pens, mugs and other rubbish marked 'For the Best Teacher in the World' or some such nonsense.

I assume that teachers go home at the end of each term laden with this junk. What the hell do they do with it all? Do they have staff room competitions? 'I had 14 cards, 9 mugs and 7 pens from Form 4B'. 'I got 17 cards, 11 mugs and 2 pens from 5A'.

Actually, it is all a bit scary and it shows just why today's kids are growing up into such whingy, pathetic, little creeps.

Marketing companies say that the millennials like natural, colourful and hedonistic products and that they upgrade their mobile phones even if only incremental improvements have been made. And then wonder why they cannot afford to buy a house.

Children are taught not to think but simply to absorb the virtuous and morally superior views which have been pre-selected and prepared for them. That's why millennials are unable to think for themselves. Schools indoctrinate pupils into believing that the EU is a wonderful organisation which will save us all from war and ruination, that those voting to remain within the EU must be wise and tolerant internationalists, and that anyone voting to leave the EU must be a dangerous, war-mongering and insular racist, that recycling old yoghurt cartons will save the planet and that the planet is overheating because we aren't recycling enough old cola cans. It's the indoctrination which has created such a stupid generation.

There are other problems with our educational system.

It is because school sports days, and their innate competitiveness, have been banned, lest pupils be faced with the damaging possibility of defeat, that the millennials always expect to get their own way.

Millennials are dogmatic and exceedingly judgemental because they were brought up to believe that they were the centre of the universe.

As a result of all this, we have a generation of people who are fundamentally flawed and psychologically damaged. They whinged and moaned when they lost the EU vote and when their unlikely champion, Jeremy Corbyn, lost the election. (Many of the most innumerate argued, quite bizarrely, that he had won and should be Prime Minister.)

And it is because of the obsession with sex lessons and unisex uniforms that we have created a generation or two of mixed up young people who are transgender, bisexual, homosexual or just plain mixed up. There has been a steep rise in sexual assaults on children by children and though this is blamed on the internet it is, in my view, almost certainly a result of the obsession with sex which seems to be rife in British schools.

In a decade, probably less, half of the coming generation will think they are gay and the other half will demand sex change surgery with half of those demanding even more expensive reversal operations a few years later. Only the growing Muslim population will be exempt from this sexual hysteria.

So, in short, I blame schools and teachers for many of the problems with the millennials.

9

I am waiting for Jeremy Corbyn and his team of 14-year-old advisors from the Young Communist Party to publish a new and improved manifesto. They are so desperate for power and excited by the enthusiastic welcome for their last, generous, gift-packed manifesto that it can't possibly be long before they publish an improved, even more exciting, revised, supercharged version.

I expect they will promise that if they win the General Election they will:

Make every weekday a bank holiday. The proposal to make four new bank holidays was massively popular. So, now they are adding five new bank holidays every week – a minimum of 260 new bank holidays a year. 'This will boost productivity enormously,' said a spokesperson.

Give everyone in the country a house worth £1 million. And a Ferrari and a yacht. At least one big yacht or two small ones.

Provide unlimited free plastic surgery and sex change surgery to everyone over the age of six.

Reduce the voting age to five. 'If kids is old enough to go to school they is old enough to vote,' said Corbyn's spokeschild.

Allow children aged two or more to choose their own sex, parents and names. 'It's wrong to force young kids to grow up with parents they might not like and names they don't like,' said Korky the cat, a cartoon character and one of Jezza's closest advisors.

Allow stuffed toys to vote in constituencies where the Labour Party does not usually do well.

Give everyone in Scotland an extra 12 extra bank holidays. This will be achieved by making the Scottish year last 377 days and it should help restore Labour's dominance north of the border.

10

The electorate's rejection of Theresa May is being seen by the metropolitan, liberal elite who control the media (conveniently) as a second referendum on Brexit.

It wasn't.

It was a rejection of a cold and arrogant Prime Minister, a Tory Party which had moved so far to the left that it has damned near collided with the Labour Party and alienated many of its traditional supporters and a manifesto which appeared to have been written by infiltrators from the Labour Party.

It seems that Theresa May is a prime example of the Peter Principle. She has risen to a point where she cannot operate efficiently or effectively.

Cameron and Blair both chose aggressive and well-known tabloid journalists as media advisors, but for some absurd reason May seems to have chosen unknown journalists – from a paper in Scotland!

11

A good friend who is a reader of mine has sent me a letter from someone called Elaine Way CBE, who is Chief Executive of Western Health and Social Care Trust in Londonderry, Northern Ireland.

My friend had written to the Trust, quoting my book on Alzheimer's disease – and the way that thousands of patients are being misdiagnosed with untreatable Alzheimer's when they are suffering from treatable Idiopathic Normal Pressure Hydrocephalus.

Ms Way consulted the Trust's three 'Memory Service Clinicians' (Dr Gillian Mullan, Consultant Clinical Psychologist for Older People, Dr Stephen Todd, Consultant Geriatrician and Dr Tuoyo Awani, Consultant Old Age Psychiatrist.)

According to Ms Way, these three told her that 'There is no definitive cure for idiopathic normal pressure hydrocephalus'.

They apparently also told her that they were unaware of any recent scientific literature that reports misdiagnosis rates for Alzheimer's disease to the degree I reported in my book.

When I read their letter, I was several hundred miles away from Northern Ireland but I wouldn't mind betting that they heard my scream of anguish.

Did these experts really say there is no cure for idiopathic normal pressure hydrocephalus?

If they did say this then in my view they are a disgrace.

Idiopathic normal pressure hydrocephalus is the one major cause of dementia which can be cured – by a simple shunt operation. The operation is very effective.

I am appalled that three people who are supposed to be experts should not know this. The scientific evidence is listed in the three-page selection of scientific references in my book entitled *Millions of Alzheimer's Patients Have Been Misdiagnosed (And Could be Cured)*. It is available cheaply on Amazon as an ebook.

My book also contains scientific evidence showing that between 5% and 10% of all individuals diagnosed as suffering from Alzheimer's Disease have been misdiagnosed and are suffering from idiopathic normal pressure hydrocephalus.

How many other hospital doctors and GPs still don't realise that Normal Pressure Hydrocephalus is a major cause of dementia and can be cured?

Thousands, I suspect.

It is, without a doubt, one of the great health scandals of the 21st century.

12

I jotted down some thoughts on politics.

Diane Abbott is rapidly turning out to be the brains of the Labour party. Who'd have thought it? It is comforting to think that Corbyn's former mistress will be in charge of a major Ministry if the Labour Party wins the election. Goody. Diane Abbott is, in my irrelevant opinion, so bereft of intelligence, so ignorant of things she should know that even in Westminster she stands out as a dangerously ill-informed buffoon.

The enthusiasm for elected mayors is entertaining. No one has yet noticed that bringing in all these new mayors is merely a crafty way to reintroduce the Regional Parliaments which the EU wanted to foist upon us and which the British electorate rejected. (The London Assembly and the mini parliaments in Scotland and Wales are merely Regional Parliaments as devised and approved by Adolf's ever enthusiastic followers.)

It's sad to see Poland and France deciding to make Brexit as difficult as possible. Didn't we save those two sorry nations in WWII when they were overrun by Adolf and the boys? Ungrateful bastards. We only fought WWII because the Krauts had invaded Poland. And now they've forgotten and they seem to take great delight in back stabbing us.

I see, by the way, that Poland is now demanding £758 billion from Germany as a result of World War II. Poland is apparently claiming it needs the money to overcome its 'national inferiority complex'. I hope Poland will be giving at least half of that to Britain since we fought that war to save their sorry asses.

Did the EU interfere with the British election?

Nigel Farage has once again proved himself to be the most able and astute politician in Britain. Keeping out of the election which saw the demise of UKIP was a masterstroke. But I bet he doesn't receive the knighthood he so richly deserves. The establishment will block any gong for Mr Farage.

Corbyn et al will probably vote against any Brexit deal. This is great news. No deal at all would be the best deal for the United Kingdom. We need the EU about as much as we need Luxembourg. The EU, on the other hand, needs to keep flogging us cars, washing machines and soggy, infected cheese. Our negotiators will screw things up and if a deal is done it will doubtless be appallingly lily-livered. So, we'll be better off without a deal. The EU has already made it clear that it hates the idea of Britain leaving without a deal. So, isn't that exactly what we should be offering?

In France, the pro EU presidential candidate is being supported by anarchists and anti-fascism groups. This is a sign of intense stupidity since the EU is acknowledged to be the most fascist organisation ever created. Still, no one ever claimed the French were bright, did they?

Populism is the latest term of abuse among the metropolitan elite. But what precisely is populism? It's political control by the people, for the people. The word 'populism' is a synonym for democracy. And that, of course, is why it is so hated by the metropolitan elite.

The SNP and the Welsh nationalists are going to be slaughtered in the General Election. The leaders of both have replaced the idea of representation with disconnected hubris and, as a result, their days are over. Couldn't happen to a nicer bunch of nonentities.

13

The National Trust appears to me to be a symbol of everything that is wrong with England.

Their task is to preserve and present our heritage and our culture but the organisation has succumbed to the virus of political correctness and is, in consequence, in its death throes.

It is now neither one thing nor the other and has betrayed its purpose and its supporters.

14

The media in Britain is totally compliant, bought and unquestioning. The BBC, of course is the voice of the leftie State. (The words 'leftie' and 'fascist' are, and always have been, interchangeable.)

The BBC is well regarded around the world by people who rarely listen to it and who, if they do, have no idea what bilge is being broadcast. Most listeners outside the UK don't understand the Corporation's purposes, obligations and financing. The wise and discerning know that the BBC is pompous, corrupt, dishonest, deceitful, unpatriotic, undemocratic, ageist, bureaucratic, racist, sexist and patronising. The BBC's news and current affairs programmes, and the majority of its dramas, are third rate at best. Its world service programmes are biased. The stuff the BBC sells to America is, of course, the pick of the bunch and so the Americans, who know nothing of the BBC's appalling bias, believe the organisation is wonderful.

The English hating staff of the BBC waste a huge amount of the British Public's money providing superficial tat and overpaying modestly talented individuals who would, without the BBC, be unable to earn a fraction of what they are paid. The organisation has repeatedly refused to allow proper debates on subjects of real importance. Instead, the staff take a position and the corporation is therefore committed.

One reason for this is that the BBC recruits staff from the readership of *The Guardian*, a painfully left wing pro EU newspaper. There are, I suspect, very few English patriots working either for *The Guardian* or the BBC.

The BBC has abandoned its public service ethos and now serves the dishonest, racist, sexist, politically motivated needs of its deeply unpleasant employees whose most notable quality are hubris and a sense of entitlement. They are also traitorous in that they seem to take the EU's side against their employers – the British people. I can understand the awful Nick Clegg and the even more awful Peter Mandelson doing a little scaremongering of the innocent and easily frightened and promoting the EU at every opportunity. They are both, after all, receiving or going to receive pensions from the EU and they have a vested interest in maintaining its strength. But although the BBC has received some money from the EU it receives most of its massive income from the British people and it should learn to be a little more respectful towards its employers. It is easy to see how bent the BBC is – just check their selection of news items (and the way they cover them) with just about any other media organisation (except, perhaps, *The Guardian* and the *Financial Times* which seem to me to be as bent as fish hooks). It is illuminating is it not to realise that the most vocal supporters of the EU are Clegg, Mandelson, Blair and Goldman Sachs.

What a bunch. Clegg, Mandelson, Blair and Goldman Sachs! Says it all, doesn't it?

Incidentally, Channel 4, the other State owned and taxpayer funded broadcaster in the UK, appears to me to be outrageously lefty, anti-Britain, anti-England, anti-English history or culture and, like its big State controlled brother, the BBC is pro EU.

The apparently left wing newspapers *The Guardian* and the *Daily Mirror* may appear to be questioning but they are not.

In many ways, they are even more committed to the status quo than any other outlet.

I have worked for most of the national papers (written columns for quite a few) and the papers take stances but don't let anyone know what those stances are. Sometimes it looks as if a paper is defending X when in reality it is promoting Y. They are very good at it.

The bottom line is that there is not one, large, truly independent media outlet in Britain. And I suspect this is true everywhere else.

As for the internet…well, you would do as well relying on the news provided by the woman behind the fish counter in your local supermarket.

15

The *Daily Mail* appears to have decided not to print the story about normal pressure hydrocephalus (based on my book) which has, so I've been told, been waiting to appear for many weeks.

Maybe the story is too scary for them. Or maybe they don't care about the elderly.

Or maybe they would print the story if the author of the book on which the article was based were 19, buxom and photogenic. Especially if she had a theory that eating sherbet twice a day would cure Alzheimer's and give you cleaner skin, shiny hair and a bigger bottom.

16

These days, every mail seems to bring another batch of problems. No company can, it seems, go a whole month without changing some fundamentals about the way it operates. I then receive a six page single spaced letter demanding that I waste time, money and effort making a choice.

It is, undoubtedly, all made much worse by the fact that I never like being told what to do.

Why can't I just put up with rules and instructions, however absurd?

Life would be so much easier.

17

NHS managers are campaigning to make tests easier for nurses.

They want to be able to employ nurses whose basic knowledge of nursing is not extensive and who don't speak or understand English very well.

I am surprised.

I thought they'd been doing that for years.

18

A politician called Tim Farron resigned as leader of the Liberal Party because he is a Christian and does not support homosexual marriage.

So that is what 'liberal' means these days.

The people who proclaim themselves to be liberal are too prejudiced and bigoted to allow others to hold beliefs.

Actually, I strongly suspect that the vast majority of British citizens do not approve of homosexual marriage. They have, however, had it foisted on them by politically correct politicians.

My guess is that 90% of the population don't approve but it is of no benefit to them to stick their heads above the parapet and so they say nothing rather than risk being pilloried or arrested.

Incidentally, I still refuse to use the word 'gay' as an alternative to homosexual.

The word gay means carefree and light-hearted. This is not, as my politically correct *Oxford Dictionary* says, a dated use of the word. It is the proper use of the word.

I am fed up with the way homosexuals have become so pushy.

A friend of mine once said that he could put up with homosexuals as long as they didn't ram it down your throat.

19

'If you play by the rules nothing can go wrong,' said the man in the café. His companions nodded sagely, clearly agreeing with him.

Wait until he gets their first full-blooded tax investigation.

He will then discover that playing by the rules does you no bloody good at all.

20

According to a 1954 edition of the *Cricketer* magazine, Essex County Cricket club had 500 odd members at the end of the Second World War.

Surely they can't all have been odd?

21

Right wing political groups have been made illegal in Britain (though it is perfectly legal to be a communist or a member of a rabidly unpatriotic left wing party).

And it is perfectly legal to be a supporter of the European Union which is the ultimate neo-Nazi organisation since it was founded by Nazis and still has entirely fascist aims.

The EU supporters ignore the fact that Britain is the most important country in the European Union. The number of British inventors on the list is far, far longer than a list compiled of citizens from all other European countries.

What have the French ever invented except a few smelly, lethal cheeses? Their most famous product (champagne) was invented by an Englishman called Christopher Merrett in the Cotswolds. And what have the Germans given the world except sauerkraut and the silly goose-step?

And now, to our shame, we sit demurely by and allow the French, the Germans and even the Poles, damn it, make demands upon us. Even a damned Luxembourger thinks he can tell us what we can and cannot do!

If we had a Government worth its salt, we would now not be negotiating our release from the EU's clutches but simply announcing our imminent departure.

Why waste time debating, arguing and pleading with such ungrateful bastards?

We should wave two Agincourt fingers at the EU and tell the sniffy little cretins who run it that if they don't roll over and let us leave as planned, we will leave now, immediately and without further ado. (The Agincourt Wave, named after the English archers who waved two fingers at the French just to show they still had their bow twanging digits, should become our national gesture.)

And we should not pay the EU one penny to leave their damned silly fascist organisation. Thanks to the cheaply bought Edward Heath, we have paid out billions to be members of a club no one in their right mind would want to join.

We should tell the EU fascists that unless they roll over quickly we will close down the Channel Tunnel, introduce an Embargo on all EU products (including German cars, French cheese and whatever the Italians are struggling to make this week) and repatriate all foreign EU citizens currently living in the UK (most of whom only came for our free money, houses, benefits and health care).

If the eurocrats object to our simple deal, we should declare war on the EU.

The whole business would be over in days.

We have beaten the Germans twice in the last hundred years and they have no stomach for a third thrashing.

The Italians always run around in circles getting absolutely nowhere if they are under threat.

The Poles are plumbers not fighters.

The Spanish are pathetic whingers who are too busy fighting among themselves. And they don't fight in the afternoons.

And the French all carry white flags in their pockets so that they can surrender within moments of any conflict starting.

Our war with the EU would be over in days; a week at most.

22

Investors are being advised that they should regularly 'rebalance' their investments. What this means in practice is that they are being encouraged to sell investments which are doing well and to buy more of the crappy stuff which is doing badly.

It is perfectly true that it is occasionally possible to do well by buying more of a share which has gone down for no good reason. In such a case, it can make good sense to buy more. I have done this to good effect myself. But to make this a general rule makes no sense at all – except for the banks and brokers who make their money from the commissions they gouge out of the poor investors who are forever selling and buying. What is sensible about selling the successful investments and buying more of the shares which are failing? It may be a brave version of contrarian investing but it isn't particularly rational or sensible and it certainly isn't safe.

Stock markets everywhere are rising and commentators are desperately trying to explain why investors are willing to take stock markets to ever greater heights. There is much talk of rising profits and of things being 'different this time' (again). This is all bollocks, of course. The real explanation for the rise in stock prices is very simple.

Central banks have been printing money for years and have kept interest rates absurdly, dangerously, unnecessarily and destructively low for a decade.

So if you have some savings, the choice is simple: put your money into a deposit account and lose a big chunk of it every year as inflation eats away at your capital, or buy shares and accept the dividends and the chances of a capital gain that will help you beat inflation.

Commentators warn that share prices will collapse. I can't see this happening for a while. Why would investors take their money out of shares and put it into deposit accounts paying noticeably less than inflation?

With interest rates so low and so many older people suffering as a result, I really cannot understand why more 70 and 80-year-olds who are struggling to cope on low incomes don't rob banks. Many have nothing to lose. If they get away with the robbery they will have won back some of the money the Government and the banks stole from them. If they get arrested they will receive warm accommodation and free food. It's a win-win situation.

As someone who has been investing for well over 50 years, I am pleased to see that people my age beat millennials hands down at investing.

The millennials are still naïve enough to think that when a share goes down, they are simply suffering a paper loss but when it goes up, they are making real money. In fact, of course, the profit isn't real money until the shares have been sold and converted into the stuff the Bitcoin generation despise and call 'money'.

23

Kids used to play at sports. They don't do that much anymore. It's a long time since I saw kids playing cricket or football.

Then they watched sports. Some actually went to stadia with the Dads. Most watched sport on television.

Then they played games on their computers.

Then the eSports industry took off and they watched other people playing games on their computers.

And soon kids will watch computers playing one another. Maybe computer robots will fight one another. The loser will lie there, bleeding oil, cogs awry and the victor will disconnect his battery to denote and define his victory.

I wonder, by the way, why it is that so many of today's generation are overweight and under fit.

I have no doubt that somewhere there is a band of fearless researchers using taxpayers' money to try to find an answer to this puzzle.

Meanwhile, I am still trying to find out what 'copy and paste into your browser' means. I don't even know what a browser is.

24

A week before the election I wondered if the Tory Party could have been paid to lose the election. There was an element of tongue in cheek to it.

Now I'm really not so sure.

Look what's happened.

The Conservative Party seems to have deliberately thrown an election. I can't think of anything they could have done to make things worse for themselves.

Now we have that worst of all worlds: a hung parliament.

Millions of sensible folk who voted Labour or LibDem because they didn't like Mrs May's hubris and wanted to give her a good spanking probably now realise how stupid they have been.

But it doesn't really matter.

The democratic dream of the majority who sensibly voted Brexit is over.

Supporters of Hitler's child, the European Union, may have lost the vote but they have won the war.

War criminal Tony Blair, aided by a small army of pathetic, whingeing remainers and middle aged Millennials are about to get their wish. (Am I the only one in Britain who believes that anyone who supports the EU in this battle, and who questions the integrity of the British people and their clear mandate for a full Brexit, is a traitor?)

The Brexit we are going to get will be so soft that we'll be worse off than if we'd stayed in the EU. We will be doomed.

We have to start the fight all over again.

And there is only one way that we can now win.

We must point out to everyone the truth that no one talks about: the EU was founded by Adolf Hitler and the Nazis. It was created to ensure that Germany won the Second World War.

(The number of people who still fail to understand this astonishes me. In his book *Flying High*, Asian businessman Tony Fernandes, who seems like a nice fellow, makes it clear that he thinks that the EU is a good idea because it was created out of the bombed ruins of WWII. How can anyone not now know that the EU was deliberately set up by the Nazis to ensure that Germany gained control of Europe? This is not a myth. It is fact.)

And, as planned, post-war Germany was dominated by old Nazis in positions of power in the worlds of politics, the police, banking, industry and the church. Germany is a fascist country and the EU mirrors that ideology.

The strange thing is that quite a number of Polish politicians seem to take special pleasure in trying to kick Britain – and to support the German controlled European Union. This is odd because it was Britain who, in 1939, fought Germany to save Poland from annexation. There are still people alive who fought in the Second World War but too many Poles seem to have forgotten how many Britons died for them.

The same is true of the French, of course. If we hadn't saved their butts, the French would now all be speaking German and kowtowing every time a German went by.

In addition to this, Britain has for years welcomed Poles to its shores. Many have made a good deal of money out of Britain (with many of them sending the money back to Poland).

I find the Poles particularly ungrateful. We saved them from Germany in 1939. Have these wretched, rude and ungrateful people no sense of gratitude? What have the Poles ever given the world except a good many plumbers and a language that looks like misprints?

25

I've written to Jeremy Corbyn. Here's what I wrote:

Dear Jezza,

The free stuff bribe worked well, didn't it? All the students fell for the gimmick about 'no fees' hook, line and sinker. Stunning. And the lots of free bank holidays and loads more benefits and great pensions – they all went down well. Voters lapped it all up. Meanwhile, those idiots in the Tory party were making loads of really dull, sensible promises which were never going to look good on social media.

But I desperately need you to win the next election so that you fuck up the country properly. I'm counting on you. The bill for all the money you're going to spend won't be paid for a few decades. By which time you and I won't give a damn. The millennials will have to pick up the tab. And sadly they won't ever be able to retire and if they don't work they won't get any sort of pension so about five million of them will be busking or begging. They will have to rediscover the joy of darning socks and making bubble and squeak with food leftovers. I bet the average millennial doesn't even know that people used to darn holey socks. So that's their hard luck, as you know. So this is a great time. And you're doing brilliantly.

Now, Jezza, I reckon we can make a bundle on the currency markets and stock markets when you become Prime Minister. The pound will crash and the price of essential imports such as food and oil will soar. That'll push up inflation, and so Carney (who seems to have turned into a full-blown party and festival attendee) won't have any choice but to raise interest rates. Actually, I wish Carney would spend more time at parties and festivals and tennis matches instead of contributing so enthusiastically to the nonsense which is Project Fear.

Whoopee! Us oldies will do well. Interest rates up, shares in gold and mining companies soaring. Great.

But you've got to do a lot more, Jezza.

If you're definitely going to win the next election you need more of those free offers. Nice big £2 million homes for everyone. Free. A nice packet containing £1,000 in freshly minted notes for every voter in the land. A cut in all taxes except for rich bastards earning over £40,000 a year – except MPs of course. The rich bastards can pay 90% tax because they can afford it. Oh, and promise £25,000 a year in tax free cash for anyone who doesn't want to work because it's boring. Make sure that it's payable to anyone who votes. And bring the voting age down to 16. And the pension age down to 30. And guarantee everyone £39,999 a year State pension, collectable at the age of 50.

That should do it.

Oh, and every time there's a disaster anywhere make sure you get there fast for the huggies and the selfies. Don't bother talking. Just hug and pose. Hug and pose. Great stuff, comrade.

You'll be in Downing Street and we'll both make an absolute bundle.

The silly millennials will eventually pay the price but what do we care?

Rock on, Jezza!

Up the Revolution!

Your comrade

Vernoninski Colemanovitch

26

A young woman who is apparently a bit famous is insisting that Corbyn had won the election and is now Prime Minister.

She seemed to me to be clinically deluded but the media are allowing her to rant on as though she were a sane person. I had never heard of her and have now forgotten her name. I have no idea who she was.

I also read that an actor called Andrew Scott says that Hamlet cannot now be played as 'mad' because audiences are too tuned in to mental health issues.

I look forward to some lefty playwright rewriting Hamlet and adding a couple of social workers and a mental welfare officer to support and comfort the potty Prince.

Meanwhile, we are now all so tuned in to mental health issues that GPs report that one in three sick notes is written for 'mental health issues'. Glory be. I doubt if there is a millennial in the country who doesn't complain that he is suffering from stress. Staggeringly, around 300,000 people a year are giving up work because of long-term mental health problems. The problem, I fear, is that people are increasingly unwilling to accept responsibility for their own lives. They always demand a solution from someone else.

When I was a GP, I refused to put full diagnoses onto sick notes because patients had to take their sick notes into their place of work where the sick note would be copied and everyone would know what their illness was. I remember one manager for a chain store telling me that if I put down that he was suffering from depression then he would lose his job. I was hauled before an NHS committee and fined quite heavily for this. That was why I resigned from the National Health Service. I was facing a lifetime of heavy fines. No one supported my stance and I was dismissed as a nutty Don Quixote character but within a year or two, the rules had been changed so someone must have been listening.

I honestly don't believe that anyone has better credentials than I have in the area of mental health issues. I have fought hard for individuals suffering from real mental health problems and I've written a number of books on the subject.

But things have now become rather silly.

The young royals (who live on their own exclusively luxurious brand of benefits and can have few complaints about what life has thrown at them) have made the whole issue fashionable and as a result every minor setback or disappointment is a depression and every hiccup is 'stressful'. People wear their mental illness with pride – as though it were a war injury.

The result is that we have a nation of people taking drugs they don't need and staying home from work. The young royals might do more good if they put a little effort into persuading millennials that life sucks and sometimes you just have to put up with it and move on.

Actually, the problem doesn't just involve mental health issues.

I saw a health website the other day which advised readers to visit their doctor as a matter of urgency if they had any pain in their chest, arms or back in case it was a heart attack. No wonder it is impossible to get an appointment with a GP.

And why, I wonder, are there now so many websites dealing with illnesses such as chest pain as though they were purely feminine problems? If there were websites suggesting that chest pain were an exclusively male problem they would be attacked as misleadingly sexist.

27

All is well with the world.

At Starbucks it is apparently now possible to order a lavender cortado from a barista who is wearing flannel rather than a green apron. The company has conducted research on what it calls 'credibility cues' and has found that baristas who have tattoos are thought to make better coffee.

Other research has shown that ice used at some Starbucks shops contains faecal matter. But who cares. As long as the faecal matter laden ice is served up by a geezer with tattoos and, preferably, served in an old avocado skin.

28

When Camden council announced that it was going to close down a block of flats (and force all the occupants to leave) because another block of flats had caught fire, all the commentators seemed to think it was a wise and good thing to do.

But it wasn't.

It was a narrow minded and very stupid knee-jerk response which will do genuine harm and it showed a complete failure to understand the concept of risk.

A girl from the council said they had done it because the local fire boss could not guarantee the safety of the people inside.

Of course he couldn't.

What a stupid question to ask the bloke.

Of course he couldn't guarantee the safety of all the people in this block'.

Can he guarantee the building won't be hit by a meteor? Of course he can't. No one can. By Camden's standards every building in the country should be emptied.

What Camden Council has failed to do is to understand the concept of risk. The residents should be told the risk and allowed to make their own choice instead of being oppressed by the nanny state. (Incidentally, French economist Frederic Bastiat defined the state as: 'that great fiction by which everyone tries to live at the expense of everyone else.')

There are in our modern world two sorts of people: the risk takers and the non-risk takers.

The people in the second group completely misunderstand the meaning of risk and they spend their lives (largely through ignorance) making life difficult (or impossible) for the risk takers who are, by definition, the people who service today and create tomorrow.

29

Today I watched a beggar sending a mate into a betting shop for him. When I asked him why he had sent his pal into the shop on his behalf, the beggar told me that he had a good begging pitch and didn't want to leave it.

I am told that in China, buskers and beggars hold up signs with details of their QR code (whatever that is) so that people can give them money via their mobile phones.

Cash is no longer acceptable.

I saw today that W.H.Smith, the newsagent, is selling next year's calendars and half year diaries.

Apparently, a half year diary enables you to write down your appointments for half the year. You then buy the diary for the other half of the year.

30

I used a telephone answering machine to move some money from one bank account to another.

I completed the whole transaction with the aid of a recorded voice which actually worked. At the end I said, 'thank you very much you have been very helpful'.

Afterwards, I watched a pair of blackbirds feeding a baby blackbird. In between mouthfuls, the baby bird sat on the back of a wooden swing seat in the garden and waited for mum and then dad to come with more food.

Mum, dad, mum, dad, mum, dad.

Fortunately, some things in the world don't change.

July

1

The Scottish government is changing the law about transplantation so that more transplants can be performed.

Organ transplantation has long worried me.

Back in the 1960s, I took part in a television programme with Dr Christiaan Barnard who performed the first heart transplant.

Many things about transplants worried me – but nothing more than the fact that it was impossible to be sure that the donor was really dead when his organs were removed.

You can't wait until the body is properly dead to 'harvest' the organs. You need them fresh and in good condition. So it's a moot point whether the donor is, or is not, still alive when his or her heart and kidneys are removed.

To start with, surgeons relied on ECG machines to tell if a patient had died. Then it became clear that this really wasn't a very safe way to decide whether or not it was OK to start ripping organs out of a patient. So, 'brain death' became the fashionable way to decide if a patient had 'died'. If there was no trace of life on the machine which measures brain activity then the surgeons could move in.

But.

This morning I read about a young Palestinian who was hit in the head by an Israeli bullet and lay in bed comatose in an Israeli hospital. The hospital doctors pronounced the young man brain dead and sent him home to Gaza strip to die. He recovered and five years later had a wife and three sons. The only sign of his injury was a limp.

And this, remember, is the same definition of death which is used as a sign for the transplant surgeons to move in and start removing vital organs.

There's another problem with transplantation.

No nation can possibly afford to perform transplants on everyone who needs one.

And so social workers, nurses and doctors sit around a big table, drink coffee, munch biscuits and decide which patients will live and which will die. The social workers pretty much run the thing.

They have a sort of points system for doing this.

So, if you're foreign and you've got 16 kids and you've never done a day's work in your life, you will get lots of points and you will probably get a new heart. If you're English and have no kids or are single then they let you die. If you happen to be the greatest composer or film maker in the country they will still let you die because the NHS selection process has become racist and politically correct.

The system is absurd, cruel, unfair and indefensible.

Mozart and Beethoven wouldn't be chosen for transplants. But an unemployed yahoo with a wife, a mistress and two council houses full of kids would be top of the list.

So, between the fact that the system is grossly unfair and no one can tell if the donor is really dead, I think we should abandon transplant surgery.

The vast amounts of money spent on transplants could be used to improve diagnostic services and to reduce waiting times for routine but life-saving surgery.

It's impossible to know what the NHS costs are for a transplant but it is known that in the United States a heart transplant costs, on average, $1,382,400. A lung transplant costs an average of $861,700, a liver transplant costs $812,500 and an intestine transplant costs $1,147,300. My guess would be that the costs in the NHS would be comparable and certainly not any cheaper.

Remember, the money available for health services is finite.

Remember that it is not at all unknown in NHS hospitals for patients to be put into beds without the sheets being changed!

Choices have to be made.

And I guarantee that far more lives would be saved if transplants were halted.

The good news today is that we have a new robin living in our garden.

2

Stephen Hawking, the author of a book which was bought by millions and read by dozens, seems to have decided that he is an expert on everything and must share his cockeyed views with the world. He appears to have claimed that the earth is going to turn into Venus and that the temperature in Wolverhampton will be 250 degrees Celsius by next Wednesday. We will apparently have acid rain. He was reported as having forecast that we are all going to have to climb into little spaceships and set up colonies on other (unspecified) planets.

I have never been convinced that Hawking had a riotous sense of humour. Maybe he has gone barking. Who knows? Although, of course, we must not lose sight of the fact that he may have been misquoted. He may have merely made a comment about the prospects of the England football team in some tournament or other. Reporters do have a way of misunderstanding.

Or maybe this is another Stephen Hawking. There are probably loads of them about. Maybe this Steven Hawking is a seven-year-old with a Twitter account and an inflated sense of his own importance.

On the other hand, if we assume that this was 'the' Hawking and he wasn't misquoted then we must remember Kipling, who wrote: if you don't exaggerate then no one will take any notice'.

The Web has, of course, taken this to heart. It is, I suspect, the tweeters' secret mantra. And it would seem to me that Hawking may have now adopted Kipling as his guide to life.

Looked at more widely, the fact is that the climate change nutters don't much care about facts or the truth.

All they are interested in is in maintaining and spreading the myth.

As far as I am aware, there is not one shred of scientific evidence to support this latest nonsense and Hawking has, in my view, just destroyed whatever small reputation he may have had as a serious scientist.

Moreover, he should surely be ashamed of himself for seeking to frighten and mislead.

I am totally in favour of creating cleaner vehicles, which go further on less petrol and which spew out less toxic gases, but that is because I want to breathe cleaner air and because I know that the oil is running out but there was never any justification for confusing these two issues with the climate change myth.

An entire global warming industry has built up with tons of folk flying around the world, having meetings, taking huge fees and thinking up new ways to punish ordinary people and sustaining the whole myth. The vast majority of people see the whole thing as the scam it is – surveys have consistently shown that most people don't believe in global warming (man-made or not).

Every time there is a weather related problem, it is blamed on climate change. Look back in history, we can see that storms and hurricanes and tempests and tsunamis have always been a part of our climatic history. Things appear worse today because the authorities insist on categorising every minor event as a major incident.

Do you remember all that talk about Cornwall being turned into a desert by 2010? They didn't quite get that right, did they?

Incidentally, why do so many people insist on writing Climate Change instead of climate change?

I have noticed that newspapers which would use lower case initials when writing about God or the Queen seem to favour upper case initials when writing about their favourite myth.

3

I have seen the light.

Modern politics is all about self-interest; the self-interest of the politicians and the self-interest of the voters.

The Millennials want Corbyn in power because he has promised them loads of free money and extra holidays. They aren't bright enough to realise that every time the minimum wage goes up a load of businesses stop hiring and thousands of workers are made redundant.

Corbyn appears to be a manipulative little bugger, and it is no wonder that liberal lefty brainless luvvies adore him. He is all promise and no policy, all tacky style and no serious substance. Most of his supporters favour higher taxes because most of them don't have jobs and therefore don't pay any tax at all.

He does not appear to be a wise or intelligent man; I get the impression that when brains were being allocated he stood in the line between the garden bench and the French accordion. Nor is he a great leader. But he seems to have the naïve charm of a village idiot and his insane burblings attract the lost, the bewildered and the resentful. His followers appear to be the sort of people who do a lot of jumping up and down on social media.

He talks about investing in our future, in a fairer society and in ways designed to stimulate the economy.

This is, of course, all complete bollocks.

Whenever the State spends money, the money just disappears and nothing ever comes of it. When administrators and politicians are given buckets full of money to spend, you can be sure that every last penny of it will be wasted and there will be no profit, no dividend and no gain. It is usually said that the fruit of experience is wisdom. This does not, however, work with politicians or bureaucrats.

Corbyn promised to abandon student loans, and to abolish fees. Then someone told him how much this would cost and apparently, he quietly abandoned the idea during the university holidays.

He wants the minimum wage to go up to £10 an hour for 16-year-olds. That will win over some of the teenagers with low paid jobs but it will soon prove unpopular when all the jobs disappear.

I assume that no one has told him that 900,000 retail jobs will go in the next few years because the minimum wage has already risen too far too quickly.

Corbyn's millennials want to stay in the EU because they are worried that if we leave they won't be able to buy BMWs and cappuccinos. A true Brexit would have led to freedom, independence, democracy and wealth. But those things aren't as much fun as camembert cheese and claret.

It all sounds superficial and selfish but it's the new socialist, lefty, way. (Socialists are mostly driven by envy so it's not surprising that most millennials are socialists.)

And Corbyn, who seems to me to have the intellectual and emotional age of a poorly developed 15-year-old, has captured the mood of the new zeitgeist perfectly.

After the recent fire in London, Theresa May did the adult, useful, boring thing. She went to talk to the fire chiefs and the emergency services. Corbyn was out there giving out hugs and posing for selfies and probably some of his trademark misplaced bosom slapping high fives too. Social media despised the sensible approach and enthusiastically applauded the promotional alternative. Corbyn is a politician in the same way that Lily Allen and Gary Lineker are politicians.

My old-fashioned sense of responsibility for the future leads me to believe that austerity was essential for our nation's survival.

Gordon Brown left Britain with massive debts which have been growing ever since.

The debt continued to grow throughout the Osborne years and it is still growing. We haven't really had any austerity yet. We've just had the warm up. Britain is still borrowing more than £1 billion a week, national debt interest payments exceed the nation's defence budget and our deficit now is greater than ever. We already have higher tax rates than at any time in the last 30 years and not many people would bet against more tax rises. The plan to cut the annual overspend by the mid-2020s is now clearly just a pipe dream.

The logical, sensible inclination is to believe that the national debt must be reduced. After all, a nation which has unpaid, growing debts eventually finds itself impoverished and unable to fund any government programmes. Ask the Greeks or the Argentinians. The UK's national debt is now worse than that of France or Italy (two recognised basket cases in Europe) because Brown and Osborne have left Britain's economy in a terrible mess. The UK's debts are massive and still growing. All attempts to deal with them are vociferously opposed by people with a personal, vested interest in resisting cuts in public expenditure. These categories include unions, public service staff and people existing on government hand-outs aka benefits.

Millennials, who now control the nation through social media, (the latest job is apparently that of 'social media influencer') don't want any austerity because it is a painful process. They don't give a damn about the future. They care only about now. They want more free money and more free holidays. And they want it now. And a cappuccino with extra double sprinkles too and be quick about it. They take offence very easily for theirs is the Diva Generation. They all think they are so very, very special, so superior. If someone thwarts them, or fails to agree with them then, in lieu of offering a sensible argument they will, like the average thick-skulled mugger, resort to violence – usually verbal, because they don't do physical unless they're in their lycra.

Well, I'm tired.

Let the daft buggers have what they want.

The nation will be utterly fucked, of course.

But that's a small price to pay.

A few decades down the line (just when today's 25-year-olds are feeling creaky and thinking of retirement) there won't be any money left for pensions, health care or anything else. And Britain won't be able to borrow because our debts will be too huge for anyone to trust us with more loans. Taxes will rise to such high levels that no one will bother to work. Everyone will want to leech off the State.

Actually, we won't have to wait long for the tax rises. New taxes are coming whoever gets in at the next election. The Tories have gone left. Labour supporters have raced into communism. Millennials don't approve of paying taxes themselves (it doesn't fit in with their feelings of entitlement and expectation) and since they control social media it will be the older citizens who will pay higher taxes. There will be wealth taxes, high capital gains taxes and so on ad infinitum.

But that's not my problem, is it?

I believe in patriotism and paying off debts because I'm an old fart.

But that's all out of fashion now.

As far as I am concerned, the present will be much better if the nation borrows more and spends more money it hasn't got. The millennials will shut up and enjoy the extra spending. And, who knows, the council might go back to collecting the rubbish as often as once a fortnight.

As I said in my letter to Jezza, we oldies will be the recipients of this borrowed largesse and we won't ever have to pay for it.

And we can make money out of it too.

The minute Corbyn gets into Downing Street, the pound will collapse. Inflation will then soar and interest rates will have to rise to more sensible and rewarding levels. Will we manage to match Zimbabwe in 1999? Inflation reached a magnificent 500 billion per cent. Sadly, I rather doubt that this sort of inflation rate is as entertaining as it might sound from afar.

We can get rich by selling UK investments and buying foreign shares and property so that we are hedged against the fall in sterling. We can hold gold, oil, dollars and even euros. (Note: the use of oil is still soaring globally – and it's running out.)

So, bring it on!

Let's have Corbyn in No 10. Let's abandon austerity, good sense and responsibility for the future.

The price will be massive.

But we old farts won't have to pay it.

The older you are the more sense a Corbyn government makes.

We will have happy, wealthy years, enjoying a present paid for by the millennials.

The millennials will eventually have to pay the price for the Corbyn largesse with very high taxes, no benefits, no pensions and a total collapse in public services.

But that's their choice.

I'm not sure that I care anymore.

4

I saw a survey today which showed that newspaper prices have soared over the last decade. During the same period, their sales have fallen by almost the same amount that the prices have risen.

This is a classic error and it's surprising to see newspapers making it.

When sales and income fall, there is a tremendous temptation to put up prices in order to help counter the fall in sales and maintain income. But if you do that then, inevitably, the sales collapse is exacerbated.

5

July 5th used to be Cecil Rhodes day. (It was his birthday) I think we should bring it back. So today, in my world, is Cecil Rhodes day. Cecil Rhodes helped free Africa from poverty by exploring and liberating the country's intrinsic wealth and then helping to turn a wasteland into a country.

Cecil Rhodes day will not be widely celebrated, of course, because those outrageously hypocritical, foreign youths who accept Rhodes scholarships to Oxford and then, when they get there, campaign vociferously to have the statue of their benefactor removed because they don't like what they think he did to earn the money which they are now so eagerly grasping. If the halfwits who protest about Rhodes had any brains, they would salute his memory and give thanks for his life.

It is no longer considered acceptable to defend titans such as Cecil Rhodes or Sir Thomas Stafford Raffles. They did great things but they were of their time, and members of the Entitlement Generation do not understand that history means that what is acceptable today will probably not be acceptable tomorrow, and that social change is a long, slow process which can, and probably will, eventually leave us all stranded on the wave washed rocks of unacceptability.

Few of the anti-Rhodes campaigners seem to have bothered to do any research. Rhodes was far less of a racist than many black and Asian politicians and far, far less of a racist than most of those who sneer at him and his work. Africans, in particular, should salute his determination and skills and respect his memory. I suspect that most know very little of what he achieved in a tragically short life. (When liberal luvvies talk about racism they never mention the fact that Arab men wear white robes while Arab women wear black. White clothing reflects the heat and keeps the wearer cool but black clothing absorbs heat and is very uncomfortable in hot climates. What's that if it isn't an expression of a racist attitude?)

How can you remove certain parts of our history, pretend that they do not exist, refuse point blank to study them or refer to them and then claim to understand the world in which we live?

Rhodes, like Raffles and many others, helped shape our modern world. They were courageous and imaginative men and just because we would do things differently now doesn't mean that the way they did things was wrong then – and nor does it make them bad men.

Standards, boundaries, expectations, beliefs were all different then.

Those who judge so enthusiastically today will doubtless find themselves with serious explaining to do about their own activities in another decade or two's time. They will then realise that to make judgements about an individual's behaviour when he lived in a different culture, when expectations were very different, is absurd and utterly unfair. I wonder how Rhodes's attackers will be viewed in 100 years' time. Maybe they will be vilified for accepting his charity. Maybe they will be vilified for criticising him. And maybe a coming generation will demand that Blair Avenue, Prescott Street and the Corbyn Primary School all have their names changed to something more acceptable.

As an anonymous reader of mine pointed out: 'The fact is that if it weren't for the imagination and energy of Cecil Rhodes, many of those who now besmirch his name would still be running around wearing loin cloths. They would be waving spears and supplementing their diet with the occasional 'rump of missionary'.'

I couldn't possibly comment.

6

Many of the residents from Grenfell tower, mostly immigrants, have refused the temporary housing offered to them, though the accommodation on offer looked damned good to me and would, I suspect, have looked damned good to most Britons.

Now, here is a thing: several hundred people die in fires in domestic properties in England every year.

How many of them are offered wonderful alternative accommodation and huge cash payments?

Some of the Grenfell residents have been put into 68 flats which cost £2,000,000 and where the rates and services charge is £15,000 a year. The flats have been bought by the council which has apparently got money to burn. The flats are in a building where some residents paid up to £25,000,000 for their accommodation.

Those who dared to question whether this is fair to the folk who had bought their flats, or the right use of taxpayers' money, were naturally vilified as racists.

The other curious thing is that the residents who owned their own apartments in the Grenfell Tower block appear to have been completely left out in the cold. They haven't been offered vastly expensive accommodation and nor have they found themselves being forced to accept huge cash payments from the charities which have been collecting voluntary donations.

Around £19 million in cash has been collected and I have to say I can't help wondering why. Do the people who give so generously to foreigners who have lost their homes also give so generously when people who live in their own homes lose everything in a fire?

(Actually, the whole thing reminds me of the Aberfan tragedy. Huge amounts of money were raised for the parents who had lost children, as though the money would help in some way, and decades later the money was still causing problems.)

The most annoying aspect of the Grenfell tragedy is that the bureaucrats and planning officers who are responsible will go scot free. Nothing ever happens to government or council employees.

And when will politicians and planners decide to stop building these monstrosities? They are blots on our landscape and unsuitable for human habitation. When I was a medical student, I spent two years living on the 16th floor of a hall of residence. And when I worked as a GP through the 1970s and early 1980s, I used to visit patients living in the damned things almost every day of my life. The people who build them should be forced to live in them. They would soon change their minds and build rows of neat villas, with gardens, instead.

7

I bought a pair of walkie talkies so that when I am in the garden Antoinette can reach me if something important happens – such as the kettle boiling. I will be spending the next few months hacking down weeds. Every summer our forest of hogweed in Gloucestershire grows to around ten feet tall. I have tried everything. The giant hogweed is the flora equivalent of the cockroach. When the world finally ends, there will be just cockroaches and giant hogweed.

I also bought a couple of helium filled balloons. They were huge. As I carried them to the car most people smiled (though one or two youths thought it would be funny to try to burst them with their cigarettes or by deliberately bumping into me).

When I got the balloons home, I took off the heavy weights which the shop had attached and Antoinette put on toy soldiers and some of that blue sticky stuff that has so many odd uses.

We then had tremendous fun watching the balloons floating around the house.

At night, we have to tether them, in case they trigger a burglar alarm. In the daytime, they float around the house eerily and move from room to room. They would, I suspect, scare the shit out of an intruder.

8

Antoinette and I watched a rather sanctimonious film called *Denial* which is about Jews who sued a chap called David Irving who made himself unpopular by making comments about the holocaust which they didn't like.

The lawsuit, as portrayed in the film, didn't seem to me to prove anything except that the two sides disagreed about the facts. The plaintiffs didn't seem to me to prove that the holocaust happened, merely that they regarded Irving as something of a monster.

There always seems to be a good excuse for suppressing facts, ideas or debate as in 'We must not talk about vaccination because if people get to hear the truth they won't want to be vaccinated and then where will we be?' The penalties for telling the truth, or daring to be original or to share a viewpoint which is out of kilter with the establishment's accepted norm are, in their way, just as bad as they were in the days of Galileo. Scientists, especially when they have been bought by drug companies and other commercial enterprises, become indignant and aggressive in defending their immorality. They also become determined to destroy any embarrassing opposition. In no area is this more apparent than in the world of vaccination. Any doctor who dares to promote or defend vaccination is a fraud and a charlatan, a professional whore or an ignorant incompetent. There are no other choices.

I always find it rather frightening when a group of people try to suppress free speech and then endeavour to justify the suppression in some way. I rather doubt that this film will appeal to anyone who does not already believe in the unproven theory which Irving questioned. This seems to me to be a propaganda film which will appeal only to people who already believe the propaganda. So, a bit of a waste of time, I fear.

I confess that at the end of the film, I found myself feeling rather sorry for Irving and disliking the lawyers representing the Jewish woman who initiated the lawsuit and seemed intent only on destroying a man's reputation. The lawyers opposing Irving made a great deal of fuss over mistakes he had made in his interpretation of history. The woman behind the lawsuit seemed to imply that the people who denied the holocaust were as daft as the people who believe that Elvis is still alive or that climate change isn't happening.

I found this a very interesting comparison for there appears to me to be about as much plain, old-fashioned evidence proving the existence of the holocaust as there is proving that Elvis is dead. And there is no scientific evidence proving that climate change is happening and is man-made. Indeed, the available evidence seems to prove the opposite.

The fact that you believe something strongly doesn't turn it into an undeniable truth. I am prepared to accept that the slaughter commonly described as the holocaust did take place (though I don't for a moment think that only Jews were involved) but the fact that I believe it happened doesn't prove that it happened. And why is it illegal or improper for anyone to admit that they have a sneaking suspicion that the numbers so often quoted might owe more to politically inspired imaginations than to fact?

A disappointed Labour Party, upset that they did not win the election, called for a million people to hit the streets and demand that Corbyn be crowned king.

Unfortunately, only 23 people turned up but they had a good time and drank lattes served in avocado skins with double chocolate sprinkles.

It was, as so many things are these days, a party for bad losers.

I wrote to UKIP offering to speak or help in any way they thought appropriate but didn't even have a reply except an automatic acknowledgement. How things change. Some years ago, Nigel Farage wanted to print 1,000,000 copies of my book

England Our England. And when I spoke at a UKIP conference, I received a standing ovation. Sic transit Gloria.

This evening an ocean going yacht parked in the sea at the bottom of our garden; close enough to pop a golf ball onto the deck with a modest seven iron. I was tempted but I am proud to say that I did not succumb. The yacht's crew and passengers swam alongside it.

The sea in many areas may be polluted but these days it is probably safer than most swimming pools. The average swimming pool contains around 50 gallons of urine and, in an attempt to counteract this, far too much chlorine. The chlorine can cause eye problems. Chest infections are commonly shared in the warm air of changing rooms and foot infections are endemic. So the sea is probably cleaner and safer.

9

According to the news today, the incidence of gender identity problems has quadrupled in the last five years. Thousands of children need gender guidance counselling because, despite the evidence which is available every time they have a bath or a shower, they aren't sure what sex they are or should be.

I'm not in the slightest bit surprised.

Schools now do everything they can to confuse kids. They have installed unisex loos and forced children to wear unisex uniforms. More and more stores are now providing unisex clothes for all those under the age of 14 years. All this is being done despite the fact that all the available scientific evidence shows, quite conclusively, that boys and girls are different, have a different outlook and different needs.

By forcing their own politically correct views on children, there is no doubt that teachers and the media (and some parents) have made gender identity problems fashionable.

The result is that no self-respecting kid wants to be without a gender crisis. The incidence of homosexuality (both varieties) is soaring. It will soon be illegal to reach 18 without at least one meaningful (and possibly compulsory) homosexual experience.

And, on top of all this, sex education is encouraging kids to experiment. Naturally, they do it in the unisex loos. And so the incidence of teenage pregnancies is also soaring and every year, thousands of children need psychological or psychiatric advice because they have sex problems or gender problems. The incidence of homosexuality is soaring.

Worse still, thousands of children (boys, of course) are put on sex offender registers because they have been caught committing sex crimes. A ten-year-old boy who pings a bra strap or draws graffiti with a sexual connotation can now be ruined for life. Thousands of primary school children have been in trouble (sometimes expelled) for sexual crimes – over 2,000 young children have been expelled from school for sex offences. This figure was welcomed by mad feminists who seemed to think it was good news that child sex offenders were being caught at any early age.

The politically correct do-gooders responsible for this mayhem aren't bright enough to connect the dots and understand that all these changes are linked. I have heard that some politically correct lunatics now want to have loos without doors on the cubicles. They claim that having no doors would prevent drug using and illicit sex and break down barriers between the sexes. I wouldn't bet against it happening at a lavatory near you soon.

In a sensible world, all sex education and gender studies classes would be done with the two sexes segregated. The classes would take place when children were 10-years-old and repeated at 14.

The lecture to boys would go something like this: 'Some of you will have noticed that there are pupils in this school who do not look like you. They are called girls and they traditionally wear skirts and blouses rather than trousers and shirts. They do not have dangly bits between their legs but they do have protuberances on their chests. These are called breasts. Your role as boys is to chase girls around the playground but not to catch them. The main difference between the sexes is that whereas you lot like playing with toy cars and guns, the girls like playing with dolls. The second difference is that whereas you don't care what you wear as long as it's scuffed and grubby, girls like nice clothes and shoes. Also, girls like to spend a good deal of time in the lavatories talking about stuff. Girls will still do this when they grow up.'

The lecture to girls would be like this: 'There are pupils in this school who are different to you. They are called boys. They are flat chested but have dangly bits in their shorts. While you and your friends are talking in the lavatories about boys and periods, the boys will be out in the playground playing games which enable them to break windows, tear their clothes and remove the skin from their knees. Boys tend to grow out of these activities when they get older but they are likely to develop an unhealthy interest in cars, sports and alcohol.'

That's it. That's all they need. They'll find out everything else they need to know.

It isn't just schools which have gone potty.

Most big organisations now have gender equality and diversity advisors and a whole host of folk eager to jump down the throats of anyone perceived as being politically incorrect.

Of course you can discriminate as much as you like against English men, especially if they're old. Indeed, you can probably go to prison now if you don't discriminate against older English men.

10

A flock of sheep escaped from their field and were gathered in the lane outside our gate. I had to go down the driveway to retrieve our big, black, plastic bin which the kindly local Non-recyclable Waste Removal Collection Specialist Executives had emptied into their lorry and I discovered that there was a police car parked right on the double yellow lines outside our gate. It took me three months to get the council to paint the yellow lines but no one takes any notice of them because we are right next to the steps down to the beach. Two men in their fifties were standing staring at a piece of road which the sheep had recently occupied. Whenever anything happens there are always two men staring at the place where it happened. I doubt if this pair had ever seen a sheep before. They'd probably tottered round to see what they looked like.

'What are the police doing here?' I asked, mildly curious.

'Dunno,' replied one of the men.

'Maybe they're here for the sheep,' I said. 'Perhaps the sheep are down on the beach making sand castles and the police are rounding them up. I don't think unattended sheep are allowed on the beach during the summer months.'

The man thought for a moment. 'Oh no,' he said at last. 'I don't think it would be that.' He and his pal gave me a funny look and wandered off.

I looked around for the police officers who had parked their car across our gate. Eventually I found one. She was wearing a bullet, knife and bomb proof waistcoat in the way that even rural police officers do these days and she looked so full of self-importance that I thought she might burst and make a mess all over the neighbourhood.

I politely asked if she was in any way associated with the police car parked on our yellow lines. She wanted to know why I was asking. I explained that the car was blocking our gateway. She asked if I wanted to get a car in or out. I said I might. She said she would have to consult her partner and see what he thought about moving the car. I said fine. She went away and consulted her partner. She came back, looking crosser and even fuller of self-importance, got into the car (which I was surprised to see they had left unlocked) and moved it away from our gateway.

I waved a hand in thanks, took the bin back in and relocked and bolted the gate.

I always feel more comfortable when the gate is firmly bolted and locked. I don't know why, except that I like to keep the world shut out. I feel happier that way.

We recently bought an iPad stand so that we could record YouTube videos without having to balance the camera on a pile of books and two umbrellas (don't ask).

Here are the instructions which came with the stand:

'Twist the adjustable valve to assemble the console bracket, then fixed the adjustable valve. User could adjust the angle of console with the adjustable valve. Open the bracket lock and Place the console on the bracket also lock fixed, then fasten the bracket lock until the console can be fixed to live. Fixator clip is adjustable According to the Tablet PC thickness.'

Brilliant. I read it three times and had a dizzy attack.

11

The millennials and the Corbynistas are again insisting that they don't want any more austerity. They want the nation to spend,

spend, spend. They want free money, lots of holidays and as little work as possible.

Those of us with brains have frowned on this Pools Winner mentality.

We have argued that Britain owes so much money that it has to start cutting the national debt – otherwise today's children, teenagers and self-styled millennials, will pay a heavy price.

But, you know what?

Bugger it.

As I have already said, old farts like me have favoured austerity because we know that in 40 to 50 years there will be absolutely no money at all for pensions, health care, education or any public services.

Britain will not be able to borrow any money because our debts will be unpayable.

Taxes will soar.

The fact is that we know that without austerity, Britain faces a bleak future.

But I'm fed up with fighting for austerity.

Fuck 'em.

Let the stupid millennials and Corbynistas have their spend, spend, spend policies.

They will be the ones who will pay the price.

I'm fed up with being 'sensible' and trying to protect a generation which is too stupid to care about its own future.

So, let's spend, spend, spend.

This will be a GOOD thing for most of us old farts.

As soon as the madness starts, interest rates will soar and the pound will collapse.

Our £1000 in the building society will pay us £100 in interest, instead of 50 pence.

Great. That will be nice.

And the millennials will find themselves paying 10% to 20% on a mortgage loan, a car loan or a loan to have more tattoos done.

Since most millennials assume that interest rates will always be in low, single figures this will come as something of a shock to the little buggers.

But we old farts won't care. Most old farts are lenders and not borrowers.

And when the spending starts, and austerity is brushed aside, we will be big winners.

So – bring it on!

I just became a Corbyinsta and a self-appointed honorary Millennial.

12

I keep thinking that things can't get any worse in Paris and then they do.

Our bank in France, Barclays, is now refusing to reply to my emails because they say they won't accept my email address. They will only ring me on phone numbers which are at least 10 years out of date. They are therefore leaving messages about my account with complete strangers who now have those numbers. They insist on writing to an address which is 12 years old.

I have repeatedly given them up-to-date information but they won't change any of the wrong information until I send them a gas bill which has our address printed on it. I sent them what I had but they demand a proper printed bill which contains my name, the address and the date. I can't send them a proper bill, the sort which they send through the post, because I don't get those now. The energy company insists on sending our bills by email.

So in the end I sent them a gas bill for a house in England, though that could have been someone else with the same name and they really wouldn't know. When I rang and managed to get through, they said that they would now post me a form to fill in and a password so that I could change my address and phone numbers.

I don't have a Barclays branch to go to in Paris because a year or two ago, without asking, they put me onto an internet/phone banking system but never bothered to explain how to use it. Nor did they send me any of the codes they now say I need. They keep telling me to use it but I can't.

I have wasted days of my life dealing with this nonsense.

13

I read an awful story about a man who was arrested because he was foolish enough to criticise the number of Muslim immigrants while talking to a customer.

Instead of just walking away, the customer complained about the conversation to the police. The police then arrested the man and took him to court where he was fined and told to pay £50 to the man who had complained, though whether this was to soothe his hurt feelings or to reward him for being a snitch I do not know.

Meanwhile, the police appear to have so far allowed Muslim men to rape at least 47,000 young, English girls (many Muslims regard white girls as a disposable commodity to do with what they will) and have done nothing in order not to cause offence to the immigrant community.

The Labour Party, exhibiting a rare degree of cowardice, seems to be so desperate to avoid being accused of being racist that it is keen to avoid offering any criticism of the responsible Muslims. Muslim rapists must apparently be left alone for the sake of community cohesion.

I don't understand why the police who decided not to charge the rapists have not been charged with a race crime for treating Muslims differently to Christians. Shouldn't they be charged with aiding and abetting the rapists?

We are accustomed to the police ignoring attacks on old people but it seems a bit thick that they ignore attacks on young girls simply because they are white.

In Dubai, on the other hand, the authorities arrested a British man, confiscated his passport and threatened him with three years in jail for accidentally touching a local man in a bar while taking a drink back to his table.

And in the UK, it is apparently illegal to point out that the massive, unexpected sudden influx of people has created all sorts of problems with health care, roads, education and housing.

The sale of our Paris apartment seems to have hit a snag. We should have signed the initial contract by now but our notaire says it will take another 2-3 weeks.

After some chasing, I discovered that part of the problem was that our notaire has taken five weeks to do what I would have thought any sensible person could do in five minutes. In France, the notaires are really just conveyancing clerks but they consider

235

themselves terribly important, have big, gold plaques outside their offices and call themselves maître.

The rest of the problem is caused by the fact that our buyer keeps disappearing for days or weeks at a time. We are told that no one knows where he goes.

And there is now some talk a translator may be necessary at a fee of 600 euros (over £500) for an hour. That works out at slightly more than £1,000,000 a year which seems a trifle on the steep side, though I realise that is probably what the EU pays its 12 million translators.

The French are impossible. If they can make things impossibly difficult they will. The delays are making it difficult and harder emotionally because I have enjoyed the apartment very much and we had many good times there.

Our buyer seems keen to delay everything.

Buying and selling property is, in my experience, always a nightmare; it is always made worse by obstructive, uncaring and incompetent professionals.

Buying and selling abroad is a double nightmare because of the language, currency and foreign bureaucracy and tax issues. The fees all these people charge are out of this world.

The one thing the French do well is to cheat.

After the end of today's Tour de France, the commissars punished two riders for taking drink bottles near to the finish. There is a rule about this since crowds mean that it is difficult for all team cars to be available to provide liquid support. Unfortunately, it was subsequently pointed out that the winner of the race, a Frenchman, had also taken an illegal drink bottle. However, instead of punishing him (and taking the stage win from him) the commissars simply removed the punishments from the other two riders.

Drug taking seems fairly uncontroversial compared to this sort of official cheating.

14

Our helium balloons are still wandering around, wafted hither and thither by every little draught. After considerable experimentation, we discovered that weighing them down with four plastic soldiers (one with the base cut off) and eight and a half sticker fixers worked perfectly.

The balloons then wander about the house.

We would be sitting having dinner, when the balloon would float into the room, hang around for a while, and then float out again. Sometimes it floated upstairs. Sometimes it hung around on the stairs. Sometimes it wandered around downstairs.

It is much more fun than tying it down with a heavy weight or fixing it to a drawer handle.

After lunch, I read that a female MP is in terrible trouble for using the phrase 'nigger in the woodpile'. The Green half-wits are hysterical. Women with their babies hanging on their chests are jumping up and down in an uncontrollable fury. The babies are probably feeling sick.

If the phrase had been used by a black man, it would have been acceptable. Isn't that racist? Actually, if a black man called the white MP a 'white honky bitch' that would be fine and if she complained, the police would probably arrest her for wasting police time.

15

The new French President, Macron, celebrated his recent win to the sound of Ode to Joy – the EU's anthem – rather than the French anthem. Macron, a thoroughbred fascist, likes to think of himself as a liberal democrat. But like all those of his ilk he sneers at populists (who are really offering what the people want).

Macron's first action was to announce a centralised tax and spend account for the EU – a new Finance Ministry for Hitler's dream: the United States of Europe. Macron wants to hand over Europe's democracy to a self-selected group of elite eurocrats.

It is, in my view, no exaggeration to say that Macron is Europe's new Hitler; he is the most dangerous leader to rise to the top of the European cesspit since Adolf attempted to turn Europe into Germany's Empire.

Like his hero, the EU founder, Macron believes that he knows best how to organise society. He wants to engineer the EU so that everyone can live in and enjoy his idea of the perfect state. He does not approve of vulgar individualism or freedom. He believes in the superiority of the French intellectual and so supposes that we will all be better off if we just stand aside and allow him to design and run the new United States of Europe.

If the new President has his way, France will soon disappear completely – lost in the new European superstate.

I wonder what the enthusiastic Macronites will think of that when they wake up and realise what is happening.

The Nazis who created the EU must be pinching themselves – unable to believe their luck. The loathsome Macron, a former banker, has sold his country to the Nazi legacy and is channelling the man whose dream was to see Germany control Europe. It is true that Charlemagne and Napoleon both dreamt of a united Europe. But their vision of a European state was quite different. They envisaged a Europe controlled by France. Macron is fighting for an EU state which will be run by Germany.

Macron is, presumably, unaware that the euro was designed to fit Germany's purposes and that it is, as a result, destroying France. France hasn't had a positive trade balance since 1997. Since then Germany has repeatedly recorded huge trade surpluses. Gosh. I wonder why that could be.

British Remainers should now be grateful to those of us who chose to leave the EU and they should work with us to escape the EU's evil clutches. The Liberal Democrats and war criminals such as Blair should be bowing down to the UKIP members who worked so hard to win the Brexit vote.

The fact is that only the most fascist of the Remainers will still support the EU; and they will doubtless be practising their 'Heil Hitler' salutes. Most Remainers are thick (Lamy, Abbott and Clegg) or criminal (Blair).

I am appalled by the fact that John Bercow, the appalling speaker of the House of Commons, has made no secret of the fact that he is a Remain supporter. The Speaker of the House of Commons is supposed to be neutral. Bercow should be fired but he won't be.

It is pertinent to point out that the vast majority of people who still want us to stay in the EU wanted us to join the euro.

There's really no need to say anything else, is there?

British political life is now dominated by some curious people.

Every time I look at the news I see little but the latest views of Allen, Lineker, Bono, a woman who sits in the Lords because she used to present children's TV programmes, a woman who sits in the Lords as a reward for selling bras and David Larmy MP, a former shadow minister of state for culture, who is probably nice and well-meaning but comes across as being a little out of his depth when trying to talk about things with the grown-ups. I really don't wish to be unkind but he, like Abbott and Thornberry are the sort who, if you ran a small shop, you would think long and hard before considering letting them take on any responsibility – such as stacking the shelves. 'No, Emily, the tins of sardines all go on that shelf and the tinned pears go on that other shelf.'

Meanwhile, over in France, I wonder if French voters will realise what's happening.

If they don't then the ghosts of Adolf Hitler and his evil chums will be dancing for joy (to the sound of Ode to Joy). The Nazis who devised the EU will be enjoying one wet dream after another now that Macron has handed them France on a plate.

Macron, surely as smarmy a little git as ever stood on the top step, is a traitor to France and to all those Britons and Americans who gave their lives defending France against the Nazis.

Meanwhile, we should ask ourselves how it came about that Macron ended up in the Elysee Palace.

A few weeks ago, the polls showed that the French were even more anti-EU than the British. A vast majority wanted to exit the EU, leave the euro and reclaim the French Franc.

The EU was in full panic mode. If the French had chosen to leave the EU then the eurocrats would have been out of work – unemployed, unwanted on voyage or anywhere else.

But on election night, the French voters chose a man who wants France to disappear still further into the maw of the evil European Union.

Puzzling, eh?

Am I the only person on the planet who is just a tad suspicious of this unbelievable result?

Surely, there couldn't have been a fiddle?

Or is it possible that the EU was terrified of losing another nation from its portfolio?

Would the crooks at the EU really stoop so low as to impede the democratic process by rigging a vote result?

Of course they bloody well would.

16

Chris Froome, the cyclist, is again being booed by the French who cannot bear the fact that they haven't had a winner of the Tour de France for 29 years since the glory days of Bernard Hinault and the best of them all, Laurent Fignon.

Later, I read that Squadron Leader George 'Johnny' Johnson was recently awarded the MBE in the Queen's birthday honours list. Squadron Leader Johnson is the sole surviving British Dambuster.

Two thoughts.

First, why has it taken so long to reward a man who took part in one of Britain's most famous (and war-changing raids)? The Dambuster raid gave Britain hope and did enormous damage to the German war machine. Our morale was boosted and their morale was damaged. Guy Gibson, who led the raid, played a vital part in helping Churchill bring America into the Second World War.

Second, why did the Queen give him a measly MBE?

These days any drug soaked professional athlete who wins a medal at the Olympics gets a knighthood. And the world of show business is full to the brim with tax exiled actors and singers who have been knighted for services to themselves.

In truth, the whole honours system has long passed its sell-by-date.

Why did Rod Stewart or Mick Jagger get knighthoods?

I am so disgusted that I have decided that everyone I know is now Sir.

The Government and the Queen should give awards to life-boatmen and others who do stuff, not for money or publicity, but because they believe it is the right thing to do and they want to help their community.

Just as potty, incidentally, is the business of universities handing out honorary degrees.

Most universities now give out honorary degrees to pop singers, politicians and wealthy businessmen and women who can be relied upon to make a financial donation.

This is the same the whole word over. For example, Bill Cosby, the American comedian, is alleged to have been given over 100 honorary degrees.

Daft.

17

We tried out our new two-way radios at last.

My call sign is Danny Boy and Antoinette is Broadsword.

We borrowed the call signs from that marvellous film, *Where Eagles Dare* which is one of my favourite war movies. We watch it from time to time and imagine that all the Germans who are shot are really French.

I wandered down towards the beach to try out the radios.

'Danny Boy calling Broadsword,' I said, in my very best Richard Burton voice (in the film I think he was Broadsword but it really doesn't matter).

'Broadsword to Danny Boy,' said Antoinette.

The radio was remarkably clear, though I was only a couple of hundred yards away.

We then had a silly pseudo-military conversation and finished with me saying: 'Wilko. Roger and out.'

As I put my radio back into my pocket, I saw a small group of holidaymakers staring at me.

'It's a military exercise,' I explained. 'I work for MI6 and we're preparing for a possible invasion by EU forces.'

They stared at me.

'But please don't tell anyone I told you this,' I said earnestly. 'Or we'll all get into terrible trouble.'

'We won't tell a soul,' whispered a woman in a blue anorak. She was carrying one of those blue metal walking sticks and had a matching blue rucksack on her back.

I thanked her and marched back to the house in my best military style.

18

Our new toys (aka two-way radio sets) are unlike mobile phones in that they don't ring to let you know that the user of the other radio wants to speak. I still haven't got used to the fact that the radio will suddenly start to talk to me without warning.

Today, I was sitting on a bench in the garden when it appeared that the ground under the bench was talking to me. I had placed my two-way radio on the grass underneath the bench and suddenly Antoinette's voice came out of the earth. It scared me half to death.

19

A bloke I know rang me. He told me in precise and painful detail every symptom and every sign of ill health he had enjoyed in the previous six months. Then, after 35 minutes, he slowed, empty of ammunition. 'Well, that's about it,' he said. 'I don't think there is anything else to tell you. Bye.'

And he rang off.

Not a 'how is Antoinette?', 'how are you?' or a 'do you have any news?' or even a 'did you enjoy hearing about my piles?'

I sometimes think I'm a bit odd.

But, to be honest, I often think other people are even odder.

Talking of nuts, our hazel bushes are already laden with hazel nuts. The squirrels are already busy picking and burying. The nuts aren't properly ripe but the squirrels don't seem to mind in the slightest. A nut is a nut is a nut is a nut is a nut as Gertrude would have doubtless said.

20

A friend of mine was looking forward to watching the Open Golf Championship on the television and had rather trustingly taken a week off work so that he could watch the tournament on television. But oddly, however, the BBC isn't showing the world's premier golf tournament this year, or any other year. Golf, like cricket, motor racing and horse racing are all regarded as too much enthusiasms for middle class, white males.

Still, I gather that the BBC will instead be showing women's rugby. That will doubtless be a joy for some.

A friend of mine who is a great rugby fan says he is unable to watch any sort of rugby on television. The organisers are apparently so greedy that in addition to making millions from the gate, and millions more from the TV rights and sponsorship and from selling advertising on the players' shirts, on the referee and on the grass, insist on setting up moving advertising boards around the touchline. These move about constantly, causing headaches and nausea.

Showing the women's rugby will doubtless gather the BBC brownie points from those who favour political correctness over all else and may help deflect some of the criticism currently directed at the BBC now that it has been shown to pay some of its female employees far less than it pays male employees doing pretty much the same jobs.

Meanwhile, anyone who pays the extortionate BBC licence fee in the vain hope that they might be able to watch Britain's cultural and sporting year highlights must again be disappointed.

The fee for a licence to watch television is now £145 (paid exclusively to the biased and prejudiced State broadcaster, the BBC, a propaganda broadcaster in the worst traditions of the USSR, a proven sexist and ageist organisation and one which is in my view both racist and treacherous) and the maximum fine for not buying the licence is £1,000 with costs. Those struggling to pay the £145 cannot, of course, afford to pay the £1,000 and so they, poor devils, must go to jail at great expense to the taxpayers.

Some might think these rather reasonable odds since if the wretched TV licensing gestapo bang on your door you are under no obligation to open it and let them in and unless they actually see or hear you watching television, I don't think they can do much about it.

Sensible people have for decades argued that the BBC licence fee is an absurd anachronism. And even insensible people have long realised that not paying the licence fee should be a civil rather than a criminal offence.

I notice, by the way, that although the BBC is a firm proponent of the climate change myth, it still sells its overpriced DVDs (programmes for which we have already paid) wrapped in two layers of plastic and one of cardboard. Indeed, I rather suspect that some of the series it sells on four DVDs could be fitted onto two disks or even one disk – thereby saving even more of our planet and reducing the Corporation's carbon footprint considerably. Indeed, if they used both sides of each disk (as some companies do) the BBC could save even more material, weight and production costs.

Still, we must not confuse 'saying' with 'doing', must we?

And we can add hypocrisy to the list of charges to lay against the BBC.

21

1973 seems a long time ago.

It was the year when VAT was first introduced in Britain.

Pink Floyd released 'The Dark Side of the Moon'.

Edward Heath was Prime Minister.

£20 million in compensation was paid to thalidomide victims.

The IRA conducted a bombing campaign in London.

Pay rises were limited to 7% and inflation reached as high as 24%

Coal shortages led to the introduction of the three day working week.

And it was the year that I first started writing about benzodiazepines – and warning that they were dangerously addictive drugs.

In 1973, I edited the *British Clinical Journal* and published a leading symposium dealing with the addictive problems of benzodiazepine tranquillisers.

In the 1970s and the 1980s, I wrote hundreds of articles about benzodiazepine tranquillisers and sleeping tablets. I made countless television programmes. I wrote three books about addiction. I made a series of radio programmes which were broadcast nationally on the BBC local radio network. I set up a help group for tranquilliser addicts. I produced a newsletter containing information and advice about benzodiazepines.

Throughout those two decades, I was violently opposed by members of the BMA and the RCGP who insisted (contrary to all the evidence) that drugs such as Ativan and Valium were perfectly safe and not in the slightest bit addictive.

And all the time I was receiving letters from patients telling me that these drugs had ruined their lives. The phrase I heard time and time again was; 'I have been to hell and back'. For years my mail from readers was delivered in grey Royal Mail sacks. Patients were numb when they were on the drugs. And they were in torment when they tried to stop them.

The size of the problem has been consistently underestimated. When my book *Life Without Tranquillisers* smashed into the *Bookseller* and *Sunday Times* bestseller lists in 1985 many were astonished because, for the first time, it became clear that the issue was one which concerned many people.

But then, in 1988, there was a breakthrough.

The medical establishment still insisted that benzodiazepines were perfectly safe but the Government took action and told GPs that benzodiazepines should not be prescribed for patients for longer than two to four weeks because of the risk of addiction.

'Dr Vernon Coleman's articles, to which I refer with approval, raised concern about these important matters,' said Edwina Currie, British Parliamentary Secretary for Health in the House of Commons in 1988.

I helped launch a massive lawsuit which had to be abandoned when legal aid was withdrawn and patients were warned (by one of the drug companies involved) that if they lost the case they would risk losing their homes. The letters were aggressive, terrifying and effective.

With surprising naivety I thought we'd won.

Sadly, doctors took no notice. GPs were as addicted to prescribing the drugs as patients were addicted to taking them. One generation of doctors retired only for another to appear and to adopt the same egregious prescribing habits. Benzodiazepines have been prescribed for every ailment known to man or woman.

And in 2011, it was revealed that in Britain a staggering 11.5 million prescriptions a year were still being written for benzodiazepine tranquillisers. And over a third of those prescriptions were for more than eight weeks supply.

Here is what I wrote in my book *Doctors and Nurses Kill More People than Cancer*:

'Any doctor who signs a prescription for a benzodiazepine (such as Valium) for more than two weeks is not fit to practise medicine and would, if the General Medical Council did what it is supposed to do, be struck off the medical register. It annoys me intensely that patients who have become addicted to these wretched drugs should be ignored by the NHS whereas whingeing idiots who take drugs such as heroin and cocaine for entertainment are, when they moan about their inevitable condition and demand treatment, instantly provided with vast amounts of support. For the record, benzodiazepines are considerably more addictive than any of the so-called recreational drugs.'

And still nothing has changed.

Doctors (mainly GPs) are still handing out prescriptions for these deadly drugs as if they were sweets.

This is the medical horror story of this century and last century. It is the most disgraceful medical scandal of modern times. It is the biggest addiction problem Britain has ever known. It is no exaggeration to say that these drugs have caused endless misery and undying pain; they have ruined millions of lives.

That is not rhetoric or exaggeration. It's fact. Benzodiazepines have ruined millions of lives. And those who created the pain still refuse to accept responsibility.

And no one in the Government, the NHS, the BMA or the RCGP seems to give a damn.

Oh, there is some modest concern.

Committees have been set up. Enquiries have been initiated. People from the Department of Health, the BMA and the RCGP have sat around tables and talked about the problem for years.

But they have, grossly misunderstood the nature of the problem, and they have underestimated the size of it.

Worse still, they seem to regard benzodiazepine addiction as being in the same category as heroin addiction or cocaine addiction. Those who are hooked on tranquillisers are blamed for their addiction as if they were in some way responsible for their circumstances.

Let us be crystal clear about this: anyone who has, since 1988, been prescribed benzodiazepine drugs for more than two to four weeks, has been betrayed by their doctor.

Any doctor who has prescribed these drugs for longer than a month, or has made them available on repeat prescription, should be struck off the medical register and banned from practising medicine.

It is, perhaps, possible to claim that doctors who mis-prescribed the drugs prior to 1988 were simply ignorant buffoons. Many could claim, with some justification, that their patients asked for the drugs. The BMA and the RCGP were roundly condemning me for drawing attention to the addictive nature of the drugs and so it was relatively easy for doctors to say 'Oh, that fellow Coleman is talking nonsense – the BMA says benzodiazepines are perfectly safe'.

But things changed in 1988.

Since the Government warned doctors not to prescribe these drugs for more than two to four weeks, the rules have been different.

Doctors are now completely responsible for the biggest addiction problem this country has ever seen. This is a far bigger problem than barbiturate addiction or other prescription drug addictions.

One Minister after another has promised help. Every promise has turned to dust.

The time for committees and discussion groups is long past. It is obscene that the BMA should now offer a view on what needs to be done. It is moderately pleasing only that the BMA and the RCGP now seem to understand that there is a problem.

But there is no need for more talk or more research. Dr Johnson talked about people being 'encumbered with help' and he could have been writing about the people still running campaigns to reinvent the wheel.

The patients who are still addicted to benzodiazepines need help now.

And doctors who are still prescribing these damned drugs without any understanding of the consequences need to be punished.

The BMA and the RCGP cannot be allowed to get away with blaming patients for taking these drugs for long periods of time.

Doctors, and only doctors, are to blame for this appalling state of affairs. (Though I confess I do sometimes wonder why so many people still willingly take them for such long periods. The evidence showing that these drugs are dangerously addictive has been widely available for decades.)

A reader of mine who is the ex-chairman of Oldham Tranx, asked George Roycroft, who is Head of Science and Public Health Policy at the BMA if the BMA might consider setting up some sort of helpline service for benzodiazepine addicts.

Roycroft replied that the BMA did not have the expertise or the resources!

At my request Barry then asked George Roycroft how much money the BMA receives from drug companies in advertising.

Silence.

Well, I can probably make a good guess.

The BMA publishes many journals, including the *British Medical Journal* and the current advertising rate for the BMJ is around £10,000 a page.

I reckon that the BMA (which is actually the official trades union for doctors) receives around £30,000,000 a year from drug companies (including the companies which make benzodiazepines). That is a conservative, low estimate.

BMA members have, through ignorance and incompetence, created this addiction problem.

And it is, therefore, the BMA and its members which have the responsibility to help clear up the mess they have made.

If the BMA does not have the expertise then who has?

The BMA certainly has the resources.

I estimate that since 1988, the BMA has received nearly £1 billion from drug companies – much of it from the makers of benzodiazepine drugs. Many BMA committee members have strong, personal links with drug companies. There are very few doctors in the medical establishment who do not receive drug company funding in one way or another.

(Drug companies buy up doctors with great enthusiasm. When in 1975 I wrote a book called *The Medicine Men*, my first attack on the drug industry, a major drug company offered to pay for me to go on a nationwide tour to talk to doctors! I obviously refused. I am probably one of very few doctors in Britain to have consistently turned down drug company money.)

Those campaigning for and behalf of benzodiazepine addicts should, in my professional view, stop cooperating with the BMA and the RCGP. Nothing good will ever come of it. It is a mistake to think of the BMA as a friend. The BMA is, and always has been, the patients' enemy.

But there is one thing the BMA understands: money.

Energy should be spent on taking legal advice about suing the BMA and its members. I would suggest demanding that the organisation, on behalf of its members, be required to pay £50,000 in compensation to every benzodiazepine addict. That should make a sizeable hole in the BMA's finances. And it might make them think a little about their responsibilities.

There are plenty of legal firms around who eagerly take on class action lawsuits.

The time for discussion and committees is long gone.

The time has come for an all-out war on the BMA, the RCGP and their members.

Doctors still prescribing these drugs for more than two to four weeks should be reported to the GMC.

Doctors, and their representative organisations, have consistently betrayed patients.

It is about time that those responsible for this on-going addiction scandal be required to take responsibility and face the awful consequences of their careless actions.

But that isn't what doctors do.

There was a cartoon in the *Wall Street Journal* a few years ago which I still remember. The cartoon showed a nervous looking patient and a very haughty looking doctor sitting behind a huge desk.

'What you need, Mr Terwilliger, is a bit of human caring; a gentle, reassuring touch; a warm smile that shows concern – all of which, I'm afraid, were not part of my medical training.'

In the old days, these essentials were provided by nurses. Sadly, this no longer happens. Nurses have been pushed (sometimes unwillingly) by ambitious professionals who wish they were doctors and are desperate to be taken more seriously as academics. Listening, soothing brows, holding hands and offering comfort are no longer within the remit of the modern nurse.

Empathy is in very short supply in doctor's surgeries and offices and almost non-existent in clinics and hospitals.

However, nothing will change for one good reason.

The people now campaigning on behalf of benzodiazepine addicts are now part of the problem. They have become entangled with the establishment and they are, I suspect, more interested in claiming grants, having meetings and collecting credit for caring to do anything likely to change the status quo.

22

I put an article entitled *Benzos, the BMA and Betrayal* on my website and it has, with one exception, attracted nothing but complaints and criticism. Some of the complaints have been patronising. Some have simply been rude. And some have managed to be both. My article was intended to be helpful, to provide some vital, historical background and some hints and clues on which way the battle might best be directed.

But it seems that everyone is now an 'expert'. And campaigning for change has become an industry. I suspect there may be grants to be won, advertising to be gained and power to be enjoyed. There is, sadly, very little understanding of how much influence the drug companies have over the medical establishment. Until there is, then nothing useful will happen. The drug industry controls the medical establishment. I've been studying the drug industry since the 60s and, as a result, I have been threatened, libelled, sued, burgled, etc. There is a good deal of innocence and naivety about. It is worth remembering that in order to please the drug industry, the medical establishment has consistently suppressed all alternative remedies – including many which work very well.

There have even been suggestions that the word 'addiction' is now less acceptable than the word 'dependence' to some benzodiazepine addicts.

This is, I fear, a result of a bow in the direction of fashion rather than a result of any scientific thought process.

As I pointed out in my book *Addicts and Addictions* in 1986 (now out of print), when this discussion was first aired, the words 'addiction', 'dependence' and 'habituation' are pretty much interchangeable. Every expert in the world agreed with this then and I believe that all would agree with it now.

Fussing about terminology is as pertinent and helpful as worrying about the colour of the tablets prescribed and is likely to lead only to confusion. It is a pointless distraction.

Since I am the only person whose campaigning has led to any positive and useful change (the legislation of 1988), it seems pertinent to point out that this was done by me working alone and it was done by fighting an all-out battle against the medical profession, the drug industry, governments everywhere and civil servants and bureaucrats. They said nasty things about me. I said nasty things about them. I spent a lot of my own money. I received no grants and no advertising. And after 15 years they rolled over and I won.

Since then, in the aftermath of that judgement, thousands of self-appointed experts, working in hundreds of small groups, organisations and charities, have, for nearly 30 years, cooperated with governments and the medical profession in a search for some sort of further solution to a continuing problem.

They have, predictably, got absolutely nowhere. The medical establishment and the Government are far too influenced by the drug industry to be truly sympathetic to the needs of patients who have been abused and betrayed. Doctors caused this problem and now have a duty to provide real help.

Over the years, I have become accustomed to the fact that so many charities and lobby groups prefer to spend their time fighting one another and arguing about terminology rather than actually dealing with the important issue which they were formed to attack. I spent many years fighting for an end to vivisection and worked, without charge, for many organisations. I gave up working with other organisations when, after a particularly passionate speech at the House of Commons, in which I produced documentary evidence proving that experiments on animals are entirely futile, a representative from an organisation called BUAV stood up and announced that his organisation was campaigning for an improvement in cage sizes for the transport of animals used in experiments.

It is my considered opinion today that most charities and organisations which appear to have been formed to fight for people or animals or whatever, will spend most of their time and money fighting one another and that their primary purpose will not be changing things for the better but merely gaining grant money and more charitable donations. I was once told by an employee of a large organisation which purported to oppose vivisection that the staff there could not support my campaigning for a total end to animal experiments because if animal experiments ended, their charity would have no purpose and they would be out of a job. An employee of an organisation purporting to oppose hunting told me exactly the same thing. It is by no means unknown for well-known charities to give no more than 5% to 10% of the money they receive to the cause for which the donations were intended. The rest goes in salaries, pensions and marketing.

Today's campaigners seem to have lost sight of the wood but prefer to stand around examining the bark of one of the trees. Today, everything is about power and money and the infighting is so ferocious that nothing will ever get done. It's more than a pity, it's a tragedy. I called my article Benzos, the BMA and Betrayal and I intended the betrayal to refer to doctors but actually I think it refers as much as anything to those self-appointed do-gooders who claim to be representing the addicts.

This isn't the first time I have had trouble with activists. Back in the early 1990s, I bought and gave away thousands of copies of my book *Life Without Tranquillisers* and I was patron of a couple of organisations.

Even earlier, back in the early 1980s, I devised a tapering programme designed to help patients wean themselves off their drugs. (At that time there were no low dose pills available and my programme required cutting some tablets up with a knife. Critics complained that the tablets didn't always break neatly and attacked me for that.) A refined version of that programme is now widely accepted and is used by doctors and patients. It has been refined and improved but I am delighted it has been of help.

A group in America who seem to think they have just discovered benzodiazepine addiction have invited me to attend a conference which they seem to think is a unique and original enterprise. They want to discuss the benefits of benzodiazepines and the hazards of using the word 'addiction'.

I think it is far more important to try to persuade patients not to take benzodiazepines – and to understand that any modest short-term benefits are massively outweighed by the vast medium and long-term problems. It is also important to try to stop doctors prescribing them.

There are no benefits to the benzodiazepines as tranquillisers or sleeping tablets.

They undoubtedly have very short-term value in anaesthesia and the treatment of certain brain disorders.

But they have no place in the treatment of patients who are nervous or anxious.

Doctors have to be educated. They have to be trained not to prescribe benzodiazepines in such vast quantities.

And history tells us that will never happen unless doctors are startled, shocked and frightened into changing their ways.

Until more people are prepared to fight the medical profession (which is backed and supported by the drug industry), this problem will never be conquered.

Unfortunately, many of those who have only recently discovered the benzodiazepine disaster, still do not realise just how evil and powerful the drug companies are and how totally they control the medical profession.

However, since I am now too old and too tired to put up with more patronising abuse I will retire from this particular fray and fight other battles.

I will leave the self-appointed experts, who are so eager to battle on in cooperation with the medical profession and the Government, to enjoy their committee meetings (sorry these people don't have meetings. Even when there are only two of them they are in conference) and their neatly printed minutes. Maybe they will eventually succeed in changing the colour of one or two of the most popularly prescribed benzodiazepines.

But that, I am afraid, is all they will succeed in doing.

You don't change the course of a steamship by worrying about the colour the funnel is painted.

23

The council in San Pedro del Pinatar, southern Spain, has issued a decree banning urinating in the sea.

Sensible move but policing that one should be fun.

Of course, the Spanish will probably still allow untreated sewage to be discharged into the sea.

At home, MCC members have been accused of snubbing a women's cricket match at Lords because hardly any of them turned up to watch.

They weren't snubbing the match.

They just knew that the cricket match wouldn't be worth watching.

Women's cricket is inordinately dull unless you can say 'Oh look there is our Thelma – isn't she bowling well?' or 'Doesn't Aunt Betty look good in those blue trousers?' No one who cares about cricket enjoys watching women playing the game, just as no one in their right mind wants to watch women playing football or rugby. It's neither seemly nor appropriate. Why cannot women sports players stick to synchronised swimming and that gymnastics thing they do with a long piece of ribbon? (I harbour the delicious thought that one day a transsexual tennis player, once a competent male amateur, will join the women's tennis tour, win all the money and use the proceeds to change back to his original sex. It would, these days, be politically incorrect for anyone to object.)

The sexist thing about all this is not that no one watches women's cricket. it is that women insist that their form of cricket should receive the same money and publicity as men's cricket. There is no doubt that there is a place for women in cricket for I have yet to meet a man who can make a decent sandwich or bake an edible Victoria sponge and so without women what will happen to those splendid teas in the pavilion which are such an essential part of village cricket?

(I put this last bit in to remind delicate millennial readers what ironic humour looks like. This sort of remark is now outlawed by the thought police who disapprove of any remark which could be construed as desecrating a sacred cow. I am not, by the way, suggesting that women rugby players et al can be likened to sacred cows.)

I used to follow sport in general quite closely.

And I was keen on two sports in particular: cricket and Formula I motor racing.

For the last decade, however, I have realised that in both sports the in-fighting and politics are far more fun than their sports. Both sports are dying but just haven't realised it yet. Financial greed has done for them because the administrators have, in both cases, sold the rights to satellite television rather than terrestrial television. The result? Dramatically falling viewing figures and little interest among the next generation. What a surprise.

Both sports also seem to be doing everything they can think of to discourage fans. Formula 1 lost fans because instead of a showcase for talent it became a playground for an endless train of plug-in drivers with interchangeable skills and personalities driving round and round circuits without boundaries. Instead of any sense of wonderment, there is now only a sense of 'so what' and 'I could do that'. Formula 1 has now decided to put metal protective shields over the drivers. They are doing this not because it is really necessary but because they can, and the organisers are frightened that if they don't do everything they can then, if there is a freak accident and someone is injured, they will be liable.

Seriously, it won't be long before drivers are done away with completely. If motor racing continues, it will be done with radio controlled cars 'driven' from the pits. To be honest, they might as well do that now since the engineers in the pits can control many things on the cars. Controlling the steering would require little extra effort on their part.

The sport has had its day; killed not by the politically correct who consider it outdated but by the fact that it has become extremely dull, monotonous and soporific. I doubt if anyone will be watching in a decade's time.

Cricket is also moribund and the MCC, once the world's premier cricket club, is now an administration club not a cricket club. It is also very politically correct, making a huge fuss of women's cricket, which no one watches. (As I have already pointed out, watching women play cricket is about as popular as watching men making jam.)

I found the other day that the MCC now has eight members of staff with incomes between 100 and 200 k plus pension funds and there is £29 million in cash in the bank. In 2012, the MCC spent £10,589,000 on administration and £11,056,000 on cricket. In 2016, the MCC spent £12,773,000 on administration and £8,624,000 on cricket. That suggests to me that the MCC is now not a cricket club but an administration club.

As a matter of principle, I have for 40 years always voted against anything the Committee recommended. I have never felt I made a mistake in so doing.

24

I spent several miserable hours trying to find out why Barclays bank has not still changed my address (as I asked them to do nearly two months ago).

My relationship with them has become entirely Kafkaesque.

I have spoken to numerous members of staff on the telephone.

They now won't change my address until I email them photographs of a variety of documents. The words 'uncaring' and 'indifferent' are far too generous.

They still want a gas bill for the French apartment and won't accept the emailed account I sent. They demanded a paper bill which I can't send because I don't get one. They did accept a gas bill for an English address but they want more.

They still won't email me or telephone me because they won't accept the email address and telephone number I give them until I have changed my street address which they won't let me do.

Instead, they prefer to keep on file a street address which is around 10-years-old and a phone number which is so old and out-of-date that I can't remember ever having used it.

In order to protect my privacy, they are still sending bills to old addresses and leaving messages for me at old telephone numbers.

Conversations with the bank staff were limited by the fact that I insist on speaking in English and although they have an English department, the people who staff it don't speak English terribly well.

So, for example, I had some difficulty explaining what is meant by the phrase 'direct debit'.

Eventually, they said again they would post me a special, very secret, password so that I could open an internet account. They said I wouldn't have to sign for the secret password since it would just come in the ordinary post.

When it comes, I can pop it on the internet for there is, I gather, now an App available wherein the innocent and naïve can store all their passwords online. I have no doubt that for safety and security, they also recommend putting your purse or wallet out on the garden wall when you go to bed at night.

25

My book listing my favourite 100 English heroes attracts constant criticism. Another reader has written attacking me for including Winston Churchill and Elizabeth I.

Both had their faults (who doesn't except for my critic) but how could anyone produce a list of England's greatest 100 and not include them?

26

Michael Spurr, the head of Britain's prison and probation service received a bonus of between £15,000 and £20,000 to pad out his inadequate £160,000 salary in 2016. The bonus was awarded after jails in England and Wales were described as 'unacceptably violent and dangerous' by the chief inspector of prisons.

Now, I know what I've been doing wrong all my life.

Can anyone explain why we pay for free internet access but we pay more if we use it?

I can only assume that the phone company's definition of the word 'free' is rather different to my own, rather old-fashioned definition.

27

A few days ago, Antoinette decided that she wanted to try some macaroni cheese. It was, she said, one of her favourite meals when she was small.

Today, she put opened a can of the stuff and put it into a saucepan on the stove. Minutes later, she came running into the conservatory where I was sitting asking me in between retches to get rid of the macaroni quickly because the smell was making her ill.

The macaroni cheese looks horrid and smells disgusting. If the Germans had used this stuff they could have got people to admit to anything. If they used this instead of beetles and bits of snake on

'I'm a Celebrity Get Me Out Of Here' they would have minor celebrities fleeing the jungle in droves.

I see that Panorama is going to run a programme next week explaining how Prozac makes people violent. I did exactly this on ITV in the early 1990s. I remember it because I was subsequently banned from that television station.

I feel like I am living in a time warp.

28

A five-year-old girl who set up a lemonade stall outside her home in Tower Hamlets (selling lemonade at the princely price of 50 pence a cup) got more than she bargained for when four (count them, four) local council enforcement officers approached her, took pictures (which, in view of her age, I would have thought would have got them into trouble with the police) and read her a statement telling her that because she didn't have a trading permit she would have to pay a fine of £150.

Barking.

Where do they find these idiotic people? There are so many of them about that I suspect the EU is breeding them in a disused mineshaft somewhere deep in Poland.

29

The threats from the EU are becoming nastier and nastier. There are tales of Brits being forced to wait four hours to have their passports checked at airports in Europe (even though we are, of course, still members of the EU) and these have led even more people to announce that they want to stay in the EU.

I feel ashamed.

Instead of waving two fingers at the EU, the Remainers are grovelling and increasingly desperate for a second referendum so that they can show their affection for Hitler.

If the Remainers had been around when Hitler invaded Poland they would have bowed down to Hitler and the Poles would all be speaking German.

The joke these days, of course, is that it is pitifully possible for outsiders to buy EU passports and if Remainers really want to keep their EU passports, they will not find it difficult.

Cyprus is an EU member state and has earned more than four billion euros in the last four years from flogging passports to crooks, money launderers and terrorists. They don't sell passports per se, of course, but they sell citizenship to philanthropic folk who want to buy property in Cyprus. And then you get the passport.

Still, it is not widely realised that the passport game is global these days.

You can buy access to the US for $500,000. The Americans flog around 10,000 visas a year. Another country which does well out of the passport game is Dominica which flogs 2,000 passports a year for a minimum of $100,000 a pop.

30

Senior members of the medical profession have at last expressed fears about the fact that statins are being given to everyone over 50 who is strong enough to swallow a pill.

I first warned about the risks associated with these drugs in 1995.

Maybe I'm stuck on Groundhog Day.

31

I spent an hour listening to Test Match Special on a chum's wireless set. What an utter disappointment.

Brian Johnson, arguably the best known and best loved of all British sports commentators, used to say that when commentating he used to pretend that he was talking to a blind friend who was sitting beside him and needed a running account of what was happening. He called upon summarisers and statisticians for support. He gave the score and details regularly and whenever you tuned in you knew within five minutes what had happened and what was happening in the day's play. Listeners felt that they were eavesdropping on a private conversation among cultured experts.

I have listened to this programme since I was a boy. The commentators were summer friends. I have made radio and television programmes while having an earpiece in – not so that I could listen to the director but so that I could listen to Test Match Special.

Today was a disaster.

After listening to meaningless, pointless, humourless drivel for half an hour, I still didn't know who was playing, where they were playing or what the score was. When a batsman was dismissed, I was not told what he had scored. Maybe it was me. Perhaps I was distracted by the sun shining or the grass growing. It seemed to me to be like listening to an endless parade of selfies. I switched off the radio, found the score from the internet, realised I really didn't care anymore and then did something else.

The commentators seemed too pleased with themselves to bother commentating. And the magic had gone completely. There was far too much coy, self-conscious awareness of the audience. The commentators, some of whom were definitely still millennials in spirit if not in body, talked endlessly about themselves, interrupting one another occasionally to mention, en passant, that a cricket match was being played in the background. Giving the score, and details of what was happening, seemed to them to be an irritation. It really was the radio equivalent of an album of selfies. I was not surprised to hear that Henry Blofeld, the idiosyncratic doyen of cricket commentators, has been told that he won't be needed in future. I bet this is true. If so then I suspect that Blofeld's fault was simple: he actually told listeners what was happening on the pitch.

Cricket commentaries in particular have lost their way and are rather pointless. But sports commentaries in general are poor too. The problem is that stations insist on hiring former practitioners of the sport in question instead of professional communicators.

Our French buyer is allegedly on holiday. But a character of the same name is a guitarist who is on tour in the U.S. I have asked our agent if this is the buyer but I have received no reply.

August

1

It was back in the late 18th century that Henry Bate Dudley, the founder of the *Morning Post* newspaper, realised that his readers wanted more than straightforward news from his paper. He filled the columns with reviews, sport, poetry, anecdotes, gossip and smut. He suddenly started to make huge profits and launched a second paper called the *Morning Herald*.

And so British newspaper journalism was changed for ever.

All other newspapers had to adapt or die.

And so they printed scandals – the activities of the royals and the rich, their divorces, their arguments, their affairs, their gambling losses. The demi-monde loved the publicity with shamelessness and their fame delighted the rich and the wealthy and the powerful such as the Prince of Wales who also became part of the game.

And so today's nonsense is nothing new.

The broadsheets pretend to look askance at the red top tabloids but they are just as bad. I have met hundreds, if not thousands, of journalists over the years and I reckon that whereas some of the nicest and most honourable people I've ever met were tabloid journalists, many of the nastiest, greediest, most devious and least honourable people I've ever met were broadsheet journalists. For the record, television journalists, editors and producers are even worse than broadsheet journalists. Many are ruthless and untrustworthy while also managing to be sanctimonious.

The only difference today is that newspapers and magazines have stopped printing news or information at all. Now all they print is gossip and opinion pieces (mainly written by 20-year-olds) masquerading as news.

In the distant old days, reporters (whether working for print or broadcast media) used to report the news. Now, all reporters want to do is share their opinions and so it is impossible to find any truths. Millennials readily admit that they do not care a jot for editorial integrity or objectivity.

In the Cotswolds, our squirrels have eaten into the large, plastic box where we keep the sunflower seeds. No sunflower seeds were available so I bought four large bags of sunflower hearts at Holland Barratt health food store

I read today that it is now quite common for large companies to employ Chief Happiness Officers. These are employed, apparently, to satisfy the demands of millennials who worry that without help they will miss out on some of the happiness to which they are entitled.

Gee whiz.

2

I spotted four strange news stories which typify the world in 2017.

First, it has now become popular to put pre-school children into retirement homes so that the decrepit old folk therein will benefit from the association.

The idea is that the oldsters play games with the children and thereby regain their youthful attitudes.

This, surely, is the most utterly patronising idea of all time.

The residents of retirement homes need to be treated with respect not humiliated in this grotesque way. But these days respect is as rare as discretion, courage, patriotism, integrity and common sense. (There is also no sense of history – but that is the result of the EU which has spent billions of our money brainwashing children and students into ignoring their nation's history.)

The woeful morons who thought this one up should be executed for initiating a crime against humanity.

Second, Britain's tax collectors, HMRC, are now charging small businesses a penalty of 30% if they fail to pay enough tax because the taxman has failed to ask for enough money. According to the taxman, small business owners now have a responsibility to check the taxman's calculations and to notify the authorities if a mistake has been made.

This is utter madness. It provides HMRC with a clear incentive to get bills wrong. Theoretically, the taxman could under bill every small business and then claim an extra 30% on every bill. And, as thousands of unhappy taxpayers can confirm, getting things wrong is something of a speciality of HMRC. Indeed, a judge recently decided that HMRC could 'challenge tax calculations that relied on its own algorithms'. It was ruled that users of tax computation software could 'not rely on its results' even though the specifications for the software had been provided by HMRC. So, the staff of HMRC can now make as many mistakes as they like without being held responsible.

Third, I read about a man who cuts his lawn six times a week. His life is clearly both a very full one and a very empty one.

Finally, it has apparently now become quite normal to propose that illegal drugs be decriminalised or legalised. The odd thing is that when I first proposed this around 30 years ago, I was mercilessly attacked for the notion was regarded as something only the devil could possibly endorse.

3

It's Antoinette's birthday so I won't even go to our post box today.

We will not be interrupted by the world.

Both our gates are locked and impenetrable unless we are attacked by a military force equipped with tanks. My mobile telephone is never on. No one has the house telephone number. My iPhone and iPad (which are the only devices which carry emails) have been switched off since the beginning of the week.

Bliss. I may never turn them back on again.

Since it is a special day, our boiler decided to stop working.

It doesn't really matter because we don't need the central heating and we have an immersion heater but since the system is less than a year old and cost about £15,000 (and we already had our own radiators and piping) it is rather annoying to say the least.

We tried undoing the filter in order to see if it was blocked with sludge but I couldn't turn off the taps properly and water poured out soaking us both.

We went and sat on the wooden bench at the bottom of our cliff top garden. The beach was deserted. Not one soul on a mile of beach. For a change, there were no dogs. There are usually two or three noisy, wild looking dogs roaming free with owners nowhere to be seen. We thought we might go for a walk and then realised that the tide was in at the bottom of our cliff. The rest of the beach was empty and our bit was wet. Unless we want to scramble over rocks, we can only walk to the nearby town when the tide is out.

So, instead, we watched the rabbits eating our lawn, our raven sitting on the metal railing which stops us falling into the sea, a thrush and a lady blackbird both looking for worms and one of our resident squirrels. At one point we had three rabbits in view (one just eating and two chasing each other round and round in ever decreasing circles, presumably in some lapine version of a turf war or more hopefully as a prelude to bunny production).

Our rabbits are crepuscular in habit and charming in every way.

I am constantly astonished that the previous owner of this house hired a man to sit in the conservatory and shoot rabbits through the open door. He didn't like the rabbits because they ate things.

Out at sea, the buoys and gulls bounced gently on the breeze driven waves. The sky was a sky of a thousand colours. Antoinette sees the sky as a painter sees it and now, thanks to her eye, I see a whole palette from amethyst to zucchini green.

'No time to turn at Beauty's glance, And watch her feet, how they can dance. A poor life this is if, full of care, we have no time to stand and stare.' Thus wrote W.H.Davies, the Welsh poet tramp.

Davies, incidentally, wrote a number of books but in my view the most moving was the very first diary of his years tramping.

But the best of his books by far was called 'Emma' and was about his young wife.

4

The prospective purchaser of our apartment in Paris is still refusing to fix a date when we can sign the Promesse, the initial part of the sale procedure.

I had suggested September 6th but no one seems prepared to say whether or not the date suits them.

Our notaire wrote to the buyer's notaire a week ago but there is still no reply.

I must say I do love the affectionate way in which notaires write to one another. It all sounds as if it has come from Jane Austen's pen.

Today I suggested to our estate agent that we should show the apartment to other prospective buyers. He says that this is against the law in France. So we are in the absurd position of having received an offer but having to wait for the buyer to decide when, or if, he will agree to take the first formal step. Until he does so, we are prevented from even offering the apartment to anyone else.

I made two huge mistakes right at the start of this fiasco. First, I signed an agreement which didn't have a concluding date on it. Second, I believed the estate agent when he told me that the buyer had the money to buy the apartment. I now don't believe he has the money.

Every piece of legislation in the country favours buyers. This is all very well if you are a buyer, and intend to hold the property you buy for eternity, but anyone who thinks that they might one day want to sell should think twice about purchasing a property in France. And then, having thought twice, they should decide against it.

According to the French, there are 100,000 empty apartments in Paris – all owned by foreigners. The Mayor of Paris has increased taxes to eye watering levels in order to try to force foreigners to sell and leave but the problem is that the capital gains taxes and property legislation introduced by the former President Hollande are so awful that people prefer to pay the local taxes in order to avoid the complexities and costs of selling. Lots of potential sales fall through as a result of boredom or inertia.

Paris has become so unpopular with property buyers that since 2012, the value of property in Paris has fallen by almost a third. Low interest rates mean that property prices just about everywhere in the world have been soaring since the financial crisis of 2008. In London, the value of property has reached absurdly high levels. But the French have shown that they are able to buck the trend simply by introducing daft laws. And as a result of absurd regulations, bureaucracy and new property taxes, the value of property in Paris has declined by a third since 2012. In an era when property prices around the world have been soaring, only the

French could screw things up so well that property prices fall by over 30% in a five year period.

Owners are reluctant to sell (because of the absurd and in some cases probably illegal taxes) and buyers are reluctant to buy because the costs of buying are absurd and they know that one day they too will have to face the problems associated with selling. Not even property developers are interested. And that's why there are 100,000 empty flats in Paris. You'd think there would be someone in the Mayor's office with the brains to see what is wrong. But there isn't. Maybe they need to hire a foreigner with some brains.

It is uncertainty that is the killer.

We also have the problem of what to do with our furniture. The depo vente, from which we bought much stuff, has closed and there are no nearby antique shops to whom to offer it. We tried to get auctioneers to handle it but they did not reply. Our estate agent, who can do snotty well enough to be on the stage, said: 'We have a partnership with Christies, but I don't think there is anything here they would be interested in'. As he said this, he looked around as though he had suddenly found himself in a low level junk shop. Snooty French bastard. I would have thrown him out of the window but the rules against littering are powerful in France.

We decided to go to Paris in the middle of September, hoping to sign the sale agreement. The estate agent has emailed to say that I must give permission if the furniture is to be removed. I emailed back to tell him that nothing is being removed until the final part of the sale has been completed and the money is sitting in our bank account. I don't trust the buyer. In my experience, serious buyers are always eager to get on with things. Our buyer has done everything he can to delay the transaction. And although I was originally told that it was a 'cash' purchase, I now don't believe this. I have a horrible suspicion that we're going to find that our buyer is either a dreamer or a crook.

I read today that in England it is now possible to complete the sale and purchase of a house within four hours. I once managed to buy a property in a week, and I have on several occasions bought properties within less than two weeks of first seeing them. But four hours is pretty sharp.

5

Today I had a letter from Lloyds to say that their overdraft fees are changing.

Now they will charge £7 for every 1p I go overdrawn each day. Or is it the other way round? Not that it makes a lot of difference. It is egregiously greedy either way – especially for a bonus-soaked bank which was bailed out by taxpayers.

So if I borrow £7 for a year they will charge me 365p which is £3.65 which is an usurious rate which would bring a smile to Shylock's face.

This at a time when the bank of England is still refusing to raise interest rates and Lloyds is paying approximately no interest on deposit accounts.

National Savings are now paying 0.01% on investments. That means that if you have £1,000,000 with them you will receive £100 a year in interest. To achieve the national average income of around £25,000, you would need to have £250,000,000 invested. And, to rub salt into the wound, inflation would have eaten huge chunks out of the capital. It is not surprising that politicians and economists are constantly complaining that people aren't saving money any more. Why the hell should they? The incentive now is to spend not to save.

Much of this is, of course, a result of the 2007/8 banking fiasco (made considerably worse by Gordon 'the Moron' Brown). But Lloyds made things considerably worse. The ill-fated takeover of the naughty Scottish HSBO bank trashed the share price and cost shareholders dearly. It was rumoured to have been done at Brown's suggestion and I still believe that. And, of course, Lloyds has been badly run for years. The bank paid out £18 billion in costs and compensation to suckers who were sold worthless insurance policies. And I've forgotten how much they've had to pay the regulators for their dirty deeds. How many Lloyds bosses have been punished for all this? Approximately none. How many have been sacked? Approximately none. How many have continued to receive indecently huge salaries, pensions and bonuses? Approximately all of them. Only shareholders and customers have paid the price for all this incompetence and crookedness.

The Bank of England's philosophy is along the lines of: 'there is a light at the end of the tunnel, so quick, build more tunnel'.

They keep worrying about the fact that no one is saving but they keep saving rates at an all-time low and don't seem able to connect the two dots. These are not people I would like to be managing a child's pocket money and yet they seem to be attempting to run the nation's finances.

6

I saw two butterflies today.

There used to be scores. Now butterflies are rare. Farmers and gardeners use vast quantities of pesticide. Gardens are covered with decking or concrete. Bushes are all torn up.

The butterflies' courtship dance is incredibly complicated and there is nothing we could do to replicate it.

Thought for the day: Is a mullionaire a man who made his fortune installing mullion windows?

7

A new law has crept in under which a business will be guilty if an employee, or an associated person, facilitates another person's tax evasion.

This will be a criminal offence even if the directors and senior management are not involved, or don't know what is going on.

Makes you want to start a business, doesn't it?

I see that Vodafone, one of the world's top 100 Evil Companies, is now charging punters £5 a day when they are abroad.

This is a brilliant way around the EU ruling limiting costs.

I never used to spend that much when abroad because I only ever checked emails.

So now, thanks to the EU and clever Vodafone I will pay more.

Mind you, it looks as though Vodafone needs the money. Despite being one of the nastiest, greediest and most uncaring companies in the world, they managed to make a loss of $6,904,000,000 last year.

We can still not get any reception at or anywhere near our home in the Cotswolds. And our attempts to get anyone interested have been ignored.

Tragically, the area around us is now as sterile as a road traffic island in a city centre. Locals pretend to love the countryside but they kill everything. They have colourless, sterile gardens with neatly clipped bushes.

When I signed the Achat for the sale of our apartment, I was told that it was merely a preliminary to the main business. I was told that it was not a legal document. My signature was not witnessed and I signed under false pretences because I was told that the buyer had the cash for the purchase but it now transpires that he does not have the cash and is struggling to raise it from his mother and a variety of banks.

I made huge mistakes in signing the Achat and the contract with the agency. But I really made only one mistake: trusting the estate agent. (The second mistake was letting him know that I trusted him. I remember telling him that I had to trust him. Oh boy. Oh boy, that was so stupid of me.)

It now appears that things have changed and the Achat has mysteriously morphed into a legally binding contract which forces me to sell to our buyer and to wait until he is ready to buy.

If, after a few years, or a decade or two, I dare to get restless then I will have to take him to court in an attempt to demolish the Achat. It seems that although the wretched document is binding on us (the sellers) it is not binding on him (the buyer). If I sell the apartment to anyone else then he will be able to sue me for an undisclosed sum.

This figures.

Recent French legislation, designed by mad socialists and barmy communists, is designed to give masses of protection to buyers but absolutely no protection to sellers who are regarded as evil capitalists who must be taught a lesson.

I am a restless, impatient person and I hate being treated with contempt. I also hate not knowing what is happening because other people won't make decisions or won't tell me what decision they have made.

According to our estate agent and our notaire, our buyer is supposed to be returning to Paris on September 15th to sign another part of the endless documentation that is required in France in order to sell an apartment. Every time I try to gouge information out of our agents, I feel as though I'm being a difficult bastard for having the impertinence to ask questions.

In the UK, a rather obnoxious British politician called Vince Cable is still moaning about the result of last year's referendum on the EU. He constantly complains that the people who voted to leave the EU were mostly over 65 and therefore too stupid to know what they were doing.

Mr Cable is 174-years-old and clearly too stupid to know what he is saying.

8

I spent an hour buying some Eurostar tickets today. Afterwards I prayed that I never have to book Eurostar tickets again.

It took them 25 minutes to answer the telephone. I protested mildly and politely at the long wait. I have no idea how much it costs to phone Eurostar. I didn't dare look. I get so infuriated at the amount of my life I waste on the telephone; usually waiting for some company which has so little respect for its customers that it refuses to hire enough operators.

'People usually wait at least 40 minutes,' said a bloke called Charlie. 'We get a lot of calls.'

There was no hint of an apology. I felt I should apologise for bothering him – them being so more important than anyone else. It's always the same with Eurostar. They really don't seem to give a fig about their customers. No one in the world is as important as a Eurostar telephone operator.

He didn't seem to me to be very good at his job.

When I told him what train I wanted, he told me there was no train at that time. I knew there was because I had tried to book it on the Eurostar website. I asked him to look again. He then admitted that he was wrong. No apology, of course.

Eurostar is keen on extra payments. You have to pay an extra £10 if you want to book seats by telephone, £3 if you want to pay with a credit card (instead of the more usual beads and trinkets which, to be honest, I find damned difficult to squeeze down the phone) and £8 if you want to have the tickets posted. You have to book by phone because if you book on their damned website you can't pick your seats until you've paid for the tickets. Antoinette and I are a bit old-fashioned in that we like to sit together when we travel. If I book online, we could well end up sitting in different carriages.

I then told Charlie which seats I wanted. He said there were no such seats on their new train. I told him that we had been on the new train and that we had sat in the seats I was asking for. He looked again and then admitted that the seats I wanted did exist. No apology. At least he was getting full marks for consistency.

I had to tell him my name several times. I had to keep reminding him that two adults were travelling. He did apologise that their system was not working properly. I politely refrained from pointing out that it never does. It is either slow or down. The bill for the seats I wanted (six weeks ahead) came to over £600. I have to travel first class because the seats in second class are so close together that I cannot squeeze into them.

'Can I use my Frequent Traveller Points towards the cost of the tickets?' I asked.

He told me that I couldn't. The Frequent Traveller Points can apparently only be used on journeys starting or ending in London. I was starting and ending in Ebbsfleet and paying the same price as if I were starting and ending in London. This must go down in history as one of the Great Rip Offs of all time.

'Shall I put your frequent traveller numbers into the system so that you can earn more points?'

I told him not to bother.

What's the point? The damned things are useless.

It took me 53 minutes to buy my train tickets. Eurostar will post them but only by special delivery, presumably so that they can charge me £8. They will no longer send them by ordinary post though it hardly matters if they are lost or stolen. This means that I will have to go to the local sorting office and queue in order to collect them.

Tonight, I will pray that we never have to travel on Eurostar again. Eurostar always tell customers that they record their calls. I rather doubt if anyone ever listens to them.

To be honest, if I live another 30 years (and hit my century) I don't think I will ever go abroad again. The hassle of travelling overseas is just too much. I gave up travelling by plane years ago and I certainly would never fly again. And now that the quality of service provided by Eurostar has sunk to a new low, I really don't want to go abroad by train either. I don't much fancy using the ferry or Eurotunnel either. Fortunately, Antoinette feels the same way that I do.

But who cares? There are plenty of places to visit or revisit in Britain. And we can go there in the car. We can rent cottages and tour around.

After my disaster on the phone with Eurostar, we went to Sidmouth for the Folk Festival.

They've been having a Folk Festival in Sidmouth every August since 1955 and we've never been.

It seems an odd time to have a Festival.

Most seaside towns are full in August and don't need any extra activity to encourage visitors. But the council there seems pretty sensible, by and large. It is certainly much more sensible than the councils looking after most seaside towns. In Ilfracombe and Weston-super-Mare, for example, the entire local councils should be taken out to sea and buried.

Since we guessed that the car parks would be busy, we paid £15 through a company called JustPark so that we could park in a local householder's driveway just a short walk from the town centre. What a brilliant idea.

Sidmouth was packed. The men were wearing those odd below the knee shorts, flowery shirts, army boots and wonderfully silly hats, many with feathers, the sort that go better with lederhosen and well-slapped thighs. The women were wearing hippy frocks and had their faces painted and flower garlands in their hair.

The vast majority of visitors seemed to be either pensioners or aggressive under 10-year-olds. (Two children elbowed me out of the way in order to get ahead of me in a coffee shop.) Maybe the ones in between were in a beer tent somewhere, manning the stalls on the Promenade or just busking.

Highlights included a man playing a didgeridoo and a group of unconnected pensioners dancing in the street while a couple of young performers (one playing a clarinet the other an accordion) looked on rather bemusedly. And there was a band of what can only be called geriatrics who were having far more fun than any of the younger buskers. I got the impression that one or two of the band members weren't entirely sure what instrument they were

272

playing, or what they should be doing with it, but by golly they were having fun and providing excellent entertainment. They would have won first, second and third prizes if I'd been judging. And they'd have received a Special Entertainment Award too. Bravo a thousand times.

I read an article by an organiser who said that 'young people were a priority'. Why? Surely, that is blatant ageism? Can you imagine the fuss if an organiser had said that 'old people were a priority'? The millennials would have been protesting in the streets, not dancing. Injustice is injustice whatever the age of the victim.

The young musicians all seemed precious, serious and very professional in demeanour if not in skill. But the members of the geriatric band were having a whale of a time with the ones in wheelchairs and mobility scooters joining in with what can only be described as gusto.

Sadly, I have to say that the general quality of busking was lower than you'd find in any old town on any old Saturday afternoon. Most of the buskers seemed to be pretentious students, earnest, precious and self-important, with plenty of attitude; most seemed to find the whole experience rather beneath them. There wasn't a smile to be seen. And whatever happened to the one man band? I used to love one man bands but I haven't seen one for decades. The EU has probably published an edict forbidding them either on health and safety grounds or because each musician is only allowed to play one instrument at a time in order to preserve job opportunities.

I hate to admit it but we found the whole experience disappointing.

The young buskers and dancers all looked as if they were revising for exams in street theatre or historical dancing. They were all trying to look different but all ended up looking exactly the same.

The local shopkeepers couldn't have been having a good time. Many shops were closed (partly because the shopkeepers wanted to open at the weekend and thanks to crazy EU laws could not, therefore, stay open during the week).

Sidmouth is, for the rest of the year, a peaceful, Victorian town with much to commend it. Though I can't see that it has a big future. Will today's millennials be visiting Sidmouth in a few decades time? Somehow, I doubt it.

But the Folk Week turned it into a rather bad tempered place. When a troupe of dour-faced Morris Dancers jiggled their way past, we stood aside to let them by and a man selling kites shouted at us accusing us of standing in front of his stall. We were there for less than 30 seconds and I don't think anyone was interested in his damned silly kites. The Morris Dancers looked as miserable as sin. How can you take yourself so seriously when you're wrapped up in jingly bells?

Part of the problem seemed to me that the whole darned thing was just too well organised. It all seemed a bit officious but, at the same time, rather woefully amateurish. I know that seems to be a contradiction but whereas the dancers were timed by the minute to appear and then disappear (the officious bit) the stalls along the promenade were made of flimsy plastic and looked as though they would blow away in a mild wind (the amateurish bit). The poor stallholders would have had to pack up their wares every evening and then fetch them out every morning.

I thought the whole thing would have looked better and been far better all round if the organisers had rented (and then hired out) a collection of the wooden chalet like shops which appear everywhere these days at Christmas time.

Next time, I'm going to the Sidmouth folk festival with my harmonica.

I have been blowing into a harmonica for over 50 years. I have never taken a lesson or studied any books.

And I still can't play the damned thing.

The truth is that Sidmouth is much more fun without its festival. The bad news is that locals want more festivals. I hope they don't go as potty as Cheltenham where there seems to be a Festival (with a capital F) at least once a week.

One sweet memory, however.

I saw a child throw down a half-eaten apple.

'Why did you do that?' demanded the angry mother.

'I didn't want any more,' moaned the stroppy child.

'Apples don't grow on trees!' snapped the mother.

I saw a headline in one of today's newspapers announcing, as though revealing a great secret: 'Avoid Alzheimer's by Staying Active'.

Crumbs.

What will they put on tomorrow's front page? I recommend: 'Stay Alive by Breathing Air'.

Later in the afternoon, we were sitting in the conservatory having afternoon tea (standards have to be maintained and we are English, after all) when one of our many regular rabbits appeared on the lawn eight feet away. The many entrances to their burrow all in our grounds.

He started to wash.

He washed his face, then his feet and then behind his ears. He spent a lot of time washing behind his ears. Then he washed his chest, and his thighs and his legs. He could not have looked better if he'd spent an hour at the furdresser's.

When he'd finished washing, he ate some grass and then finished off his meal by eating half a windfall apple which he had found in our courtyard. The apple had fallen from apple trees high up in the garden and rolled down the garage roof before rolling under the car.

The other half of the apple he carried off with him, presumably to take to his burrow. I have seen rabbits running around with a whole apple in their teeth. Despite their huge eyes they have terrible eyesight, however. If they drop an apple, it takes them ages to find it again. If they take the apples into their burrow, which I assume they do, I hope they don't leave them until they start to ferment. Squirrels often get drunk on windfall apples. Maybe rabbits do too.

9

We are living in the age of the sneak. And it is deeply unpleasant.

A couple of hundred years ago, when I was younger, there were few lower forms of human being than the sneak.

Children who 'told tales' on their classmates would be ostracised.

Neighbours who maliciously spied on others and spread gossip would find themselves 'sent to Coventry'.

Back in the ridiculously simple days of honesty and decency and respect and privacy, sneaks were strongly disliked. Sneaking was not the right thing to do. It wasn't what good, honest people did.

Indeed, rather than tell tales on their contemporaries people would lie, take the blame themselves or claim that they'd walked into a door.

Sneaks were thought to be bad, bad people. They were traitors; the lowest of the low. They were people who happily sold their souls for a mess of potage or anything else that was on offer.

But today every other person is a sneak, damn their hides.

It is the new fashion, the new industry, the latest trend. And the little bastards are everywhere.

They are the cyclists with little cameras fitted to their helmets. The slimy, little, Lycra-clad toads will turn you in if they managed to catch you sliding a wheel into a bus lane.

They are the motorists and lorry drivers with dash cameras. If they catch you hogging the centre lane, they send off their little films to the police. If they film you eating a toffee then they report you to the authorities. (And yet I have, on numerous occasions, spotted lorry drivers reading books, reading newspapers or, in one case, working on a laptop which they have resting on the steering wheel. It is still commonplace to see drivers using their telephone to talk or to text. And I cannot, for the life of me, see why using a hands-free telephone should be allowed. It is still a serious distraction and certainly far more of a distraction than nibbling while driving – an activity which requires no more loss of attention than smoking or trying to work out what all the road signs mean.)

They are the concerned local citizens who set up private speed cameras and report motorists to the police if they travel at 22 mph in a 20 mph school zone even if it's 6.30 p.m. on a Saturday night.

They are the people with mobile phones who film you if you dare to put your rubbish bin out an hour early or cram a little something forbidden into your wheelie bin. And then they send off their bit of film to the council.

They are the people who film you parked on double yellow lines while you pop into the chemist to pick up a prescription. And then put their little film online and send a copy to the local Plod.

They are the doctors who dob you in to the police at the drop of a hat and the accountants and lawyers who dob you in to the tax people if they think you might have forgotten to declare £1.09 in interest from a forgotten savings account.

(I discovered earlier this week that there are now 693,000 lawyers and accountants working in the UK. Could this possibly have anything to do with the fact that our laws in general, and our tax laws in particular, are ridiculously overcomplicated and incomprehensible?)

They are the relatives and neighbours who dob in the woman next door to anyone who will listen, if they suspect she is sharing a bed and seeking a little human warmth on cold winter nights, heaven forbid.

They are the neighbours, friends and relatives who will telephone the tax people with tidbits of information, in the hope of claiming a handsome 'snooper reward'. ('The bloke next door has just bought a new lawnmower. I don't know he can afford it.')

In the old days, it was Us versus Them.

Now, it seems that everyone has joined the forces of Them.

It hasn't happened by accident, of course.

It has been engineered deliberately to make us all feel uncomfortable, threatened, anxious and, most of all, oh yes most certainly most of all, paranoid.

The people who do the sneaking, bought with bribes if they do or threatened with prison if they don't, think they are doing the right thing; probably believe (like the naïve citizens who wash out their yoghurt pots and their beer cans and think they are saving the planet from certain doom) that they are making the world a better, safer, fairer place.

They aren't, of course.

They are doing just the opposite.

It may seem difficult to blame the ones who are sneaking because they are forced to do so: the doctors, the accountants and the lawyers who spill the beans on their clients.

Individually they don't have much choice.

But as a group they should have resisted and refused to cooperate with laws which threatened their relationship with their patients or clients.

But the ones who choose to sneak just for the hell of it, and because they can, are despicable and treacherous.

They have sold out to the bad guys.

And now they are the bad guys.

Everyone is terrified of being dobbed in.

And there appears to be no escape.

'We can evade reality,' said Ayn Rand. 'But we cannot evade the consequences of evading reality.'

News from France is that Paris is now going to triple the taxes that foreign property owners must pay. That seems to me to be a racially motivated tax. If you aren't French you pay three times as much as the French pay.

How can that possibly be legal?

Racism is, after all, defined as prejudice or discrimination against someone of a different race.

And how can it possibly fit in with EU law?

The EU is trying to introduce standard taxes across all member nations.

And Macron, who is already on course to be another despised French President, wants the EU to have the power to introduce standard taxes across EU countries.

So how can Paris introduce special taxes for Europeans who don't happen to be French?

And, while we're on this subject, why does Paris hate foreigners and tourists so much? Dante Alighieri, one of the first package tourists, the fellow who went on a guided tour through the nine circles of hell, would have found that modern Paris reminded him of his previous adventure.

The new taxes will backfire.

Foreigners, now knowing that they are unwanted, will not travel to Paris.

Tourists (who provide the French city with much of its income) will stay away.

A fear of what else might happen will stop foreigners buying property in a city which already has the lowest capital city prices in the world.

There are said to be just 100,000 foreign property owners in Paris.

But my guess is that many of them are influential.

And the city just pissed them all off.

There is already talk of a boycott of the French capital by investors, businessmen and tourists.

Though, sadly, tourism levels in Paris are down so much that I doubt if anyone would notice. Paris, always renowned for its rudeness to visitors has become even ruder and less welcoming in recent years. It is now known as the rip off capital of Europe. And it has become mean and nasty. The damned city even cut off all the much admired and rather wonderful love locks attached to a couple of bridges.

Macron and co don't have the brains to realise it but the EU has destroyed Paris. It was the EU which forced millions of immigrants and terrorists into France. It was EU rules which have led to the street lights being turned off at night. It was EU regulations which mean that cafes and shops are now shut on Mondays (giving the city two Sundays). It was EU rules which have meant that the city is now awash with rubbish.

The socialists who now run Paris don't understand that there are 100,000 empty apartments in Paris because absurdly nasty rules and tax laws make it unprofitable and risky to let out an apartment. There are awful rules if you sell an apartment and awful laws if you keep one. It is no wonder that property prices in Paris are the lowest in the developed world. Only a fool would buy, only a fool would hold and, it seems from my experience, that only a fool would attempt to sell property in the city.

Finally, as an Englishman, I am rather peeved that the French want to punish me for having fallen in love with their capital city.

In the last century, foreigners twice saved Paris from the Germans.

You'd think the frog-eating bastards (all of whom carry a white flag in their knapsack) would be just a teeny bit grateful, wouldn't you?

10

In my last diary, I mentioned having taken shelfies (photographs of books on shelves).

It seems that Antoinette has added a word to the English language, for millennials are apparently now busy taking loads of shelfies with which to impress their friends. The idea, apparently, is to buy a load of books (paperbacks by the yard will do) and stick them on the shelves of a bookcase. You then take pictures and send them to all your friends, put them on your Facebook page and distribute them via Twitter.

This is actually rather sad.

Millennials are always trying to impress other people with their petty achievements. Instead of enjoying a view or an experience, they have to take a picture of it to prove that they were there.

And now they want to pretend that they read books.

The problem is, I fear, that millennials have no foundation in their life. They have no sense of their place in the world around them and this is because they were brought up without rules, taught to exist in a world where they were encouraged to believe that the world belonged to them. We have a nation of divas. Everyone is now a royal; full of self-importance, filled with a sense of inner certainty and deprived of the capacity for fun.

And in trying forever to live for the acclaim of others, they fail to live their own lives. It is all a bit sad really.

I tried reversing our Mitsubishi up our driveway today. The Bentley was parked in the courtyard next to the house which is the only place where I can turn round. To my astonishment, the damned Mitsubishi Barbarian had enormous difficulty in getting up the hill. Even when I tried out the quartet of four wheel drive options, the car just span and struggled. There was no ice, no wet leaves, no spilt diesel – just a slight dampness caused by a little light rain. Our Ford Ranger would have got up easily. And so would the Bentley (which is four wheel drive). Maybe it's just me. Maybe I need to learn a few words of Japanese so that I can offer appropriate encouragement. What, I wonder is Japanese for 'Giddy up'?

I had to leave the Mitsubishi parked half way up the drive where we have a space where two or three cars can be parked. The Mitsubishi is toast. I think maybe I'll get one of the new four wheel drive Maseratis.

When I looked at a recent car magazine, I was disappointed to see that most of the advertisements now give carbon dioxide emissions and miles per gallon in every imaginable circumstance but never give acceleration, maximum speed or price.

Well bugger it all, I am going to add a Maserati to our garage. I realise I am paying a chunk for the name but sod it, it is a Maserati. Money needs to be spent otherwise it has no function other than to enrich bankers, money managers and other riff raff who will steal whatever they can lay their hands on. Funds which are superfluous to purpose of staying warm and fed (and for fuck you money) need to be spent on toys.

Meanwhile, I have rediscovered Dandelion and Burdock.

If the Americans and the North Koreans start a war I have no doubt that Britain will somehow become involved. Antoinette and I will hide under the table with a bottle of Dandelion and Burdock and a packet of Hula Hoops.

11

A few weeks ago, I ordered a jacket from an American company called Orvis. I like their jackets because they are equipped with a variety of pockets – several of them large, zipped and inside the coat.

The website told me that there would be a delay of a week or two but that was fine. I ordered the coat and paid extra for express delivery. Orvis sent me an email letting me know that the jacket would be available on 8th August.

But when I chased them by email the other day, they told me that the jacket would now not be available until December.

I was cross not because they didn't have the jacket but because they twice told me that they had it and gave me a date when it would be delivered. That's sloppy and unprofessional. When I cancelled the order and told them to remove my name from their mailing list, I received nothing but a simple confirmation. They offered no explanation and made no effort to keep me as a customer. I'm glad I don't have any shares in the company. If I did, I would sell them. And I bet I continue to get a zillion advertising emails for the company.

It was raining again today. It has been a pretty miserable summer. Still, we can perhaps enjoy the parallel universe occupied by the climate change mythologists who claim that we are once again experiencing one of the hottest years on record.

They claim indeed that for the past several years the weather has been hotter than ever.

Why does anyone with a brain still listen to these completely discredited buffoons?

The climate change industry fiddles the figures and makes up the 'facts' to suit its own commercial and political purposes.

After a massive manhunt police arrested a jogger who had apparently pushed a woman pedestrian and nearly knocked her under a bus.

They were not helped by the fact that the CCTV pictures were, as usual, pretty useless and told them only that the culprit was almost certainly two legged.

The man they named, after their extensive manhunt, quickly claimed to have been in America at the time. It seems a pity that the police didn't do a little basic checking before arresting the poor fellow. And an even bigger pity that they didn't check before releasing his name. These days I rather suspect that the police are more interested in getting publicity than in getting things right. Naturally, they still haven't arrested the culprit.

I have noticed two things about public car parks.

First, the width of each space will be in inverse proportion to the age of the car park. The newer the car park the narrower the spaces will be.

Second, in a busy car park the car selfishly parked across two spaces will always be a black Audi.

12

Students who claim they are suffering from ADHD, OCD, hyperactivity and dyslexia (not just one, you understand, but all these and more) are suing universities which do not allow them more time than other students to learn their stuff and then regurgitate it at exam time. They want special privileges too – such as a room of their own.

Maybe they would also like an hour beforehand with the answers? And perhaps an adviser sitting at each elbow while they sit the examination.

If you think about it logically, it will soon be necessary to offer all intellectually disadvantaged students the chance to study for four, five, six or more years in order to master their course. And then give them double or triple time to sit their exams. Academia will become like a golf club – with the brighter students given a handicap so that the less intellectually endowed students have a chance to compete with them.

Actually, I am surprised that students aren't suing universities for making them sit exams at all.

'Not taking my word that I know the stuff is insulting and defamatory.'

I have no doubt that universities will roll over when faced with new demands. They have become soppy. If one student complains that a book has upset them (for some undisclosed reason), the university will remove it from the curriculum. Students demand to feel 'comfortable' at all times. They never want to be stretched, offended or faced with anything controversial. They want to rewrite history to remove the bits which distress them. It is, apparently, official National Union of Students policy to prevent controversial people from speaking at universities because they might imperil the 'safe space' of university campuses where students must now be protected from 'upsetting views'. I despair, I really do. And these, remember, are members of a generation which seems to worship at the shrine of disruption. The only disruption they will tolerate is the sort they themselves initiate. Any disruption offered by the over 30s is regarded as terrifying, appalling and entirely unacceptable.

13

I read yet again that Zuckerberg, the Facebook billionaire has promised to give away 99% of his wealth.

Am I nit picking in pointing out that until he says exactly when he is going to do this, the promise is rather meaningless.

Talking of wealth, I see that someone called Glynis Breakwell, who is the vice-chancellor of the University of Bath (I wonder how many people knew they'd got a university there) receives a salary of £451,000 plus £19,000 in living expenses. The university (for which I suspect we can, in part, read 'taxpayers') also paid her utility bills, council tax and £8,000 laundry bill.

There is, of course, absolutely no connection between the absurd salaries paid to university vice chancellors and the massive debts incurred by students.

Someone Antoinette knows was bitten by a tick while walking in the countryside. She rang her doctor's surgery. The receptionist told her that they didn't deal with tick bites.

Maybe someone should tell the receptionist and her employers about Lyme disease.

14

I spoke to three people who all said it took at least three weeks to get appointments with their doctors, though one said they could get an appointment with a trainee or a locum but that these stand-in doctors 'never seem to know anything and never like to change anything prescribed for them by one of the principals'.

There are few doctors available these days because a majority of GPs are women who all want to work part time with no evenings, nights, weekends or bank holidays. This attitude doesn't matter in banking or architecture but it does matter in medicine.

Many female GPs work only two or possibly three days a week. Some female doctors like to share jobs. One works half a week and the other works the other half of the week. This suits them very nicely. It means that they earn quite good money, have lots of time off and pay very little income tax. Unfortunately, of course, it means that patient care is somewhere between terrible and awful. A patient has little chance of seeing the same doctor more than once. And since the female doctors don't like providing night time cover, or working at weekends or on bank holidays, the patients get a really rough deal. (The establishment should have known this because it has been a problem for decades. When I was in practice over 30 years ago, it was well-known that some women doctors did not want to accept their full share of out of hours responsibility.)

This was a result of government policy years ago to increase the number of women doctors. It has been a disaster not least because with women doctors working part time there is no continuity for patients. Patients prefer to see the same doctor and it is safer for them to do so. Many patients find it harder to share confidential information with a doctor they don't really know well enough to trust. There is absolutely no doubt that the increase in the number of women doctors has resulted in a massive increase in patient morbidity and mortality – not because women doctors are poorer diagnosticians but because their personal working preferences disadvantage their patients.

The latest bit of politically correct nonsense to hit the world comes courtesy of those promoting a gender neutral world. These idiots claim that there is no difference between boys and girls and men and women and that allowing girls to dress in pink or giving boys toy cars to play with is a major sin. Apart from being scientific balderdash, this is dangerous and damaging nonsense and it is frightening that some people are apparently taking it seriously.

In schools everywhere pupils of both sexes are now expected to share loos. In Berlin, someone has allegedly opened a loo where urinals designed for women to use have been installed alongside traditional male urinals. Who, I wonder, is responsible for this absurd nonsense? Why were they let out without supervision? If it isn't stopped now, I have no doubt that the gender neutral movement will lead to a massive increase in gender confusion among children and teenagers. Young girls going through the menarche will be devastated. Sex assaults will rocket and indecent exposure (accidental and deliberate) will become endemic. If we don't stop it this is another piece of social engineering that will be accepted and eventually become compulsory.

15

I found an old album recorded by Emperor Rosko, the greatest disc jockey of all time. It occurred to me that nothing since the 1960s (certainly not the internet) has been so big a cultural shock as pirate radio.

Have you noticed that people will often say 'they must know what they are doing' when talking about people in authority. Most people assume that the folk in authority know what they are doing. This is wrong. The people in authority may know what you are doing and they almost certainly know what I am doing but they don't have the faintest idea what they themselves are doing. Most of the time they are too busy feathering their own nests to know which way is up or what day it is.

The Eurostar tickets for which I paid an extortionate £8.50 postage charge still haven't arrived. Rather than waiting for 40 minutes for one of their agents to speak to me I sent them an email asking where the tickets are.

And I was right about Orvis. I am being bombarded with advertisements for the coat they couldn't provide until December.

16

A woman has noisily complained that every woman in Britain has been the victim of sexual harassment. Many others have joined in and endorsed the claim though just how they know this is true is a mystery. Every female Z list celebrity in the country now claims to have been fondled, propositioned or touched inappropriately at some time in the 1970s or 1980s. One woman complained that back in the 1980s, she was asked to do a twirl to show off a new dress. Another complained that her boss told her that she looked 'nice'.

'Give us a twirl!' is harassment? What the hell is wrong with these people? What strange world do they inhabit?

The folk complaining, of course, mostly celebrities of a certain age and most seem strangely eager to talk about (in surprising detail) things that happened half a lifetime ago.

Suddenly, there is fame to be revived, sympathy to be garnered, victimhood to be enjoyed, interviews to be done, and television programmes on which to appear.

As a result, reputations are being ruined with nary a shred of real evidence. The accusation is, it seems, usually enough for the court of social media.

Moreover, there seems no interest in the fact that the culture was different then and, dare I say it, some women were as guilty of touching as were some men and many were more likely to be disappointed if they weren't touched somewhere than if they were. The world was very different and expectations were a world away from today's much stricter, politically correct environment. It may have all been wrong but it was the way it was, and to judge behaviour of the 1970s by the rules of the 21st century seems as wrong as making judgements about Cecil Rhodes et al according to the world in which we now live. You can't fairly judge one generation by another generation's standards.

In reality, I confess that I rather doubt this claim is true but I do think it is true that every man has most certainly been the victim of sexual harassment.

Women use sex in many ways, the most obvious of which is the wearing of provocative clothes, sexually appealing make-up and scents.

It is not difficult to argue that women who wear revealing and sexually provocative clothes (short skirts, lots of cleavage) when they are at work are just as guilty of sexual harassment as are men who make sexual comments. No one ever dares say this might be true because it is politically incorrect to say so. And yet I have frequently read about women (actresses, journalists, businesswomen and politicians) who have claimed that they 'show a little leg' or 'flash a little cleavage' in order to attract attention to themselves. Many women who are successful in business have admitted, without criticism, that they have deliberately used their charms to help advance their careers in some way. And how many actresses dress in polo neck sweaters and old jeans when attending events where the press and public will be gathered?

It is worth remembering that it wasn't all that long ago that in Britain an Act of Parliament was passed allowing men to annul a marriage if their wife had used perfume, padding, attractive clothing or make-up to enhance their appearance.

If it is true, as has been claimed, that every woman in the world has been the victim of sexual harassment (though there are doubtless many would argue that the word 'victim' has been misapplied in many of these cases and there are others who would simply argue that the claim is a wildly emotive exaggeration) then I would say it is absolutely rock solid certain that every man in Britain has been a victim of sexual harassment by women and none of the guilty women has been charged with anything, let alone convicted.

I realise with some horror that I would not dare to make this point online for it would immediately result in trolling, abuse and, quite probably, the arrival of a couple of dozen police officers at our front door.

Today I ventured further into the nightmare world of modern banking as exemplified by Barclays France.

I still hadn't received the statements and other documents which Barclays in France had been promising me since early June.

So, today I telephoned again.

I have lost count of the number of times I've rung and emailed, and my phone bill must be a serious drag on Britain's national economy. Barclays in France makes the Post Office look like a citadel of efficiency. Indeed, I suspect that the star pupils from the Finishing School for British Post Office staff, la crème de la crème as Miss Jean Brodie might have put it, the rudest, the most incompetent, the most brazenly uncaring, are all selected by Barclays bank to work in France. Barclays surely have an option on each year's prize pupils. It is no doubt quite the thing to get the call. For pupils at the Post Office Finishing School a posting to Barclays must be a tribute to be savoured and boasted about. To be so rude and egregiously incompetent that you are picked to work for Barclays in France, is doubtless an honour to be savoured.

With one thing and another, I am now full up with disputes and anxieties. There really is no room for any more.

The Barclays employee to whom I spoke today confirmed that absolutely nothing I had asked them to do had been done. They have not cancelled the direct debits they promised to cancel weeks ago. I have a suspicion that they perhaps have some sort of staff bonus scheme whereby employees are given extra money according to the number of emails and phone calls they generate when asked to perform simple tasks. Their files still show my phone number as two numbers I last used nearly a decade ago. When they do bother to communicate with me they insist on trying to use these ten-year-old numbers because they refuse to update their records. I don't think I have ever encountered such gross incompetence.

And the French staff who are supposed to speak English are so unilingual that I talked to them in French (it doesn't say much when my French is better than their English). Pleasantly, they do not complain about my French when they realise just how hard it can be to discuss complex banking procedures in another language.

Feeling as though I had died and gone to some cruel French banking hell, and having completely run out of patience, I told them today that I now wanted to close the account.

I was told that I must send more email instructions and that once the instructions were received it would take three weeks for someone to pluck up the necessary energy to press the button required to make the closure. I was told that an email instruction would be acceptable if I photographed a written instruction and sent the photograph with the email. I was also assured that someone would ring me to confirm that the emails had been received. I also sent yet more emails cancelling my unwanted direct debits and updating my phone number.

Some hours later, when no one had telephoned, as promised, to confirm that Barclays had received the emails I rang again.

This time, another employee told me that an email instruction would not be acceptable and that I would need to put the same instruction in the ordinary mail. I couldn't help feeling that this was all being done to slow down the whole process still further and leave them controlling my money for a little longer. I wrote myself a euro cheque for the bulk of the money in the account and sent it to my bank in the UK. Maybe it will be possible to salvage some of the money Barclays are holding.

Everything in France seems to be done at a snail pace. Appropriate, I suppose.

I jotted down a list of all the calls I've made and letters I have written and I reckon I have so far wasted just under a week of my life trying to persuade Barclays France to do things which should have taken me at most 15 minutes. Writing needs a routine environment and peace. It doesn't need constant interruptions and uncertainties.

Looking at the news later in the day, I saw that four senior Barclays executives from the British part of the bank have been arrested. This does not seem to be enough. Surely more should be charged. Actually, why waste time with charges and trials. Why not just put all Barclays staff into jail?

Thanks to the French, we have had a summer of discontent, deceit and disloyalty. I suppose we should not have been surprised. It was, after all, the French, in the person of Cardinal Richelieu, who perfected the modern art of manipulation and deceit. The

French are, in addition, an exceptionally ungrateful and grasping nation.

Antoinette and I spent half an hour looking for a film in which lots of French bankers get slaughtered. In the end, we settled on 22 Bullets (in which Jean Rcno slaughters a good many Frenchmen) and 'Attack on Wall Street' in which an aggrieved citizen kills a lot of bankers.

Anyone contemplating buying a property in France should think again. Buying is a nightmare. Selling is a double nightmare.

I'm now also fighting the French gas and electricity suppliers who know damned well that our consumption is light (partly because we haven't been there much recently). They know that our consumption is light because I've given them the readings. However, they still insist on charging us more than we owe and then generously telling us that we can eventually reclaim the overpaid sums. Bugger that. In future they will get paid what I think we owe rather than what they want. What are they going to do? Cut us off? See if I care.

Having decided to sack Barclays, I realised that I would still need some sort of banking facility with a euro account so that I could carry on paying bills relating to the damned apartment in Paris. Having done a little research, I telephoned Lloyds Bank who appeared to offer a simple euro account, complete with a euro cheque book facility.

I then entered the nightmare world of the bit of Lloyds Bank which deals with poor sods who want to open euro accounts.

In a call which lasted over 50 minutes, and in which I spoke to several people, I endured the sort of interrogation which usually requires a powerful light and ends with the removal of some fingernails.

Having told me that they didn't offer cheque books ('None of our customers requires them,' said a teenage banker who was completely stumped when I asked him how he knew this if the bank didn't offer them to their customers) I was passed from one interrogator to another.

They wanted to know if I had any political affiliations, where my money came from and where it was going. They reserved the right to share my personal information with Uncle Tom Cobbleigh and they wanted to know my income (and who paid me) and what

I was planning to do with the money which went into my account (and where it would be coming from). They wanted to know my street address, my national insurance number, my date of birth, where I was born and my bank details (I pointed out that I had five accounts with their bank but they said they were a different department). They wanted me to take my passport into a local branch (where it would be copied) and they wanted the usual utility bill to prove that I heated the house and had electric lights. They wanted a copy of a bank statement issued by themselves. They wanted to know my nationality and they wanted my telephone number and my email address. I lost track of the questions and eventually when I demurred, someone actually assured me that all this information was being collected for my benefit and that it would be 'kept secure on file'.

I was told that there would be another form to fill in before I would be told whether or not I would be accepted for a euro account. I would have to print out the form myself, sign it and return it. I asked if they could post me a form but they didn't seem to think that would be possible.

In the end, I pointed out that their interrogation would help identity thieves and terrorists but would not help me and that they could keep their damned euro account. I pointed out that they could not promise to keep my information secure since they were a bank and banks had an appalling record when it came to preserving information gleaned from customers. I forgot to mention that they had already told me that they intended to share the information I gave them with whatever other organisations they felt would benefit from it (or, perhaps, pay them for it). I was also told that the absurd questions were set by the Isle of Man Government since the Isle of Man is a separate country (though I bet it isn't a separate country if the Germans threaten to invade).

I ended the conversation by making a formal complaint about their absurdly impertinent and completely unnecessary questionnaire. I am willing to guarantee that I will never receive a response to my complaint.

I am now left with no way of paying bills on the apartment but I really don't care about that either.

17

I bought a Bosch grass trimmer. It is battery operated and rather feeble looking but it will, I hope, be a useful back up to our collection of petrol strimmers.

The Bosch product came with a thick book (in many languages) but the book doesn't seem to contain any instructions about how to put the device together. This is presumably a crafty German ploy to avoid having to hire one of those illiterate Japanese people who usually write instruction booklets.

The strimmer doesn't seem very strong. Indeed, I have nail clippers which seem to weigh more and which appear to be considerably more robust. Still, it will probably do for a little light strimming where required and it should be useful for cutting back the nose and ear hair which seems to grow with such enthusiasm these days.

I read today that all comments on the internet should be written in a light and entertaining way.

Hmmm.

Announcing the start of World War III should be something of a challenge.

'Hey, folks! You'll never guess what Germany just did...'

18

I received an automated acknowledgement from Eurostar in response to my email complaining that our tickets have not arrived. But no one has bothered to reply to me. I don't think I have ever known a company fall so far and so fast. When Eurostar started, it provided an excellent service. Today it must be one of the worst and least caring companies on the planet. Thankfully, Antoinette succeeded in downloading the tickets from my iPad. Still, it would be nice to have received the tickets since I paid extra to have them posted by special delivery.

After months of consideration, and consultation with one another, Britain's top experts on terrorist attacks have published advice on how citizens can best survive an attack.

The advice can be summed up neatly in two words: run and hide.

Crumbs! It's nice to know that we have experts looking after our interests.

Without them which of us would have thought of 'run and hide'? I hope and expect these geniuses will all receive massive bonuses and knighthoods for their wise advice.

I have written their advice on a small piece of cardboard which I have placed in my wallet, lest I forget.

'Run and hide.'

Maybe the Government might like to print 60,000,000 small reminder cards with these words printed on them. Then every one of us could carry a reminder card with us at all times. Nike or Adidas would doubtless buy advertising space on the reverse of the card.

Oh, and the experts also suggested that later, when it is safe to do so, we should tell someone what has happened.

I don't know about you, but I'd never have thought of that either.

Actually, Antoinette and I are much better prepared than this.

Whenever we go to London or Paris or any other popular terrorist centre, Antoinette wears a simple black headscarf around her neck (or carries one in her handbag) so that in extremis she can wrap the scarf over her head and cover her hair. I refrain from shaving, dress scruffily and scowl a good deal. We have both learned the words Allahu Akbar which we will, if necessary, shout with great gusto.

We had a sudden attack of thunder at 1 p.m. today. It hadn't been forecast so I checked the Met Office website to see what they were saying. They said we were having a nice sunny day. Outside a real storm was developing.

At 5 p.m. this afternoon the sun was shining and I checked the Met Office website again. They said that it was now raining heavily with thunder and lightning.

Sadly, it seems that the Met Office staff have not yet mastered the art of looking out of the window to see what the weather is like. If they can't get the weather right when it is happening then it's perhaps not surprising that they can't get tomorrow's weather right. And it is, perhaps, no wonder they seem to think this is the hottest summer ever in the entire history of this or any other planet.

Most surprising is the fact that they seem able to pontificate on the dangers of global warming when they can't even tell us what today's weather is like when it's happening.

Still, all is not all gloomy. It has been announced that Met Office forecasters will split a £1 million bonus (the biggest since the Met Office was set up 163 years ago) for making 'more accurate' weather forecasts. 'More accurate' than what I don't know but my guess would be 'more accurate' than a drunken sot dangling a piece of seaweed out of his window.

Actually, I am, I confess, completely fed up with the hubristic bastards who read us the weather these days. They, almost more than anyone in our patronising society, seem determined to belittle us and to pat us on the head at every possible opportunity. They have the affrontery to tell us when to use umbrellas, when to use sun-cream and when to stay indoors. And we must keep warm and put on a clean vest and wash behind our ears.

It would be nice if they could, just occasionally, get the bloody weather forecast right.

19

A couple I read about today want to know when they will be able to buy a house. They are both in their mid-20s and have a combined income of around £40,000. They are not married but live with parents. They pay around £5,000 a year in board and I doubt if their tax bill is much more than £5,000 so they have an available £30,000 to spend on themselves. They have so far managed to save just £2,000 from this considerable disposable income.

They seem to me to typify the millennials. They expect to be able to buy a house without having to make any real sacrifices. I have no idea what they spend their £30,000 a year on but I'm willing to bet that there are some nice cars, good holidays, expensive coffees and quite a few internet expenditures.

The sad truth is that members of the entitlement generation cannot afford to buy a home of their own because:

They don't like work very much. They expected to be millionaires at 25 but don't want to have to do much to earn the money. They prefer to spend their days sending Twitter messages and updating their Facebook page. They are addicted to taking selfies which they much prefer to work. I discovered today that Cirque du Soleil now has 'selfie breaks' built into its shows so that entitlement generation customers can take pictures of themselves.

They spend vast quantities of money on gadgets and games. They feel deprived if they don't have the latest mobile phone, the latest iPad and the latest laptop. They also spend a fortune on shoes, clothing and grooming. Strangely, male millennials now spend more on clothing and grooming than female millennials.

They spend much of their cash on tattoos. These silly expressions of self-self are far more expensive than most people realise. A moderately successful tattooist can earn £240,000 a year and a fashionable one can enjoy an annual income of £320,000. Overheads and the cost of ink are almost insignificant. This sort of money is considerably more than a trained consultant surgeon can earn – even with a large private practice. I suspect that the training to be a tattooist is rather less extensive and expensive than the training to be a surgeon. Those absurd bits of graffiti with which members of the entitlement generation have themselves decorated cost a small fortune to have done. I don't wish to spread bad news but many will become infected and produce serious blood poisoning problems in the years ahead. The long-term problems with tattoos mean that no one under the age of 65 should ever have any part of their body tattooed. Tattoos were all very well when they were confined to a neat anchor and the word 'Mum' tattooed on a sailor's upper arm. These days just about everyone seems to be tattooed. I have seen several individuals with their faces covered with tattoos. It is a peculiarly British fad and today women are as likely to cover their bodies with tattoos as are men. I have even seen nurses with visible tattoos. Awful.

The average entitlement generation couple spend over £27,000 on their wedding and a quarter of couples borrow money not to buy a home of their own but to pay for an expensive shindig for their chums. That sum alone would provide a big chunk of a down payment on a new home.

The entitlement generation waste vast amounts of money. For example, they spend £310 million a year on Halloween fripperies.

They don't save any of their money. To be fair, I can see their point. For the last 10 years the rewards on savings have been somewhere between derisory and non-existent. But the real answer to this problem is not to save less but to save more. It is worth noting that the low interest policy was at least partly designed to transfer wealth from the elderly to the entitlement generation. It has done this very successfully. The elderly, who saved hard for much of their lives, are now rapidly become impoverished. Someone who saved £100,000 out of their taxed income, and who might have been expecting that the interest would help them live more comfortably, will now be lucky to receive an after tax income of £1,000 a year. The money has been stolen from the cautious and the prudent and transferred (in a variety of ways) to the pockets of the greedy millions of the entitlement generation.

20

I occasionally buy the *Daily Telegraph* on Saturdays since it provides around 2.3 acres of inflammable newsprint with which to light fires and to trigger my double twin incinerators into action. I don't usually bother reading it because there isn't usually anything in it worth reading (and, if I take my time and look at everything and do the crossword I find I have wasted five minutes of the day) but this afternoon, while lighting a fire in the incinerator, I noticed that according to yesterday's paper the National Trust has sacked a gardener who has 50 years' experience because he doesn't have the requisite paper qualifications. The gardener's main task was cutting grass with a ride on mower but it seems that the National Trust demands that those responsible for such delicate work must have formal qualifications. Gosh, how I dislike the National Trust. Has there ever been a more aggressively worthy, more sanctimonious organisation?

The National Trust has become the Eurostar of charities: once respected now reviled. They were in the news recently for exposing a donor as homosexual and for trying to force volunteer staff to wear ribbons, ties or whatever celebrating homosexuality. They seemed surprised when there were complaints.

Sacking people because they don't have paper qualifications happens a good deal these days.

We know of a delivery driver, with many years' experience, who was threatened with redundancy because she didn't have the required certificates. And Antoinette knows of a cleaner, keen and eager to work, who was fired because she too didn't have the paperwork her employers deemed necessary.

And here's another odd thought: Why is it so difficult to buy decent cheese these days? Most of the stuff on sale seems to have been made from old car seats.

Ah, well. They probably do make it from old car seats as part of the recycling process.

Cutting the grass in Gloucestershire with our massive and frighteningly powerful wheeled strimmer, I suddenly discovered that I had cut through the armoured cable which supplies the outside lights in the garden with electricity. It made me realise just how strong the strimmer blades are. I must remember to keep my toes out of the way in the future.

I blame the EU for allowing manufacturers to sell strimmers which can cut through armoured cable. Mind you, I also blame the EU for allowing manufacturers to sell armoured cable which can be cut through with a strimmer.

And, of course, I blame the EU for the fact that the grass grows at all.

Since our esteemed neighbour His Serene Highness the Prince of all Gloucestershire ordered trees and bushes to be banned from his small estate and, with council approval, had them hacked and cut and burnt and sprayed, the deer have disappeared and the squirrels have virtually gone. There are very few blackbirds, virtually no butterflies, no cowslips, and far fewer other birds too.

What's the difference between this and city vandalism?

Well, rural vandalism is worse because it affects many other creatures and it affects the health of our environment.

21

The newspapers are warning of snow and blizzards later this year.

When I look, I always find that the snow is forecast for Scotland.

Who cares? It always snows in Scotland.

It snows in Iceland too but I don't much care about that either.

Stephen Hawking is in the news again, again, this time complaining about the NHS. It occurs to me to wonder whether any NHS money has been spent keeping this intolerable, old windbag alive at the expense of other less media savvy individuals.

A helicopter comes round once or twice a day and takes a close look at our Jolly Roger flag. It then flies over the bay and disappears. If it is a sea rescue helicopter then I have to confess, I fail to see the point of these regular fly pasts. If you are drowning at 11.37 a.m., when the thing flies overhead, then you will doubtless be saved. But if you get into trouble a minute later you've got a long wait before it comes around again. It seems as pointless an exercise as health screening.

Five minutes later another helicopter came round for a look at our flag. It is, I think, a commercial flight and probably taking tourists for a ride.

Time I think to do some kite flying. That should keep them away.

22

Most medical research has always been sloppily done. In my second book (*Paper Doctors*, 1977) I drew attention to just some of the many flaws in published research papers. Despite the sloppiness, much medical research gets reported as front page news by medical journalists who seem to me to know little or nothing about medicine or journalism.

I saw research the other day which showed (or claimed to show) that people who drink even small amounts of alcohol are more likely to develop cancer.

Here are the problems with the research I saw.

First, some drinkers also smoke. Some drinkers do not smoke. The researchers did not separate the two groups. I think it is a fair bet that people who drink alcohol and smoke are more likely to develop cancer.

Second, no attempt was made to divide the drinkers (or the non-drinkers for that matter) into groups who ate meat and groups who did not eat meat. Since it has been proven beyond doubt that meat eaters are more likely to develop cancer it was essential to do this. If there were more meat eaters among the drinkers than among the non-drinkers then they would inevitably be more likely to develop cancer. (I would expect there to be more meat eaters than vegetarians among a cohort of regular drinkers.)

Third, no attempt was made to measure the amount of stress endured by the two groups. Maybe the drinkers suffered more stress than the non-drinkers. That would, I suspect, be possible. And we know that people who suffer from a lot of stress are more likely to develop cancer.

It seems that medical researchers are still as ignorant and as sloppy today as they were when I wrote *Paper Doctors* in 1977.

When I wrote *Paper Doctors* I suggested that we would all benefit if medical research were stopped completely and we used the freed resources to use the information we already have. The fact is that we already know tons of stuff which could save millions of lives but we don't take advantage of it because the facts we have are commercially or politically inconvenient.

For example, (and this is just one example) the evidence shows quite clearly that eating meat is as big a cause of death as smoking cigarettes. Governments know this. The World Health Organisation knows it. But no one dare take useful action because the meat lobby is too powerful.

And so we ignore the evidence which would save millions of lives and we continue looking for 'magic bullet' cures which are probably never going to be found and which are not at all necessary.

23

I read today that someone called Kim Kardashian (I hope I have spelt that correctly) who is apparently a television reality performer (i.e. someone who has no talents or knowledge but who is filmed breathing and walking and who is therefore a person of considerable importance in the social media world) charges £380,000 for one photo on something called Instagram (I hope I have spelt that correctly).

Maybe this is what they mean by the New Economy.

I saw an advert in the September issue of a magazine called *Boat Trader* for a ketch priced £37,500. The advert included the following phrase: 'Lying Portugal UK Owners'.

I bet they now wish they'd put the comma in.

Curiously, the word used 'lying' used to be popular on land too.

A chum's grandmother once received a card from a very straight-laced friend in which she said 'Lay at Shrewsbury with your husband'.

I ordered a couple of paperbacks containing *The Times* crosswords. I got them from Amazon and today, I opened one of the books. I discovered to my astonishment that most of the crosswords had been completed by a previous owner.

This is a case of life imitating art.

One of the regular characters in my Bilbury books is a shopkeeper called Peter Marshall who is, to put it politely, a bit of a chancer. One of his tricks is to buy old crossword books which have been filled in with a pencil, rub out the completed entries and then sell the crossword books to customers.

But at least Mr Marshall used to rub out the completed answers. Whoever sold me this crossword book didn't even bother to do that.

Out of idle curiosity, I checked out the practice where, many decades ago, I used to work as a GP.

A friend and I founded the practice in a purpose built centre and for years we ran it together.

To begin with there were just the two of us with a small handful of receptionists. I think we had two full-time receptionists and two part-time members of staff. For nights and weekends and bank holidays, we had an arrangement with another local practice which had three doctors and together the five of us provided all our patients with care for 24 hours a day every day of the year (including Christmas Day).

Today, that same modest building where my friend and I ran our practice is occupied by eight doctors, five nurses, one health care assistant, a phlebotomist, four administrators, nine receptionists and three secretaries. That's a total of 31 people now employed by the NHS in that small surgery.

I suspect some of the medical and nursing staff work part-time. If they don't then they must be sitting on one another's laps to do their work. But that's still a hell of a lot of staff. I wonder how many patients see the same doctor every time they need help.

The sad thing is that with all those doctors and nurses and other staff there is no out of hours service provided. Patients who fall ill at night, at the weekend or on bank holidays must either drag themselves to the nearest hospital, call an ambulance or take their chances with the NHS helpline.

It's not surprising that Accident and Emergency Departments are overloaded.

24

Today I found a letter from a neighbour in our mail box. I don't know when it was written or sent. Most of our mail goes to other addresses in different parts of the country. The mail that comes to us at the seaside house goes into a box on a seven foot high locked gate. I open the box only every day or two.

The neighbour wants us to cut the top off one of a row of a dozen beautiful beech trees because it interferes with his view of the sea. He claims that the already mature tree has grown 25% since he bought his apartment two years ago. He has couched his request (his word) in the sort of way that the police usually couch their 'requests' when inviting motorists to explain why they were doing 41 mph in a clearly marked 40 mph zone.

The tree is at least 50-years-old and is quite beautiful. If we have the top lopped off one tree then we will have to have the whole row seriously damaged. The entire balance and integrity of our garden will be destroyed. I am tempted to ask the council to apply TPOs (tree protection orders) to all of our trees.

The roots and trunks are all on our land and if I spot that anyone has been messing with the trees in any way I shall be consulting the police and lawyers. I gather that in some seaside towns it has become commonplace for residents to poison trees which interfere with their view of the sea.

I had an email from Barclays in France today. They need to speak to me urgently. They say they have tried to call me but I suspect they must still be using the ten year out-of-date phone number which they refuse to remove from their files.

I rang them (the call on my Vodafone mobile cost me around £20 because the EU's abolition of absurdly high roaming charges doesn't seem to apply when calls are made from England to France) and eventually they rang me back. They insisted on my confirming all my bank details on an open mobile phone, while I was sitting in a busy café. They will now, presumably, send the contents of the account over to England. Once again, I spoke to two English speaking employees whose English is worse than my French. But I'm English and I try to be a gentleman so I said nothing.

I had hoped to put the money into a Lloyds account but Lloyds have taken a week to post me the form I needed to put the cheque into my account. (The form went via Andover for some reason). So stuff them. The money will go somewhere else.

Thinking of France, is Emmanuel Macron the vainest and most stupid man in Europe? The news that he spent 26,000 of taxpayers' money on make-up in just three months must certainly make him the vainest. (I bet Frau Merkel of Germany didn't spend a tenth of that).

What the hell did he buy? Where does a Frenchman put 26,000 euros worth of make-up in just three months? And his absurd pro EU policies must put him in line for the title of 'the most stupid man in Europe'. If he could read, and knew the history of the EU, he would know that the EU was Hitler's brain child. So where does that leave poor old Macron? Probably blushing so much he needs more make-up.

Actually, of course, French presidents are notoriously generous to themselves with taxpayers' money.

Sarcozy was so generous to himself that even French voters got fed up with him.

And the shallow and unpopular Hollande, spent 30,000 euros a quarter on make-up and an additional 10,000 euros a month on barbers. Have you seen a picture of Hollande's hair? The man only had about three strands. I doubt if any of Hollywood's most extravagant madams spend that much on hairdressers. What a loathsome slug of a man he is.

Macron, the new President of France, is the Donald Trump of Europe. In fact, Macron is beginning to make Trump look modest and intelligent.

The new Chief Frog, told the press they weren't bright enough to understand him and his thoughts.

Oh dear.

Hubris takes many forms.

The little fellow loves the EU and wants France to be part of a super state. But he also wants to restore the French economy.

Can't do both, I am afraid.

Macron has now discovered that the German run EU won't let him do what he plans. Anyone who understood the EU could have told him that would happen before he made a complete idiot of himself and showed that he doesn't understand the first thing about the purpose of the EU.

I already predict that Macron, who seems to think that he is the new Sun King, rather than merely its President, will lose the next French elections and the National Front will get in. The French people will be fed up with his anti-French policies and his support for the Nazi created EU. His supporters talk as though he won the last election by a landslide but it was in reality a close run thing and the French are already fed up with him.

Over in the United States, La Trump has been a great disappointment to me. Within minutes of swaggering into the White House, the Diva of the political world hurried to recruit men from the arms industry to run the nation's bloated defences and men from Goldman Sachs to ruin what was left of the nation's economy.

Although he promised to put an end to it, he is also continuing with Nobel peace prize winning President Obama's insane war in Afghanistan. That little adventure (for which no one can divine a purpose apart from the protection of some part of the oil industry and the expenditure of vast amounts of money on bombs, drones, bullets and mines, for which the arms industry is doubtless truly grateful) has already resulted in the deaths of nearly 2,500 American soldiers.

25

Singapore is now intending to take 10% of my Indian royalties. I'm not sure why or how this can possibly be legal. In fact, it seems more like mugging than tax collecting.

If I want to avoid this tax I will have to fill in a gazillion forms and send them to an address in the Ukraine. Honest. To avoid the tax people in Singapore taking a chunk of my Indian royalties I have to download some forms and send them to the Ukraine.

This sort of thing happens with monotonous regularity and I have pretty well given up filling in forms and sending them off to reduce foreign taxes. The British Government loses out. Since they take half my income, they will be losing 5% of my Indian royalties to the Singapore Government which appears to have financial representatives in the Ukraine.

Maybe that's what they mean by globalisation.

26

'I've waited my whole life for this', said a 16-year-old, quoted in the papers after some success or other.

Wonderful. Her whole life!

Antoinette says I must not tell anyone about this but I have bought myself a year's subscription to the *Beano* comic. I some time ago decided not to renew my subscription to *Fortune* magazine. It is woefully parochial and contains far too much stuff about millennials and internet companies and is therefore rather juvenile and pathetic. Every internet impresario is a genius, previously unparalleled in human history, and every profile is hagiographic. The magazine seems to me rather like an old man who wears a wig, has plastic surgery and wears clothes usually sold for 25-year-olds.

All very sad.

Amusingly, the magazine recently published an issue containing a list of companies which are, the editors claim, making the world a better place. They put J.P.Morgan Chase, the bank, number one on their list. I almost fell off my chair laughing when I saw that. The top Ten also included Apple, Novartis, Walmart, Toyota and Johnson and Johnson. It's impossible to take a magazine seriously which considers those companies to be making the world a better place.

Reading the *Beano* may not give me more smiles but it will give me a rounder, more thoughtful appreciation of the modern world.

When I want to read something I don't read a newspaper. I read PG Wodehouse or Dickens or Ambler. Or even an old *Dandy* annual.

I spent much of the afternoon sitting on the bench at the top of our stretch of private Devon cliff, looking down onto the beach and the sea. There were many Lego people on the beach (a kindly term which refers only to their apparent size from where we are) and quite a few boats of varying types and sizes in the sea. Quite a few brave souls were using those boards which are used like punts, with the user propelling themselves forward with a paddle.

From where we sit the seagulls, cormorants, crows, rooks, jackdaws and our two resident ravens fly past at or below eye level, sometimes with their young families. We have a huge jackdaw colony at the top of the garden. Several times a day the jackdaws practise communal swooping over the edge of the cliff. They disappear and then reappear as if by magic and for our entertainment.

Bees buzz around the clover and we now have a few peacock and admiral butterflies sunning themselves. A few cabbage whites flutter about.

There is so much to do: grass to cut, hedges to thin, a book to write. But I sit here watching, looking and seeing. A rabbit munches quite noisily on grass and daisies. In the distance, across the bay, I can see a couple of golfers trudging up the hill. Down on the beach I hear children shouting and a small dog barking. There is a splash as someone falls off one of those boards. A motorboat roars across the bay with a water skier in tow. There are all sorts of flowers around me. The noisy rabbit moves a few yards and starts again on a fresh piece of grass. A squirrel bounces about the lawn burying nuts. This is my life.

I sit here, away from the world, and never want to be anywhere else. This is where I want to spend the rest of my life. I no longer have any yearning to travel. Indeed, I feel positively opposed to travel. The world is too big, it is changing too fast and too much of the change is pointless. Travel used to be exciting and educational. Now travel is all about waiting and queuing. I think I will burn my passport if we ever manage to sell the apartment in Paris. The world is simply too rich for my taste; like a Christmas cake or pudding that contains too much fruit, too many nuts, too much brandy, too much richness. The world has become too greedy and mean.

Here, on this cliff, is where my spirit will rest for eternity.

I can see the Channel to the east and to the west and if I made the effort to walk to the top of the garden, and I borrowed Antoinette's powerful, new binoculars, I would be able to see France to the south. But I don't particularly want to see France.

You cannot sit here and not believe in God. I feel closer to God here than anywhere else I have been; this is nature's cathedral. I am at peace.

Our home is tucked into a sheltered nook. The people who built our house chose the spot with great care.

After a little while, Antoinette came out and joined me on the bench.

We sat and watched the world, as though we were ringmasters.

This evening, two DVDs stopped working.

We tried the usual tricks (wiping the disk on something innocuous) but neither resumed normal service. There were no scratches to be seen.

In the bad old days videos occasionally used to stick and sometimes not work at all.

The wonderful indestructible DVDs sometimes stick and occasionally don't work at all.

Progress.

28

I sat in a café while Antoinette was shopping and I was embarrassed when a 20-year-old employee loudly showed a new 50+ employer the ropes.

'This is where we put the trays'.

'When you are collecting the dirty crockery I find that if you put the plates on top of one another you can get more onto a tray'.

The word 'patronising' leapt into my head and wouldn't leave.

In the end, I was so embarrassed for the 50-year-old that I had to leave.

I was reading a splendid book called *Patently Absurd* which describes a variety of objects which have been patented. There is a device for producing dimples, a mouth closing device, protecting armour for cyclists, a combustible gas-powered pogo stick, a birthday cake candle extinguisher, a derriere exerciser and a transparent brassiere in which the breasts float in water.

Most of those inventions were never turned into reality but they produced smiles.

Today, the world is full of inventions which have done an enormous amount of harm. And no smiles.

I amused myself today by making a list of ideas and inventions which have done more harm than good and which I would, if I could, happily uninvent.

I doubt if anyone else will agree with much, if any, of my list. But it's my list. I could have gone on to 100 without any difficulty. Here it is: Health and safety rules with no concept of relative risk values (if something can happen and something can be done to prevent it happening then it must be done to avoid litigation or worse); political correctness; electric cars; the European Union; biofuels; the global warming myth; compulsory recycling; the continental quilt; computers; the internet; the atom bomb; guns; television; powered flight; genetic engineering; electric cars; comprehensive schools; university for all (the idea was that this would keep unemployment levels down among the young but the result has been to saddle countless thousands with worthless degrees and huge debts. Most graduates would be better off without the degrees and the debts); high rise residential blocks; mobile telephones; big hospitals; the NHS; the benefits system (one of the great mistakes of the 20th century since it has encouraged dependence upon the State); aeroplanes; the Beeching report; landmines and self-service tills.

29

One of the most popular videos on YouTube at the moment is a very short film in which a man is on a train. The train stops and the man jumps off shouting 'I've shit my pants'. That's it. Apparently 36 million people have watched this clip and think it is the funniest thing available. I think I have lost touch with the world. The world of YouTube is quite alien to me.

When we put up some short, home-made films which I had recorded, I ticked the box to ensure that no one could leave rude comments. It seemed sensible.

Within hours, I received an email telling me that my presence on YouTube was not credible because I had not allowed folk to abuse me online.

Surely, if people want to say things about me there are plenty of other ways for them to do so without my making life easy for them.

Antoinette bought me a small silver pen knife made by Tiffany of New York. There was a modest customs payment of £4.97. Royal Mail charged us £8 to handle the £4.97 payment.

30

Often, when we fall out of love with something (a food, a drink or a place) it is a result of something which has happened to us. We have changed. We have matured. We are no longer convinced that we could survive for the rest of our lives on a diet consisting exclusively of sherbet dip and dandelion and burdock.

But sometimes we fall out of love with something because the object of our affection has changed beyond all recognition. The cheese we once admired is manufactured by a process better designed for the production of car tyres than for the production of a favoured comestible.

And thus it is with Paris.

I have fallen out of love with the French capital because it has changed beyond recognition and now all that are left are the faults.

In the once wonderful parks, the weeds are high and the birds have gone – all killed. The parks now look like abandoned allotments except that they are silent.

It is illegal to feed the birds in Paris. Last year, when I bought packs of bird seed in the supermarket we have patronised for years, one of the uncivil staff members asked me if the bird seed was for birds in the park. I smiled, thinking it was a pleasant question, and said that it was. The next day all the bird seed had been removed from the shop's shelves. The bird seed has never returned. Owners of caged birds must presumably now buy their bird seed elsewhere.

So the last time we were in Paris I managed to cause some concern.

When I bought a loaf of bread one day, I smiled at the loathsome assistant, held up the bread and said 'Pour les oiseaux!'.

The woman stared at me in horror and when I left, I saw her scurrying away to see the manager.

But I bet they don't dare stop selling bread.

Actually, looking for bird seed was rather a waste of time. There are hardly any birds left in the city. They have killed them all. Pigeons, sparrows and crows have pretty well all gone. It seems strange to me that the French worry so much about a few sparrows shitting on the grass when the streets of Paris are ankle deep in merde de chien. (The French never 'pick up' – they consider it beneath them. They prefer to walk around with their noses in the air and, indeed, they do so with good reason.) London, of course, is the same. Both cities are sterile and unwelcoming. I really don't understand the mentality of those who want to destroy all our wildlife. It even happens in the countryside where death squads are constantly out searching for squirrels and badgers to kill. The fact is that politicians do far more harm than any wildlife. We would do better to exterminate them.

Those whose knowledge of Paris is confined to short stays in smart hotels will hate me for saying any of this, and they probably won't understand. Many reviewers of my book on Paris (which was, believe me, written from the heart) attacked it because they had spent a week in the city and therefore claimed to know Paris better than I do.

They remind me of the P.G.Wodehouse character who spent a weekend in Brazil in order to write a guidebook.

31

A couple of decades ago, I received several invitations by promoters to tour Britain, speaking in town halls, village halls, parish halls and draughty halls. It was, I was told, to be a David Icke sort of tour. (Indeed, it was at one point suggested that David and I should do a tour together. That would have caused some fuss inside Special Branch.)

I decided against the tour for a variety of reasons.

But it is one of those things I wish I had done not because it would have started a new career or made a lot of money (I don't think for a second that it would have done either of those things) but because it would have been a good way to see the country.

I used to tour radio and television stations and back in the 1980s and early 1990s, I frequently spent a month or so doing nothing but wander the country making appearances on radio and television chat shows. I found it an excellent way to see what was happening in parts of the country I would never normally visit.

I couldn't do any sort of lecture or promotional tour now, of course. (No one alive has heard of me.)

But I would like to plan to tour Britain with Antoinette for a while.

The trouble is that we both like our house on the cliff too much to want to leave it.

Flicking through the papers today, I discovered the following:

English churches and cathedrals are now charging hefty admission fees. The average entrance fee is £10.17 and the church authorities seem surprised that fewer people now want to go into their buildings. Do they charge worshippers, I wonder? Or is it possible to sneak in and take a look around at Matins or Evensong? What a bloody world we live in. Still, we do now know the value the church puts on the provision of comfort and sanctuary from the world outside.

The metropolitan police are apparently asking for yet more money for their Madeleine McCann inquiry. They've spent around £12 million already and now want more taxpayers' cash. Am I missing something here? Wouldn't the police serve the public better by demanding that the McCanns answer some outstanding questions about their own behaviour before any more taxpayers' money is spent on what has so far been an entirely fruitless search? The current official 'value of a preventable fatality' in the UK is £1.83 million. That's what the Government thinks is fair to spend to prevent a single death. Every year thousands of people who could have been saved die because the Government didn't think it was worth spending money to save them. Thousands of people die because the NHS isn't allowed to spend money on needed drugs. Road safety improvements aren't made because there isn't enough money available. I estimate (and I admit it is an estimate) that the

£12 million already spent on the McCanns could have saved at least 5,000 lives if the money had been used to reduce waiting times for essential hospital tests. The McCanns, of course, have been backed by numerous Prime Ministers and cabinet ministers. No one is quite sure why. And the McCanns are reported to have the best part of £1,000,000 still sitting in a Madeleine fund. If they think detectives would help, why don't they spend that money? Wasn't that why it was donated? (When I last looked, I noticed that around half a million was in an investment account.) Oh, and how much have the McCanns spent of their own after tax income on the search? If I lost a loved one and believed they could be found I would spend every penny I could raise. Finally, it is worthwhile pointing out that thousands of other children go missing – but virtually no public money is spent looking for them. The official figures show that in Britain a child goes missing every three minutes. Why are the McCanns getting such special treatment? If the police are still working for us perhaps they wouldn't mind giving us a few answers.

A 17-year-old thug who killed a 65-year-old man who didn't have a cigarette to give him has been sentenced to four years and four months in prison. So he will doubtless be out in a couple of years. Once again the courts have shown that they do not value an elderly life very highly. Can you imagine how long the sentence would have been if the victim had been a 30-year-old MP or a 30-year-old policeman? Ageism is as rife in our courts as it is elsewhere in Britain.

A Google employee recently wrote a memo about the relative abilities of female programmers which caused some controversy and resulted in him being fired. Here's what Susan Wajcicki, the CEO of YouTube, said in response: 'While people may have a right to express their beliefs in public, that does not mean companies cannot take action when women are subjected to comments that perpetuate negative stereotypes about them based on their gender.' Ignoring the appalling, cliché ridden, politically correct English, there are two things about this which actually frighten me. First, the use of the word 'may'. So now we 'may' have a right to express our beliefs in public. And this from the boss of YouTube – a company which is owned by Google. If we may have a right to express our beliefs then, presumably, we may not have a right to express our beliefs in public if they offend one of the most powerful individuals on the internet. The comment which has caused so much offence did not break any laws. It was not inciting terrorism. It did not reveal privileged or secret information. No one was trolled. It was merely an expression of a perfectly valid opinion. But it clearly upset Ms Wajcicki and was, therefore, unacceptable. Second, I am startled by her suggestion that companies have a right to take action when selected individuals are offended by comments which other individuals have made. Isn't that how we define censorship? Scary stuff. And this from Google which is, in my view, one of the most evil companies on the planet.

September

1

Antoinette discovered that the loaf of bread which Tesco delivered is turning green so, wanting a bit of exercise and some fresh air, I walked along the beach to the nearest town in order to buy an edible staff of life in a colour we prefer.

We forgave Tesco this error since I worked out the other day that buying roughly the same weekly shop from Waitrose cost us around £3,000 a year more. That's £6,000 a year after tax.

We only switched because there is no Waitrose locally.

Apart from the financial saving, I'm glad we changed. The Tesco drivers are much jollier than the Waitrose staff.

It's only about a third of a mile on the shingle and another few hundred yards to the nearest shop but there's coming back as well as going so it's two thirds of a mile on shingle and if you've ever walked that far on shingle it becomes tiring, especially when the return journey is done carrying a shopping bag which gets heavier by the yard. While I was there, I bought two loaves, a bag of onions, a couple of magazines and, as a reward, a bag of doughnuts.

Oh, and I almost forgot, there are about 150 steep steps down to the beach.

That's 150 on the way down and another 300 on the way back (a step up takes twice as much effort as a step down).

But there's always something interesting to see on a walk on the beach.

I saw seven dogs running free, off their leads, and two clear notices which stated unequivocally that dogs must be kept on a lead at all times. Councils don't bother to enforce the laws about dogs.

I believe that if people are allowed to break the dog control laws then the rest of us must be allowed to carry Tasers and pepper sprays as protection.

Why don't the police uphold the laws which have been passed? They would do us all a favour if they arrested more dog owners and fewer motorists. The number of people injured and killed by out of control dogs has rocketed in recent years and will doubtless soon rival the number of people injured and killed on the roads.

On the beach, I saw a woman walking along with a papoose strapped to her chest. There was no baby in the papoose. The man walking with her had no baby either. Where was it? Did the woman routinely walk around with an empty papoose strapped to her chest?

I saw half a dozen people, all seemingly in their 20s, walking along in a group. Each and every one was studying a mobile telephone. I don't know whether they were texting or playing games. Every few steps they took they tripped on large pebbles. They blundered along regardless of the sea, the cliffs, the birds, the sky – seeing nothing of their surroundings. They were a menace to other walkers. I read somewhere that in Honolulu they have introduced a 'distracted walking' law, making it illegal for pedestrians to wander about staring at a small screen and taking no notice of other pedestrians or traffic.

I saw a middle aged woman wearing a headscarf in what is now the accepted Muslim style. She was self-consciously fingering the knot at her neck as though worrying that people might wonder if she was Muslim or a Muslim sympathiser. I suppose she might have just been wearing a headscarf in the way that women do, to protect her hair from the weather. Or maybe she really was a Muslim. I don't really care but I bet the sale of jolly headscarves with pictures of horses on them has nosedived. A year or two ago, the Cotswolds were the headscarf centre of the universe. Today you hardly ever see a headscarf of any description, except on the head of a woman walking three paces behind her husband.

At the top of the beach, I counted around 100 beach huts (I think the preferred technical term is chalets but they are to all extents and purposes nothing more than huts in that they look like garden sheds and are not equipped with either water or electricity) and although it was a lovely sunny day, only two of them were open. That is about as many as are ever open.

The council says that all the huts are sold, leased, rented or whatever they do with them so why do all those people bother to pay out good money if they never use them?

Just along the coast, a beach hut is for sale for £275,000 plus £3,000 a year to the council and no security because the council can tell you to take your hut away at any time.

You could buy a house on the beach front for not much more.

I suspect that many of those who rent, lease or own these huts find that, like boats, they seem more appealing than they really are.

Talking of boats, there are at least 100 very nice looking boats parked in the harbour. And most of them stay there. On a warm, calm Sunday, there may be half a dozen of the smaller boats out and about. But the bigger ones never move. It's probably just too much trouble to do all you have to do in order to go to sea. Most people probably just buy a boat so that they can say they own a boat. But I'm tempted by the prospect of messing about in boats, and all that.

I took my half of our set of two-way radios on my walk. They're supposed to work for about three miles but they don't, of course. They stopped working about half way along the beach. I didn't expect more so I wasn't disappointed. That's the way these days, isn't it? Don't expect too much in order to minimise disappointments. And that's rather sad in itself.

Still, I got there and back without collapsing so that's rather pleasing.

I went to bed grateful that I don't live in Birmingham.

The Unite union has said that its dustmen members are going to strike until the end of 2017 and that no rubbish will be collected this year. I think that if they go on strike for months on end, endangering lives and making millions of people miserable, they go back to being dustmen, possibly even binmen, rather than waste product redistribution management consultants. I am astonished that so many binmen should treat their neighbours with such complete disrespect. I have often thought that it if the Nazis had been recruiting in Britain they would not have found it difficult to recruit an endless number of concentration camp guards. Still, I suppose the same thing goes for most other countries too.

This is, of course, the problem with state control monopolies. It is true that the residents of Birmingham will be able to hire private rubbish collectors but then they will be paying twice and most people cannot afford to pay twice. (Those who pay for private health care or private education are paying twice of course).

It seems to me that strikes are becoming commoner again. But they don't always work well.

Paris tax drivers went on one of their regular strikes when Uber was making inroads into their business. It was not, perhaps, the brightest thing they could have done for the result was that all their stranded customers rang Uber and started to use the new alternative. Many would have probably never have dreamt of trying Uber if their usual taxi service hadn't been on strike. The Parisian taxi drivers found that their strike worked against them and made their lives much more difficult.

Serve 'em right, some might say.

2

As an experiment, in a mischievous moment I posted a comment on a well-known web forum (Linkedin since you ask) in which I argued that eSports as they now exist will have changed dramatically in three to five years and that players and commentators will have been replaced by computers. It was a rare and temporary excursion onto a social media site and I blame the coffee and walnut cake I ate the other evening.

The disruptors, I suggested, would have themselves been disrupted.

There are several good reasons for this and all relate to the psychological make-up of the millennials (sometimes known as 'snowflakes') and the Z generation – almost exclusively the sole consumers of eSports. For the sake of simplicity, I will refer to them collectively as 'snowflakes' though the more I think about it the more I think that the word 'divas' would be more accurate.

First, today's generations of divas are loners. They may be well linked on social media but intrinsically they are loners. They communicate with one another almost exclusively through mobile phones and other gadgets. They are poor at communicating face to face. One inevitable result will be that the market for arena eSports will collapse within the next few years. The demand will be exclusively for battles fought online – which can be viewed on personal screens, without any human contact. Excluding the human factor from eSports will improve the quality of the sport but it will also exclude people from the equation – and that is exactly what tomorrow's generation will demand.

Second, the enthusiasm for genuine violence has been increasing apace for decades. Horror films which were successful a generation or two ago (and regarded as terrifying by previous generations) are now regarded as so feeble as to be comedic. The problem is that each generation becomes immune to levels of violence which shocked the previous generation. Today's enthusiasts require a much greater level of violence. Tomorrow's enthusiasts are going to require even more violence. Games such as Grand Theft Auto and television programmes such as the BBC's appalling Eastenders have constantly and consistently encouraged violent attitudes.

However, the rise in the power of the health and safety police will mean that it will not be possible for there to be any real danger when humans are battling. (Incoming health and safety requirements will also dramatically limit the amount of time humans are allowed to spend playing games on computers.) Watching computers fight each other to death will satisfy all the new urges – while satisfying legal requirements. The viewing figures for battles between self-controlled humanoid robots will be huge. The humanoid robots will battle to the death – until the vanquished collapses in a puddle of cogs, wires and oil.

Third, divas are innately selfish. They see the world only as it exists to them. Tomorrow's divas will not want to watch other divas doing anything – let alone playing computer games. They are interested only in watching people humiliate themselves (as on reality television programmes). It is clear, therefore, that watching inanimate objects warring will allow them to be entertained without any genuine human contact being necessary and without them being expected to idolise other divas – an anathema to the next diva generation.

When I first suggested that eSports will change dramatically in the coming half a decade, the response from millennial eSports enthusiasts was immediate and dogmatic.

They insisted that what I suggested was quite impossible and, implied that people simply wouldn't stand for it. (As though the planned changes were going to be forced on people – rather than arising from human demands).

I was assured that the status quo was rock solid and that there could be no changes.

(One clearly offended individual admitted that what I postulated was possible. But not yet. Not in a way that might impinge on his career.)

This amused me for the millennials who control the internet have happily disrupted thousands of other businesses. They were happy to destroy other people's lifestyles and careers but they are clearly terrified that the same thing might happen to them.

Complainants seemed to think it was impossible and unthinkable that such a thing should happen to their industry. They are making a good living out of eSports and they are horrified that anything could happen to interfere with business.

The astonishing thing is that eSports people don't realise how fast things change. This is bizarre. Their entire industry was born just a blink ago. You would think those involved would recognise that they too could be obsolete in another blink. Most significantly they don't seem to understand the importance of human psychology and the way that rapid changes in human behaviour are having an impact on every aspect of our world.

The eSports industry is proud to boast that 380 million fans follow eSports. That is truly extraordinary. A few years ago, it would have seemed inconceivable – absurd even – that human beings would pay to watch other human beings playing computer games.

But those 380 million, and the next generation of fans, will follow new developments with matching eagerness.

And those who want to make money out of the new versions of eSports will have to adapt their business models. Those who are currently earning a living playing computer games will have to accept that they will need to look for some other way to pay their bills. The future in eSports lies with software engineers and mechanical engineers who can build robots and warring computers.

I took great delight in putting on another note telling the unhappy whingers to embrace the change (as the millennials are always saying) and to remember that progress is inevitable. I reminded him that thousands of publishers, bookshops and record shops hadn't thought that the internet would disrupt their business models.

Hours later, the responses to my original thesis were still coming in. And they were, I suppose, fifty fifty in that half of the people responding thought my scenario perfectly possible and said they rather liked the idea of watching computers playing against computers. (I can't imagine anything less fun myself but there you go). The other half, consisting exclusively of millennials involved in the eSports industry in one way or another, were hysterical and abusive, aggressive and, I thought, bullying in nature and accused me of trying to destroy their industry. One said I was trying to force him to accept my opinion. The majority of these respondents were bigoted, narrow-minded, intolerant and humourless and they clearly could not accept the possibility that they might be wrong or that the status quo could possible change in any way that they did not approve. All these respondents rejected outright and quite dogmatically any possibility that their tiny world could possibly be disrupted in the way I had outlined as a possibility. I was told that I must withdraw my prediction. The overriding attitude was 'we don't like what you say and therefore you must not be allowed to say it'. These were not children. They were, judging by their photographs, all in their 20s or early 30s and all male. Most were well educated. What struck me most was that the responses were judgemental and abusive, aggressive and threatening, rather than germane.

And when they weren't being personally abusive they were being, well, stupid.

In response to one complaint, I pointed out that many strange things had happened with startling speed and had shocked experts within a number of communities. As an example of something that had not been expected and which had shocked people, I gave negative interest rates. This immediately produced a response from a millennial eSports player who wanted to know what negative interest rates had got to do with eSports and who then compounded his ignorance by claiming that everyone expected negative interest rates and that hadn't come as a surprise to anyone. What can you say to people like that? I can't deal with these people.

Ah, the hubris of the millennial disruptor who only likes disruption when it doesn't affect his life or income. If it were not so alarming, the irony of it would make me smile.

(As an aside, millennial software designers all say they believe in disruption but what they really believe in is profit. All those kids with new software just want to be billionaires. I see that someone has become a billionaire after inventing a social messaging site called Snapchat. The selling point of this vastly over-valued site is that it destroys messages within a few seconds. Brilliant, eh? I'm expecting to become a trillionaire with my site called Crapchat which destroys messages before they are sent. People who subscribe will be able to send messages without worrying about there ever being any unpleasant consequences.)

The eSport afficionados should, more than most, have been aware of the possibility of change and they should have been anxious to confront any possibilities of change. But they were less able to comprehend the very idea of change than 70, 80 or 90-year-olds.

You would have thought these divas would have heard of Kodak, Polaroid and Xerox. All three thought they had irreplaceable technology and were, therefore, producing indispensable products. All were wrong. It is truly amazing that eSport fans, born in the Amazon generation, should not understand how quickly things can change.

My conclusion has to be that many millennials are not going to be able to cope as the next decade or so brings changes which will destroy all their plans and expectations. They are so hypersensitive that they actually seem to me to be mentally ill. They have no empathy, they misinterpret quickly because they don't read properly and their stupidity is matched only by their aggressiveness.

Now, even making allowance for the fact that these replies came from grown people who were dedicating their lives to playing computer games (and who are, therefore, nerdy beyond most nightmares) it seems to me that even the most avid disruptors lose their affection for disruption when it looks as though it might affect their own area of interest.

The fact is that no one is immune to change and sticking your head in the sand is a sure route to extinction. (It's also likely to result in your getting sand in your ear but that's another story.)

To be honest I found the responses alarming and rather frightening.

Free speech? Not acceptable.

Off the wall, original opinions? Not acceptable.

New ideas? Not acceptable.

Really, that's the way the world is now.

The millennials, or a large chunk of them, are so insular and self-absorbed that they reject anything which seems to them to threaten their view of life. They are like adolescents in that they think the world is about them. And when things don't go their way they whinge. They seem to be constantly surprised to discover that life isn't fair.

I have also noticed, by the way, that millennials welcome censorship. They love it. They can't get enough of it. As a generation they are uniquely, exclusively fascist. But when they are threatened by the censorship they become hysterical.

Maybe they need to read about Sisyphus who spent his days in Hades, pushing his damned boulder up the hill and then watching it roll down again. Or, at the other end of the cultural spectrum, listen to Homer Simpson who described life as 'just one crushing defeat after another'.

Alternatively, as usual, no one put it better than P.G. Woodhouse.

'What is life, asked Bertie Wooster once, 'but a series of sharp corners, round each of which Fate lies in wait for us with a stuffed eel-skin.'

No one has ever put it succinctly.

Life is one surprise after another, most of them unpleasant. And, just for fun, life usually ensures that the problems we worry about most, usually turn out to be of little consequence. It is the problems we don't see coming which really hit us hard on the back of the neck. Life's thunderbolts have a tendency to hit us all from time to time.

In a way, I think I understand squirrels, rabbits, cats and other animals more than I understand the millennials.

The people truly are a new breed.

I am certain that some of these critics will celebrate the fact that I deleted my remarks and that they succeeded in silencing me and forcing me to withdraw.

What happened, and what they won't understand, is that I have such complete contempt for these people that I no longer want to try to communicate with them. I can have a more sensible conversation with a rabbit.

Most of the millennials who responded appear to be spoilt brats; precious, touchy, selfish, greedy and headed for a life of endless disappointments. The world is now full of meddlesome, irritating, know it alls, who take instant and permanent offence at so many things, and must qualify as professional offendees.

Teachers who over-protect children from failure (by banning sports days and ensuring that no one fails an examination) and over-indulgent parents are partly to blame for this strange new breed of sub-humans.

Television is to blame, too, of course.

Rudeness is now endemic, both in drama and in entertainment. It isn't just joshing. It's deliberately conceived to be cruel and hurtful.

And the internet itself must be blamed too for it has divorced people from reality in a way that makes them feel able to be abusive and threatening from the safety of their armchair, their bedroom or a café table. They feel safe because the person they are abusing is miles away and doesn't know who they are or where they are.

Occasionally, of course, the person being abused will track down and punch the abuser. And the abuser will demand that the authorities deal with the retaliator.

A year or two ago, an author whose book had been savaged by a reviewer traced the culprit and punched her on the nose. As an author, I can't really blame him for that. My pseudonymous novel *Balancing the Books* (written by the deliciously named Donald Quixote) would have been my fictional extension of that incident if I hadn't written the book before the incident occurred. *Balancing the Books* was fun to write and contains lots of gruesome murders. It's about a sweet woman whose husband, an author, is destroyed by wicked reviewers. She sets about killing them – but making their deaths look like accidents. And she succeeds terribly, terribly well. She is probably still out there somewhere; plotting and killing, plotting and killing.

Incidentally, I have noticed that an increasing number of reviewers will complain that they do not like a book or a film or a whatever because it is not something else; it is not what they wanted it to be or wish it had been.

They are not reviewing what exists but what they wanted.

That is, of course, a fair criticism if the reviewer were misled. If you buy a movie which is promoted as a gentle romantic comedy and you find that it consists of Jason Statham killing people for 90 minutes then you are entitled to feel aggrieved.

But if you buy a movie which was advertised as consisting of Jason Statham killing people for 90 minutes, and you find that the film does include footage of Jason Statham killing people for 90 minutes then you do not, in my view, have a right to complain that the film was not a gentle romantic comedy starring the egregiously self-satisfied and sanctimonious Paltrow woman.

The problem today is that the needs, requirements and demands of the reader or viewer now over-shadow the importance of the artist's ability to produce the work which he had intended to produce.

People used to enjoy a book (or a film) even if they disagreed with the author's point of view. They would respect the writing and maybe learn something from the content.

These days it seems to me that too many reviewers (and I include professionals who write reviews for a living) write reviews in order to express their own view and to substantiate their own view by damning the author's opinion, point of view or carefully marshalled facts.

Young authors are already censoring and Bowdlerising their own work in order to avoid seeing their work destroyed.

People say that authors shouldn't take reviews personally. That, I am afraid, is a rather silly thing to say. Every book I write has some of my soul in it. I give my books some of my life. So of course I take it personally when someone slams a book because it isn't the book they wanted or because they bought it by mistake but still managed to find the right way to write a seering review.

Now here is what I find really scary: most authors would not dare write any of these paragraphs for public online consumption – either on a website or in a book.

The readers of these diaries are tolerant, intelligent and compassionate and sensible enough to understand that human beings cannot all agree about everything and that it is perfectly possible to debate issues, even those about which we feel passionate, without resorting to abuse and threats and violence.

That now sounds patronising but it wasn't meant to be.

What I'm trying to say, and perhaps doing it clumsily, is that the sort of people who read this book have to be tolerant and able to accept my foibles and eccentricities because if they aren't they would have given up at page two, written a one star review and deleted the book.

Silly complaints mean that writers amend how they write. And, in an important way, that is the beginning of the end of civilisation.

In their tone, the responses I saw reminded me of the gang led by a self-righteous and painfully vindictive author whose main objection to a book of mine seemed to me to be the fact that it had been published before his own book on the same subject. He rounded up his social media disciples, wound them up like clockwork soldiers and marched them off in my direction. The only thing that can be said for them is that they obeyed his implicit instructions to blacken my book to make room for his own tome with commendable enthusiasm and efficiency.

'Let's destroy all his books,' wrote one disciple. And thus it came to pass.

Once a book has been slaughtered on the internet, it is ruined for life. An initial one star review is often all it takes.

(It is possible to mine some comedy from the reviewing game. In my novel, *The Hotel Doctor* I described how customers at a Parisian brothel began to rate the girls working there and how, in response, the girls set up their own website and began rating the customers. In my book, that was the end of that particular piece of silliness.)

And so with a shudder, and the sound of jackboots in my ears, I deleted all my comments about the eSports business and vowed never again to enter into any online conversation. The thought of wasting my life with such people is frightening. How, I find myself wondering, do these people deal with one another? What sort of future do they have? I shudder to think.

I do think some of the people who communicate online have lost all sense of proportion. The other day, while sitting in a café, I overheard a conversation which included the following remark: 'It was the worst day in history,' he said. 'There was something wrong with my connection. Even Twitter was down for an hour and a half.'

Ah, what joys and adventures lie ahead for these poor lost souls as they tip toe through life with such attenuated fears and high expectations.

Am I alone in thinking that Twitter has simply provided millions of self-obsessed, self-important millennials with a modern megaphone through which they can broadcast every stray, irrelevant, superficial and unconnected thought which pops into their heads? (The subsequent generation, known as Generation Z, is just as worryingly self-obsessed.) We now have a whole generation of self-obsessed individuals. Doubtless, psychologists will try to find a name for it. There is no need to bother. It's known as narcissism and it has (appropriately) been recognised for millennia.

I have this vision of a 1970s world in which everyone is given one of those push button megaphones which police inspectors use to control crowds. It is a world in which the air is thick with the isolated, bigoted, promotional bleatings of the half and quarter witted; a world in which good sense is drowned out by the screaming of several million Linekers.

That's what Twitter and Facebook have done.

The creators of social media are bad, bad people who have done a bad, bad thing.

3

One of the jailed Libor traders from Barclays has been whingeing. After serving less than half of a 33 month sentence, Alex Pabon, an American millennial, has been released. He complains that because of his legal costs he is not as well off as he used to be. A lot of other people could say that. Barclays shareholders had to pay £290 million in fines. And millions of people around the world lost out because he and his chums were fiddling interest rates.

Pabon claims he didn't know that what he was doing was illegal. That may be true (though I have always understood that ignorance of the law is no excuse and I would have thought it was reasonable for a banker to have a pretty good idea that fiddling interest rates might break a law or two) but didn't he think there might be something immoral about dishonestly manipulating interest rates for profit?

That's a rhetorical question for he clearly still doesn't see that there was anything immoral about what he did.

Is this yet another example of a millennial unable to comprehend the difference between right and wrong?

Many millennials seem to be completely out of touch with reality; too many of them think that what they believe matters more than reality.

And the ignorance of young people is staggering. One in eight people aged 18-24 has never seen a cow. One in five young people has never left the town or city in which they live. The young have virtually no contact with nature. Most have never played conkers or made a daisy chain or planted an acorn or a lemon pip and waited with baited breath. Hardly any have ever built a dam across a stream. Few have ever seen, felt or acquired any understanding of nature in her raw beauty. Vast numbers have never heard of Adolf Hitler and have no idea that we fought two wars against Germany. (A History channel study of 2,000 adults showed that many thought that England and Germany had been on the same side during the Second World War, a third had no idea that the Blitz took place in the Second World War and several hundred did not know that someone called Adolf Hitler was involved in the War.)

Moreover, the millennials have more hang ups than the M&S women's wear section. We have bred a nation of wimps who parade their feelings (especially when hurt) as though they were achievements. Their petulant, selfish, childish whingeing serves only to create more mental illness. If anyone asks them a question, or heaven forbid, dares to criticise, they become hysterical. Too many millennials think they own the world, and that the world exists solely for their benefit, delight and satisfaction. Their expectations are endless and eternal and their sense of entitlement is embedded in their souls.

The young Royals have jumped onto this out of control bandwagon and have made things infinitely worse by talking endlessly about their own apparent suffering. What we really need (and are unlikely to get) is a firmer understanding of what mental illness is and (just as important) what it is not. The young royals, and their fawning acolytes, have made it infinitely more difficult for professionals to provide essential care for those who are really in need because they have encouraged everyone to believe that their minor disappointment or unwanted setback is mental illness which requires full-blooded therapy. Especially with those magic drugs which they all believe are available at the squiggle of a pen.

The young Royals whinge constantly that they want to live 'normal lives'. And yet they are self-obsessed and self-important and what they really mean is that they want the privileges without paying the (modest) price.

'Yes, thank you, we will keep the titles, the privileges, the work-free money, the castles, the special medical care, the palaces, the holidays and the kudos but we want a normal life. Like Greta, we want to be left alone. We will take the cheering crowds and the taxpayers' money and the absence of any real responsibility and obligation but we will take a rain-check, thank you very much, on the opening of cupboards and the intrusive photography and the endless bloody on-line carping and criticism.'

It's pure, 22 carat millennialism.

4

A surprisingly small group of militant communists, most of who seem to hate England and a good many of who are foreign, now appear to control the Labour Party and they are campaigning hard for the referendum vote to be ignored. They clearly do not believe in democracy. Anyone who does not believe in democracy and who tries to interfere with our democratic process is our enemy and should be treated as such. What seems to be widely forgotten is that there is no practical difference between communism and fascism. And since the EU is the most fascist organisation in history, it is hardly surprising that the unelected left wing nutters who now control much of Parliament are also enthusiastic supporters of the EU and are demanding that, contrary to the will of the British people, we remain members of the EU.

Meanwhile, I am learning a few words of Russian.

Antoinette, who is brilliant at learning languages and can already converse in Mandarin, is learning Russian and I have learned a few words so when we are out together Antoinette, who is going a storm, can chatter away in Putin-speak and I can reply with a word or two from my limited vocab, just to confuse people.

5

Two weeks ago, I thought I had succeeded in persuading Barclays to close my account in Paris. They were supposed to send the proceeds of the account to a bank in England. Since I had heard nothing, I telephoned today to find out what had happened. They could not tell me anything because none of their computers was working. Has there ever, in the history of banking, been a bank quite as disorganised, inefficient and grossly incompetent as Barclays in France? It is absolutely no exaggeration to say that if you add up all the time I have spent telephoning, trying to telephone, waiting for the telephone to be answered, photocopying documents, taking documents to the post office, emailing and so on I have wasted a vast amount of my life trying first to persuade Barclays to change my address and then to persuade them to close the account and send me the money it contained.

Meanwhile, of course, they continue to have the use of our money.

There's only around 6,200 euros in the account but if they are doing the same nasty trick with everyone else and taking weeks to close accounts then they're giving themselves a ton of free money to play with. And then the bankers wonder why they are hated so much.

My attempt to sign a cheque to myself failed miserably, with the cheque I wrote being suffocated by bureaucracy and paperwork.

When I rang Barclays to see how they were getting on with closing my account, no one seemed to know or to care. They had, apparently, received the paperwork a fortnight ago.

One Barclays' employee, when doing a security check, told me the number of my bank account and asked, 'Is that your account number?' I said it was. That apparently satisfied him that I was the owner of the account. Bank security, Barclays style.

I spent about three quarters of an hour on the phone and spoke to several people.

In the end, someone promised to ring me tomorrow. They won't, of course. Time and time again they have promised to ring me 'this afternoon', 'tomorrow', 'immediately', 'this week' and every single time they have let me down.

I hate that because I cannot work when I am waiting for a phone call, so that too is time wasted and lost forever.

Still, today, some of the statements that they promised to send in June arrived. If the damned things had arrived a couple of months ago, I wouldn't have wanted to close the damned account. I know that without a bank account in France I am going to be in trouble.

I wonder what sort of mail they used. I must remember to find out and use it when sending off cheques to local councils and utility companies.

This evening, I got myself into such a state over the stressful on-going Barclays fiasco that I cleaned my teeth with antifungal cream, applied gum lotion to my toe nails, put toothpaste on my athlete's foot and patted some mouth wash onto my cheeks.

To calm myself down I studied the Church Commissioners annual investment report.

Next time you slip five pence onto the offerings plate remember that the Church Commissioners have an investment fund of £7.9 billion. In 2016, their investment managers produced a return of a very impressive 17.1%.

Wheeee. That's seriously good.

Finally, I had some good news.

I have managed to order a complete set of James Agate's diaries (the first was called *Ego 1*, the ninth was called *Ego 9* and the ones in between were named appropriately). They are among the best diaries ever kept by anyone anywhere in the history of the universe.

The books are out of print in the UK and second-hand copies are difficult to find. This set is being sent over from Belgium so I hope they arrive safely.

Agate wrote a series of diaries (each called *Ego* with a number) in which he wrote with rare honestly about his life.

For example, in the entry for June 29th 1932 he wrote, 'A common fault with playgoers is to dislike a piece because it is not something else.'

How I can sympathise with that. A reader has written to complain that he bought a copy of my last diary, *Life on the Edge*, expecting it to contain a collection of Bilbury stories. He complained bitterly and threatened me with all sorts of terrible consequences. I can't help feeling that it is a bit like buying a coal scuttle and then complaining when it turns out not to make a very good teapot. The books are clearly labelled but it seems that as always authors are expected to write the same book time after time. Any variation is likely to cause trouble.

And here is another wonderful Agate quote: 'I don't know very much, but what I do know I know better than anybody, and I don't want to argue about it. My mind is not a bed to be made and remade.'

I don't know why Agate is so little read these days.

The rather nauseatingly saintly Reverend Kilvert is far more fashionable but extremely boring. ('I went for a walk and saw wonderful primroses on Wenvale Hill. Later Miss Pilkington played upon the organ with great success; giving me much pleasure and leaving me greatly satisfied.')

Pepys was the Diary Master, of course, and Fothergill the most outrageous and politically incorrect.

But James Agate was probably the consistently funniest and he undoubtedly provided the very best account of early and mid-20th century life.

6

In the US, less than 10% of retail transactions take place online. But in the UK, the figure has already risen to over 15% and is rising fast.

I was astonished to read that a quarter of all clothing sales in the UK are now made online.

Why could this be?

I can think of two explanations why shoppers in Britain don't like going to bricks and mortar stores.

First, car parking, usually controlled by local councils, is expensive and difficult. Greedy councils everywhere are putting up charges and making the spaces ever smaller. Nasty councils (naming and shaming Carmarthen, Dorchester and Buxton) are also insisting that drivers put their car number plate onto their ticket. This is done to prevent Good Samaritans giving tickets with unexpired time on them to other motorists. What sort of message does that send to people? Kindness will be punished? And, to save money, public loos are being closed and the space used to provide parking for another half a dozen vehicles.

Second, the whole shopping experience in Britain is painful. Staff are rude and unhelpful and have, in many stores, been replaced by self-service tills. It doesn't say much for the retail experience when many shoppers prefer to do their buying online because although it is impersonal it is friendlier than the sort of experience available in shops.

(Why, incidentally, are modern tills designed in such a way that the customer cannot see what they owe but must rely on understanding the assistant's mumbled demands. Old-fashioned tills used to show the total value owed to both the customer and the assistant. As our population ages and becomes increasingly hard of hearing, it would make good sense for those tills which remain, to offer this simple facility.)

Yesterday, Barclays in Paris promised to ring me today. They did not.

I think ill-manners come naturally to them. They refuse to email me for security reasons (though they will email me when it suits them because presumably the security issues don't matter then).

I hate Barclays France with a deep and inconsolable loathing. The company policies are absurd beyond belief and the people who work there are foul. They lie, lie and lie again. It is all the bastards seem to do. They have promised more times than I can remember to post me my statements. I haven't had one. Not one. They promised repeatedly, repeatedly, repeatedly that the statements were in the post but they never arrived. My main problem is the feeling of being betrayed, lied to and let down. If Barclays had said 'Look, old bean, we're all French and unreliable and we lie a good deal and you can rely upon us only to let you down' I would have accepted it and had correspondingly low expectations. But they feigned efficiency and competence and pretended they were a bank. And every time I obeyed the one set of absurd instructions they found another set of absurd instructions and when those were obeyed, suddenly they would find another hoop for me to jump through. It is intensely frustrating to be promised that this will happen and then that will happen – and for nothing to happen.

I gather that today Barclays sold the parts of the bank that are in France.

I've never heard of the company which has bought the branches being sold. I don't really care who they are, they can't make things any worse.

In a way, this is good news. I hope the new owner of Barclays France turns out to be an asset stripper and that he fires all the staff. With luck, they will all end up walking the streets of Paris searching for crusts of bread in the gutter. I know I should not feel like this. It is truly not my nature. But I do. The staff of this damned bank have wasted so much of my life since the beginning of June that I fear that my hatred for them will be sustained until I die. And at the rate I am going that won't be long.

Today, we got home to Devon to find that a man had parked half outside our gate on the double yellow lines which I persuaded the council to repaint. I tooted lightly, in that non angry way which means, 'Excuse me please do you mind very much just moving your car a few feet so that I can get through my gates and into my driveway.'

The driver didn't move an inch though there was plenty of space behind him. Instead, he watched while I jiggled and turned and tried to get the truck into the driveway around him.

In the end, predictably, I caught the front wing on one of the stone gateposts.

Only then, when he heard me do about £500 worth of bodywork damage to the paintwork and metal, did he condescend to move a few inches.

(Proving that things really do go in threes, over the next two days I managed to damage both our other cars. The Bentley I scratched on a twig while driving in a narrow, Devon lane. You'd be surprised at the damage a twig can do. The Ford I succeeded in backing into a tree which had evaded the sensors at the back of the vehicle and which I couldn't see because of the mud on the back window. I consider it a Parisian style parking adventure. Three out of three in three days must surely be some sort of appalling record. I shall not, of course, be claiming any of this on the insurance.)

When I remonstrated with the driver who was sitting in his car and watching my vehicular contortions, he just stared at me uncaringly and unseeing.

I think I have been abducted by aliens and moved to another planet. I want to go back to the old one where there were at least some kind and thoughtful people around.

When we got in, we settled down and picked out a suitable film to watch.

I feel so enraged by the world (particularly Barclays France) that I have a constant (and, I hope, temporary) need to watch violent films in which bad people are killed in huge quantities. I sit and imagine that the Russian or Chinese gangsters or Arab terrorists are all employees of Barclays France. It is a joy to watch them die bloody and painful deaths.

Suitable movies include *Where Eagles Dare*, *John Wick*, *The Equalizer*, *22 Bullets* and almost anything starring Jason Statham. In all these films, the baddies are all employees of Barclays France.

To be honest, I'd really like to watch something with Cary Grant, William Powell or Robert Donat but I know I wouldn't be able to concentrate on anything requiring brain matter.

If I didn't have Antoinette to love and to cherish I would dissect out a vein and bleed to death on the cliff top.

I don't think I have ever felt so bloody low.

7

Barclays France still refuses to send me my banks statements. They won't telephone or email me. But now they have managed to write to the UK address I gave them demanding the return of my cheque book. The letter is unsigned.

In the 17,000 conversations I have had with Barclays France, no one has previously mentioned the need for me to return my cheque book. I had assumed that burning it would suffice and it is a miracle it hasn't already gone into the incinerator because yesterday I tossed it into the bin in my study.

I must now go into town, queue in the Post Office and post them the cheque book by registered mail. If I don't send it registered they will lose it or simply say they've never received it.

Whenever they want me to do something, Barclays France usually writes in both French and English. For this letter, they wrote only in incomprehensible banking French. They have also sent me, by separate post, a form I can fill in if I wish to change my telephone number in their records and get rid of the two phone numbers which they still hold on file – one of which has never been my number and the other of which is around a decade out of date.

Actually, they have sent me two separate and quite different letters about the telephone number.

And the letter demanding the return of the cheque book seems to contain something threatening about what will happen if I do not do as they demand. I do not give a fig what this is because I would rather welcome a chance to confront Barclays in court – even a French one.

I give thanks to the banking gods that if we ever sell our bloody apartment in Paris, I have no intention of using Barclays France to move the money back into a proper currency.

I took an aspirin tablet to help prevent my first heart attack and a decent measure of 23-year-old Bunnahabhain to help wash it down; one of my favourite scotch whiskies. (Do not try this at home. Only doctors are allowed to wash aspirin down with whisky. It was a soluble aspirin, dissolved in a little water.)

I wonder why the Bunnahabain people bottled it at 23 years of age.

Perhaps they intended to wait until it reached a quarter of a century but got tired of waiting.

'Nearly there, folks.'

'Oh bugger it. I'm tired of waiting. Let's sell it now.'

I thought I would open the bottle because I hate the thought of dying and leaving it unopened. Whoever acquired it after my demise would never appreciate it as much as I will. As I think I've said before, it is like drinking Christmas.

8

David Lammy, the black MP who seems to me to have an ego the size of an Alp and the brainpower of a mushy pea, has apparently led an inquiry into young people in British prisons.

He found that a lot of them were BAMEs (an acronym which I had never heard before but which apparently stands for Black Asian Minority Ethnic) and that although BAMEs make up just 14% of the population, they make up 25% of our prison population.

One of Lammy's solutions is brilliantly simple: give potential prisoners the chance not to go to prison.

This, he reckons, will reduce the number of BAMEs in our prisons.

Gosh, I suppose it would.

'Would you like to go to prison or not go to prison?'

'Can I ask my mum?'

Lammy seems to suggest that there are a lot of BAMEs in British prisons because they have been victimised.

No one seems to be brave enough to offer the politically incorrect theory that there might just be more BAMEs in prison because they are more likely to break the law.

(Surprisingly, I am pleased to say, there is not yet any suggestion that they are there because of a toxic combination of BREXIT and climate change.)

The suggestion that there is a high proportion of black and Asian citizens in prison because of racism in our judicial system is utter bollocks.

No one seems to have noticed that there are (literally) twenty times as many men as women in our prisons.

Is that because our judicial system is sexist as well as racist?

Or could it possibly be because men are more likely to commit crimes than women?

Similarly, is it not possible that people of different racial backgrounds might, just might, regard property and life in different ways?

Thanks to the efforts of the politically correct, we are all so busy trying to pretend that we are all the same that we sometimes forget that we are not.

The fact is that today London is far more dangerous than New York.

And there are only two possible explanations for this terrifying fact.

Either the police have become much more incompetent or the tremendous influx of immigrants has changed the nature of the city – and it is the immigrants who are responsible for the increase in violence. I am no apologist for the police but I know which answer I believe to be the correct one.

Another annoying piece of news came to light today.

Apparently, the NHS is planning to recruit 5,000 foreign GPs because of a shortage of home-grown doctors.

The new GPs probably won't be able to speak English very well (if at all) and they certainly won't understand idiomatic English.

So the recruiting campaign will be a disaster as far as patients are concerned.

But why does the NHS recruit so many foreign doctors when British medical schools are turning out more new doctors than ever?

Simple.

The first problem is that the General Medical Council (the bizarre and utterly useless charity cum quango which controls the licensing of doctors in the UK) has introduced mad rules which mean that many doctors – particularly older more experienced ones – are being forced out of the profession completely in their 60s and even 50s.

I have said before that I believe that the General Medical Council's mad policies are responsible for thousands of deaths every year.

And now that they have effectively forced the NHS to recruit more foreign doctors, I believe that the problems are going to get worse.

The second problem is that the Government (acting on sexist rules imposed by the EU) has forced medical schools to train more female doctors than male doctors. And thousands of female GPs want to work part time – many working just two or three days a week and refusing to do night time or weekend calls.

The result of all this is that all over Britain, patients are going to have to see doctors who understand very little English and next to nothing about our culture, our fears or our way of life.

What can we do?

Well, the first thing to do is to close down the General Medical Council – which does far more harm than good.

Patients would be far safer without it.

If we don't do something now then the NHS will continue to kill more people than it saves.

(And that is no exaggeration).

Finally, today, in the same news bulletin I discovered that the Government is claiming that the flu vaccine works with children though it doesn't work well with older folk. (Naturally, the fact that it doesn't work very well doesn't stop them trying to persuade the over 65s to be vaccinated against the flu.)

Just how did they arrive at those figures?

The reports I saw contained no background information of any value.

Did they just see how many children who had been vaccinated subsequently developed the flu?

If they didn't compare the vaccinated children with unvaccinated children then the study was utterly pointless and of no value whatsoever.

None of this is much of a surprise.

In my experience, much of the research work involving vaccines is of little or no scientific value.

Amazingly, no research has been done into the long-term effects of vaccination, the effects on the immune system or the consequences of mixing numerous vaccines in one small body.

Our current vaccination programmes are one huge experiment – with no one watching to see what happens. No one assesses compatibility of the consequence of interactions with other substances. We do know for sure that vaccines are often worthless because they don't work very well, and not safe because they can cause real and lasting damage. Maybe we will discover the answers to the unasked questions in a decade's time. Maybe the whole issue will continue to be smothered in silence with no one allowed to question vaccination programmes and with all debate systematically silenced.

Anyone who dares to question the establishment's authoritarian but unscientific claims is dismissed as a renegade, hounded and oppressed.

Here's an off the wall thought: could the strange and often inexplicable behaviour of the millennials be explained by the fact that they have all received vast numbers of vaccinations and are, therefore, brain damaged?

I am not kidding. That's a serious thought.

9

It's the Last Night of the Proms this evening: a night much enjoyed by all those who take delight from English and British traditions. It is part of the tradition of the event that people attending the event wave union jacks or flags for their part of Britain. It is a patriotic celebration of a patriotic event.

Knowing this to be the case, EU supporters (all, by definition, members of the Establishment) are handing out 10,000 of those horrid blue and yellow EU flags to those going into the royal Albert Hall. I suspect they are doing this solely because they know it will annoy, upset and spoil the occasion for the vast majority of those watching. I half suspect the flags are being paid for by the EU itself.

There is no doubt now that those who wanted Britain to remain in the EU are poor losers. It is perfectly clear now that we are going to leave the European Union and that nothing, however mean and nasty, will change that outcome.

The only conceivable reason for handing out so many EU flags, and encouraging those attending the music to wave them for the television cameras, is pure spite.

'You're going to make us leave the EU so we're going to do everything we can to spoil all your enjoyable experiences that celebrate Britain.'

Mind you, the BBC have done that very well. They appear to have politicised the Proms as they have politicised just about everything else they touch.

For example, when did the Proms last include a proper tribute to Gilbert and Sullivan, our most loved and most successful authors of opera?

I am left with a mystery.

Why do so many people still love the European Union so much that they are prepared to wave flags in support of it?

I can understand politicians like Blair, Mandelson, Clegg and Cable promoting the EU. Blair, who is so discredited that he has no chance of a second career in British politics, probably still believes he can be EU president but to attain that goal Britain must remain within the EU. Could it be that Clegg and Mendelson, who are both former EU employees, are loyal to the organisation which will pay them hefty pensions? Is Cable just a self-important, publicity seeker who sees the EU as a way to attract attention to himself?

All of this is despicable, but it is at least self-serving enough to be understandable.

But why do thousands of non-politicians revere the EU when the organisation has made them poorer than they would have been without it, has endangered their lives and has done a great deal to make their lives worse?

I think there are probably several explanations.

Some have undoubtedly been institutionalised. They feel threatened by the prospect of freedom and democracy. Some are monumentally ignorant and do not realise what the EU stands for, how it is run or what its future will be.

Some hate Britain in general and England in particular.

And, of course, many either do not realise that the EU is a Neo-Nazi organisation which was founded by Adolf Hitler. There are doubtless not a few fascists who do realise that the EU was founded by Nazis and who support it for that very reason.

So, the bottom line is that we won't be watching Last Night of the Proms when it doesn't come out on DVD. Instead, we will buy and watch the recording of the New Year's Day concert from Vienna. The Austrians have retained all their traditions and their event is a highlight for millions around the world. The Proms, in contrast, is now just a sordid and pointless embarrassment.

In Devon, we have so many hazelnuts in our garden that the nuts are thick like leaves on our driveway. Rather than crush them all (and make them worthless for the animals) I kicked a few hundred off the drive but the drive is too long and there are simply too many nuts to move them all. When I drove the car along the drive last night, the sound of crunching and cracking nuts seemed like a demented crowd of nutcracker wielding uncles at a wild Christmas party. I have a feeling that our resident squirrels won't eat nuts which have landed on the driveway because they don't approve of the smell of them. Squirrels, like all rodents, have an amazing sense of smell. I know of squirrels who can smell a nut when it is buried inside a solid wooden box.

I read a report today showing that 23% of consumers trust pension companies, 40% trust banks and 30% trust utility companies.

Why so much trust?

How can anyone with any functioning brain tissue trust any of these organisations?

Every pension company, bank and utility company in the country must be regarded as crooked unless proved otherwise.

And so far none has proved otherwise.

10

I am always astonished at how sports stars often react when they win things or do good things. So, for example, a golfer who has won a tournament will go to hug and kiss his children before he hugs and kisses his wife. And a sportsman will often mention his children before his wife.

So, for example, in yesterday's *Daily Telegraph* there was a quote from a cricket player who said he felt a bit emotional because 'I knew my family were there in the crowd: kids, Mum and Dad, my wife.'

The poor wife is mentioned last. Maybe last is best in sporting terms. Seems odd.

Something called Bitcoin is in the news again.

An anonymous bloke invented this currency. It doesn't exist except as a blip in a computer but he said it was a currency and so lots of people bought it, paying good honest dollars or pounds or euros for it. It is particularly popular with millennials who are very greedy and gullible. Greed and gullibility are a toxic mix.

For the last few years, the price has gone a zillionfold so that now people who had £50 in bitcoins are millionaires.

But nothing actually exists. You don't even get a tulip bulb.

The joke is that the people who are keen on Bitcoins think they have invented something entirely new. They haven't, of course. People have been inventing currencies since men decided that living in trees wasn't much fun. The advocates of Bitcoin claim that there is no opportunity for fraud. But this is rubbish. There have already been massive Bitcoin frauds.

The advocates also claim that the idea of a currency which only exists in computers is brilliant and innovative but this, too, is nonsense. When you buy a house and the bank moves money from one account to another, does anyone actually see any money? Of course, they don't. The money exists only in computers. When Central Banks 'print' more money they don't actually 'print' more money. They just tell the computers that the stuff is there.

Bitcoin is just another way for confidence tricksters to scam the gullible and the greedy. It will end in tears.

I don't really care about the greedy idiots who have invested in the scam. But I do worry that when Bitcoin collapses, the real economy will be affected. Internet investing is now all interlinked and a huge dotcom like crash in one area will doubtless affect other parts of the financial world. And many of those who have borrowed to buy Bitcoins will have to sell other investments to pay off their sudden debts.

The Bitcoin fever is just like the tulip fever that tore Holland apart. It is no more logical than the dotcom fever which led to a financial rout. And it is no more sensible than investing in mortgage based securities which were built upon the greed of estate agents, banks and speculators.

Incidentally, I have it on good authority that because of all the computers involved the whole Bitcoin nonsense uses up more electricity than Serbia. Honest.

11

We have an appointment to sign documents to sell the apartment in Paris. But we have to sign them in offices on the other side of the city. I asked our notaire in Paris why we couldn't sign the documents at her offices instead of at the buyer's notaire's office. Since the buyer has set the date and the time I thought it seemed fair that we had a choice of venue. But no, this is not possible.

Apparently, when a property is sold in France, the transaction must be conducted at the offices of the buyer's notaire. This is the law. The French have a law about everything. It is the way Napoleon Bonaparte wanted it.

It's a good job, I said, that the buyer's notaire isn't in Nice.

'Oh, if it were then the transaction would be conducted at my offices', responded our notaire.

It seems there is a law about that too.

The French don't rely on common sense for anything. There are laws governing absolutely every aspect of human behaviour. And whereas in the past the French used to regard the laws merely as an excuse for a little imagination, the modern French regard the law as the law and they take everything very, very seriously.

12

It is a little breezy today. The met office has given the breeze a name and called it a storm. We have been told to keep the cat indoors and to prepare for bits of tree to fall off.

The authorities will doubtless do this all through the winter so that they can say, at the end of the winter, that we have had more storms than ever. This will please the idiots who run the world and who believe in climate change.

(I note, incidentally, that in recent months both the Governor of the Bank of England and the Pope have become expert spokespersons on climate change. When, by the way, is there going to be a female Pope?)

The pound has strengthened and Barclays have still not sent our money. This incompetence has cost us the equivalent of several decent bottles of malt whisky.

13

My nine diaries by James Agate arrived safely and in good condition. Most of them are first editions. Looking through them, I am delighted that I bought them. The volumes I have are all 'best of' the diaries and selections taken out of a diary don't carry the flavour of the original. It's a bit like watching a DVD of the best of a favourite comedian. I once saw a DVD which consisted of highlights of Tommy Cooper's shows and contained very little but punch-lines. Without the build-up, the background and the patter, the shows weren't at all funny because the timing had disappeared. In good writing, like comedy, timing is everything.

We are off to Paris next week and so I have prepared some idioms to teach the French. As I mentioned earlier, I like to use idiomatic phrases such as 'Tally ho!', 'Right ho old boy!'. 'Odds bodkins', 'What ho!' and so on whenever I am speaking with foreign people. I particularly like to use the phrases 'crave a boon' and 'the game's afoot'. Other favourites include 'Hither and yon', 'Pip pip', 'Right ho!' and 'My dear old thing', as made famous by the irreplaceable Henry Blofeld.

'May I crave a boon?' I might say to the Frenchman who thinks he speaks excellent English. (All French folk think they speak excellent English. Even when they are unintelligible they think they speak excellent English.) Then, when he seems confused, I will explain and express surprise that he has never heard the phrase. 'English is a very tricky language,' I will say kindly. 'Foreigners always have difficulty in mastering it. But you're doing quite well. You should persevere. You will soon reach a point where English people will be able to understand you without too much difficulty.'

The ones who like to sound English always pick up these idioms and try to use them. And nothing sounds funnier than an earnest Frenchman saying 'He cocked a snook!' or 'The game's afoot, eh?'.

The trick, I find, is to bring the adapted idiom into an ordinary stretch of conversation. Usually the French person (though this works just as well with Germans and Belgians and would probably work well with the Italians and the Spanish if you could ever get a word in edgeways when talking to them) asks what the phrase means. If they don't ask then you repeat the idiom with an explanation casually tacked on after it. If they say, 'doesn't it mean XYZ?' you say 'Oh no that's something completely different,' laughing lightly and derisively as you speak.

It is, of course, more fun if you create slightly bastardised idioms. Here are some I created for distributing among the French: 'He dug himself into a corner'; 'Never punch a gift horse in the mouth'; 'He was as healthy as a harp'; 'It was like looking for a milkmaid in haystack'; 'Never steal someone's lightning'; 'Give someone the cold elbow' and 'He punched the bucket'.

Today Barclays have closed my account and sent me the euros it formerly contained. They have still not sent my statements. I've had no official notification of what was in my account, nor what was taken out of it, since May.

I changed the euros into sterling and bunged them into an investment account. The UK end of the operation took less than five minutes.

I then went onto the internet and gave Barclays a one star review. I've never done anything like this before but I couldn't help myself. There wasn't much point. They have over 600 reviews and 86% of them were for 1 star. The average rating is, therefore, 1 star.

Wouldn't you think a major clearing bank would be embarrassed enough to want to know what they were doing wrong?

No, of course you wouldn't.

14

The Greens want to stop us using oil, gas, coal and uranium. They want us to get all our energy from renewables such as solar and wind power. Through their power in the EU, they are forcing through policies which fit with these aims.

They say we should leave all the oil and gas in the ground. They want the big oil companies to go bust. Numerous investment companies (including pension funds) are refusing to invest in oil companies because of pressure from the silly, ignorant Greens who want to fly to their regular conferences by solar powered jet and power up their laptops with wind power. (Good luck with those, boys and girls).

Bless them, aren't they the little sweethearts? We need a jolly giant to whom we can say: 'Please eat up our greens.'

Sadly, there is a teeny weeny problem which the Greens haven't noticed.

Actually, there are several teeny weeny problems.

First, electricity, though very nice and useful stuff, only provides about 20% of our energy needs. The other 80% comes from nasty old gas, oil, coal and nuclear power.

Second, it is nigh on impossible to increase that proportion. It's impossible to power ships, aeroplanes, lorries and so on with electricity. It's a bummer but that's the way it is.

Third, an awful lot of people rely on gas for their central heating and cooking. If all those people are forced to use electricity for heating and cooking then there is going to be a great shortage of electricity because we are already using up every drop of the stuff that we can make.

Fourth, renewables such as solar energy and wind power provide only a quarter of our current electricity needs. We would need to carpet the countryside with solar farms and wind farms to increase that proportion significantly. And without subsidies (paid by consumers to rich landowners) the electricity produced would be horrifically expensive.

Fifth, (and this is a real heartbreaker for the Greens), manufacturing and maintaining windmills and solar panels requires more energy than the windmills and solar panels actually produce. The much loved renewables are actually a negative source of electricity.

Sixth, electric cars don't work either. Making electric cars (and the batteries they need) requires vast amounts of energy – far more than is needed to produce a non-electric car. And the electricity which electric cars use when they are running is taken from the 20% of our energy supply which is provided by electricity. (This is where it gets really painful for the Greens.) Moreover, despite all the subsidies which have been introduced, we still obtain 75% of our electricity from oil, gas, coal and nuclear power. So, three quarters of the electricity which keeps electric cars on the roads comes from (wait for it) oil, gas, coal and nuclear power. Despite all these simple truths, Britain and France have announced their intentions to ban the sale of all petrol and diesel cars. India wants all cars to be electric by 2030. And China has announced its intention to phase out the sale of all petrol and diesel powered cars.

Still, we mustn't despair.

If the Greens insist that we stop using gas, oil and so on then we must do that rather than upset them.

However, since renewables only produce electricity we will have to survive on a source of energy which provides just 20% of our current needs. (You can't make oil or gas from windmills or solar panels).

And since renewables only provide a quarter of our electricity we will have to survive on just 5% of the energy we use at the moment.

This is a bit of a problem because we can hardly cope on the energy supply we have now.

We can only cope with the Green's demands if we give up:

All forms of powered transport (including cars, planes and ships)

All forms of entertainment which require electricity (e.g. television, radio, computers, mobile phones, etc.)

All forms of heating

All factories which make things

All mechanised farming and all fertilisers

All hospitals, medical treatments and drug production

Of course, the real bummer is that the 5% of our energy which we have left will be needed to maintain and service our solar panels and our windmills.

If there is any energy left over, we may be able to boil a kettle and make a cup of hot water, though there won't be any tea leaves, milk or sugar to put in the hot water.

The good news is that our inability to use tractors and fertilisers will mean that most of us will starve to death, so we won't mind too much.

Welcome to the Green World.

All this is accurate. It is true and it is terrifying.

If the Greens have their way, our planet will plunge into the biggest war of all time. The survivors will be those countries which retain fossil fuels and use them to manufacture armaments and to make and fuel bombers and tanks. The citizens of countries which decide unilaterally to rely on renewables will die.

Our energy policies define our future.

And our current energy policies mean that we have no future.

15

Antoinette bought us each a pack of Whitworth dried apricots from Tesco. And then she noticed that on the back of the pack it said that the apricots had been hand stoned and left out in the sun to dry. All this had been done in Turkey. How well did the people who did the picking and the laying out wash their hands? Were the apricots laid out on the dirt or on old bits of carpet or old newspapers? How many birds shat on the drying apricots? Were the grubby apricots washed at all before they were packed?

We threw the two packs away.

16

'What do you think will kill you first?' asked Antoinette. 'The North Koreans nuking us all? Planet Nairobi smashing into Earth? Yellowstone Park erupting? The Green's crazy energy policies?'

'Oh, definitely the bastard who is or is not supposed to be buying our ruddy apartment in Paris,' I replied.

I am exhausted, full of anger and weary from the frustration, the feeling of uncertainty, the helplessness. I have been repeatedly ignored, lied to and I have felt unable to influence any of it. I've been depressed, suffered from repetitive brain strain. I have felt like bursting into tears through impotent rage. Fortunately, I know that there is no drug in the world that will help bring an end to the pain. The only solution is to push and push for conclusions. I have to remind myself of the Chinese saying: 'We cannot help the birds of sadness flying over our heads, But we need not let them build their nests in our hair.'

Long ago, I wrote a book called *Toxic Stress* in which I argued that much of the stress which harms us is completely beyond our control. It is not there because we work too hard or put ourselves under pressure. It is there all the time; a result of society's demands and uncaring. Stress comes not from what happens to us but from how we react to what happens to us. Well over forty years ago, I pointed out that it is how we react to what happens to us that does the damage; and part of that is how we perceive ourselves in the aftermath of stress. Chronic, persistent stress creates uncertainties, desperation and self-destructive behaviour as we lash around looking for unavailable comfort and invisible solutions.

17

A spider walked across our living room. It was so big you could hear it walking on the rug. We caught it with one of those suction tube things. It was then a toss-up whether we should send it to Longleat for their wildlife park or release it into the garden. We chose the latter for convenience but warned the spider not to come indoors again. There are plenty of suitable outbuildings.

There is no doubt that our spiders are becoming bigger and more powerful and I have no doubt the mythologists blame this on global warming.

I saw a cobweb yesterday which was tethered to a tree by a strand of web which was over fifteen feet long.

I don't think any of this is a result of global warming. It makes just as much sense to blame the European Union.

18

We are off to Paris tomorrow and for the first time in my life I am not looking forward to it. I really don't want to go.

A short while ago, looking through my library for something to read on the train I picked out a beautiful leather bound copy of *Barnaby Rudge* by Dickens. I realised the other day that when I was working my way through Dickens as a boy, I must have missed this one. What a joy. It is genuinely pocket-sized (six inches by four inches and two thirds of an inch thick). There are 668 pages but it is printed on Bible paper and that's how they kept it so thin and light. I love small books which can be fitted into a pocket or shoulder bag and I cannot understand why publishers seem to make books bigger and ever more cumbersome. When I was publishing my own books as 'proper' books, I repeatedly, but unsuccessfully, tried to find a printer who had machinery which could print on Bible paper.

When I found this copy of *Barnaby Rudge* I looked on eBay to see if anyone had any more of this pocket sized leather bound series of Dickens. I have a fine collection of first editions but you can't read those in the bath or on a train or in the garden. To my delight, I found a bookseller in Scotland prepared to send me all 14 books in the set for £20 plus £6 postage. I suspect that the price is low because Dickens is now out of favour.

The politically correct arbiters of taste (aka the sanctimonious censors) disapprove of Fagin because Fagin is both an unpleasant character and a Jew. In the same way *Guardian* readers, schoolteachers and the BBC disapprove of Shakespeare because Shylock, in the *Merchant of Venice* was a Jew. You can have bad Christians and bad Muslims but you aren't allowed to have bad Jews.

Both Dickens and Shakespeare must also struggle against the huge disadvantage of being white, male and English. These are impedimenta of crushing weight.

Modern theatre directors dislike Shakespeare so much that when they are pressured into putting on performances of his plays, they frequently put the actors into modern dress. This is appalling bad manners and quite notably stupid since it creates an uncrossable schism between the words (which are clearly Elizabethan) and the costumes (which are clearly not – or at least not the right Elizabethan.) Also, it is a nonsense to insist on having a black actor play Othello. (It would make as much sense on insisting on finding someone with royal blood to play Lear or deliberately casting a Jewish moneylender as Shylock.) It is equally obscene to have all female casts, as is also popular now. This is merely feminism on a mad rampage. The director might as well have the actors naked and walking about on stilts. That would draw attention too.

The seller of my collection of Dickens even agreed to split the parcel so that it could travel by Royal Mail rather than a courier who would doubtless get lost and never arrive. (Our postman in the Cotswolds puts parcels into a huge, plastic storage box we keep hidden behind some hazel bushes near the front door.)

The books arrived today. What a dream. Well over 100-years-old but in beautiful condition. The leather is generally unmarked and the paper feels like silk. I'm going to reread the Master.

We are travelling to Paris for an appointment to sign the initial documents relating to the sale of our apartment.

But today, I received an email from our notaire in Paris telling us that the buyer will not be attending the signing.

We (and she) were initially assured by our estate agent that the buyer had the necessary cash and would be buying the apartment without any outside assistance.

Now it transpires that the buyer does not have the just over one million euros required and has co-opted his mother as joint buyer.

Unfortunately, they have just discovered that even together they don't have enough money and they have to apply for a bank loan. I don't understand this. You would think, would you not, that someone preparing to spend over a million euros on an apartment would know early on whether or not they had a million euros kicking around in a bank account.

Coincidentally, we are told that the mother of the buyer cannot attend the signing because she has decided to go into hospital on Wednesday for an operation. Her failure to sign is, allegedly nothing to do with a shortage of funds but entirely a result of this sudden desire for surgery. Our notaire doesn't have the foggiest what is going on.

The cancellation came with a promise that they would be able to sign the necessary paperwork on or after the 9th of October. It appears that they know for a fact that mother will have recovered from her surgery on that date. And they will have found the money by then.

I sent a note expressing sadness and hoping that the operation went successfully. I don't think anyone on our side of the fence believes that this is anything other than a clumsy delaying tactic. Still, they cannot keep using it.

The whole business is becoming tiresome beyond belief.

What I find most annoying is the fact that selling the apartment is, for me, a rather sad affair. Having owned it for nearly 20 years I have grown very much attached to it. It is spacious, light and airy and although Paris has changed dramatically, the apartment has stayed loyal. It is a little scruffy it is true (it is 17 years since Antoinette and I painted it ourselves because we couldn't find any reliable French workmen prepared to do it for us.)

19

When we arrived at the apartment, we found seven letters from Barclays bank. Each envelope contained at least one bank statement.

Each of the statements had been posted after we had officially changed our mailing address to an English address.

Sadly, when I turned on the boiler it made a hugely expensive sounding noise. I rang our boiler service people. They cannot come until tomorrow afternoon.

The apartment is cold. The water is cold. We could boil pans and the kettle for baths but the bath is huge. I turned on the electric fire. It blew up. The damned thing actually blew up and stopped working!

Things were not going well.

'Let's try the boiler again,' suggested Antoinette.

So I turned it on and we both ran out of the kitchen and hid in the hall while it made a hell of a lot of noise.

Suddenly the noise stopped and the boiler started to purr.

We tried a tap.

Hot water!

The radiators started to warm up.

It had been nothing more substantial than an air lock.

20

I'm 250 pages into *Barnaby Rudge*, which is subtitled *A Tale of the riots of Eighty*.

There is still no sign of riots.

And *Barnaby Rudge* hasn't been seen for so long I'm thinking of starting a search party. Only Dickens could get away with it. But I'm still reading and captivated.

Our telephone went early this morning.

This was odd because our phone in Paris never rings. We use it only for ordering workmen and taxis. The caller, a young woman, spoke in English and asked to speak to Henry. When I said that there was no one around called Henry she asked to speak to Richard. I apologised and said that she had the wrong number. (I am English and so I always apologise if someone makes a mistake which inconveniences me in some way.)

When I had put the phone down, I explained to Antoinette that I had received a very strange call. She spotted instantly that the call had come from the estate agent's office and that our deeply unpleasant agent had doubtless been endeavouring to find out if I had come to Paris despite the buyer pulling out of the meeting.

Although we were no longer due to sign anything, I visited our notaire to discuss what we should do next.

While I sat in the reception area waiting to be seen (reading my *Barnaby Rudge*) our estate agent turned up.

He wanted to know if the buyer could call around the following day to measure up for alterations, carpets and so on.

I said that this would not be possible since we were sorting our possessions and that the apartment floor was covered entirely in books, CDs, DVDs and clothes. He was clearly put out by this and said that he would have to try to ring 'her' to cancel the appointment.

Is it possible that the woman who had an operation yesterday (on the arranged day of the signing) is now well enough to totter around our apartment armed with a tape measure? If so then I feel insulted that the deceit is so badly managed.

'By the way,' I asked him. 'Do we have to empty the apartment completely before the final signing?'

'Yes,' he said sternly. 'You must.'

They have a lot of laws in France and everything is taken very seriously.

'What about the kitchen equipment?' I asked. 'Cooker, fridge, sink, washing machine, dishwasher, boiler and so on?'

He thought about this. 'You can leave those,' he said at last. He made it sound as if he were doing us a favour by agreeing to this.

'And the bathroom?' I said. 'Should we leave the bath and the sink or should we have those taken out?'

He thought again and then nodded. 'You may leave those,' he said, making it clear that we shouldn't expect this sort of generosity as a rule.

We decided (or, rather, I decided and the notaire agreed) that we would give the bastard and his mother an ultimatum: 'Sign on the 9th October and complete the transaction by the end of the month or you're not buying it'.

The notaire admitted that she had never known a transaction go as badly as this one.

Why does everything strange happen to us?

The real problem is that right at the start of this procedure I and the putative buyer both signed an Achat. I was assured that this simple document (very short for anything produced by the French) was merely an indication of interest. I agreed to sell the apartment to the buyer and the buyer agreed to buy the apartment from me.

(The apartment is in my name because I bought it a few months before I met Antoinette and I was living by myself at the time – intending to move to Paris. Putting the apartment into both our names would create legal and tax problems that would keep the entire French judiciary busy for a century.)

The Achat is not supposed to be a legal document but it has, over the months, acquired legal standing. The estate agent (whom I now loathe even more than he doubtless loathes me) has warned me that if I do not sell the apartment to the putative buyer he will be able to sue me. The Achat is undated and it appears that the buyer can wait ten, twenty or a hundred years before buying the apartment if that suits him. He will then be able to buy the apartment at the price mentioned on the Achat.

The real problem is that the Achat contains no date.

If I ever sign one of these things again I will write on it that the Achat is only good for 30 days or whatever I deem appropriate at the time. Come to think of it, I don't think I will ever sign an Achat again. They can manage without one.

French law is now notoriously and absurdly in favour of the buyer of property. This is fine and dandy except that most buyers will eventually become sellers and then discover that laws which seemed rather jolly at one end of the procedure have become grotesque at the other end.

It seems logical that if the Achat has legal standing for the buyer then it must also have legal standing for me, as the seller.

But it doesn't seem to work that way.

The notaire then showed me a list of the taxes and deductions which will be made before I receive any of the proceeds from the sale of the apartment (if it is ever sold). There was one deduction for 600 euros.

'What is that for?' I asked.

'That is for the agents who look after the building,' she explained. 'They have to provide a letter confirming that you have paid all your bills – for repairs and maintenance.'

'And they charge 600 euros for that?'

'I'm afraid so. It is outrageous but it is the law. They are allowed to charge.'

I then handed over 200 euros in cash to pay for copies of some documents which had been obtained.

(I had already given copies of the documents to the estate agent whose office is probably 200 yards away but it had apparently proved impossible to find anyone willing or able to carry the copies that enormous distance. So the process had to be delayed another month and I had to fork out another 200 euros.)

After I had finished at the notaire's office, Antoinette and I filled another half a dozen boxes with books to post to the UK.

Each box weighed just under 5 kilograms and should have gone by the cheap book rate. Unfortunately, when we arrived at the French post office, the official on duty was a young girl who obviously hated foreigners.

'Are all the books in French by French authors?' she demanded. I said that sadly they were not. 'Then they cannot go the special cheap book rate,' she told me sternly.

I told her, in English but with a smile, that it was an enormous comfort to me to know that she would most likely spend her entirely pointless and miserable life working behind a Post Office counter.

There was a hearty round of applause from some English tourists who were standing behind us, queuing to buy stamps for their postcards.

Can it possibly be legal to charge more to post books written by English authors than it is to post books written by French authors?

It sounds racist and ethnicist and completely contrary to the principles of the European Union.

Is this the world of Macron, I ask myself?

The answers don't matter a damn, or course, because the girl behind the counter is the one with the all the sticky labels and rubber stamps and all I have is a wallet stuffed with their silly euro money.

When we returned to the apartment, we continued sorting out.

I found a packet of balloons, blew them all up and put them into an empty cupboard which I could only just reach.

The French are all dwarves and when one eventually manages to open the cupboard he will be overwhelmed by balloons falling out onto and around him.

I then sent the estate agent (technically he is 'our' estate agent but he is 'ours' in the same sort of way that 'Macron' is our President of France and Mrs May is 'our' Prime Minister) a note in which I apologised to both him and the member of his staff who had made the phone call earlier in the day.

'I am sorry,' I said, 'that I was confused by the call.'

He did not appear to be in the slightest bit embarrassed by this.

He sent me an email in reply which contained one of those childish smiley faces constructed out of punctuation marks.

In France, the estate agent is paid by the buyer not the seller (and so the fee of 5% of the price will be added to the bill). This is, it seems to me, one of many flaws in the French procedural process. It means that the estate agent's loyalty is probably to the buyer not the seller.

Sometimes, I think I would like to have been born more patient and more tolerant. And then I realise that I would have been a completely different person if I had been. I think I have always been compassionate (a trait which has caused even more trouble than my impatience) but if I had been more tolerant of other people (such as vivisectors for example) would I have fought so hard for animals and people?

I rang to book a taxi for Saturday. The woman who took the booking insisted on taking my mobile phone number so that they could send me a text to let me know that the taxi was on its way. I thought this was pretty impressive.

When I'd done that I telephoned our phone company to cancel the phone. The woman to whom I spoke said they would not send the final bill to another address. It has to go to the address where the phone is registered. It would be sent out in one month's time, undoubtedly so that we would have to pay for a month's rental that we did not require.

'But we are leaving Paris,' I said, hopefully.

She shrugged. I could hear the shrug of indifference at the other end of the telephone.

'It is the law,' she said.

'How do I pay the final bill?'

'You must tell the postman to redirect the bill.'

Or not.

21

One of America's most successful hedge fund operators, a man called James Simons, has revealed one method he and his firm used to make money.

He noticed that there was a correlation between weather data and stock market returns and that in Paris, in particular, the stock market did slightly better on sunny days.

So, by using leverage (with borrowed money) Simons' hedge fund made huge profits out of this absurd correlation.

22

Leaving the apartment today with two huge bags of rubbish, I turned on our stairs and asked Antoinette if I had my sunglasses on. (I couldn't remember if I was wearing my sunglasses or my reading glasses.)

'Yes, you are,' she replied.

'That's odd,' I said. 'I can see very well.'

'You're looking over the tops of them, just the same as you do when you're wearing reading glasses,' said Antoinette patiently.

I am delighted to see that the NHS is now warning that it is important to differentiate between Alzheimer's disease and normal pressure hydrocephalus because 'the symptoms of NPH can be relieved with treatment'.

I am delighted by this for it shows that my campaign to improve awareness of normal pressure hydrocephalus is beginning to have an effect. A few months ago, the NHS officially regarded NPH as very rare and made little official effort to encourage doctors, nurses and others to differentiate between the NPH (the curable dementia) and the other forms of dementia (such as Alzheimer's).

Antoinette spent much of the evening teasing me about my sunglasses remark earlier today. We finished our packing and then found five crystal champagne glasses in a cupboard. I stuffed them into Jiffy bags, wrapped them in clothing and crammed them into a suitcase.

'We're bound to break one of them,' said Antoinette.

'OK,' I said. 'Which one do you think will break? We might as well leave that one behind.'

23

Today we took the train from Paris to England.

When I booked our tickets I made sure that there were no big events in Paris today. No visits by Presidents. No major football matches. No marathons. No events likely to snarl up the city and prevent us travelling from the apartment to the Gare du Nord. Paris shuts down at the drop of a hat and I knew that we would have a number of heavy suitcases to carry.

When I checked this morning I discovered, to my horror, that Macron's opponents were planning a huge demonstration in Paris, that there were a number of transport strikes in operation (including a blockade by petrol tankers, preventing fresh supplies of petrol and diesel reaching the city) and that Eurostar was having trouble with its trains. Selfish civil servants of all kinds (who make up the larger part of what is laughingly and inaccurately referred to as the French workforce) are protesting that they may lose the chance to retire at 50 on full pay.

There are always big demonstrations in France whenever a President tries to drag the labour laws out of the 19th century. Macron wants employers to have the right to fire bad employees or make employees redundant if times are hard. Without any such rights, many employers are unwilling to expand or take on new staff.

But we were lucky.

Our taxi driver took us on a very pleasant route which took us past les Invalides and the Opera and managed to miss all signs of the demonstrators. After we'd been in the taxi for about twenty minutes, I received the promised text from the taxi company to let me know that our taxi was on its way. Perhaps they need to work on this use of modern technology.

As a result of the strikes, Paris was deserted. It looked like a Sunday. The shops and cafes which have not been permanently closed and shuttered were quiet and doing no business whatsoever. Macron may as well roll over now instead of dragging out the pain. Every French President since de Gaulle has tried to change French labour laws. Every single one has talked tough. Every single one has capitulated in the face of protests. Macron, who is very inexperienced politically and who has an ego bigger than the Eiffel Tower will give in quickly when the jeering becomes serious and he realises that he has become even more unpopular than the saucy Hollande.

Macron has made things worse for himself by describing his opponents as stupid slackers. Demonstrators have taken to the streets wearing T-shirts and carrying banners describing themselves as stupid slackers.

Macron's problem is simple: his arrogance drips off him. He is typical of the sort of French snob created by les grandes ecoles – the same colleges which train eurocrats and rulers of France. Macron et al are the sort who regard democracy as government by cobble hurling riff raff; something to be avoided at all costs.

At the bottom of the escalator leading up the Eurostar terminal (they put it on the first floor so that travellers have to go up with their baggage and then, when boarding, go back down) a genial black fellow stood with a board containing pictures of various types of guns, bullets and explosive devices. He showed it to Antoinette. She shook her head.

'No bombs?' said the black fellow with a huge grin. He seemed disappointed.

When he showed it to me, I studied the items on the board and then shook my head. 'Non merci. Je ne veux pas acheter quell que chose aujourdhui.' No thank you. I don't wish to purchase anything today.

He laughed.

I went through customs wearing a thin shirt, a thick shirt, a jumper I didn't want to leave behind, a jacket, a coat I had found, a scarf and a Grosvenor style hat made by Bates of Jermyn Street in London. I was cooking.

There were the usual long queues.

As always only one carousel was working (they have three but two always remain idle) and so there was a big queue of people waiting to hump their bags onto the conveyor belt.

Between us, Antoinette and I had seven cases and bags. No one at Gare du Nord offered any help whatsoever but just stood and watched as we struggled to load the bags and cases onto the conveyor belt. To be fair, the damned things were so heavy that they were probably outside the allowable range for health and safety reasons.

(Yet another thing that annoys me about the French is that they are such dirty people. It has always annoyed me that whereas travellers in England are told to put their jackets and outer clothes into a plastic box before putting the box onto the conveyor belt, travellers in France are offered no such facility and must put their jackets et al straight onto a filthy conveyor belt. Now that I have come to loathe the French I realise that many things which previously looked quaint and charming, such as dirty, dented motor cars, now look simply scruffy and lazy.)

My jacket pockets contained my small, leather bound copy of *Barnaby Rudge* by Charles Dickens, a paperback of *Uncommon Danger* by Eric Ambler, a rather fine French pepper grinder, some portable weighing scales, a pair of pliers, a silver hip flask full with Cardhu malt whisky (the remains of a bottle), three CDs, a DVD, a roll of sellotape, two clean pairs of socks and an unopened tube of toothpaste.

In short, the normal sort of detritus Englishmen slip into their pockets when travelling between countries.

Since porters are a thing of the past at the Gare du Nord and trolleys not provided (they are an unnecessary expense and their presence would add nothing to the SNCF's bottom line) I was dragging and carrying a pile of suitcases and bags while wearing enough clothing for an expedition to either Pole. I was, therefore, pouring with sweat.

Fortunately, the two dozen French security people who were standing around were too busy chatting to one another to remember their training and the bit in the manuals about bombers sweating. Or maybe they just didn't care.

We got all our cases and bags through customs without anyone bothering to take a look. Pity, really. Antoinette's largest suitcase contained, inter alia, 74 CDs, a full bottle of Cardhu and a very realistic stuffed cat. I had been looking forward to her case being opened.

'Francois! This woman's case contains a pile of CDs, a bottle of whisky and a dead cat. What should I do?'

'Is she English?'

'Yes.'

'That's OK then.'

I was waiting for someone to look at all our bags and cases and ask 'Are you moving house?' so that I could reply 'Yes.'

The Gare du Nord has now replaced many of the seats with benches which have no backs. Travellers must, therefore, sit on unbelievably uncomfortable benches.

Moreover, Eurostar express their solidarity with French socialists by putting the first class carriages at the far end of the train so that passengers who have paid the most (and who are, on the whole, the oldest and frailest) have furthest to stumble, dragging, carrying or pushing their luggage under the watchful eyes of unhelpful railway staff.

On the train back we sat across the aisle from a Frenchman who looked perfectly sane but who spent the whole journey reading a magazine out loud. Occasionally he would comment on the article he had read out. It was, I suppose, a variation on the rather eccentric habit of talking to yourself and then commenting on what you've said. Why do people do this? I glowered at the fellow several times but he was so captivated by the sound of his own voice that he didn't notice. I don't think he would have noticed if the train had gone across the English Channel without bothering to use the tunnel. I suspect that to describe him as an idiot would have been an upgrade.

This reading aloud business isn't just a French peculiarity because there is a fellow in Cirencester who favours a café we patronise and he is often in there sipping his latte, or whatever, and reading his book out loud. We always try to sit as far away from him as possible but the problem is that everyone else does too.

360

I read the papers (quite silently) and managed to do so without even moving my lips. This is a trick which I learned at school.

I was annoyed by an article written by someone called Tim Harford in the wretched and loathsome *Financial Times*.

Mr Harford obviously regards himself to be as much of an expert on vaccines as Jade Goody's ex-boyfriend. In an appalling piece entitled, 'The fatal attraction of cynical falsehoods' (in which he attacked people who misuse facts) Harford stated categorically that the flu vaccine cannot cause the flu.

He perhaps did not know that some flu vaccines are attenuated not killed and could revert. The nasal vaccine, for example, is not killed.

Second, he stated with equal certainty that vaccines cannot cause autism.

However, this is an open question and there is much convincing evidence that they can. Who knows what evidence will appear in the coming months and years?

Cynical falsehoods indeed – though it is easy to see why he made what I consider to be elementary mistakes.

Time and time again doctors, nurses and drug companies claim that vaccines are safe and effective. By this they imply that all vaccines are always safe and effective. They don't say 'some vaccines are safe some of the time' or 'a few vaccines are occasionally effective'. They say: vaccines are safe and effective. This is the establishment, official line but it is not true, of course. It is, indeed, a lie. All vaccines are potentially dangerous. And none of them is entirely effective for everyone.

Researchers don't look for problems with vaccines because they get paid by drug companies, and drug companies don't want anyone looking for problems. 'We think it appears safe' really isn't terribly reassuring when vaccines are being given to millions of people in the biggest drug trial ever. And no one is looking for problems.

I sent a letter to the *Financial Times* correcting the writer's errors but naturally, the Letters Editor declined to print my contribution. It would, I suppose, have been contrary to the *Financial Times* in-house philosophy to allow inconvenient facts to be given consideration on the pink pages.

The *Financial Times* is so appallingly, embarrassingly biased and bent over in favour of the EU that it makes the BBC look positively fair-minded. It is relentlessly in favour of the EU and establishment promoted myths such as vaccination and global warming. What a despicable newspaper it is; quite possibly the most treacherous and irresponsible newspaper ever printed in Britain. It is worse, I suspect, than Pravda and whatever the Nazis printed, because it pretends to be honest and fair when it patently is not.

And why would the *Financial Times* want to bother their readers with the uncomfortable fact that for a number of diseases far more people die of the vaccine, or are severely injured by it, than die of the diseases themselves, the ones for which the vaccinations are given?

This is a fact but no one cares about facts any more.

The prejudices and the propaganda must come first.

There is absolutely no point in complaining about the *Financial Times* which is a biased, prejudiced, bigoted and relentlessly inaccurate newspaper.

Indeed, to whom could I possibly complain? No one in the media cares about the truth.

So, the myths are strengthened and more people will suffer and die as a result.

When our train approached our stop, a sign came up on a screen above us: 'Enjoy Your Stay in Ebbsfleet'.

I laughed so much I nearly cried.

How can you enjoy your stay in Ebbsfleet? It's a soulless railway station and a windswept car park. But maybe the Russian railways put up a sign saying 'Enjoy Your Stay in Siberia'. Actually, I don't suppose Russian signs have little signs that light up. Maybe a bloke in a furry hat wanders about carrying a piece of cardboard with 'Enjoy Your Stay in Siberia' scrawled on it with a piece of charcoal.

When we left the train, Antoinette and I dragged our cases and bags a mile and a quarter along the interminable platform at Ebbsfleet (I could see no trolleys available there either though I heard a rumour that some had been seen huddled together out of the way – though my bet is that they required travellers returning from abroad to have British coinage in order to release them from confinement) and I muttered a silent prayer that I would never have to board another Eurostar train. An old couple struggled to get aboard with their luggage. Two young men in Eurostar uniforms just stood and watched as they struggled. Antoinette and I helped the couple onto the train. Travel has become an unpleasant business and I concluded some time ago that no one should now travel with more luggage than they can comfortably carry themselves for at least half a mile, including hauling it up or down several long staircases. Travellers should practise at home against the clock.

The Eurostar service has deteriorated dramatically in the nearly two decades we have been using it. The conductor no longer even bothers to warn travellers that the time is changing an hour forwards or backwards and no one announces that the train is entering the Channel Tunnel.

As far as I could see, there are no longer any individual lights and the overhead lights are so harsh and glaring I find it difficult to read on the train.

(It is well known to everyone except Eurostar carriage designers that general lighting is a lot less helpful than direct, focussed lighting. Those of us with developing cataracts find the absence of specific lighting makes life excruciatingly difficult. For example, I cannot see to read if an overhead light is switched on but I can see to read if I have a focussed light source. Even Samuel Pepys knew this for heaven's sake.)

The carriages now appear cheap and nasty.

Eurostar is just a faint imitation of the service which I first used nearly a quarter of a century ago. At one point I was travelling on Eurostar once a week, then we moved to once a month. When we have sold our apartment, I hope never to have to use it again. Even buying tickets is hard work and takes half an hour on the telephone. This is probably because they want everyone to use their damned website. One of my favourite Mont Blanc pens was stolen on the train. Antoinette and I both nodded off and someone took it from the table.

On our way back home on the motorway, our satellite navigation device wanted us to take the M3 but the gods were with us and I refused. I don't know why. It just didn't seem a good idea at the time.

Within minutes, we saw a sign warning that part of the M3 was closed. For the next 60 miles, we saw conflicting messages saying that the M3 was now open, that it was still closed, that it was now open, that it was still closed and so on.

As usual, the police and highways people seemed determined to cause confusion.

It turned out that a 12 hour closure was caused by some liquid being thrown onto the motorway. Huge traffic jams were created though for the life of me I cannot see why they couldn't test the liquid, confirm it wasn't deadly and then remove it from the motorway in less than 12 hours.

I am convinced that Britain's police forces are run by our nation's enemies (there are now many) and that the plan is to disrupt the country as much as possible.

I seriously believe that 'managed motorway schemes' are designed to increase the size of traffic jams and use up petrol and create traffic jams and more pollution. Britain is known to have the busiest, most overcrowded motorways in Europe and the Ministry of Transport seems determined to make things ever worse.

And why are motorways invariably shut down for a standard four hours or so whenever a selfish, attention seeking idiot threatens to throw themselves off a motorway bridge? Surely there must be a quick way to deal with the problem. Think of the pain, stress and distress caused to tens of thousands of motorists. We will never know how many innocents are made ill by these exhibitionists. (Motorway bridges aren't particularly high and if you jump then death is not an inevitability.) I did some basic sums and a four hour delay on a motorway will lead to a traffic queue of between seven and ten miles. That means around 10,000 cars being held up. And in cold weather those cars will use up between £150,000 and £200,000 of fuel just to keep the drivers and passengers from freezing to death. Just think of the pollution caused by all that wasted fuel. Just think of the missed appointments, the disappointments, the business disasters. How many surgeons and anaesthetists are caught up in these jams? How many patients miss vital hospital appointments? How many trains don't run because the driver couldn't get to work? How many children must wait on the pavement because their mothers can't get home on time? The big problem is that the publicity given to those who threaten to jump off motorway bridges means that it has become a popular way of attracting attention. It really is time that the police found a quicker way to deal with the problem. Nets or tranquilliser darts would speed up the process and save much stress and many innocent lives. Or park a few furniture lorries under the bridge. Or a row of bouncy castles.

Many people have supported the would-be jumpers (who hardly ever jump but usually abandon their suicidal thoughts when they become cold or hungry) but I rather doubt if those supporters have been stuck in a four hour motorway traffic jam.

The official estimate is that, overall, traffic jams cost Britain around £9 billion a year so, given the tendency of government agencies to under-estimate costs by a factor of two or more the cost is bound to be at least twice that.

I am not in the slightest surprised. Why has it taken until now for anyone in power to notice?

Back in the 1970s and 1980s, I used to do long radio and television tours which lasted for three or four weeks at a time. Each day I would visit three, four or five radio or television studios to do promotional interviews for my latest book. I often used to travel quite long distances between interviews but I don't remember ever missing an interview.

These days our roads and trains are so bad that I find I have to allow at least two extra hours for breakdowns, holdups, accidents or those stupid 40 mph signs which the police put up on motorways when the traffic is moving too freely and they feel the need to do something to bugger up everyone's journey.

One motorway was recently closed completely because a lorry needed to have a tyre changed. It would have been cheaper to have airlifted the lorry off the motorway with one of those massive helicopters – or to have blown it up. (Why doesn't our sat nav find us a route around the blockage? Why aren't sat nav devices pro active? Why doesn't my sat nav tell me I am approaching a problem and then guide me round it before I get there? Isn't that what satellites and computers are supposed to be able to do? To be honest, most sat nav schemes seem woefully primitive.)

These days when Antoinette and I have to travel on a motorway, we put a bag into the car containing enough food and water to last us 12 hours. I am not kidding. We don't stop at motorway service stations longer than we have to because we're conscious that the longer we are on or around a motorway the more likely we are to find ourselves in a motorway traffic jam. And as we trundle along at slightly more than walking speed, we entertain ourselves by trying to find Christian names to fit the personalised number plates which are now so ubiquitous. So GBW would be Gilbert Bertram Wilberforce and RTE would be Reginald Theophile Everard.

The real problem is, I suspect, that self-important traffic policemen and absurd health and safety rules are the cause of the huge queues which are now a regular aspect of our motorway system. All these unnecessary traffic holdups endanger lives, add massively to air pollution, waste millions in fuel and cost Britain billions in wasted time and lost production.

It seems safe to assume that variable speed limits on motorways are used in order to catch drivers speeding – and therefore make money out of them. The constant changing of speed limits means that drivers are forever braking and accelerating and that means that accidents are more likely. It also means that more fuel is used and more polluting gases are emitted. Moreover, there has, for years, been clear evidence that forcing motorists to drive slowly causes more accidents and that when speed cameras are removed there are fewer accidents. Drivers lose concentration when they are forced to travel at inappropriately low speeds. (Incidentally, am I the only one to have noticed that the police seem to use a good many grey, unmarked estate cars for motorway patrols? Wouldn't they do better to ring the changes occasionally?)

Too many policemen seem to take pride in the length of the queues on 'their' stretch of motorway.

Surely police forces should be fined if the queues on their piece of motorway are exceptionally lengthy?

Public service officials in Britain are far too fond of bonuses. We should use negative financial incentives more often.

We went back to our home in Gloucestershire and the minute we'd walked through the door, we decided to go back to Devon instead of staying in the Cotswolds. So we climbed back into the Mitsubishi truck and trundled on again. By the time we got to Devon, we had travelled across a chunk of France and much of

England in one day and had, during the course of the day, visited all three of our homes.

When we unpacked the cases, we found that the crystal champagne glasses were all intact. What a miracle.

One final thought for the day: I hate the fact that so many motorway service stations now seem to be run by or for Messrs Marks and Spencers.

Our favourite service stations all seem to be converting to M&S and instead of selling decent doughnuts and edible snacks, they now sell overpriced and inedible food designed for nutty, Fairtrade millennials.

24

I tried to fix up a new email address. By mistake, I put in the wrong birthdate. 'Your application is rejected,' said the website sternly. 'You are too young to have an email address.' Realising my mistake I corrected the birthdate.

The website then accepted my application and allocated my chosen email address in the name I had selected. (The name, for the record, was Patchy Fogg. I think everyone should have an email in the name of Patchy Fogg. I use the poor fellow's name whenever possible.)

Surely this rather defeats the purpose of trying to exclude children from having email addresses? Or don't the people who make up these rules realise that nine-year-olds are probably perfectly capable of lying about their date of birth?

So, it is official, Mrs May has betrayed the country and makes James Joyce (Lord Haw Haw) look positively patriotic.

We voted to leave the EU but Mrs May seems to have decided not to bother. She now joins the long list of traitors in British politics. Britain voted to leave the European Union and it is a disgrace that we have as Prime Minister a woman who wanted us to stay in the EU. May is shovelling money into the EU's coffers, seemingly without a thought for the people who will be paying for it. A billion here, ten billion there. Politicians always talk about billions as though they don't matter. But they damned well do. And the irony is that these are the same politicians who will submit an expenses claim for an aspirin tablet or a biscuit if they are spending their own money. Our money doesn't matter so much.

We have too much politics.

Politicians should just look after things and keep quiet. But these days they have massive egos, hidden agendas and a yearning for the wealth they believe they deserve. Their only skill is making simple things complicated and using other people's money to make themselves obscenely rich.

This is something they have mastered and they are assisted in their endeavours by regiments of bureaucrats and eurocrats.

Anyway, Mrs May has now nailed her colours to the mast. She's come out of the closet as someone who clearly loves the EU more than she loves Britain. And in my book that makes her a neo Nazi.

And a pretty craven, weak, wishy washy neo Nazi too.

I suspect that calling that daft election was either done for her own benefit (so that she could say she had won an election rather than inheriting Number 10 from David Cameron) or it was done to wreck the Brexit process. I find it impossible to think of any way in which the election campaign could have been more badly run.

Britain is at a critical juncture. Never, since 1939, have we needed strong leadership more than we do now. And never have we had such weak leadership.

Is Theresa May a worse Prime Minister than the awful Gordon 'the moron' Brown?

Well, Brown just destroyed our economy.

May could destroy what is left of the country by failing to take advantage of the Brexit vote to leave the EU and frustrate Hitler's plan.

25

In Victorian days, a reformer was more likely to be successful if he could suggest that the victims of injustice whom he was trying to protect were in moral danger.

In his amazing and enormously readable book *Roads to Ruin* (published in 1950 and subtitled *The shocking history of social reform*) E.S.Turner points out that 'what shocked the middle classes, who read the reports on conditions in the mines a little more than a century ago, was not so much the system under which children crawled on all fours dragging sleds behind them, or in which men ruptured themselves lifting loads on to their daughters' backs; it was the revelation that lightly-clad young women working in proximity to naked men at the coalface made no strenuous efforts to save their honour when molested, which was fairly often'.

Turner's book should be daily reading for everyone interested in campaigning for reform. He points out that 'even if he suspects that he is a crank (and a crank rarely suspects any such thing) the reformer must not give up. 'Normal' people rarely exert themselves in the direction of reform, and sometimes fanatics draw added strength from being derided. How far would 'normal' persons have advanced the cause of the suffragettes?'

And Turner points out that moderate reformers (who begin small) always do better than those who push their principles to extremes. Moreover: 'It is hardly necessary to say that a reformer must not count on receiving any help from the victims of injustice'.

Shop assistants who were working fourteen hours a day were little interested in the Early Closing Association.

Seamen had little interest in Plimsoll's campaign to prevent the overloading of ships, and it took Samuel Plimsoll much of his life to improve safety at sea.

Until Plimsoll fought against the industry norm, it was customary for ship owners to overload their ships and then, if a ship sank, claim on the insurance. Plimsoll may be remembered by the load line that bears his name but today he is a largely forgotten man who deserves to be remembered alongside William Wilberforce.

And the women working in the mines mocked newcomers who 'were eccentric enough to wish to preserve their virginity'.

'When the reformer has risen above all the foregoing obstacles, when he has moved inertia, exposed self-interest, pricked apathy, dispelled ignorance, stimulated imagination, refused to be blinded with technicalities, shaken off undesirable supporters (ready to add their own enemies to his), and even moved those who are prejudiced against him because of his political colour, he must recognise that he is less than half way to success,' writes Turner.

And history shows that Turner was right to be pessimistic.

'The first of the chimney sweeping Bills was introduced into Parliament in 1788. It laid down that no boys should be apprenticed under eight years of age, that no sweep should have more than six apprentices, and that sweeps should be licensed.'

The apprentices, of course, were the boys who were sent up chimneys.

And the House of Lords moaned about that bill, only passing part of it.

The result was boys were still being sent up chimneys years later.

In 1819, the MP for Barnstaple in North Devon, F.M.Omnaney, introduced a petition from sweeps complaining that the boys who were recruited to clean chimneys were taken from poorhouses and that if Parliament prevented them from climbing chimneys, MPs would be depriving the boys of a way to earn a living.

Other MPs claimed that it was better that boys sweep chimneys than lie idle in the workhouse and one called Joseph Foster Barham boasted that he had introduced climbing boys into the Stockbridge area of England.

(Incidentally, though most of the children climbing chimneys were boys, Windsor Castle was at one time swept by two girls.)

The Earl of Lauderdale wrote a booklet called *The Young Chimney Sweepers* in which he suggested that boys who had been chosen to sweep chimneys by a 'gracious God' should be grateful for their good fortune.

Women were united in support of keeping chimney sweeping boys. Virtually no women campaigned against the practice. Most middle and upper class women wanted to have their chimneys swept 'the old fashioned way'.

As the protests about chimney boys continued to grow, the Marquess of Londonderry joined in the campaign in favour of sending boys up chimneys, pointing out that if boys were not allowed to climb chimneys there was a chance that children would not be employed in other work.

It was not until Charles Kingsley wrote *The Water Babies* in 1863 that opinion was moved in favour of stopping the practice of sending boys (and girls) up chimneys. A Bill was passed making it illegal for a sweep to take children under 16 into a house with him. Naturally, neither magistrates nor police took any notice of the bill.

Eventually, in 1875, the practice of sending children up chimneys in England was finally stopped by an effective Act of Parliament. The practice continued abroad however and it was still practised in Italy up until the Second World War.

Turner's book is extraordinary. It's a pity more people don't read it – but it has been out of print for years.

I read today that one of Britain's biggest producers of postcards has given up the unequal struggle. It seems that people are no longer buying and sending postcards. They send emails instead. This is so sad. I am an enthusiastic sender of postcards but I understand that the cost of the stamps is probably a disincentive.

We have decided to go to Gloucester Cathedral tomorrow. I intend to write an extensive study of the cathedral architecture and decorations. There are, so I am reliably informed, no less than 46 misericords dating from the 14th century.

The excitement is gripping. I don't think I shall sleep tonight.

26

I have long argued that the Internet has done far more harm than good and I realise that this is an unpopular viewpoint.

I have a number of concerns but the most significant perhaps is the way that the big, powerful internet companies (such as Google and Facebook) have damaged entrepreneurial activity, removed the last vestiges of privacy, polarised political views and discouraged people from daring to express their opinions. And these companies are evil. Not for nothing was Google recently fined 2.4 billion euros. Aggressive and vocal minorities now control social media and sensible discussion is suppressed.

It seems that everyone in public life (especially politicians, senior police officers, charity bosses, health service executives, etc.) will do or say anything (usually on social media) to obtain publicity and glory for themselves and to promote their over-rated view of their own status and their extremely modest achievements. This is Coleman's First Law of 21s Century News.

The rise of Corbyn could not have taken place without the internet.

We did not go to the Cathedral in Gloucester.

It was a nice day and so, instead of travelling up the motorway and spending six hours sitting in a queue while a lorry driver changed a wheel, I sat in the garden and watched boats bobbing about in the bay. There was nary a misericord to be seen.

In the evening, I sorted through my collection of charger leads. Some of them are for mobile telephones, others for laptops and cameras and the rest for heaven knows what. In the old days people collected stamps, beer mats and matchboxes. These days we all collect charger leads.

(Why, incidentally, aren't mobile phone companies instructed to make standard connectors? That would be a sensible rule which would save an enormous amount of waste, improve productivity and reduce pollution.)

In the end, I didn't dare throw any of my leads away because one of them is bound to be vital. The day after I throw it away I will discover that I need it.

27

Sainsbury's, the supermarket people who sells groceries to families who drive Volvos and read *The Guardian* newspaper, has an advertisement which shows young, bright millennials happily texting one another. The millennials text away slickly, quickly and with smiles of delight. Oh, aren't they clever little darlings. They are so terribly pleased with themselves that you can feel the smugness.

The shots of the beautiful, young folk merrily texting is intercut with shots of an old man pecking at the keyboard on his phone as he struggles to send a message. The old man is of course white and pretty obviously English because no one in advertising or commerce would dare take the piss out of anyone black or brown or female or obviously ethnic. (The English can't be 'ethnic' because legally England no longer exists as a nation.)

The advert is outrageously ageist and offensive but Sainsbury's clearly doesn't give a damn. The fact is that old people don't seem to count. I suspect that the copywriters, and the people at Sainsbury's who commissioned the advertisement, are themselves too young to realise that although the young have a tendency to say a great deal they do so without ever saying anything worth listening to. And nor are they old enough, or wise enough, to realise that the older citizens are often reluctant to speak but, when they do speak, are far more likely to say something worthwhile.

I wonder whether Sainsbury's would be quite so happy to have an advertisement taking the piss out of Muslims, gays, lesbians or young housewives.

Here are some ideas for Sainsbury's adverts:

How about laughing at Muslims not being able to tie their shoelaces.

Or gays who get lost when trying to use the Underground.

Or young mothers failing to use a television remote control properly.

Or a black man lost on a motorway and trying to work out how to get where he wants to go.

Or a Muslim woman in one of those full face thingies bumping into lamp posts. That would be hysterical and Sainsbury's would be bound to get some sort of advertising award.

(I note, by the way, that the wearing of face masks by Muslim women has been compared to the wearing of masks by surgeons in the operating theatre. That there are people around who seem to be taking this seriously convinces me that the lunatics really have taken over.)

Of course, Sainsbury's won't make any of my ads because they are snivelly, cowardly bullies who will take the piss out of elderly, white males because they don't count and as an ethnic group they are invisible and don't matter.

So I'm going to boycott Sainsburys.

Sadly, they won't notice because I don't shop there anyway. I'm already boycotting them for something. I can't remember what.

28

The would-be buyer of our apartment in Paris is now offering to sign the first bit of paper on the 16th October rather than the 9th of October. Although I was originally assured that he had the cash, the little bugger is apparently still struggling to raise the money. The one thing I have learned from this sad experience is that no sentient being should ever buy a property in France. If you do then the French will cheat you, resent you, lie to you, deceive you, harass you, and manipulate you. Cheating and lying are, I fear their national sport.

I wrote to our estate agent saying, 'You never understood why I distrusted our buyer. But it was simple. Everyone buying a property for themselves wants to do it as quickly as possible if they have the money. It's human nature. They don't go away for weeks and they don't delay without good reason. Our supposed buyer was never going to buy the apartment.'

I have told our notaire that we will accept the signing on the 16th October if the buyer tears up the dishonestly obtained Achat and accepts that if he (and his mother) don't turn up on the 16th then they are not going to be allowed to buy the apartment. The last signing was due to take place on the 20th September and the buyer's mother (who had been co-opted as a signee without anyone bothering to tell us) couldn't attend because she had a hospital appointment.

Why, oh why does everything in France take so damned long? Buying and selling property in the UK is a slow and tedious business. But, compared to France, it's a process on speed.

Part of the problem is, obviously, the French obsession with deliberately doing things slowly. It takes weeks for bits of paper to travel from one desk to another. But I also have a suspicion that dishonesty and deceit are far more commonplace in the French system. In my experience when the French open their mouths, they are practising their lying and deceiving. It is no wonder that there are few successful private businesses in France. And how many great inventors, creators or artists have there been born in France in recent decades? To save you looking it up the answer is none. Their best invention was the guillotine (invented by Dr Guillotine) which, I once discovered to my surprise, they used until 1981.

Meanwhile, since I no longer have a French bank account I am having a little difficulty in paying our French bills. I expect someone will threaten to sue me but what exactly are they going to do about it? And do I care? If the Mayor of Paris sues me for my local taxes it will presumably be a civil case and I don't think they can extradite me for a civil debt. Let's hope we get out of the EU speedily, just in case.

The snotty agents who look after the administration of our building (and whose unbelievably pushy and self-important employees seem to think they own the place and are allowing us to stay there out of the kindness of their hearts) are refusing to take payment in any form other than a direct debit on a French bank. I have explained more times than is decent that I do not have a French bank account and I have offered to pay with a credit card, through PayPal or with a euro cheque drawn on a British clearing bank but they steadfastly insist that they will only accept payment via a direct debit made through a French bank. I would pay in cash but the current bill is for over 700 euros and it is illegal in France to make payments for such amounts in cash. I have now received an armful of emails from Twattus Gallicus insisting that this is the only method of payment they will accept.

Since I will vote communist before I open another French bank account we seem to have reached some sort of impasse.

29

We went to Cirencester today. I had an appointment for an eye test. I've been putting it off for months but I really needed to go and have my cataract checked – to make sure that it isn't ready for treatment. It took us 50 minutes to find somewhere to park the car (we tried three car parks and all were overflowing) and eventually I dumped the Ford in the Waitrose car park and made a dash for the opticians while Antoinette bought some groceries we didn't need in order to justify our place in the car park.

I can't imagine why all the car parks were full since Cirencester was looking very glum. It seemed that a large proportion of the shops were closed and the town looked very forlorn. These days, Cirencester is not the place to go for a shopping expedition unless you are looking for a headscarf with horses on it (not surprisingly, there appears to be a glut) or a pair of bright red trousers.

Saddest sight of all was the huge number of conkers lying untouched or crushed on the pavement. It seems that the boys of Cirencester no longer play conkers. Have they been banned by health and safety or just given it up because it requires string rather than batteries? I bet they'd play if the game were available as an app.

I noticed that Cirencester is twinned with somewhere called Itzehoe. I have never heard of Itzehoe and I find this habit of town twinning quite bizarre. I can't help suspecting that the only people who benefit are the local councillors who use taxpayers' money to enable them to have regular beanos in their home town and abroad. I am convinced that the whole 'twinning' scam was set up by the European Union to break down very sensible cultural barriers.

I'm thinking of twinning our house with somewhere abroad. Maybe I could twin it with the Elysee Palace.

Yes, that will do nicely.

I'll get a sign made saying that our house is twinned with the Elysee Palace.

I hear that the Mayor of London is thinking of making log fires illegal. I assume he thinks that electricity is a far cleaner fuel which causes less pollution.

I wonder if he realises that much of Britain's electricity is produced by burning coal. And much of the rest is obtained by burning wood. (Maybe no one has told him that 'logs' and 'wood' are the same thing.)

The only effective way to reduce the level of pollution in London would be to reduce the population. And the best way to do that would be to reduce immigration. Maybe the Mayor would like to consider that as an option?

When Daniel Defoe toured England in 1724, researching his amazing book *A Tour Through the Whole Island of Great Britain*, the country was mainly rural. At least eight out of ten people lived in hamlets and villages – most of which had only a few hundred people living in them. Towns and cities are a relatively new development and most Britons have little real cultural experience of town life. We are, at heart, country dwellers who have still not properly adapted to the restrictions of town or city life. Town planners and politicians still don't understand this.

Defoe's book is full of fascinating bits and pieces.

For example, I read the other day about a man who had been married nine times. The previous eight had all died. This is unusual for these times but it was something Defoe had seen a good deal.

In Essex, Defoe discovered men who had 25 or more wives (though not all at once). Defoe reported that the men were bred in the marshes and coped with their soggy surroundings quite well but when they wanted wives, they went to the hilly country. They took young girls from fresh country air and introduced them into the marshland where it was foggy and damp. The girls usually became ill and died within a year. So the farmer went back upland and found another wife. Defoe said that the men regarded the acquiring and losing of wives as a variety of farming.

I've been looking through my library, picking out the best books about England and the English. My favourites are: *Rural Rides* by William Cobbett; *English Journey* by J.B.Priestley; *Britannia* by William Camden and almost anything appropriate by John Hillaby and H.V.Morton.

I received an email from our estate agents in Paris. Apparently, the putative buyer of our apartment has had it re-measured and will want the price of the apartment to be reduced. We have been waiting for this since it was the only thing the buyer had not yet thrown at us.

Our apartment is a loft, the whole top floor of a six storey building in central Paris, and there are two ways of measuring the size.

The first is to measure the whole floor area: the horizontal stuff between the walls. There is no dispute about this measurement. The floor area is over 90 square metres. This isn't a lot but in central Paris, in the 7th arrondissement, the most expensive part of the city, it is a valuable chunk of real estate.

The second way to measure the apartment is to measure the floor area that is high enough for a typically tall Frenchman to walk around on. In our apartment this area is, of course, rather smaller than the first measurement since there are spaces under the eaves and so on. These spaces are perfectly useable but unless you are small, you can't stand up under those bits of ceiling. In practice, the whole thing is balanced by the fact that the ceiling in other areas of the apartment is so high that you could, if you wished, install a mezzanine floor.

Before we were allowed to put the apartment on the market we had to pay a specialist to come and do a zillion and one tests (his report was over 100 pages long and about as useful as an old Metro ticket).

One of his jobs was to measure the amount of floor area where the ceiling is high enough for the average Frenchman to walk about. This is called the Carrez surface. He said that while the overall floor area was more than 90 square metres, the Carrez surface was 79.8 square metres. The whole thing is a farce because anything which isn't 70.866 inches high is regarded as being under the Carrez surface area. But now that General de Gaulle has gone to his Algerian heaven, it is rare to find a Frenchman who is close to six feet tall or above. Most of them are midgets. And lying, cheating, devious little midgets too, it has to be said.

Well, it seems that our would-be buyer decided that he wanted to have the floor measured by his own man with a tape measure and a clipboard.

And his man found that the Carrez surface was just over 76 square metres. The difference between our measurement and his measurement was well under 5% and therefore of no financial value. In France, in the real estate business, size matters enormously and our buyer was clearly someone for whom every centimetre had great value.

Presumably disappointed by the result of this measurement (one can imagine the anguish) the buyer then either sent back the same man or sent in another man to do some more measuring. This second attempt was successful in that the measurer managed to find that the Carrez was 74.87 square metres.

The whole business of this measuring is, of course, woefully and patently unscientific. You point a little laser gun device at bits of ceiling and the machine works out the answers for you. But the answers depend entirely upon where you point the laser gun device.

This figure of 74.87 square metres was significant because the French have a law which entitles the buyer to demand a reduction in the price if the Carrez is more than 5% smaller than the original, quoted measurement. And, of course, the difference between 74.87 and 79.8 is slightly more than 5% of the total. It seems to me that as a buyer you just keep having measurements taken until you get one that you like. Our problem is that you can take Carrez measurements (as they are called), and claim a refund on the purchase price for up to a year after buying an apartment. And a really bad person could, of course, easily stick up a bit of false ceiling, have the place re-measured, demand a refund of 100,000 euros and then tear down the bit of extra ceiling. Would a French buyer do that? Of course they bloody well would. The French don't have property surveys done. Instead, they cheat and fiddle and sue whenever they can.

Alarmed by this measurement, our estate agents then sent our guy back in to repeat his measurements and he found that a new Carrez measurement of 77.25 square metres.

So, now we had four different measurements.

But actually we had five different measurements because when I bought the apartment just under 20 years ago, the Carrez was measured at around 71 square metres. So the apartment has been growing steadily over that time.

I find it difficult to take any of this seriously but if I don't, we could get sued by a crafty buyer.

Our estate agent told us that the buyer will probably now demand a reduction in the price. Gosh, what a surprise that was. You could have knocked me down with a tank transporter. I thought it odd that he didn't suggest to me that we simply amended the official figures on our sale documents (which had, in the French way, never even been printed) or that I tell the buyer to fuck off. Instead, this bozo in the smart jeans and blazer, whom we had hired at someone else's enormous expense, was suggesting that we roll over and cut the price by some presumably substantial and acceptable amount. What's 100,000 euros here or there between enemies? No one, after all, goes to all the trouble of commissioning Carrez measurements in the hope of having a mere 10,000 euros knocked off the price.

When I heard this nonsense about reducing the price of the apartment (and I think a piece of real estate in the French capital which is valued at one million euros deserves the title 'apartment' rather than 'flat') I couldn't help remembering that old crook Robert Maxwell.

Before he started taking the swimming lessons which he couldn't finish, the fat man in the baseball cap was renowned for renegotiating prices at the last minute. If he and a seller and a team of lawyers had spent six months working out a mutually satisfactory price, Maxwell would walk into the meeting where the papers were ready to be signed and demand a cut in the price. Naturally, because everyone had been expecting to sign the papers there would be consternation. But in order to keep the deal alive, the sellers would usually agree to Maxwell's demands.

The French government, never slow to do something idiotic, has enshrined Maxwell's infamous little trick into property law.

The really odd thing is that French politicians are desperate to get rid of foreign property owners by encouraging them to sell their properties and to allow local French folk to buy them. Someone should tell them that they are going about things the wrong way. The rules and regulations seem designed to punish anyone who owns property.

And it seems to me that there is now a new negotiating ploy in France.

The buyer finds a loft apartment and says he would like to buy it. He then messes the seller around for four months by making repeated promises and then breaking them. And when the seller is suitably softened up by all the delays, the buyer sends in his tame measuring team with instructions to find that the Carrez floor area is more than 5% smaller than the Carrez floor area listed on the sales particulars.

In our case, I did find it strange that the buyer didn't send in his own measuring team until long after the passing of the dates when the first contracts should have been signed.

I may well be an old cynic. But who wouldn't be.

I was so incensed by this blatant trick that I immediately sent back an email suggesting that the buyer might like to prepare a pan of water, add a few mint leaves, stick his head in and boil it.

I also sent an email to our notaire telling her that I was planning to make a formal complaint about the buyer's notaire. There's a fairly straightforward complaints procedure which involves writing to the Chairman of the Disciplinary Chamber. I also pointed out that since I agreed to the sale only after I was misled about the buyer's financial situation, I intend to sue the buyer to recover damages and costs of 250,000 euros. This was to a large extent a warning shot across everyone's bows – just to let them know that although I am elderly and not French I am not prepared to lie down and allow myself to be bullied.

And just for fun, I sent along an email expressing my intention of writing several articles for national British, American and French magazines analysing the peculiarities and peccadilloes of the French house selling business.

I had used the same jolly little trick when confronted with a problem with a French bank the best part of two decades ago. The bank had allowed someone to empty our bank account and to send all the money, around £6,000 I seem to remember, to an account in Monaco. I was pretty sure that it was an inside job and that someone working in the bank had siphoned off the money. No one at the French bank was in the slightest bit interested in our loss until I went to see an absurdly expensive lawyer on the Champs Elysee and told him, en passant, that I intended to write some articles about the bank and its refusal to pay up. Within hours, we received an invitation to visit the bank. When we did so, every centime of the money which had been stolen was handed to us in cash. (Oddly, if I'd tried to pay in £6,000 in cash I would have been arrested.) And the funny thing was that the expensive lawyer never sent us a bill. I have always believed that he was paid off by the bank to ensure that they could deny that the whole thing had happened.

Remembering the French bank mystery, reminded me of some of the other bad things that have happened to us in France.

I remember, for example, the decorator to whom I gave money for materials and as an advance on his wages. (I can be very stupid at times.) He disappeared, together with my money, and I never saw him again. Antoinette and I ended up carrying all the paint and brushes over from England and decorating the apartment ourselves.

In Paris, our letterbox is constantly filled with leaflets and catalogues. Once we found a large packet of cocaine pushed into the box. I flushed the stuff down the toilet. Most annoying are the hundreds of promotional cards containing telephone numbers to ring for help with a variety of household problems – plumbing, electrical, lost keys and so on. Early on, full of innocence, we used the numbers on these cards. We paid £2,500 to have a simple electrical fault repaired. We paid £350 to have a cooker hood removed. (We had to have it removed because a boiler servicing company had snitched on us and reported us to the authorities for having a perfectly serviceable but apparently illegal cooker hood.) We had to throw out a pair of crooks who insisted that our new boiler needed replacing (it needed a replacement fuse) and who demanded several thousand pounds to do the work.

And out in the streets we avoided being mugged a couple of times only because I am 6 foot 3 inches tall and, in the winter, have a penchant for wearing thick coats and an Irish tweed cap which hides my greying and disappearing hair and gives me a rather menacing look.

When I stop to think about it, I realise that we have had far, far more unpleasant experiences than pleasant ones in our encounters with Parisians.

The best workmen we met were Russians who came to repair a stretch of our ceiling. They worked hard for two or three days with unfailing courtesy and good humour and they tidied up when they'd finished.

Back to the flat, the Carrez measurement and the alleged buyer.

I think we've found a way to stop this little trick.

I instructed the notaire to alter the measurement on the apartment particulars so that our second measurement is now the Carrez floor area. This means that the buyer's second attempt is not less than 5% lower and therefore we don't have to reduce the price. I have also told our notaire to obtain a written agreement from the buyer that our measurement is the correct one. French law (which is, incidentally, hand in hand with EU law) is neither logical nor sensible but this should protect us.

I had to think up this ploy myself. I have learned that in France you are on your own and you should never assume that anyone is on your side.

30

Health care in Britain is bad because the NHS is like British Railways; a flabby organisation run for the benefit of the employees rather than the customers.

All nationalised industries fail because the people who work for them never care enough for the people they work for – the customers.

The BBC is the same.

Organisations always tend to become fascist and socialist (the two are, of course, the same) because left wing agitators are invariably more vocal and determined than anyone else.

This tendency is particularly true for large organisations and always true for taxpayer funded organisations where the 'customers' are captive and have little or no right of reply and no opportunity to control the service they are given.

I was strimming an area of rough grassland today when, just at the last moment, I spotted a tiny oak tree. It was about two feet tall. The acorn must have been planted by a squirrel because there is no mature oak tree in sight. I tried to pull away but I was too late. I strimmed the little oak tree. I was devastated.

And finally (as they used to say on the news programmes) a friend of ours is opening a pastie shop in the South of France. He is calling it 'Corniche Pasties'.

October

1

The dandelions are back. They're better than daffodils because they come twice a year. They are the first of the year to provide sustenance for the birds and the bees and they are the last to provide sustenance.

I've been collecting and cutting wood for the fireplace. It takes two tons of good firewood to produce as much heat as one ton of coal but there is, without a doubt, something very special about a log fire.

The Victorians went off wood fires in a big way when coal became readily available and much cheaper. To burn coal instead of wood the old-fashioned huge open hearths (sometimes big enough to contain an old man or woman sitting in a corner) were often converted to small coal-burning grates.

Fortunately, our home in Devon has two hearths big enough for logs. And in the Cotswolds we have a log burner which I usually use with the door open. (I don't much like log burners. A proper old-fashioned hearth is much nicer. And log burners can be dangerous. It is suicidal to install one in a cottage with a thatched roof because log burners make the chimney so hot that the thatch is likely to catch fire. Log burners can, I think, also cause wooden floors to catch fire.)

Not all wood burns well. And wood really needs to be dry and mature to burn satisfactorily. Green wood contains much moisture and when the wood gets hot it just drives the moisture up the chimney. Generally, woods which grow slowly burn slowly, making a good hot fire whereas quick growing wood burns quickly with flames.

I have, over the years, learned a few useful things about logs for burning. Dense woods only smoulder unless they are very dry after being stacked for a year or two. Orchard trees such as apple and pear make fragrant firewood and burn quite well. Coniferous trees produce spicy scent but spark a lot. Elm needs to be dried for at least two years. Hawthorn, holly and yew burn green and give very hot fires. Lilac wood produces good heat and a very pleasant smell. Sycamore and walnut are good and willow is fine when it is very dry. Old fence posts and stakes make good kindling. Silver birch and willow are always losing branches which make excellent kindling. In the Cotswolds we get almost all our kindling from one huge and very healthy willow tree. Dead branches drop off in high winds and are easily broken up.

We have several magnificent yule logs for the Christmas period – big enough to burn for hours. You just keep pushing the log into the fireplace as it burns.

2

The company which hosts my websites sent an email note asking me to update my credit card details on their automatic payment site. When I inputted all the required details, I was told that I would be charged £1 for the privilege of updating my information.

Is there no end to the greed of computer and internet related companies?

Any remaining doubts I might have had about the sanity of the world were removed today when passengers on board a packed rush hour train forced the doors open and fled onto the tracks (with a live electrical wire) when a man started to read from a copy of the Bible.

Another traveller had told the man he was scaring people but that didn't stop the lemming like rush. In order to avoid seeing passengers fried on the live rail, the power was cut causing massive disruption.

A guard who escorted the Bible reader from the train was praised for 'compassion, restraint and bravery'.

'Bravery'?

In a separate story, I discovered that wedding couples are paying £350 for 50 small boxes containing butterflies. The guests hold the boxes while a Native American poem is read out. And then when the poem is over the boxes are opened and the hapless butterflies released for a 'photo opportunity'.

There has been no reply at all from our Parisian estate agent or from our notaire. Antoinette and I have decided that we will go back to Paris in the New Year and find a new estate agent to handle things.

I picked up one of my favourite 'odd' books today. Entitled *The Clumsiest People in Europe*, it is a guide book to the peoples of the world which was written 150 years ago by a Victorian author called Mrs Mortimer.

Speaking of the French, Mrs Mortimer says 'It is too common in France not to speak the truth'.

Dear old Mrs Mortimer.

Nail on the head and bang on the button. Give that woman a travel rug.

But no rug for Theresa May who appears to be consumed by fear.

Instead of seeing the positive, exciting future for Britain without the dead hand of EU bureaucracy hovering over every decision and ambition, she (led and advised by the blind men of the Treasury, whose forecasts have been discredited and the Bank of England, which has no credibility at all) can see only problems and dangers.

The Office for Budget Responsibility, The Treasury and the Bank of England are no better at forecasting what the economy will do than I am at picking the winner of the Grand National.

If these were people who were accountable and required to produce reliable figures in return for the massive salaries and pensions which they receive, they would have all been fired years ago.

Mrs May's answer to the problems ahead are solutions which involve still working with, and under the thumb of, the EU. She is even talking of handing over £40 billion to the EU just because they have demanded it (and desperately need it). No one has yet bothered to explain why we should give £40 billion of taxpayers' money to the eurocrats. You can build a lot of hospitals and roads with £40 billion and we need more of both now that our island is crammed to the coastline with EU immigrants.

I gather that much of the £40 billion will be used to pay the fat cat pensions of eurocrats.

And why don't we get a refund from the EU for our share of all those EU buildings that we helped pay for?

3

More than one in five pensioners still have to complete tax returns.

Astonishingly, 1.7 million people over the age of 65 have to complete individual tax returns and a quarter of a million of those are aged 80 or over.

I have a vested interest in this, but I can't help feeling that if you're retired and you've paid tax for more than 40 years then you should be exempt – in the same way that if you've paid a club a subscription for long enough then you may receive free membership. It seems utterly crazy to me that someone who is receiving a pension should have to hand some of it over to the Government.

We were going to register with a local GP in Devon but then discovered that although the practice is quite large (there are at least four full-time doctors working there) they do not offer any out of hours cover. The entire practice is shut down at night, at weekends and on holidays and patients are told to telephone one of those pointless out of hours numbers which are manned by a single doctor working in an office in Sheffield or Milton Keynes or Karachi.

I find this disgraceful, unprofessional and frighteningly uncaring.

Why bother training to be a doctor and then be satisfied with providing a mediocre service?

The practice is at least 30 miles from the nearest hospital offering accident and emergency facilities.

I know doctors are entitled to opt out of providing 24 hour cover but they are also allowed to opt in. And they receive an additional fee for doing so. If the local doctors agreed to provide cover for 168 hours a week it would involve them in working no more than two nights a week. Indeed, the fees they received for providing out of hours cover would easily pay for the cost of hiring an additional doctor.

So, the bottom line is this: what is the point of registering with a practice which provides only office hour cover? We can obtain almost immediate medical advice through the internet if we need it. It is now quite easy to obtain prescriptions and even arrange blood tests through doctors who work online. (Ironically, these are probably GPs who do not offer their own patients a decent service and, specifically, do not provide 24 hour cover.)

And if we need emergency help then we have to cut out the middle man and telephone for an ambulance. If we really need to see a local doctor then we can demand to be seen as temporary residents. Most practices are very happy to see temporary residents for the simple but excellent reason that they receive another fee every time they do so.

4

Most of today's pensioners were keen savers. They saved as much as they could and have subsidised Britain for years. It was 'small' savers and taxpayers who paid all the costs of Gordon Brown's bank bailouts.

Today's older folk paid 10, 15 and 20% in interest when they bought their homes. Now that they have a little money saved for their old age they are receiving less than 1% in interest. After inflation and tax, their savings are earning a negative rate of interest.

Not surprisingly, the Bank of England has expressed considerable concern at the fact that savings rates are lower than they have been for decades. Millennials aren't saving anything. They are the spend, spend, spend generation.

It doesn't seem to have occurred to the politicians or the Bank of England that when interest rates are considerably lower than the rate of inflation then there isn't much point in saving money. Today most interest rates seem to be around 0.01% and the official inflation rate is 300 times higher. (If there is another crisis, there is no doubt that negative interest rates will be introduced. The politicians and the bankers want to get rid of cash completely not just because it will make their lives easier but also because if there is no cash they will be able to force anyone with savings to accept negative interest rates.)

The Government has deliberately stopped people investing in property and so the few people who are saving are putting their money onto the stock market and into a variety of very risky investments. Most are putting money into Unit Trusts and OEICS.

These are desperately bad choices for most people because the costs usually far exceed any profits which may be made. Anyone who invests in a Unit Trust cannot be regarded as a serious investor but is, rather, a dilettante, lining the pockets of greedy fund managers.

Inevitably, low interest rates are encouraging people to borrow more and more and individual levels of debt are reaching levels never previously seen. So, many people are now borrowing money in order to purchase expensive new motor cars. The greedy millennials who are making millions out of banking are selling one another car loans in exactly the same way that they sold house loans.

Today I received an email inviting me to lease a £30,000 car for £100 a month. How can that possibly make sense?

Millennials frequently claim that they are being financially disadvantaged by the elderly. This is the sort of spin that Goebbels, Campbell and the EU would be proud to have created. The reality is that absurdly low interest rates and incredibly low mortgage rates have made it astonishingly easy for young people to buy homes if they are prepared to cut down on the tattoos, the lattes and the other luxuries they regard as essential. Heavens, the Government is even lending money free of charge to young home buyers. The Help to Buy scheme gives millennials a loan of 20% of a property's value (up to £600,000) for 25 years, without any interest.

Strewth, back in the dark 1980s, when today's oldies were paying their mortgages, the banks were lending out money at 17% interest and inflation was well into the mid 20s.

Our society is cruelly unbalanced with everything in favour of the young and contrary to the interests of the older citizens. The young and inexperienced take power and responsibility as though it is their right, even though they don't know anything and are far too arrogant to ask for help. They also appear to have absolutely no understanding of money – allowing themselves to be distracted and attracted by all the wrong things. Most of them are heading for decades of penury.

The millennials need to be careful with their money and they really should be saving hard. It isn't difficult to see that they are pretty well screwed. Robots will shorten working hours and working lives but pension shortfalls will mean an ever-increasing retirement age. Today's 20-year-olds will be out of work at 50 (if they are lucky) but won't receive a pension until they're 70 (if they're lucky). They will, I suspect, be regarded as stupid and worthless at the age of 50.

Incidentally, the IT people drool about robots (some of them have argued that robots should be given employment rights and pensions) and seem to think that robots will soon take over our planet completely. This is bollocks, of course. Robots are no threat to us at all. If they get uppity all we have to do is unplug them or remove their batteries. And if they are solar operated we throw blankets over them and move them all to Scotland

5

The buyer for our apartment has now disappeared and will be unavailable all week to answer our simple question about whether or not he accepts the new Carrez figure.

This is vital because if he won't agree to the new size he could sue us after he has bought the apartment.

In the end, I gave an ultimatum: if they didn't get an answer by the end of the day then he wouldn't buy the apartment at all. I am fed up to the incisors with him being unavailable when it suits him.

There was no reply by the end of the day and so we no longer have a buyer for our apartment. Antoinette and I rejoiced. We are going to go over to Paris, fasten the shutters, lower the blinds, turn off the electricity and take the apartment off the market until next spring.

I have from the start been convinced that our buyer had decided that I was old, poor, desperate, dilapidated and weak – easy prey for a sharp Parisian. I think he has spent four months softening us up in order to demand a reduction at the last minute. There had to be some little trick. It's been like dealing with a bucket shop crook or an internet phisher.

I am, I confess, utterly exhausted by all this and by all the crap in general. Why do property deals always seem to bring out the worst in people? Or is the world now just populated with intrinsically ruthless bullies? Or is the lack of any sense of control which I find so painful?

Right from the start, I told the agent that our buyer was not serious and did not have the money available. The estate agent insisted that he had the money and was serious. But what serious house buyer makes an offer to buy a property, signs a preliminary purchase agreement and then disappears for months? Psychologically, it made no sense to me and as the weeks went by, I became increasingly convinced that the sale would not go through and that we were dealing with a hornswoggling horbgorble.

And we still don't know the real identity of our buyer. Our agent has refused to give us any information. I am beginning to think that our agent has deliberately allowed us to get confused about the buyer so that we won't notice that the money is not forthcoming.

I think it was William James who wrote that 'Need and struggle are what excites and inspires us; our hour of triumph is what brings the void.'

Well, bring on a bit of void. I've had enough need, enough struggle, enough excitement and damned near enough inspiration.

I have been sent a US tax form. If I don't fill it in the American tax authorities will deduct 30% of all my US earnings. I spent an hour trying to fill in the form online and failed miserably because the form refused to accept my signature.

I get these damned forms regularly from publishers and agents all over the world and I usually ignore them.

Because I sell a lot of books there, I regularly receive tax forms from Portugal. The forms are, not surprisingly, in Portuguese and they are lengthy and quite incomprehensible. The UK is, in my experience, the only country in the world to print all its official documents in as many languages as can be found. Other countries save money and insist that foreigners learn their language or hire a translator and this seems to me to be fair enough.

I throw away the forms from Portugal, give the Portuguese Government a big chunk of money and claim it back against my UK income.

I am convinced that foreign governments deliberately make their forms impossible to fill in so that they can deduct the tax from writers' earnings. I spent hours earlier filling in an incomprehensible form from the Japanese Government because my agent over there insisted that I had to do it or else really terrible things would happen. I will probably find that I've joined the Japanese air force.

I suppose I will have to find a way to fill in the American form. I earn enough in the US to make this form well worth completing so I will have to hope they take pity on me and tell me what I'm doing wrong.

IRS tax forms as issued by the American tax people are notoriously demanding and I gave up buying American shares on US exchanges because the paperwork defeated me.

Apropos of nothing, I wonder how widely it is known that the EU is now proposing to give itself the right to freeze the accounts of all depositors who have money in any bank within the European Union. The previous plan was to block the accounts of anyone who had more than 100,000 euros in their bank. The latest plan is to hit the accounts of all savers. The EU intends to give itself the right to control all bank accounts and people will only be allowed to take out enough money to pay for their day to day needs.

The keen Remainers do not know this, of course, because they never bother themselves with facts.

(The Remainers lied and exaggerated constantly before and during the referendum on the EU but, with outstanding cheek, have consistently made absurd allegations against those voting to save Britain from the Nazi dream. It is also relevant to note that the Electoral Commission fined the Liberal Democrats £18,000 for failing to provide full invoices and receipts for their spending on the Brexit campaign. The official Remain campaign was fined for similar offences.)

6

My joy on getting rid of the alleged buyer for our apartment was short lived.

While preparing a letter to sack the agents, I spotted a clause in the small print which means effectively that we have to pay them 50,000 euros if we don't sell the damned apartment to a buyer they find.

So I have told the notaire they can sell the damned apartment. I feel so fed up with the whole thing I don't want anything more to do with it. This whole extended and frustrating business has made life miserable for both of us. I can understand a buyer changing his mind. We all do that. We've done that. But our buyer, aided and abetted by our estate agent, has turned an apparently simple procedure into an unending process: a chronic nightmare.

Today is a day of idiocy.

I found out that the reason I couldn't sign the American tax form sent to me by Amazon was that I have to give my permission for me to sign the form, and the box I have to tick to give myself permission to sign the form is on the page after the page upon which I am supposed to sign. The form won't allow me to sign the form until I have gone to the next page and ticked the box allowing me to sign the form on the previous page.

If this were a form that had come through the post, this would not be so bad.

But it is an internet form.

I no longer understand the world or anything in it. The men in the white coats have clearly buggered off and the inmates have taken over completely.

I realise that I have to step back and care less. I have to cut myself from outside problems, put on blinkers and keep my eyes, my mind and my heart focussed on things that really matter: looking after Antoinette is way up top. And writing a few more books comes next. Filling in forms is nowhere.

After luncheon, I did some cosmetic surgery on a stuffed toy cat which had an ear which wouldn't stand up properly. He now looks much better. Stuffed animals are damned nearly as good for you as real ones. They bounce back the love and they never fall ill or die.

I then spent an hour this afternoon cutting ivy off the garage in Devon.

I like ivy, it provides food and housing for a good many creatures, but the stuff has finished its journey up the walls and is now working its way across the roof and between the tiles. One of the garage walls abuts a local footpath and small lane and as I was snipping away, three couples walked along the lane. They all said 'hello' in a cheery, jolly sort of way.

What a nice change from Gloucestershire where our garden also runs alongside a narrow lane.

Cotswoldians and visitors who pass by are invariably rude and surly. While folk in Devon smile and say hello, the folk in Gloucestershire sneer and grunt and generally behave as though they must, by definition, be vastly superior to anyone who is reduced to spending any of his time trimming bushes, strimming weeds or tinkering with a dry stone wall.

I have never forgotten that a friend of mine, a former Literary Editor of the Birmingham Post, once interviewed Tolkien when he was very old. My pal says that Tolkien lived almost exclusively in Middle Earth. Who can blame him?

Lying in the bath this evening reading the new Le Carre (a first edition but a reprint and therefore of no financial value) I was very disappointed.

Le Carre has turned George Smiley into a European, a supporter of State Fascism. We are now told that Smiley did everything for Europe and not for England.

Peter Guillam gets a repaint too and is unrecognisable.

An author can, of course, do whatever he likes with his characters but if he wants to retain the interest and enthusiasm of his readers, he can't go too far and I don't think he should impose his own political views onto well-established characters.

Le Carre is a well-known supporter of the EU but I don't think the enthusiasm fits comfortably into Smiley's character.

The Smiley whom Le Carre gave us originally was an Englishman through and through; a loyal servant of Queen and Country and not a traitorous hound likely to brown nose Juncker et al.

I like to think that Le Carre himself is simply ignorant and I don't care about that but I don't like to think that Smiley doesn't understand and is a supporter of Hitler's dream. He wouldn't, would he? It's like discovering that Robin Hood was a secret supporter of King John and a snitch for the Infernal Revenue Services. Or that Dickens's Tiny Tim was a benefit fraudster with three separate families and a flourishing drug smuggling business. Or that the Pied Piper of Hamelin was a Troop Leader for the Nazi youth party.

I put down the book and found myself thinking yet again about our alleged buyer in Paris.

It is, I decided, a debacle.

If it had been left to us, he would have been told to fuck off some months ago. But we have been told that we might be sued if we do this. We have said firmly that if he doesn't sign on the October 16th then he won't buy the apartment even if he sues us and M.Macron delivers the writ himself.

Incidentally, our notaire showed me a letter she received from the buyer's notaire.

From this it is clear that although we were encouraged to believe that the money was ready and waiting, the fact is that the buyer still needs a bank loan which he is having difficulty in arranging.

The endless delays are, it seems, all designed to give him more time to find a bank prepared to part with the necessary funds. He has had since June to find the money. Unless he wins the Euro-lottery it doesn't seem likely that he is now going to find the money in the next week or so.

I wonder if our estate agent knew that the money had to be borrowed? Maybe he and the buyer were being rather clever or disingenuous in telling us that the buyer didn't need to sign a Promesse contract dependent upon a bank loan?

(There are two types of promesse. In one, the buyer admits that he has to borrow the money. In the other, the buyer says he has the money available.)

Our buyer has, I suspect, always needed to borrow the money from somewhere but didn't want us to know this because he knew (quite rightly) that we wouldn't have accepted his offer if we had known this. I rather feel that we have been played for suckers. Or, to switch metaphors, we have been led up and down the garden path for months. What if we had needed the money to buy a house we wanted?

Four and a half months after the start of the process, we are no further forward than we had been at the start. Indeed, we are worse off for we are committed to a buyer who has no money and, apparently, no prospect of finding any. No one, least of all our estate agent, seemed to give a damn about our situation.

The sad thing is that at the end of this (if an end ever arrives), I know I am going to loathe the French, detest France, hate Paris and feel an overwhelming sadness at having parted company with an apartment which was the source of so much joy for Antoinette and me.

Our buyer has disappeared again and has been unreachable for over a week. I am assured that neither his notaire nor the estate agent knows where he is and neither can reach him by telephone or by email. He is mysteriously incommunicado.

And so, when we repeatedly asked for confirmation that he accepted the new Carrez reading there was no reply. I made the elementary mistake of telling them that they had made my Antoinette ill. This seemed to be seen as a sign of weakness to be exploited.

I am so cross that I think I am turning into the sort of character Jack Nicholson played in *As Good As It Gets* and *Bucket List*.

I usually think Jacques Tati is my cinematic alter ego but I've gone way beyond Tatisque confusion and bewilderment. Besides, Tati was French and I don't like French anything anymore.

We desperately don't want to sell the apartment to the buyer we are supposed to have. We want to get rid of him. We want to sack our wretched agent, collect our keys, close the apartment shutters and put this miserable experience behind us. The fact is that keeping the apartment will be far less tiresome than trying to sell it.

Maybe we will try again in 2018 with a different estate agent.

In nearly twenty years, I cannot think of a single French transaction that was decent and honest. The woman from whom I bought the flat delayed the final handing over of the keys to suit herself – and then removed fixtures and fittings which she agreed to leave.

I remember the people who own the cellar next to ours demanding that we switch cellars. I did so, carefully making sure that our cellar was clean and swept. They promised to do the same but when I eventually managed to get the key out of them they had left the cellar chock full of rubbish – including an old mattress. (Why would you bother putting an old mattress into your cellar when in Paris the bin men will take anything left outside?)

The worst thing about the Barclays and the apartment fiascos is the time I have wasted.

There have been genuine financial losses (currency losses, changes in taxes and opportunity costs).

But it is the time I will never recover. I am more and more determined to do my best to make sure that these damned people never buy the apartment.

You have to fight these bastards don't you? If you lie down and let them ride roughshod over you the anguish, the suffering, the frustration are all so much greater.

This whole process has been replete with inexplicable delays and cancelled or postponed appointments and promises. I find it increasingly difficult to accept the frequently offered assurance (proffered by our estate agent) that this is normal for the French process. Disappointments are, of course, good for character building but to be honest my character has been pretty well built, altered, rebuilt, knocked about so much that if there is any more building then I fear the drains will stop working.

7

One of our squirrels has just discovered the Joy of the Apple. Today he picked up one of the apples which had been partly eaten by the wild rabbits, nibbled some of it and carried the remainder up onto a wooden table next to a wooden swing seat which we have in the garden. The only possible reason to do this was to keep it for later and to ensure that the rabbits didn't finish it off for they, of course, cannot climb up the table legs. When the rabbits get to an apple first, they pick it up by the stalk and carry it off to be eaten in their burrow. (We give apples without stalks to our resident pheasant and keep apples with stalks for the rabbits and the squirrels.)

I am now having to put out several apples a day. The rabbits prefer them to grass. The squirrels still like their nuts but they enjoy an apple too. The Hereford Russets still seem to be favourite.

At a vote of the EU parliament, a number of MEPs elected by Britons (two representing the Tory party and 18 representing Labour) voted against the UK's interests and for the EU.

I suppose it is inevitable that some MEPs will be miffed at the prospect of losing their comfortable jobs (complete with marvellous expenses and pensions) but to vote against British interests when you are paid to represent British interests seems to me to be the ultimate betrayal and act of treachery.

The 73 British MEPs who sit in the European Parliament will receive around 6 million euros in golden goodbyes when Britain leaves the EU. Some MEPs will receive more than 200,000 euros – paid by us, of course. MEPs will also receive lifetime private health care and massive pensions.

I have pretty well given up writing new material for my website. I'm not at all convinced that anyone bothers to read the stuff. If I want to build up the website I must become a social media fanatic and tweet every hour or so. I refuse to do that. What can anyone say in a sentence or so that is worth saying?

Antoinette has been painting for a few years now. She began with watercolours and turned to oils some months back. She has already produced some stunning work of gallery level.

After much experimentation, she has settled on a style known as tonalism which is a variety of impressionism and which was favoured by an American painter called Inness.

I love her paintings not because they are hers but because they are beautiful pictures. Her aim is to get her paintings into a gallery. She will succeed.

('You are not to buy a gallery so that I think I've succeeded,' she told me.)

8

Our two yew trees in Devon are laden with big, juicy, fat berries – as big as raspberries. Oddly, however, our yew tree in Gloucester has no berries at all.

I worked in the garden in Gloucestershire today and had a great bonfire.

I emptied a spare freezer which contained out-of-date bread, chips and ice cream and burnt the lot. I specialise in lighting bonfires in the rain and now claim to be the only person in the world to have successfully started a bonfire in a heavy snowstorm and to have burnt out-of-date ice cream in an incinerator. The frozen bread, the frozen chips and the frozen ice cream were all turned into ash.

The secret to a good bonfire is, of course, the provision of plenty of air.

If you are burning a pile of garden rubbish you need to ensure that the stuff doesn't become compressed. I find that a few small cardboard boxes and empty, plastic water bottles, hidden deep within the stuff I'm trying to burn, are a vital ingredient.

Antoinette wants me to write a book on bonfire lighting. She's even got the title: 'Insania Pyromania'.

At six o'clock in the evening, I found myself searching through my pockets for coins to send the ferryman home, thereby making it impossible for me to cross the River Styx.

I really thought my time was up.

I spent a couple of hours working in the garden, had dinner and slumped down in an easy chair with a coffee and a Richard Stark novel which I am re-reading for the umpteenth time. Suddenly, I felt strange. I checked my pulse. It was fibrillating and so fast I couldn't begin to count it. I checked my blood pressure and pulse with a machine we have. My pulse was 156 and upwards and my blood pressure alternated between absurdly high and absurdly low. The machine lit up with all the little warning lights with which it is fitted.

I had no chest, jaw or arm pain but I had a great deal of wind.

My fault.

Since I managed to clear my once crippling IBS with a potent mixture of acidophilus, an ultra violet light machine which I use to destroy the fungal infection of my toenails, and a diet rich in onions and garlic, I have been getting a little millennial (the new word for 'cocky'). A couple of weeks ago, I started eating rough, brown, wholemeal bread packed with seeds. It was wonderful to taste good bread again, after years of eating nothing but white bread.

Doctors, relying on what they have been taught, supplemented by what they have read in medical journals and medical textbooks, still believe that IBS is best treated with a diet heavy in roughage. This is like trying to treat diabetes mellitus by telling patients to eat more sugar. The professions don't take IBS very seriously because there is no effective pharmacological remedy available. The healing professions are, I am afraid to say, dominated by the needs of the pharmaceutical industry. Modern medical care is dominated by, and run for, interventionists in general and drug companies in particular. As a result, doctors can be hidebound and worryingly unimaginative. And, because IBS is neither a dramatic disease, nor a fashionable one, doctors remain blisteringly ignorant about it. I have lost count of the number of patients who have told me that their doctor has told them that their wind is not caused by IBS because 'the tests came back negative'. That's clever of them because I know of no comprehensive and truly effective tests for IBS. The diagnosis has to be made on the basis of the symptoms and signs.

I have studied IBS a good deal over the years and have found the medical and nursing professions to be steadfastly slow to accept new information. A quarter of a century ago, I was the first doctor to notice that intestinal wind can cause kidney bleeding.

I had first-hand experience of this since I very nearly lost a kidney to doctors who were keen to rip out what they thought was a cancerous organ. Only my insistence that a scan be done had saved one of my favourite kidneys from ending up as someone's breakfast.

In recent years, I had pretty well controlled my IBS, and was feeling far too over-confident. I had forgotten that IBS is not a disorder to be treated lightly. As a result, I overdid things. Yesterday I ate four slices of the darned stuff and today I am bloated and suffering. Unusually for me it is my stomach, rather than my large intestine, which is most bloated. Who would have thought that a few slices of rather tasty bread could cause such awful disruption.

Antoinette wanted to call an ambulance but I wouldn't let her. I felt certain that my crazy heart antics were a result of the massive amount of wind that was in my intestines in general and my stomach in particular.

The stomach and the heart share a common nerve supply (the vagus nerve or tenth cranial nerve) but although doctors recognise that burping may, rarely, be a sign of cardiac dysfunction they do not recognise that cardiac dysfunction (including palpitations, fibrillations and so on) can be a result of intestinal wind. If A and B are known to be linked and A can cause B you would not think a huge stretch, would you, to suspect that maybe B can also cause A?

Am I being too cynical in supposing that when doctors diagnose a cardiac malfunction they can always recommend some expensive intervention (prescribe drugs, recommend surgery, etc.) but if they diagnose a wind problem there is really absolutely bugger all that they can do? As I have pointed out many times before, the medical profession is dominated by, and ruled by, the pharmaceutical industry. If there is no suitable drug therapy available then the problem will not be recognised. Moreover, doctors and nurses are dedicated to the interventionist philosophy. Doing something is their default. And, sadly, too many patients are eager to accept whatever treatments are offered. The truth is, however, that discretionary medical care is not only very expensive in financial terms but it is also very dangerous and deadly in human terms.

It took about six hours for the fibrillations to slow and for my heart to start beating normally again. I was exhausted, inevitably, and yawning frequently too. The vagus nerve also triggers yawning. To the orthodox professional, yawning is therefore a sign that a patient is having a heart attack. And the vagus nerve can cause pains in the left arm too.

How many people, I wonder, are being treated for heart disease when their initial signs and symptoms were caused by wind? A million? Probably more. How many are taking potentially lethal anticoagulants such as warfarin which they do not really need?

And how many patients (let alone doctors) know that all the drugs used to treat irregular heartbeats have potentially alarming side effects – including irregular heartbeats. Oh, and that ultimate side effect known as death.

This is yet another undiscovered health scandal.

The older I get, and the more I know, the more I realise that medicine really is still in the dark ages. We have to remember, I suppose, that it isn't all that long ago that doctors claimed that smoking was good for the lungs. Now they say that vaccination is good for the whole organism.

Both my parents were killed by incompetent doctors (the details are in previous diaries) but I particularly remember the way my father was killed. He had a terrible kyphosis (due, in part, to his enthusiasm for creating software on his computer) which led to an inevitable breathing problem. A nurse diagnosed him as suffering from the new-fangled and nonsensical conglomerate disorder of Chronic Obstruction Pulmonary Disease (COPD) and prescribed some pharmaceutical rubbish to help his breathing. One of the side effects of the rubbish she prescribed had atrial fibrillation as a known side effect. But when my father duly developed a heart irregularity, the nurse didn't take my father off the drug. Instead, she gave him something else to 'cure' the irregularity. And, naturally, that made things worse. By the time doctors finally managed to kill him by prescribing an inappropriate drug, my father was taking so many medicines that when he died we filled two black bags with the leftovers. Inevitably, the drugs included digoxin and warfarin.

Given my symptoms, I would be lucky not to end up with a fistful of prescriptions for heart drugs. Statins, of course. Something for the high blood pressure I don't have. And a few expensive delicacies for the heart irregularity.

The problem, you see, is that the medical literature shows a single case of a man in his 60s who presented (that's medical jargon for he turned up in a doctor's surgery) with wind and turned out, on investigation, to have problems with his cardiac arteries. (Please don't ask why they checked out his cardiac arteries when he complained of wind.)

Now, you might imagine that it would be possible for a man of that age to suffer both from some sort of intestinal disorder and a heart problem. But doctors like to tie things up neatly. And so it was concluded that the wind was a symptom of heart disease.

And so that's it.

According to medical literature and medical teaching, wind is now a symptom of heart disease.

It does not seem to have occurred to the people who write articles for medical journals that when heart symptoms and wind do occur together, it might be possible that the latter could be the cause of the former. I suspect that wind induced heart problems could be another one of those diagnoses which are missed – like normal pressure hydrocephalus.

Of course, I could be wrong.

I could have heart disease and, maybe, have just endured a silent heart attack.

I rather hope not. And I am prepared to bet my life on my diagnosis.

Anyway, all this explains why I am wary of seeing a doctor.

Or one of the new-fangled practice nurses (known as 'nurse prescribers') who has the authority to prescribe drugs about which she probably knows next to nothing.

9

When I awoke, I was feeling more alive and so we drove into Cheltenham. There was, inevitably, a massive queue causing a lengthy delay. When we got to the front of the queue we found that it was caused by a workman's truck parked on the road. Traffic lights had been set up but there were no workmen and no activity. This seems to happen often in and around Cheltenham.

As we were heading back to the car (or, more accurately our truck) Antoinette spotted a CD rack in a charity shop window. One of those tall, thin things, made out of solid wood and capable of holding a 100 or more CDs. We went in to buy it (the advantage of having the truck with us was that we could take it home) and as I prepared to leave, I suddenly noticed that Antoinette was engaged in an earnest conversation with a young man who was pushing a pram.

'I thought the baby was dead,' she told me, as we headed to the car. 'So I had to stop and look more closely. But it wasn't a real baby. It was a very realistic, life size doll.'

The young man told her that the 'baby', which is apparently called a 'newborn' was called Isobel and that she was due to have a birthday soon. There were toys in the pram and the young man told Antoinette that he had spotted a better pram in the shop that he wanted to buy. It was a little smarter and larger than the pram he had and he thought Isobel deserved an upgrade.

'So I gave him £20 towards the cost of the second hand pram,' said Antoinette. 'He was so pleased. He's looking forward to taking his baby daughter for long walks.'

Apparently, this is by no means an uncommon occurrence. Quite a number of adults, of both sexes, have life size, realistic dolls which they treat just as gently and lovingly as parents treat their real children.

10

I don't follow Twitter but today I heard about a twitter which reminded me why I eschew social media.

A celebrity tweeter wrote a tweet slightly sneering at world champion boxer Chris Eubank for being adopted. (His father, Chris Eubank, was also a world champion boxer.)

That is such a nasty, horrid, cruel thing to do that I find myself hoping that the tweeter was drunk when she wrote it.

It seems to me to be quite awful that one human being could use the internet to attack another for being adopted – maybe just for a bit of cheap publicity. And no one else seems to think this is a bad thing to do.

Oddly enough, I remember that another champion boxer, another Briton, Tyson Fury, was vilified on social media for daring to express perfectly sound and valid opinions about marriage, his faith and homosexuality. Fury, a kindly seeming bear of a man who is 6 foot 9 inches tall, ended up depressed and out of his sport for two years. Once again, the people doing the criticising seemed to me to be real Z list celebrities grabbing any cheap publicity they could find. One critic, I seem to remember, was a homosexual whose main claim to fame was his ability to do the hop, skip and jump successfully. (I've always thought of that as the athletics equivalent of solo synchronised swimming.) I don't know whether this individual's nastiness had anything to do with Fury's depression but it truly can't have helped. Whatever happened to Christian charity, understanding and warmth towards one's fellow man?

Why is it that so many people become aggressive, rude and patronising when they enter a chat room or an online forum? Is it, perhaps, because they feel distant from other people and therefore safe in attacking them?

The more I read and hear about it the more I am convinced that the modern witch hunters (politicians, police officers and minor celebrities) who seem willing to gather around to stone anyone who seems to be a worthwhile target – regardless of the presence or absence of any evidence – are no better than the flash mobs who persecuted midwives testing them for witch hood by immersing them in the village pond. If the women drowned, they were innocent. If they did not drown, they were guilty and would be burnt at the stake or hung.

I did something very silly this morning.

In a hurry, I picked an Earl Grey teabag out of an airtight container and dunked it into a cup full of hot water. It was only afterwards that Antoinette noticed that the tea bags were mouldy.

Out of curiosity, I looked on the internet to see if I was the only idiot to have made this silly mistake. I found that I wasn't. (There aren't many things you can confess on the internet and not find yourself a member of a large club.)

One woman who had accidentally drunk tea made with a mouldy tea bag had posted a sad plea asking if anyone knew what would happen to her. 'You will die', wrote someone – anonymously, of course. I suppose it was intended as a joke. But it wasn't funny. And it probably gave the unfortunate woman some sleepless nights. How can people be so damned cruel?

There is no news about whether or not our buyer and his mother are going to turn up to start the real process of buying our apartment in Paris. It is like waiting for the other shoe to drop. But maybe our buyer only has one leg and there is no second shoe.

Our bet is that he thinks we are going to Paris (we aren't because I have signed a power of attorney form with the notaire) and wants to make sure that we not only have our tickets but are also on our way. His hope, I suspect, is that we will be so fed up when he demands a reduction in the price that we will give in and accept whatever deal he wants to offer. A dirty trick but it would not be out of character. We suspect that there is something dark going on here. Maybe the buyer is planning to do up the apartment, increase the price and resell it with the same agent – who will, in that case, make over 100,000 euros in commission.

I can't help wondering if he is mad.

I have long wondered if he is a fantasist with 12 euros in a checking account and no job.

Antoinette suspects that they have a property to sell. I think she is right. Maybe the mother has to sell something and either won't or can't. Or maybe she is not as keen on our apartment as her son.

Either that or they are waiting for someone to die and leave them the money they need and clearly have not got.

Actually, if they do have a property to sell maybe that explains why our estate agent told us that they did not need a bank loan to buy our apartment. Maybe he was simply being disingenuous. If

405

they were waiting to sell a property that would explain the variety of delaying techniques and it would also explain why no one seemed to want to tell us what was going on.

No one involved in this sale seems to want to tell us anything.

But my guess is that Antoinette is right. If she is (and she usually is) then we've been played like suckers throughout this whole disgraceful process. Maybe we were the only people involved in the whole damned saga who never really knew what was going on.

None of this explains why I get so upset by this nonsense.

It's not that we have to sell or that we need the money now because we have some specific plans for it. The problems are uncertainty, frustration and resentment at the fact that an outsider (and his mother) are deliberately delaying, changing their minds, letting us down and treating us without any respect at all. Every time they delay, I have to exchange another flurry of emails with our notaire. I have so far sent and received hundreds of emails and I have wasted at least a week of solid working time on this damned nuisance. (The same thing happened with Barclays Bank of course.)

It is the constant making and breaking of promises which is so intensely stressful. All made worse, of course, by the incredible unfairness of French property laws which seem to be designed to give the buyer all the power in the world and the seller absolutely no real power at all. I dare say this happened because there have been bad sellers in the past. But now the system is designed to aid and abet bad buyers.

From experience, conversation and investigation, I know that the French have always had a reputation for playing dirty and for being devious and underhand. They are innately selfish and indifferent to other people's needs.

I am beginning to realise why the frog crunching, snail munching, white flag waving bastards have such a well-deserved reputation.

This evening, in Devon, I went down the drive to pop a plastic, black bag full of rubbish into our black plastic wheelie bin. I usually wear disposable, plastic gloves while doing this, to avoid catching any of the multitude of germs left on the lid by the dustmen, but today I forgot to take any gloves with me. I then had a brainwave. I had immediate access to a disposable item with which I could safely lift the lid – and of which I could afterwards easily dispose. A leaf. A large sycamore leaf. You can't get any greener than that, can you?

While walking back up the drive I noticed, in the distance, that some of our neighbours are away. I know this because all their curtains are clearly closed and there is no car in the driveway. Why do people close all their curtains when they go away? Don't they know that they might as well put up a big sign saying 'House Empty'?

11

Yahoo was hacked back in 2013 and they've just noticed that the hack was worse than they originally thought. Instead of affecting just a few customers it actually affected three billion customers. That's three billion as in 3,000,000,000 customers who had their personal information stolen. How did Yahoo not notice? Why does no one seem to care about this sort of carelessness? 'Oh, by the way, I lost the personal, private, information of 3,000,000,000 customers who are now liable to have their identities stolen and their lives ruined.' 'Oh, don't worry about it – it happens to everyone.'

We stood on our balcony and looked out across the bay. An exquisite moon was reflected in the mill-pond calm sea and lights from the houses around the bay were reflected in the water too. On the beach, we could see a dozen small twinkling lights: fishermen settling down for the night, with their absurdly long sea rods resting on their tripods, their vacuum flasks filled with soup or tea and a plastic box with their sandwiches by their side. Some of the fishermen had put up small tents so that they had a little protection from the elements. They weigh down the corners with stones from the beach. There is no sand into which they could drive stakes or pegs. At dawn, they will all go home with, if they are lucky, a small catch of mackerel. It's a strange hobby but a romantic one in a way.

12

Another portion of England's coastline has fallen into the sea. Shaped, concrete barriers, built along Britain's coastline, would prevent coastal erosion for a fraction of the cost of HS2 – the absurdly expensive and almost completely pointless railway line improvement on which the Government plans to spend untold billions. Even old-fashioned Victorian breakwaters would be useful. Anything remotely effective would improve coastal communities in every conceivable way and so produce a huge and lasting economic dividend for the nation. Looking far ahead, we should be preserving our coastal communities. When international travel becomes too expensive except for a chosen few, or is banned by the global warming mythologists, our home-grown seaside communities will provide vital holidays and relaxation.

I read today that eBay told the UK authorities that its UK revenue for 2016 was £200 million but told the US tax authorities that its UK revenues were $1.3 billion. And Netflix appear to have the same approach to accounting. Netflix had estimated UK revenue at $520 million in 2016 but reported its revenue at only 22 million euros. How surprising it was to discover that both companies paid peanuts in tax to the British Government. What makes me think that if I told the UK tax authorities that my UK income was X and then told the American tax authorities that my UK income was Y, I might have men with boots banging on my door?

I bought a copy of the *Financial Times* (the publishers seem to have stopped producing weekly copies of my preferred choice *The Dandy*) and was pleasantly amused to see a full page advertisement for a *Financial Times* event entitled Kilkenomics at which various *FT* journalists were due to speak. I was amused because the event was promoted with a puff describing the event as 'Brilliant' from a journalist called Simon Kuper. My amusement was inspired by the fact that Kuper was listed as one of the speakers.

Maybe the *FT* is breaking new ground here. How much more fun it will be if authors, musicians and film makers write their own reviews.

This afternoon, I received an email from our stand-in notaire in Paris. (Our long-suffering main notaire has gone on holiday).

Apparently, our wretched buyer now wants to delay the signing by two more days. This renders the power of attorney useless and so if the signing is going to go ahead on Wednesday instead of Monday, I am told that the whole thing will have to be redone. Making things more complicated is the fact that the estate agent has agreed to cut his commission from 50,000 euros to 40,000 euros. My guess is that the buyer demanded a cut in the price of the apartment and the agent, knowing that we would not knock anything off the price, agreed to take 10,000 euros off his fee in an attempt to keep the deal live.

Since I am in Devon and not in Paris, the notaire has sent me a new six-page power of attorney (in French) which I must immediately read, scan, email and then return as a hard copy via DHL or some other overnight courier.

I wrote back asking why the buyer thought that another two day delay would make any difference. 'I think it is reasonable to ask the buyer to explain exactly why he cannot sign on Monday but can sign on Wednesday. What magic will happen in two days that has not happened in four months?'

Antoinette and I agree that we cannot trust this buyer at all and so I think I will suggest that if we give him the extra two days to raise the money then he must accept that if he cannot complete the purchase before or on the 20th November then he will lose his deposit.

I have long favoured the 20th November as a completion date because the Chancellor of the Exchequer has a Budget on the 22nd November and I fear there is a chance that there will be a change in capital gains tax rates. A two day delay in the signing could easily result in an extra bill of £100,000 or more.

(Governments have tried backdating capital gains tax rises but the last time they tried this they had to give it up and capital gains were taxed at two different rates depending on the date of the transaction.)

I am also going to insist that he sign a document agreeing that he will not in the future ask for any compensation, refund or anything involving money. We don't trust him an inch and we're concerned that he might try something crafty. I wouldn't put it past him to complain that he didn't realise that the apartment was on the top floor. Or maybe he will sue us because he thinks the kitchen needs a lick of paint.

What a truly miserable, painful, exhausting, debilitating experience this has been. And throughout, our agent has insisted that these sort of delays are normal in France. It seems clear that foreigners should never, ever contemplate buying property in France unless they know that they will keep it forever and never have to try to sell it.

We watched *Wag the Dog*. It is one of my favourite films. The author of the book upon which the film was based was Larry Beinhart who has also written the utterly amazing *Fog Facts* – the seminal work on media manipulation.

13

I have always thought that the most important question is 'Why?'.
I still do.

Our notaire in Paris is away and another notaire has taken over. He tells me that the buyer cannot now attend the signing which he agreed would take place on Monday the 16th because his mother has suddenly decided that she has a meeting elsewhere. I have no idea where. He didn't say. Possibly she is taking the dog for a walk. Possibly she has made an appointment to see her hairdresser. Possibly she is going for a joyride on her broomstick.

I cannot believe these people. Are they mad? Are they simpletons? Or are they just thoughtless, selfish and plain nasty? I really, really, really do not want to sell our apartment to them. But the French system seems to make it impossible to do anything but put up with their machinations, excuses and nonsenses.

It also appears that the proxy I signed is even more useless than was previously thought. I now have to sign another version of the damned thing because the estate agent has cut his commission from 50,000 euros to 40,000 euros. He has done this, I assume, because the buyer demanded a cut in the price in view of the adjusted Carrez figure. I had already made it clear that I would not reduce the price of the apartment. So the buyer has negotiated a 1% cut in the price by thugging the estate agent. And because the proxy contains the whole price, including the fee for the estate agent, I have to sign a new version.

I suggested that it would be far easier all round for the buyer and the estate agent to sign a separate document in which the estate agent promised to give the buyer 10,000 euros when the deal was finalised. But the notaire says we cannot do this because if we do the buyer may have to pay another few euros in tax.

So, in order to protect him from this very modest eventuality, I have to sign another proxy and somehow get it to Paris by yesterday. I suspect that the cost of sending the packet to Paris will exceed the tax liability I am helping the buyer to avoid.

The bottom line is that anyone who is thinking of buying property in France should think again and then do something more sensible. Buy a shark and keep it in the bathtub. Sail around the world on a homemade raft with sails made out of string vests.

If the tide is out tomorrow, I will totter along the beach to the local Post Office and get rid of the revised proxy.

A British economist called Richard Thaler has been awarded the 79th Nobel Prize in Economic Sciences for pointing out that people aren't always analytical, rational and clear minded. Instead, we apparently feel financial loss more than we enjoy financial gain. We treasure things we have – and overvalue them. We rate new information more highly than the stuff we already know. And we hate change.

Nobel Prize for that stuff?

Crumbs.

Economics is in a worse state than I thought.

People hate change, eh?

Who'd have thought it.

14

I've been told again by our stand-in notaire that I must send the signed proxy document to Paris by DHL or some other courier. To comfort our buyer, I must travel several miles to the nearest Post Office (I have told them it will have to be a Post Office because there is no DHL office for miles and miles) and arrange for the document to be sent.

I have been given around 24 hours to get this form back – though the buyers seem to delight in taking weeks to reply to any query I send.

I got up early this morning and went to the bottom of the garden to check the tide. It was in and so I couldn't take the short cut along the beach. It will take forever to find a car park space on a Saturday morning so I had to walk the long way round, taking a short cut through some woods and then walking along the road to the Post Office.

Before I set off, I checked to make that the Post Office was open on Saturday mornings. It was supposed to be.

But when I got there the door had a handwritten, misspelt notice stuck on the glass, apologising for the fact that the Post Office was 'closed due to illness'.

So I walked all the way back home, stuck some stamps and an Air Mail label on the damned packet and stuffed it into a nearby post box.

What else can possibly go wrong with this damned stupid sale?

At least my heart seemed to cope with the exercise without having forty fits. It seems as though my diagnosis was correct. Just as well, really.

Still, it is worth reflecting that if I had gone along to the Accident and Emergency department of a hospital when I had my fibrillations, I would have doubtless ended up with a fistful of prescriptions for drugs which might well have killed me. And, I have no doubt, my theory about vagus nerve interference would have almost certainly attracted nothing but sneers, raised eyebrows and a diagnosis of dementia.

15

I've been around long enough to know that we are due a major financial crisis. It will be a big one: as big, if not bigger, than the crisis of 2008.

The basic reason is simple: the central bankers have been steadily making things worse in their clumsy attempts to save the big banks from the consequences of their actions. And none of the leading bankers and politicians who caused the 2008 crisis (and subsequently made things worse) has been punished or learnt anything from what happened. All the evidence proves (not suggests) that central bankers have absolutely no idea what they are doing or why.

Central bankers in general, and the Bank of England in particular, have steadfastly, and with unerring accuracy, got everything wrong. They caused the dotcom bubble, they over-emphasised the impact of the Millennium Bug, they over-reacted over the attack on the twin towers and they helped create the huge debts that began in 2000. They pushed up prices, encouraged risk taking, and then introduced emergency policies in 2008, which they have still not been brave enough to change. As a result, companies which should have gone bust are struggling on, productivity has collapsed, property prices have soared, savers have been punished by absurdly low interest rates and the rise of very left wing socialism has been an inevitable result. Pension models have been destroyed and pensioners severely disadvantaged (except, of course, for those receiving pensions from the Bank of England or Parliament).

Low interest rates, and low returns on savings, have forced companies to stop investing and to shovel all their available cash into their pension funds.

It is difficult to imagine how anyone could have screwed up more than Carney et al. All the Canuk has done for us is give us bloody horrid plastic money that no one likes.

Now, on top of that, we have a number of serious problems around the world in general and Europe in particular. Nationalism (dismissed and derided as populism) is not dead, despite the fact that the EU (and Macron, their appointed winner) succeeded in defeating the National Front in the French elections. People in Catalonia want to leave Spain (which could lead to a major crisis within the EU). Scottish nationalists want to leave the UK. Welsh nationalists want to leave the UK. The Basques want to leave Spain. The Corsicans want to leave France. The people of Flanders want to leave Belgium. The people of several regions in Northern Italy want independence. None of this is going to go away. The allure of Hitler's European superstate is diminishing daily. (Not that any of this is new, of course. Not long ago, both Yugoslavia and Czechoslovakia were countries.) Greece is a financial basket case and Italy isn't much better.

If any of these regions achieve independence, they will be outside the EU and the EU's power and authority will be massively diminished. There will also be enormous bureaucratic and legal complications, of course. And that is why the EU will do everything it can to prevent any break away states forming. Unfortunately, for the EU, rounding up a bunch of feral cats could be easier.

In an attempt to deal with its problems, the European bank has printed three trillion euros in the last couple of years.

I suspect that Greece is still the EU's real problem. And the underlying everlasting fault is that Greece was taken into the euro fraudulently with figures cooked by Goldman Sachs. The odd thing is that one former Goldman Sachs boss was an Italian called Mario Draghi.

And guess who is now printing euros like mad to try to cover up the Greek problems? That would be the chief of the European Central Bank.

And that is (surprise, surprise) the very same Mario Draghi.

As well as running the ECB, Signor Draghi finds time to be a member of the Group of Thirty founded by the Rockefeller Foundation. The Group of Thirty is a private group of lobbyists in the finance world.

(As an aside, it is worth mentioning that lobbyists pretty well control the EU, of course, spending nearly £2 billion on bribing parliamentarians and eurocrats within the EU. Lobbyists want rules and laws to be introduced which protect their clients' interests and the result is that small, growing companies have no chance of succeeding within the EU. There are no democratic checks on EU officials and regulators and so in practice it is the lobbyists, working for big companies, who make up the laws.)

It seems odd to me that the man running the EU's finances should also be a financial lobbyist for there seems to me to be ample room for conflicts of interest.

Draghi's home country of Italy is in an even worse state than Greece. The banks there have debts of 360 billion euros.

And Draghi's European Central Bank itself is in an even worse state, having borrowed 7,800 billion euros from the Bundesbank.

In Germany, the teetering Deutsche Bank has derivatives worth 46 trillion euros on its books. That is 14 times Germany's Gross Domestic Product.

Other banks throughout Europe are in a similar mess, though everything is carefully orchestrated (fiddled) to make it look as though everything is fine and dandy.

The rest of the world isn't much better off than Europe.

In Venezuela, the government is pretty well bankrupt and certain to default on its bonds (big chunks of which are held, I am pleased to say, by Goldman Sachs).

Meanwhile, back in Europe, the people (derided as populist hordes by the EU's fascist supporters) are rising up against the undemocratic rule of the Nazi creation. The opposition to the EU comes largely from young Europeans who see the EU for the fascist state it has become. Austria, for example, has just elected a 30-year-old leader who loathes the European Union.

It is only in Britain that the young people are so ignorant and superficial that they support the European Union in the mistaken belief that once we are outside the EU they will no longer be able to go skiing or drink their favourite style of cappuccino.

Hubristic central bankers who created the global financial crisis a decade ago are still pursuing policies (zero or negative interest rates and the endless printing of money) which make things ever worse. They themselves have, of course, remained above the financial carnage. Their huge salaries, generous expense accounts, massive, inflation-proof pensions and absurd severance payments have protected them from the consequences of their own bottomless stupidity and unrelieved arrogance. The other day I read that an employee of Santander in the US, is apparently leaving the bank and taking with him a total of $713 million before tax. That is beyond silly and obscene and well into the realms of science fiction.

To counteract the crash they caused, the world's bankers have produced a collection of bubbles which will, when they burst, produce unavoidable penury, inescapable unemployment and inevitable hardship for millions.

If inflation rates go up a little too much (the bankers and politicians hope they will rise but not too far) then interest rates will follow. And the result will be chaos, bewilderment, outrage and confusion among the many who currently assume that interest rates will always stay close to zero (or below). If interest rates go back up to normal levels of 6% or 7% there will be forced selling of houses, a collapse of house prices and mass poverty among the middle classes.

So, what else is there to worry about?

Donald Trump seems to want to nuke North Korea and he has a stockpile of 1,240 nuclear warheads with which to do it. It matters not one jot that North Korea has no capacity to attack America. Russia is still classified as an enemy, though no one can remember why, and Iran is officially an enemy again though the Iranians haven't invaded anywhere since the Battle of the Eurymedon in 466 BC.

It isn't really difficult to explain the preponderance of America's enemies.

America spends over $300 billion a year on arms and the arms industry spends $1 billion a year on lobbyists trying to persuade the politicians to spend more. When you have that many bullets you have to find someone to shoot them at or else your stockpiles grow so big there is no room to put everything.

And then there is Brexit.

Brexit should have been exciting and given politicians a chance to grasp the future and shape it to our advantage. Brexit was an opportunity. The people gave the Government a mandate for change; a chance to throw off the chains of the European Union.

But our politicians have proved totally inadequate and are running around like trouserless characters in a 1960s Whitehall Farce. The three leading members of the Government which is supposed to be negotiating for us to leave the EU (May, Green and Hammond) are either supporters of the European Union or are giving a very good impression of supporting it. It seems that all three voted Remain. Once every five minutes someone in the establishment issues a warning about some aspect of our life which will be wrecked by Brexit. We've been warned that aeroplanes will stop flying, that all the bankers will leave the country, that cancer treatment will halt and that our courts will cease functioning. And we won't be able to buy anything that isn't made in Birmingham or Leeds. There will, I suspect, be no more slippers, no more hairdressers and no socks on sale. (There will, thankfully, be plenty of bras on sale because they are all made in China which was not, when I last looked, a member of the European Union.)

In any negotiation you only have strength when the other side honestly believes that you will walk away from whatever deal is on offer.

Our woefully incompetent Government has steadfastly refused to countenance the idea of leaving the EU without a deal in place. Worse still, a bunch of treacherous MPs are insisting that they will vote against any attempt to leave the EU without a deal having been made. These idiot politicians have clearly never worked in the real world and they have certainly never been involved in any real negotiations.

Without the ability to walk away and leave the EU without a deal having been made, our negotiators will have no power. And so we will be slaughtered if and when serious negotiations ever take place. Imagine two people walk into a garage to look at new cars. If one of them says, 'We must have that. We simply must buy that today!' then they are screwed. They have no negotiating position because the salesman knows that they cannot leave the showroom without buying the car.

The Brexit fiasco is made infinitely worse by the fact that Theresa May's full cabinet of 23 men and women contains just six individuals who campaigned for Brexit. The other 17 members of the cabinet did not want us to leave the European Union but are now charged with arranging our departure. And this is democracy?

So those are just some of the problems ahead.

We can take our pick.

But, whichever way you look at it, our politicians and the Bank of England have ensured that there is a major financial crisis just around the corner. A lot of people who thought they were quite well off are going to become poor. For those who have saved a little money, who are not greedy but who want to protect their savings against inflation and political mayhem, and who would like a modest income or some growth, finding the best way to invest is like threading your way through a snake infested pit. (For anyone who is interested, everything I know about the general principles of investing is in my book *Moneypower* which is available as an ebook.)

The politicians and the bureaucrats, blessed with taxpayer-funded salaries and fat, inflation-proof pensions, will, of course, remain wealthy and above the turmoil, anxiety and misery which face those of us who pay for their security.

16

Our buyers were supposed to be signing the first part of the purchase paperwork today. I have lost count of the number of appointments which have been made and broken.

This was their suggested date but they have backed out of signing because the mother has suddenly acquired another appointment which is more important than the appointment she and her son agreed to less than a week ago.

These bloody people are unbelievable.

In France the laws seem to favour the buyer so much that the seller seems to have no rights whatsoever. I really don't want to sell the apartment to these damned people. I told Antoinette that I would sell it to them over my dead body and that if I'm allowed, I will leave instructions that even then they won't be allowed to buy the damned place.

The problem is that our damned contract with the estate agent contains a clause which says that if they find a buyer I have to sell it to that buyer. There is no let out clause. Technically and legally the buyers can probably keep us hanging on until the year 3000. By which time, we will all be dust, the apartment will be worth a million times as much and their descendants will be able to buy it from our descendants for the same price as it was last May.

Today, we are on our third notaire.

Our first notaire has gone on holiday (doubtless exhausted by the whole affair) and the notaire who took over from her has also disappeared.

On this singularly unsuccessful journey, the buyers have passed through rude and manipulative, nodding en route at absurd and the barely believable, passed through the villages of farce and fiasco and have finally reached the Dombey style Dickensian gloomy conurbation of Madness where the only redeeming feature lies in the brightening suburb of Good Copy and Grotesque Entertainment.

Our new notaire told me this morning that the mother has now decided that she cannot sign the documents on Wednesday either (as she agreed when she cancelled because of another appointment which had suddenly leapt into her clearly over-crowded calendar) because she is going to do something else instead.

I have no idea what this is.

Another trip around the city on her broomstick, perchance.

I suppose they feel they can't re-use the 'hospital appointment' excuse. Or maybe there is a law in France that people must think up new excuses every time they break agreements. It would not surprise me.

The buyers have steadfastly refused to provide any evidence that they have the money to pay the deposit, let alone the rest of the money they will owe, and our new notaire told me today that he is doubtful that even if they sign they will have enough money to complete as I have asked on or before November 20th. And he implies that there is nothing we could do about it if they do sign and then break the contract.

Our estate agent still believes that the deal can be done. I suspect he also still believes in the Easter Bunny and the Tooth Fairy. I also fear that he is desperate to be paid his reduced commission of 40,000 euros without having to do any more work.

I asked (begged would probably be a more appropriate word) our new notaire to do whatever he can to extricate us from this nightmare of a mess.

I am not hopeful.

When I still hadn't received a reply by the end of the day, I sent a firm note to all three notaires telling them (again) that the deal was now finally over.

Actually, I don't think it's such a bad thing. I may be rationalising but there seem to me to be at least six reasons why holding onto the apartment might prove to be a decent investment after all.

If we had sold next month as planned, I would have probably invested much of the proceeds on the stock market. But stock markets are high. Maybe this isn't the best time to be turning property money into share money.

If Macron does succeed in taming the French unions (even a little bit) there is a chance that France could grow stronger. That would help property prices enormously.

French tax law allows sellers to reduce their tax liability according to the number of years they have held a property. If we just hold onto the apartment for another six months or so, our profits will be enhanced considerably – far more than the holding cost.

American companies are moving employees to Paris because of Brexit. One bank alone is moving 300 highly paid employees to Paris. There will be a growing demand for reasonably expensive properties. And there isn't much on the market because of France's absurd legal restrictions.

The Parisian property market has fallen for several years (largely as a result of Hollande's damaging policies). It is now rising again. The apartment should be worth more by next summer.

Sterling has recovered a little. Where it will be in six months' time? I have no idea, and nor has anyone else. But if we time the sale carefully we could add 100,000 euros to the gain.

We were, to put it bluntly, lied to by someone at the beginning of this fiasco.

I don't believe our buyers could raise the money to buy our cellar let alone the apartment. Time and time again they disappeared, ignored requests for information or quite simply declined to answer essential questions. The result has been frustration, uncertainty and a stressful sense of powerlessness.

We will stick with the estate agent for now and do so for two reasons.

First, neither of us wants to travel to Paris to find a new agent at the moment.

And second, we feel curiously comfortable with our current agent because we feel we can't trust the bastard any more than we could throw him. Sometimes it is good to believe that you cannot trust someone in a situation like this than it is to believe that you can.

What now, I wonder?

Antoinette is worried that the bastards will find some way to sue us now that we have told them they can't buy the apartment. Maybe they were trying to trap us into throwing them out so that they could sue us. Or maybe there was some other plot. Maybe our agent will sue us. Maybe the French Government will confiscate the apartment. Actually, I no longer much care if they do.

But, stuff them all.

We will defend ourselves.

One thing we know for sure is that the buyers don't have much money. Antoinette and I have given ourselves a 100,000 euro budget for starters to cover legal and marketing fees. And since we have been misled and have suffered real financial damage, I rather think that we can, if necessary, counter sue both our buyers and the estate agents for a small fortune.

We have added another lesson to our ever-growing collection. We have learned that the French have absolutely no sense of fair play – particularly where the English are concerned. Indeed, in my now considerable experience, the French are insufferably rude, arrogant and selfish when they are involved in any transaction or activity which involves money. Trusting a Frenchman is like hanging a sign around your neck saying 'Trick Me'.

I made things worse at the beginning by saying to our loathsome estate agent: 'I don't understand how a French property transaction works so I'll have to rely on you.'

Evidence shows that the greatest risks for illness occur when people have little or no control over their lives.

Our buyer had power over us because he had the right to buy the apartment, the ability to decide when to buy it, the power over all the rules. And he and the agent had the knowledge of how the system worked (entirely in his favour).

Amazingly, three notaires agree that the way the law stands he can probably sue us if we try to sell the flat to anyone else or if we do not keep paying the bills, maintenance bills and taxes, and keep it available for him to buy if and whenever he has the money to complete the purchase.

So, he has a good deal of power over us.

We wanted to sell, wanted the whole thing over and finished so that we could get on with the rest of our lives.

But, thanks to French laws which even Kafka would have found astonishing, we are stuck in a nightmare.

However, our plan now is to keep the apartment and not sell it to this buyer even if he finds the money. In the spring of 2018, we will find a new agent, sign a better contract and find a proper buyer with the money to buy the apartment.

We felt better. We can kid ourselves that we have taken back control and liberated ourselves from these evil people.

Today, I have finished the 12th Bilbury book. I think it is the best.

17

Elvis memorabilia has apparently lost its value. I am not surprised. Most of his former fans are dead or dying or selling and not buying.

Similarly, comics and toys and cigarette cards which were valuable are now not valuable. Cricket books have lost their value too because the sport has become a minority interest.

Today, I sat on my bench from Lord's cricket ground, high up on our own stretch of the Jurassic Coast and read old cricket magazines. I found myself reading about C.B.Fry again. His life always makes me feel laughably inadequate. Fry played cricket and football for England and played in an FA Cup Final. He played rugby for Oxford University and held the world long jump record. He was a Captain in the Navy and wrote a number of books. He worked as one of the first radio commentators and was a regular panellist on radio programmes such as Any Questions and the Brains Trust. In his seventies, he was still fit enough to be able to jump backwards, from a standing position, onto a mantelpiece. The Albanian people were so impressed by this English superman that they asked him to be their King. He declined, presumably because he couldn't fit it into his schedule.

In the old *Cricketer* magazine which I was reading today, King Fry had written a review of a book by Australian all-rounder Keith Miller. Fry's articles are always firmly forthright and slightly bizarre but make wonderful reading.

I also enjoy reading the results of the schools matches. The players who later won England caps invariably stand out head and shoulders above the rest.

Down on the beach a dog was barking at the sea. It was the spaniel which comes down every day for half to three quarters of an hour. The dog stands on the edge of the sea and barks continuously while its owner stands proudly on the beach and watches. This presumably makes them both very happy. I find it rather irritating.

An actress I have never heard of complained today that at the start of her career she was 'made' to do an almost nude audition for a part. I suspect she wasn't forced to do anything of the kind. I suspect she was asked to do an almost nude audition and she agreed because she was desperate for the part.

And the corollary is that the other girl, the unknown who didn't want to take her clothes off and who said 'no, thank you' to the producer, is probably now working in Walmart.

The girl working in Walmart is neither famous nor rich but maybe she feels better about herself.

Who knows?

Life is about choices.

Not even self-important actresses have a right to whinge in public if they made choices they later regret.

Am I the only one getting tired of the endless line of minor celebrities complaining that they were molested or propositioned 20 or 30 years ago? If the incident was so bad, why didn't they complain at the time? If they kept quiet to protect their careers then aren't they guilty of aiding the offender? Could they possibly be taking advantage of the current media obsession with the subject to gain a little publicity to help their careers? Where does prostitution start and stop?

We didn't hear a peep today from our flashy estate agent. Maybe he is trying to rescue the deal. I suspect we haven't heard because he thinks that we are desperate to sell. We aren't. We were never desperate to sell. For the last few months, however, we have been desperate to escape from an appalling and fraudulent deal and take back control. And we are happy to wait. I think the Brexit deal is going to be disastrous for Britain. The pound will collapse and our share of the sale price will be much higher because the French will take their capital gains tax on the euro value not the sterling value.

I spent an hour clearing away some of the leaves on the drive. Both sides of the drive are lined with deciduous trees (and one Yew which drops its berries). Most of the trees are beech and silver birch. I cleared away a vast number of leaves with a wide yard broom, a pair of large gauntlets and one of those massive bags builders use for sand and waste. I had already prepared a space at the bottom of the drive where I could dump the leaves. Last year I made the mistake of pulling the bags full of leaves up the drive to a space I had prepared. This year they are going down the drive.

And in a few weeks' time, the hazel trees will start losing their leaves so the whole process will have to start again. (I know that hazel is technically a bush but when they are 40 foot high it seems more sensible to think of them as trees.)

18

I've been trying to buy fireworks without much success. No one seems to sell them anymore. Newsagents always used to be a good source of fireworks. No more. It seems that the laws, rules and regulations controlling the sale of fireworks are now so onerous that no one wants to sell them.

A gardener came to the house in Gloucestershire today to give us a quote for dealing with our overgrown garden. I've had a hell of a job finding someone to come round and cut our grass and weeds. Most Cotswold gardeners describe themselves as 'landscape gardeners' but they won't demean themselves by handling lawnmowers and hedge trimmers.

I found this fellow through one of those internet tricks which seem impossible to avoid. I had typed in the name of our village and the words 'gardener required'. And, immediately, there were the names and contact details of several gardeners in our village.

Only it turned out later that they weren't gardeners in our village. They were gardeners all over the country who were looking for work (and, quite possibly, a chance to scam anyone stupid enough to try to hire a workman through the internet). I suspect that most of these business folk specialise in ripping off the elderly who are tiptoeing through the internet and who, like me, are still cursed with some remnants of trust

Our selection turned up in a smart uniform, driving a lorry that was full of leaves and tree trimmings that I subsequently suspected he had purchased as a job lot from a local branch of Leaves-R-Us.

I should have sent him away when a pheasant saw me and came strolling down the garden towards me.

'Oh, do you keep chickens?' asked the gardener. This, remember, was a man who earns his living looking after gardens.

'It's a pheasant,' I said. I didn't explain that his name was Percy. (All pheasants are, for historical reasons, known to us as Lord Percival and the ones at our house in the Cotswolds are very tame. They come running when they hear my voice.)

'Oh,' he said, clearly surprised.

We walked around the garden. He seemed to recognise grass and he correctly identified an apple tree (not difficult because there were still apples on it) but I wasn't confident that he recognised anything else.

He was, however, very good at spotting things he could do to put up the price. He said he could clear our overgrown patio (whereupon the oak table, bench and chairs were almost hidden by weeds) and trim some beech trees overhanging our garden shed as well as strim and tidy the rest of the garden. They were all things which needed doing. He called me Vernon a good deal. 'Well, Vernon…', 'And so, Vernon…', 'Ah, Vernon…'. It's what all good confidence tricksters do. It makes the mark feel comfortable.

And then, after these gentle preliminaries, we got down to the nitty gritty.

At this point, I am rather overcome with shame and I feel great pain at having to write what comes next.

I was, I suppose, thinking of something in the region of £500; maybe £750. If he had said £1,200 I would have sent him on his way.

'How much is this going to cost me?' I asked.

'£3,000. For that, Vernon, I'll clear your patio, trim the trees and tidy all the garden.'

I stared at him. If he'd asked for the Koh-i-Noor diamond I couldn't have been more surprised. I had been thinking in hundreds rather than thousands. £3,000 was so far out of my ballpark that I lost my frame of reference. I lost all touch with reality. I thought that maybe I was just out of touch. I just stared at him. My lower jaw probably fell an inch and a half.

'I couldn't do it for less than £2,500, Vernon,' he said, while I stared at him and struggled to think of something to say. Naturally, this now seemed cheap.

'There will be three of us for four days, Vernon,' he explained. 'And the equipment and the fuel. All my equipment is top of the range, Vernon. We can start tomorrow.'

Why do we succumb to these smooth talking conmen? Or, more precisely, why did I succumb? I think I know. It was because I am tired of people promising a good deal and not doing anything.

And my new best friend seemed convincing.

I thought he probably would turn up – if for no other reason than that I had no intention of paying him until he'd done the work. And I am tired of people not returning calls; of workmen expressing eagerness and then disappearing to the Maldives for three months. A workman who turns up on time and seems keen is a rarity.

(I still don't understand why workmen don't ever write down the instructions you give them. You tell them what you want. They nod and say 'of course'. But they don't write anything down. And when they come to do the work they've completely forgotten what you want doing. Instead of putting up a shelf in the bathroom they put up a new ceiling on the landing. Instead of painting a bathroom light green they put flowery wallpaper up in the dining room.)

'How would I pay you?' I asked.

'When I've finished, Vernon,' he said. 'You can pay by bank transfer. Or cash would be best.'

'Cheque?' I asked.

'Cheque?' he said, as though I'd suggested paying him in shells or glass beads.

'I could write you a cheque,' I said. 'You know where I live,' I added with a little laugh.

'I do, Vernon,' he said, with just the hint of a hint of a thought of menace. I had visions of gardeners turning up at midnight armed with chainsaws, rakes and bags of potting compost. 'But cash would be best.'

We shook hands. He said his father had taught him to shake hands to cement a deal. You can't argue with a man who trusts a handshake, can you?

I couldn't help wondering to myself if it was legal to pay £2,500 to a gardener in cash. But then I remembered paying that much at auctions where I had bought furniture. They always liked cash. And I'd expect a receipt, of course.

'I don't do internet banking,' I told him.

'So, it's cash then, Vernon,' he said, with a big smile. He didn't seem to mind the prospect of having all those notes to carry home.

'We'll be here in the morning, Vernon,' he promised. In turn I promised to leave the side gate unlocked and I showed him where to park his lorry.

It occurred to me later that it would have been cheaper to ring Harrods in Knightsbridge and ask them to send up a couple of men to do the garden.

19

There's a blues song called 'Born Under a Bad Sign', written by William Bell and Booker T.Jones which contains the line 'If it weren't for bad luck, I wouldn't have no luck at all.'

(Actually, on hunting around I find that pretty much the same words appear in a song called 'Bad Luck Blues' by Lightnin' Slim. That must be a bit of a pisser for Mr Slim or, more likely, his estate.)

I was reminded of this when our new and very expensive gardener had been today.

Oh dear, I've really done it this time.

It quickly transpired that this was about to become another in an apparently unending series of disappointments and frustrations.

He turned up at 10.45 a.m. with his son. There was no sign of the third man who seemed as elusive as Orson Wells in the film of Graham Greene's novel. They brought with them a Heath Robinson contraption which consisted of an engine, an oil drum, a good deal of hose and a power pressure lance of some kind.

Antoinette and I then went out to Bourton-on-the-Whisky for a few hours. (The famous Cotswold village is officially known as Bourton-on-the-Water but these are trying times and so I have renamed it.)

Our first visit was to the Christmas shop; something we'd been looking forward to for a while. To begin with, it seemed to be disappointing.

The crackers they had for sale were awful. All contained the usual mixture of a plastic shoehorn, bits of plastic stationery and a tiny pack of playing cards. Why can't cracker makers be original occasionally? Every damned thing in this year's crackers had been in last year's crackers and the crackers from the year before and the crackers from the year before that. We decided, sadly, that we are not going to bother with crackers this year. First time ever. We had thought of filling our crackers with tiny toys we'd bought ourselves. But both of us had been for weeks looking for suitable bits and pieces that would fit into crackers. And we had both failed. Maybe that's why the manufacturers of crackers for children stick with a small plastic yoyo and a tiny set of skittles.

Next, I wanted to buy some more candles for our Christmas decoration which whizzes round when the heat from the candles rises. The man in the shop told me that they hadn't got any of the thin candles which would fit our device but they did have some thicker candles.

'Well, do you have a device that will take the thicker candles?' I asked.

He said, rather sadly, that they didn't but that they did have some of the things which took the smaller candles.

'So you have the decorations which take the thin candles but you don't have any thin candles and you have the thick candles but you don't have the decorations which take the thick candles?'

He agreed that this was an accurate assessment of the situation.

We looked around and bought three or four new Christmas decorations and some Patchouli oil incense burners and then, while I was paying, I noticed, behind the salesman, a beautiful wooden thingy which was part of the window display. Maybe he had forgotten they had it. The thingy had vanes on the top which were clearly designed to be turned by three candles. It seemed a bit crazy to have a candle powered wooden toy but we like to live dangerously and my Dad used to light real candles on a real Christmas tree festooned with paper streamers so what the hell I bought it. And I bought a large box containing 50 of the thick candles that would almost fit the candle holders.

The rest of our trip was a disappointment. It still seems impossible to find a café, pub or hotel selling decent coffee in Bourton-on-the-Whisky. I still have to resort to buying coffee in a cardboard cup from a local supermarket in order to find something remotely resembling coffee.

And two men with hammers and lots of boarding were shutting up Lloyds Bank which had apparently just closed permanently. There was a notice informing visitors who might want to take out some money that there was another branch with a cash machine in Stow-on-the-Wold. I'm sure that will be a great help to local shopkeepers struggling to stay in business.

And so the world improves and progress marches on.

When we got back home at 3.30 p.m. the gardener had gone. No sign of him. He and his son can't have been at the property for more than around four hours or so.

Now, I have to admit that the patio at the back and the paving at the front of our cottage were transformed. The weeds which had overgrown the whole area were gone. I was pleased. We won't use weedkillers or anything else which might harm the wildlife so this was a huge success.

There were, however, a few problems.

The place was in a terrible mess. The patio areas were covered in mud. The ground floor doors and windows were covered in mud. The inside of our front porch was covered in half an inch of mud. The floor of the conservatory was muddy. Our letterbox was wet and muddy. The front gate had been blasted off its supporting post. There was evidence remaining of what they had eaten. The outside tap had been left on (and was now, apparently, stuck in that position because someone had been rather too rough with it) and the side gate had been left open. None of this was excusable.

That evening I emailed to point out that when I had agreed to the absurdly inflated price for dealing with the garden I had been told that three people would be working for four days. I said how pleased I was with the patios but that we would be obliged if they would hose down the mud they had left behind them.

Knowing what workmen charge in the Cotswolds, the price seems high but by no means impossible. To hire almost any sort of workman, even for labouring work, costs around £200 a day. ('Cash would be fine, thank you', invariably follows any quote.)

I wrote a short limerick to celebrate our new gardener:
There was a young gardener quite thin
Who mowed and who strimmed with some vim
He made such a mess
That I have to confess
I'm thinking of doing him in.

20

The gardener emailed back to say: 'Hi Vernon the cleaning was a
bit quicker than expected so worked hard and fast so all being good
we may be finished late Tuesday or if not we will be finished
Wednesday I always estimate on the longest time as not to
disappoint my customers but we always pride ourselves in how we
work super hard and fast (no tea brakes)'.(sic)

He also told me that he was going to Ireland for a long
weekend.

What can you say?

A promise of three men working for four days had suddenly
become two men working for one and a half days. That is, twelve
working days of labour had been stripped down to three working
days of labour. Taking out the cost of hiring the machinery and so
on, that turns a steep but not unreasonable £166 per man per day
into an utterly outrageous £750 per man per day.

The trouble with conmen is that they don't just take advantage
of greed. They also take advantage of honesty, ignorance and
gullibility. The price of £2,500 was now clearly a con. But I agreed
to it because it seemed to me that the work involved probably
would take 12 man days. And that was what I was told.

My main mistake was, as always, in being too trusting.

I sent the gardener a lengthy email pointing out, as tactfully as I
felt able, that he had told me that he would need three men for four
days and that he had not explained that for half of the allotted time
he would be away in Ireland. 'You can't cram a 12 day job (three
men for four days) into a 3 day job (two men for one and a half
days).

'You won't finish on Tuesday. Not if you are going to do the
good job you and I want you to do. I know how much work there is
and you can't strim faster than a strimmer strims. The banks of the

stream are tricky. And you need to take care around the young trees we have planted.'

I then listed all the work that was left to do.

'Please take care with everything. The outside tap was fine before. And your pressure squirter has damaged the front gate. We obviously don't want any more mishaps. I know you want to do a good job. And I am sure you will. It's what we both want. But you won't be able to do that and finish on Tuesday.'

Later I received a reply.

'Hi Vernon there will be three people working on your job from Tuesday. I'm not going to rush the work or lower my standards so please don't worry everything will be done as agreed however many days that takes so please don't worry it will all be done for you. Please don't worry I'm not going to rush or compromise the job.'

Do I believe him?

Actually, I think I do. This may merely show more gullibility on my part. But there is a carrot dangling over the horizon. Because when I invited him to quote, I told him that I was looking for someone to look after the garden on a regular basis.

I am so tired of workmen. They fuss, they whinge, they complain and they are incessantly greedy and demanding. They must have cups of tea and chocolate biscuits and if you don't provide them they ask for them. They must be allowed to arrive when they want to arrive and to leave when is suitable for them. They leave a mess behind every day and they break things without ever bothering to explain or apologise. And they are largely incompetent. Our back door still has a knob which has to be turned counter-intuitively because the idiot carpenter who repaired it put it on the wrong way round. I am so tired of workmen that I haven't called anyone to take down four dead trees which need removing and half a dozen which need some serious pruning. One, a beautiful silver birch has grown right over our drawing room chimney and the other day I found a singed branch in the fireplace. I am so tired of workmen that I haven't called the carpenter we need to do a dozen jobs or the man about new gates or the man to fit solar panels onto the garage only so that we can survive the next power cut. When we get round to it we will need a storage battery too. I don't remember power cuts in the 1950s. We're getting something we didn't get then so it's progress of a kind, I suppose.

At least our expensive gardener will do the work without our having to be there. And I don't have to do anything except pay him. I'll settle for that.

A huge tree at the bottom of our drive in Devon has died quite suddenly. It is not unknown for trees to die mysteriously by the seaside – especially when views are impeded by trunks, branches and leaves. This one was a lovely silver birch.

21

Yesterday we were warned that Storm Brian would arrive today. All coastal properties have been warned to beware. I can't take the name Brian seriously for a storm. Not that, Brian isn't a perfectly decent name. Of course it is. I don't want legions of Brians reaching for the one star review button. I have, in my life, known and supped with several Brians.

But Brian is not a name for a storm any more than Cuthbert or Sidney are suitable names for hurricanes. What drives this yearning to give silly names to bits of the weather? What next: Cloud Claude? Sunny Day Samuel?

I do think it was much better when hurricanes (and hurricanes alone) were given feminine names – like ships. It was, of course, protests from feminists which led to this change. I notice that they didn't complain about the fact that ships are always given feminine names.

(Talking of feminists, why are female actors known as actresses and female poets known as poetesses but female authors and composers simply known as authors and composers?)

It is not generally realised, particularly by those involved in naming storms and hurricanes, but there is something of an art to choosing a good name. Oscar Wilde always named the characters in his plays after places. So, in *The Importance of Being Earnest*, he had characters called Basildon, Bracknell, Goring and Worthing. I have started to do the same and many of the characters in my fiction have been taken from signposts we have passed on our travels. I also found that 18th century pirates provide a wonderful variety of good names. The important thing is that the name has to fit the character since, unlike real life, one cannot rely on the character eventually growing to fit into the name.

As it turned out, Storm Brian was more of a Stiff Breeze Brian rather than as advertised.

What a surprise.

The meteorologists will doubtless be terrifying us all with loads of false scares in the years to come – partly to justify their existence and partly to fit in with the global warming myth which is so popular these days. Every breeze, every snowfall, every warm day is now officially a sign of climate change. Everything must be exaggerated. A hot day becomes a heat wave. A windy day is a hurricane. But in truth our weather hasn't changed; it is our way of reporting it that has changed. There has been snow in Scotland and the Peak District for centuries.

(Numerous so-called 'experts' are still claiming that last summer was the hottest on record. I think they must have confused the records for Britain with the records for some other country.)

The Paris authorities seem incapable of following the simplest of instructions.

A few years ago, I tried to persuade them to change the address to which they post their annual tax bills (there are two of them). We went into the town hall in Paris, waited for ages and completed forms for a change of postal address. Men with rubber stamps did a lot of stamping. We were assured that the address had been changed. It hadn't. The bills still went to an old address. It took a host of emails and a score of letters (including several sent by registered mail and two to the mayor of Paris) to persuade the clerks at the Town Hall to make the necessary, very simple alteration.

A year ago, I asked the Town Hall to change my address again.

Naturally, they have ignored the request. The first of this year's bills has been sent to an old address.

You would think, would you not, that they would try harder to ensure that bills went to the correct address?

I'm not writing to the idiots again.

I collected the bill which they sent and put it on the bonfire.

I'll pay their bills when they can be bothered to send them to the correct address. I feel comfortable about this because I am damned sure that if they send the international bailiffs round they will be sent to the wrong address.

22

Louis L'Amour was one of the world's best and most successful storytellers. Pseudo intellectuals (the sort who write reviews for *The Guardian* and who wrote for *The Independent* before it went bust) sneer at writers such as L'Amour. They really shouldn't.

Louis L'Amour wrote Westerns and he wrote them with affection and with an unparalleled knowledge of the world about which he wrote. He was brilliantly concise but I'm willing to bet he was not well or often reviewed on the literary pages. His books have sold over 300 million copies and counting.

Here is the first sentence of his novel Fallon: 'Marco Fallon was a stranger to the town of Seven Pines, and fortunately for him he was a stranger with a fast horse.'

That one sentence sets the scene brilliantly. It tells you a good deal about Fallon and the town of Seven Pines and gives you a good idea about what is going to happen. You want to read on and to know more. You can't write better than that.

I still think the best training ground for writers is writing drama reviews. The writer has to produce 300,500 or 800 words to fit a slot which has been kept for a precise number of words in 30 to 45 minutes after the end of a performance.

Ah, those were the days.

When I was a medical student, I wrote play reviews for a number of publications including *The Birmingham Post* and I spent many an evening in a smelly, cold telephone box, struggling to read notes which I had scribbled in the dark. I was, I seem to remember, paid £3 per review but the newspaper allowed me to use their contract with a local taxi service in order to get back home afterwards. You could buy stuff for £3 in those days.

23

London is now going to charge the drivers of vehicles which were registered prior to 2006 an extra £10 (in addition to the £11.50 congestion charge) to enter central London. The Mayor, Sadiq

Khan says that the new charge will cost taxpayers £7 million to collect. Just how it will cost so much to collect all those hefty fees he did not explain. It is, perhaps, a good job that Mr Khan doesn't run a corner shop.

The year 2006 has been selected because vehicles which were registered before then do not meet EU directives regulating vehicle emissions.

The important point, however, which no one seems to have noticed, is that the new charge will discriminate against the poor.

Only people who can't afford posh new cars and vans drive vehicles which are over a decade old. And because they are poor, those individuals will be penalised.

Every time he does anything, the Mayor of London goes further and further down in my estimation. I read recently that he is forcing builders to make houses without car parking spaces. I assume he thinks that if people don't have a garage or a driveway they will not buy cars. This is nonsense. They will simply waste time struggling to park their cars on the street – where they will be prey to vandals. I wonder if Mr Khan walks to work every day? Or maybe London's tax payers pay for a nice limousine with a chauffeur.

As part of my on-going education process, I look into betting shops occasionally. I don't really know why I do this except for the fact that it always cheers me up because everyone in there, punters and staff, looks seedy and glum. No one ever laughs in betting shops, do they? No one ever seems happy? Even the occasional winners look as miserable as if they'd just been told they had been selected for a tax audit.

We heard today from one of our notaires in Paris. It seems that our buyers are back, like a metastasising cancer.

Unbelievably, our erstwhile buyer is now threatening to sue me for not selling the apartment to him even though he does not have the money to buy it. I wrote to our notaire to ask how long we must wait for him to find the money. I do not like being threatened; especially by a scum sucking, snail crunching, frog amputating French branleur.

Apparently, it does not matter that the estate agent told me that the Achat was not a legal document.

It does not matter that I was lied to and tricked into signing the Achat under false pretences (I was told he did not need a loan when he does).

It does not matter that the buyers have repeatedly broken promises.

It does not matter that one person signed the Achat but two are now buying.

It does not matter that according to our notaire, the buyers agreed to rip up the Achat and agreed that if they did not attend the signing on the 16th October they would withdraw from the whole procedure.

And it certainly doesn't matter that they don't have the money to buy the apartment.

The French, it seems, don't care much for logic or common sense. I get the impression that the only thing that matters is that the French bastard must prevail.

So, the bottom line is that I am not allowed to take the damned apartment off the market. I am forced by French law to sell the apartment to people who do not have the money to buy it and who have failed to borrow the money to buy it.

The threat of a lawsuit means that we are not allowed to offer the apartment to anyone else. The estate agent refuses to offer the apartment to other potential buyers. And the notaire refuses to handle it.

So we are stuck, in limbo.

A buyer can, it seems, legally spend years prevaricating and preventing us from finding another buyer. During that time, the value of our apartment will doubtless go up so the buyer can eventually hand over his cash in two years' time and then put it straight onto the market and make a huge profit. (The French property market is rising at last and is out of the doldrums in which it has been settled for years.)

I wrote to our notaire saying that the deposit must now go back up to 10% because if the buyers do not complete the purchase (very likely) and we have emptied out all our furniture (which we have to do before the completion signing) then we will have an empty and useless apartment.

I also said that they must produce evidence that they have the money for the entire purchase before they sign. And I asked to be told the maximum time they can delay after the first signing. I do not trust these damned people an inch. I loathe and detest them. They have cheated and lied and behaved like scum. Moreover they have, so it seems to me, been aided and abetted by our estate agent.

And I pointed out that if the buyers won't do all this then I will hire a lawyer to take action. It now seems possible that according to French law I can force the buyers to buy an apartment they cannot afford so, presumably, they will then be willing to tear up the Achat they signed in bad faith. I also pointed out that the publicity will not be terribly good for the agents, the buyers or, indeed, the notaires.

If the French insist on playing tough then we will play tough too. We have been manipulated and bullied by these bastards ever since last June.

Afterwards I went outside and stood on our cliff, faced across the Channel and waved two fingers, Agincourt style, at France. I then went back indoors and destroyed everything I have which was bought in France, made by the French or which could be thought to have any sort of French connection. Once loved CDs by Charles Trenet, Maurice Chevalier, Mistinguett, Edith Piaf, Jean Sablon and Fernandel all ended up in the charity bag. I kept the Johnny Hallyday because he was so pissed off with France that he emigrated. I also got rid of all my French born notebooks – the ones which are printed with squared, mathematical style markings.

We have just two bottles of champagne left.

Some lucky local charity shop can have those. It is, incidentally, a nonsense that the EU says that champagne must be made in one region of France. Champagne was invented in England, which is not yet part of France.

24

I've decided to keep the champagne. It is, I have decided, perfectly possible to loathe the French but to drink champagne.

Legend has it that the musk deer wanders the forests constantly searching for the source of the beautiful odour it can smell, but never realising that the scent is its own.

There's a moral hiding in there somewhere.

25

We planned to go up to Gloucestershire today to see how the world's most expensive gardener was getting on. We planned to arrive at around 2 p.m. and left in plenty of time. We managed to get all the way up the motorway without any lane closures (something of a miracle on the M5 now that the police have introduced Time Wasting Motorway Regulations and are doubtless given bonuses if they manage to create big queues) but once we got near to Stroud we found ourselves in a massive queue.

Thirty minutes later, we found the cause of the hold up. It wasn't a sweet wrapper in a gutter or a leaf on the road. Nothing as serious as either of those. Workmen who had been doing something to the road had departed but had left their traffic lights in operation on a very busy roundabout. There were enormous queues in all directions and the queues were rapidly lengthening. Thousands of motorists were wasting time, becoming dangerously exasperated and burning up vast quantities of diesel and petrol. The air around the town was thick with poisonous fumes. No workmen. No machinery. Nothing happening. No hole in the road. Just traffic lights set to cause maximum disruption.

Gloucestershire really is the home of the needless traffic jam. The Highways Department seems to have total contempt for road users.

Well, he may have been expensive but our gardener has done what he said he would do. The slabbed areas at both the back and front of the house (he calls them our patio but we've never thought of ourselves as patio people) are sparkling and weedless. Remarkable.

We took a tour of the garden to see what had been done. I had been to the bank and had the fee (£2,500 in cash) in my pocket.

We were about half way round when I heard a plaintive cry behind us. Antoinette, who was bravely attempting to keep up with us, was breathless and at a standstill. She suffers terribly from palpitations and all the manifestations of a malfunctioning heart if she tries to do too much.

The grass and bushes have all been cut. (So, too have my twenty lavender bushes, my huge sage bush, my mint collection, the new hedge I had planted and my rosemary bushes. I can't blame him. They were all so overgrown that they were invisible.) It is comforting to know that while we have been away the air has been rent by the constant sound of three strimmers a strimming.

Naturally, one of our particularly nasty neighbours had taken advantage of our absence to ask the gardener to cut our hedges to improve his view of the countryside. Fortunately, I had warned the gardener that this would happen.

This is the neighbour who complained about us parking our vehicles on our land outside our garage because they spoilt their view and prevented them parking on our land. They also complained when a builder dismantled a gateway which was dangerous and collapsing. And when the previous owners of the property applied for planning permission to build a stable for the children's ponies they objected – even though the stable would not have interfered with their views in the slightest way. And it seems that every time a gardener or a utility van comes within shouting distance they ask for our bushes and trees to be cut back. Nasty people.

The gardener who did the job with his wife and son, may be absurdly, egregiously, indecently, obscenely overpriced but I don't mind for two reasons. First, he came when he said he would come. Second, he finished the job without disappearing in the middle of it. It was all over when he said it would be. And those are rare and special qualities these days. He was also polite without being unduly false or obsequious.

Those are, I suspect, qualities which are the secret of success for anyone in a service industry. If you do things then you can overcharge with impunity.

When the gardener had gone, I looked around the garden. 'Well,' I said, looking up at the beech trees which had been pruned. 'There will be less leaves to sweep up from around the shed.'

'Fewer leaves,' said Antoinette, automatically. 'It's a countable noun.'

Antoinette edits my books and has studied the vagaries of the English language at far greater length and depth than I have.

439

'Who fucking well counts leaves?' I demanded.

'Good point,' replied Antoinette. 'But you could if you wanted to.'

I looked at her.

'OK,' she sighed. 'Less leaves.'

26

We went into Cheltenham to do a little light and early Christmas shopping. There was, inevitably, a lengthy hold up, caused by some traffic lights which were there all by themselves. There were no workmen, no lorries, nothing happening – just traffic lights and long queues. This happens everywhere these days but seems particularly likely to happen in Gloucestershire. I assume that the problem is that the department which does the digging is separate to the department which puts up the traffic lights. A little coordination would save motorists many hours and improve the nation's productively massively. But I suspect that no one working for the council cares about these things.

I went into Holland Barrett to buy more sunflower seeds for the birds. (It is nigh on impossible to find sunflower seeds or peanuts elsewhere and my attempts to have them delivered by courier have been disastrous.) Two small girls of about ten were standing in front of me. When an assistant decided to do a little light serving he picked up one of my packets which I had placed on the side of the counter because they were heavy and I had a lot of other things to carry.

'This little girl is in front of me,' I pointed out.

And then an awful thought occurred to me. Are elderly, white males allowed to even mention the existence of little girls? And are they allowed to call them little girls.

'Sorry,' I said, correcting myself. 'Young lady.'

The two girls giggled.

I then watched in horror as a male assistant of about 30 asked the girl for her email address. I realised that he was trying to sign her up for some sort of customer programme.

When I'd finished my shopping I sat in the Old Restoration (which remains mercifully unrestored, I'm pleased to say), read and worked on my next book. At the next table, two men in their fifties compared mobile telephones and talked endlessly and knowledgeably about all the things they could do. Sadly, instead of doing them they just sat there and talked about them.

Later, I tried to persuade a BBC employee to watch my YouTube video on the history of the EU but he simply refused. He obviously didn't want to be confronted with the truth in case it upset him. It has been established, to no one's surprise, that during the Referendum on whether or not Britain should leave the EU, the BBC continued its outrageous bias in favour of the EU. Far more pro-EU speakers were allowed to air their views on BBC programmes and the BBC consistently drew attention to perceived problems which might arise if Britain did leave the EU. (The BBC was of course, worried that if Britain left the EU it probably would not receive any more money from the EU.) It is beyond outrageous that the BBC should continue to demand that it receives vast amounts of taxpayers' money (through the absurd licence fee system) rather than paying its own way. The BBC is already corrupt. Let it take money from whomever it likes – but not from British citizens who dislike its politics.

I decided to move my pair of stone eagles down to Devon. A few years ago, I had to leave the stone bases behind because I simply couldn't lift them. (When I was younger, I could move them easily so I assume that the lichen they have accumulated must weigh more than you would think.) I picked up the first eagle, knees bent to spare my back, and hugged it to my stomach and chest. There was a hoot or toot of protest. I nearly dropped the darned thing. I put it down and picked it up again. Another toot. It frightened the living daylights of me. Whoever heard of stone eagles tooting? Or hooting for that matter?

And then I realised that I keep an old-fashioned bicycle horn in my jacket pocket. (The horn is there, at Antoinette's insistence, so that if I fall while working in the garden I can call for help.)

Phew.

I managed to carry the two eagles up to the top gate and put them both into the back of the Mitsubishi pick-up truck. The back of the truck (which carries a ton) went down noticeably.

When we got back to Devon we found that the Bentley, which we had left parked, was covered in snails. We spent twenty minutes picking them all off and putting them back into some bushes. I hate to think what the folk at the Bentley garage would have said if they collected it for cleaning and found that before they could start work they had to remove a slime of happy snails.

When I got indoors, I found a selection of bills had been sent to me from France. The electricity and gas company want paying. The phone company wants paying. The agents who make a mess of running the building want paying. And of course the city of Paris wants its taxes.

Most of these used to be paid by direct debit. The others were paid with a cheque drawn on our account at Barclays in Paris. However, now that I have closed the account, but still not sold the apartment, the paying of the bills is rather more of a problem. So I stuffed the paper bills into the bin (to be incinerated) and deleted the bills that came by email.

Sorted!

27

Have you noticed with websites these days that if you cannot remember your password they will send you a link so that you can create a new password? So anyone who hacks into your emails can easily and quickly create new passwords to replace all the ones you chose yourself.

I've still been trying to buy fireworks without success. Antoinette and I thought we would have our own firework display on the cliff top but it looks as though our fun is going to be thwarted.

The problem is that no one seems to sell fireworks. There was a time when every corner shop sold them. No more. The rules and regulations are so strict (with everyone in Westminster worried that someone will empty all the gunpowder out of the Roman Candles, use an unfurled Catherine Wheel as a fuse and wake up Parliament) that hardly anyone sells them anymore.

Eventually Antoinette found that it is possible to order them from Tesco.

So I gave my date of birth and ordered £150 of rockets and things that go fizz in the night. They will be delivered tomorrow. This is good because our groceries are also delivered on Saturday.

And Monday we are off to a local auction. We've been looking forward to it for weeks.

Well, that's what we thought.

But later, we had an email from Tesco to say that instead of bringing them on Saturday, as agreed, our fireworks will now be delivered on Monday between the hours of 7 a.m. and 7 p.m.

Great.

If they think I am getting up at 7 a.m. to take delivery of my fireworks then they have another thing coming. But it still means that we have to stay in all day and listen out for the doorbell.

And now our trip to the auction is impossible. Thank you, Tesco. We've put hefty advance bids on four lots but we won't be able to go there to see what's happening.

There has, of course, been no email from our notaire offering another date on which the buyers can fail to sign to buy our apartment.

Antoinette has come up with what I think is a slightly amended version of our excellent plan.

Our plan now is to go to Paris in January and take the keys back from the agent. We will then fire the useless bastard.

Before we go, we will fix an appointment with a lawyer in Paris. And when we are there we will give him fistfuls of euros so that he can sue the buyer.

The law allows the buyer to sue us and force us to sell the apartment to him but I am now told that the same stupid law also allows us to sue him to force him to buy the apartment from us. It isn't difficult to see why the French have a reputation for being mean, devious and grasping. It probably has something to do with the fact that they are mean, grasping and devious. Since he doesn't have the money to buy the cellar, this will be a silly waste of time but it should bring the whole sorry business to a head. It is vital for this plan to work that we can tell the lawyer that we are able to show that we have been keen to sell but that he has steadfastly avoided buying the apartment. And so the longer we go without hearing from him the better it will be for us. I no longer look at my emails hoping that there will be something from the notaire.

(The strange thing is that in France it is illegal not to go to someone's aid if they are in need. And yet nothing causes more illness and death than stress and the French property system seems to have been designed to cause the maximum amount of stress to the seller. Buyers who enjoy the system should remember that they too will probably become sellers one day. The other irony is that the Paris Mayor has pushed up taxes in order to encourage foreigners to leave the city. Well, Madame Maire, we tried. But our apartment has now been empty for six months thanks to your system.)

The global financial situation has changed.

Brexit is said to be turning bad but despite the problems created by the EU (and by Poland, France and Germany in particular) the official figures show that Britain is growing at a rate unforeseen by the so-called experts at the Treasury and the Bank of England. Britain will save £90 billion in EU trade tariffs alone when we leave the EU. Despite the politically biased prognostications of the Bank of England, the Treasury and slavish, neoNazi newspapers such as the *Financial Times* there seems no doubt that Britain will boom if and when we finally quit the evil conspiracy which is the EU.

Meanwhile it seems clear that the Bank of England is certain to raise interest rates and so sterling is rising. Every 1% rise in the currency means a £10,000 loss to us. We no longer want to sell the apartment at this time and we will do whatever we can to avoid selling it at the moment. (The rise in the currency is also particularly painful since most of my income is in American dollars.)

And when all this sorry business is over it will be a joy to write some articles for British and American magazines explaining why people shouldn't buy property in Paris.

28

The tax people are now surely the greatest threat to our privacy. They obtain information about us all from our tax returns, of course, but they also acquire information from banks, credit card companies, Land Registry reports, and social media.

Lawyers and accountants and all other professional advisers must give information to HMRC and HMRC has acquired the right to force Apple, amazon and companies such as Airbnb to give them data too.

PayPal gives HMRC information and so do currency exchange services. I suspect that eBay does so too. Overseas governments hand over information and so do local authorities.

And, of course, there are the 113,000 reports a year which HMRC receives from members of the public (aka snitches). Each year the taxman pays out £500,000 to sneaks.

And then there is the information which is stolen. If you or I buy stolen information (or anything else) we will get arrested but when HMRC buys stolen information it is members of the public who go to prison. I really don't understand how that works.

The odd thing is that HMRC regards all taxpayers as criminals who have not yet been caught and its modus operandi is to strike fear into the hearts of every citizen. Tax inspectors sometimes forget that they are servants of the State and that the State exists to serve the citizens.

These days, the authorities everywhere are buying up stolen bank details and using taxpayers' money to do so.

The German police, for example, have just handed over five million euros of German taxpayers' money for a large stache of documents stolen from a Panamanian law firm.

The *Financial Times* is becoming ever more desperate in its fear and loathing of Brexit and Brexiteers. Today I saw a news story about a hedge fund manager called Crispin Odey who has had a bad time recently and whose funds have done poorly. The *FT* cannot resist describing Mr Odey as 'The Brexit-backing investor'. The phrase is irrelevant but the implication seems to be that his Brexit-backing has led to his downfall.

Ignorance about how and when the EU was founded continues to astound me. Today, in an editorial, the *Daily Telegraph* repeated the nonsense about the EU's founding which is now so widely believed. 'It was founded in the post-war years to create a more unified, democratic Europe, one that would be so rich and stable that extremism would wither away.'

This is such total bollocks.

29

Thinking again of the War, I remember my father. It is strange how the Second World War brought comradeship to so many and is remembered with a strange nostalgia which the First World War (aka the Great War) never brought.

My father was a company director and an inventor and designer (he invented domestic circuit breakers though sadly on a ridiculously modest salary at the time) but served in the Navy in the Second World War and throughout his 80s he referred to himself exclusively as being an ex-Royal Navy man.

In the 1880s, Germany's Chancellor, Otto von Bismarck decided to prick the balloon of developing demands for a more socialist approach to politics, by introducing a State pension programme for older Germans who had stopped working.

Bismarck and the German Emperor William the 1st argued before the Reichstag that people who had reached the age of 70 should receive a State pension. This was later reduced to 65 since 65 was, at the time, the average German life expectancy.

In Britain, the Old-Age Pensions Act of 1908 proposed a weekly pension of 5 shillings a week to the half a million citizens who were over the age of 70. Married couples received 7 shillings and 6 pence a week. The pension age in Britain was also later lowered to the age of 65.

(The large number of individuals eligible for a pension will probably startle those who wrongly believe that until 2016, average life expectation was no more than 30 or so and that anyone surviving into their 50s was a freak worthy of a starring role in a fair, billed alongside the bearded lady and an obligatory dwarf. Life expectation for adults has hardly changed in the last century. What has changed is that infant mortality figures have fallen dramatically. It was high infant mortality figures which brought down overall life expectation figures.)

In 1935, Germany's proposed retirement age of 65 was selected for a retirement age in the US when President Franklin Roosevelt introduced the idea of State pensions into the US.

And the same age has, for years, been the generally accepted age at which workers could expect to retire and receive a pension.

It seems entirely reasonable that older people should be entitled to retire at some pre-determined age, should they wish to do so.

But although it seems equally unreasonable that many older people are forced to retire, little or nothing is done to stop it

446

happening. It is against the law in most civilised countries to force individuals to retire at a certain age. But that doesn't stop it happening.

For a quarter of a century, I have been warning that Britain's pension system is screwed. Every Government I can remember has made things more complicated (and therefore worse) and Gordon Brown's greedy grab from private pensions buggered things up for everyone not entitled to receive a civil service (or MPs) pension. But things are getting worse by the year. In my book *Stuffed!* I pointed out that even people working for the Government and for local authorities can no longer rely on the pensions they have been told to expect. There simply won't be enough money.

The UK now has a pension shortfall of £4 trillion. This is rising rapidly and will reach £33 trillion by the middle of this century. That is serious money – even more than Tony Blair earns from advising American banks et al. This means that our current shortfall is greater than the country's GDP and so things can only get worse – much worse.

Workers throughout the developed world can usually rely on government pension schemes to replace two thirds of the income they enjoyed when they were working. But in the UK, pensioners receive only just over a third of their working income. British pensioners are worse off than pensioners anywhere in the world. (Apart from countries where loin cloths are usual daily wear.)

I paid National Insurance stamps for over 40 years but my State pension wouldn't pay our heating bill.

Future pensioners in the UK will have four choices.

They can build up a pension. (This is tricky because successive governments keep changing the rules).

They can save and put money aside for their old age. (This is not very productive with interest rates at 0%.)

They can keep on working. (Not easy if you are bricklayer. And anyway this option means that younger workers can't find employment.)

Or they can choose between eating and keeping warm.

I opened the water bill for our house in Gloucester today. It came a few days ago but I like to keep these exciting things so that I can savour them for a while.

For the first time in my life I actually looked at the Severn Trent bill for some reason and noticed that a big chunk of the price was for 'Surface water drainage', described as 'water that comes off roofs, driveways and other parts of your property, which ends up in our sewer network.'

But we don't have any drains around our place in Gloucestershire. And Severn Trent must know that. So I've written asking for a reduction in our bill and a refund for the last umpteen years.

If they don't simply ignore us they will probably argue that I should have told them before now that they are charging for a service they don't provide.

But they know where our house is and they know where their drains run. Don't they have a responsibility to send our honest bills?

30

I got up late and only just managed to cram breakfast in before lunchtime.

Antoinette did suggest that I might miss breakfast completely, or combine it with lunch in what it is now, I believe, known as 'brunch'.

But I suspect that this is a slippery slope.

Once standards start to go then where will it all end? One has to ensure that the days are properly structured: breakfast, elevenses, luncheon, afternoon tea, dinner, supper.

So, I had just about finished munching my way through my toast and marmalade when Antoinette put luncheon on the table.

I see that researchers from the London School of Hygiene and Tropical Medicine have reported that MRSA, the antibiotic superbug usually associated with hospital infections, is now widespread in the general community.

To say that I am not surprised would be an under-statement. I have been predicting exactly this for more than a decade.

Inevitably, patients will get the blame.

But patients aren't the problem.

And nor are hospital visitors (most of whom happily wash their hands with cleanser every time they go into or out of a ward).

It is the staff who are the problem.

Every time I see another nurse doing her shopping in her hospital uniform I want to scream at her.

Hospital staff, particularly those working in the NHS, seem to have absolutely no understanding of how bugs are spread. And so they wander around in their contaminated uniforms. And I wonder how many of them wash their hands before they go out into the world? Those nurses are a deadly danger to us all. Now we must all be extra vigilant all the time. We must all wash our hands and use antiseptic wipes frequently. MRSA kills fast.

Every time you see a nurse walking down the street or in a shop you are looking at a health care idiot who doesn't understand the first thing about hygiene – or how dangerous bugs are spread. It is pointless to tell visitors to wipe their hands with antibacterial gel when the staff are too stupid. Last week I stood in a queue next to a man wearing theatre scrub greens and theatre slip on shoes. Later I saw two nurses in the street – both wearing their uniforms.

I called a tree surgeon this morning about our tree problems. He is coming around this evening at around 7 p.m. I wonder if he realises that it will be dark then and that our garden is fairly large and rough going even in the daylight.

We won two of the four lots that we had bid on at the auction we visited the other day. We put bids down on paper though I always feel this is terribly risk, especially when you don't know the nature of the auctioneers. It is frighteningly easy for a corrupt auctioneer to take advantage of bids left by bidders who can't be present. All he has to do is take a few bids off the wall in order to ensure that you pay a price which is at or somewhere near to your final bid price. We won a beautiful bronze bull in the style of the sculptor Barye and another bookcase to add to our growing collection. We missed out on a rather dull looking wardrobe for a spare bedroom and a beautiful Victorian scrapbook. I really wanted to buy the scrapbook for Antoinette but I was the underbidder. I should have been braver. I always say that when I miss out on something.

I asked a solar company to give us a quote for putting solar panels on our garage. They emailed back to say that they wouldn't do it because the rake on our garage roof isn't sufficiently steep. It is a fairly normal roof, it cannot be seen from the road and if you try to find it on a Google satellite map all you see are trees so I'm not sure why they have come to this conclusion.

Later a good friend who runs a manufacturing business emailed me and mentioned, en passant, that when he needs new staff, he only interviews applicants who are 45-years-old or older.

He says that younger workers make useless employees.

31

The tree surgeon didn't turn up yesterday evening. He got lost in the lanes. He turned up this morning. He agreed that it was probably a good thing that he got lost in the dark last night and didn't come to look at our trees in the black of a moonless night. He looks about 16 and I suspect that tree surgeons are, like ski jumpers, all young because anyone over the age of 35 has more sense than to shin up a tree and cut off branches. He told me that he is properly trained and went to college, courtesy of his Grandma, and he certainly knows his trees. He told me that it is unusual to find anything other than fir trees this close to the sea and said he thinks it's because of something in the sea air. We live in a very sheltered spot and maybe that has something to do with the fact that we have an astonishing variety of trees in the garden.

The tree surgeon is going to take down four trees which are dead (three of them being silver birch and one a spruce), top and shape a silver birch which hangs over the chimney to the fireplace we use most often, and remove dead branches from another three trees. He estimates that it will take him and his companion two and a half days to do the work and wants £700. I think that is fair and we shook hands on the deal. It is certainly rather cheaper than the £2,500 (in cash) which I paid last week to have our grass cut in Gloucestershire. Having a garden is an expensive business these days. Having two is twice as expensive. But that's entirely our fault. We have (literally) thousands invested in mowers and strimmers and other equipment.

I asked the tree man about the beech which a neighbour wants us to trim so that he can see more of the sea but the surgeon agreed with me that if we take the top off one beech then we will have to take the tops off all the beeches in that particular row. And that will take a week, cost us thousands, and lose us some privacy. So the beech trees are staying as they are and the neighbour will have to put up with a partial sea view. The tree surgeon, whom I now decided looks about 14-years-old, said he'd be with us early Thursday morning and would stay until six p.m. He said that he could clear away and chop up branches in the gloaming. (He didn't actually say gloaming.) Naively I was impressed by this.

After he had gone, I spent the best part of an hour sweeping up more leaves. Few things are more annoying than sweeping a long driveway almost clear of leaves and then walking back up the driveway across a carpet of newly fallen leaves. A neighbour in Gloucestershire proudly told me the other day that he had bought himself a new powered leaf sweeper to save him the effort of sweeping up his leaves. He sees no irony in the fact that a couple of months ago he joined a gym so that he could get some exercise.

A friend of mine died today. He was loveable, vague and forgetful. Antoinette and I were once invited to dinner with him and his wife. We got there on time but when we pressed the doorbell there was no response. Since the door was open, we let ourselves in. Within the next fifteen minutes three other couples arrived. So then there were eight of us in the living room. But there was still no sight of a host or hostess. We could smell food cooking in the oven and we were all worried that our host and hostess might have been kidnapped or had an accident.

Half an hour later, the host turned up. He had been playing golf and had stopped in the clubhouse for a drink. He had forgotten about the dinner party.

Twenty minutes later, the hostess turned up. She had been to her Art Class and had been chatting to a friend. She hadn't forgotten us but didn't think we would mind waiting.

How could anyone be cross with such folk?

I told Antoinette that we have to be half an hour late for our chum's funeral. It's only polite and he would appreciate the gesture.

We'll get there half way through.

I decided today to start writing a new Mrs Caldicot. I often wonder what she and the crowd are up to.

The Mrs Caldicot books were ignored by critics when they came out, although the film of the first book started a trend for movies about older citizens and spawned a series of films about feisty old folk. *Mrs Caldicot's Cabbage War* (the movie) has proved enormously popular and enduring yet when it came out it was roundly criticised by reviewers who presumably could not abide the notion of a film about older people and who were, I seemed, particularly offended by the thought of an old woman sticking up for herself. (The *Guardian* was, predictably, particularly scathing. How dare anyone write something celebrating the independence and spirit of older folk?)

Fortunately, readers and cinema audiences loved the book and the film.

So I'm now going to write a third book about Mrs Caldicot and her chums.

I have decided to send her and the residents of her nursing home to Paris (Mrs Caldicot had always wanted to go there).

So I need to find an excuse to send her there for a short holiday.

In the second novel about her (called *Mrs Caldicot's Knickerbocker Glory*) Mrs Caldicot married Jenkins, the newspaper editor who befriended her. But I can't let Jenkins go to Paris with them because he is far too competent and would sort out the inevitable problems far too quickly – thereby destroying the story and the fun.

So I also need a reason for him not to go. And do I send all the residents to Paris? And do I send the staff?

Then, of course, the fun really starts. What adventures will they have? What will go right? What will go wrong? What disasters will there be?

I'm very looking forward to seeing what happens. I'm hoping that once I get started, Mrs Caldicot and her chums will write the book for me.

I was going to write another thriller. Indeed, I had spent a few weeks writing the plot for one. But the problem is that it will confuse readers.

I've already written a couple of thrillers (*Deadline* and *Tunnel*) and a science fiction satirical docudrama about the European Union in the future (*Revolt*) but the readers of books with my name on expect me to write light comedy.

Authors and others always used pen names because it was assumed that readers wouldn't be able to cope with one person being a tennis player and an astronomer.

I was told that people don't like anyone masquerading as anything remotely resembling a Renaissance man or woman.

At least that was the thought a few decades ago. I suspect things have changed a good deal

However, if I write under a pen name no one will buy one unless I promote myself on social media. And I really can't bear the thought of doing that.

I can't bear the thought of literary agents either. I never had much luck with them. The first one I had (a posh London agency called Curtis Brown) sold a number of books for me but seemed confused because I didn't write the same book over and over again.

When I wrote *Tunnel* (a novel about a fire in the Channel Tunnel – which I wrote many years before the real Tunnel was built) my agent refused to handle it because she said it wasn't the sort of thing I wrote. I then put a pen name on it and sold it to Robert Hale.

Another agent refused to handle a diet book I wrote (*Eat Green and Lose Weight*) because she didn't want to become type cast (she had just sold a diet book for an acquaintance of mine to whom I had recommended her). Luckily, however, I sold the diet book very successfully to Century.

And my third agent refused to handle *Alice's Diary* (even though it was written anonymously) because she said it wasn't the sort of thing I wrote.

I had books published by all the leading paperback houses (Arrow, Pan, Penguin, Corgi, Mandarin and Star, etc.) and most of the leading hardback publishers (RKP, Thames and Hudson, Sidgwick and Jackson, Macmillan, etc.) but the failure of anyone to see the potential for Alice depressed me somewhat. That was when I started self-publishing. And for years, *Alice's Diary* sold and sold and sold. We printed 10,000 at a time and could hardly keep it in print. If it had been published by a main stream publisher, it would have been in the top ten fiction lists for a decade. But the people who made up the bestseller lists in those days were snooty bastards and they didn't count books which were self-published.

I seem to have wandered a long way off the point.

I had spent two months planning the new thriller so it's sad to abandon it. I think it would have been quite fun to write. But it could have been frustrating and disappointing.

Having said that, I am writing the Mrs Caldicot because I want to write it, rather than because I want it to sell loads of copies.

As a writer, true liberation comes when you write stuff you want to write, rather than stuff you have to write.

But first I need a bible – a list of all the characters who appeared in the existing two books, together with their appearances, ages, peculiarities, likes, dislikes and so on. In the past, I have written books in which characters changed age and appearance with rather startling frequency. I am by no means the only author to have done this.

I wrote *Mrs Caldicot's Cabbage War* in 1993 and *Mrs Caldicot's Knickerbocker Glory* in 2003 so I need to read them both again and take fairly extensive notes before I can start on a third volume of Caldicot adventures.

We had a promotional letter from Severn Trent water. The headline was, 'Be prepared for unexpected problems with this plumbing offer.'

I wonder what unexpected problems there could be with their plumbing offer?

How amazingly honest of them.

November

1

Antoinette noticed this morning that I now have curly hair. Or, more accurately, what hair I have left is curly. This is strange. I had curly hair when I was very small but for over six decades, I have had dead straight hair. Now it's gone curly again. Maybe this is God's idea of symmetry.

Moreover, Antoinette has noticed that my hair (what there is of it) goes very curly just before it rains. This phenomenon is, she assures me, far more reliable than the Meteorological Office. I am thinking of renting my hair out to companies who need an accurate weather forecast.

As I now do every morning, I threw two apples out onto the lawn. Before the apples stopped rolling, a rabbit who had been waiting just out of sight darted out grabbed one of the apples, and ran off up the slope of our upper lawn. It was a brilliant interception. And I was absolutely delighted to see that at least one rabbit enjoys his daily apple so much that he is prepared to wait for it to arrive.

After breakfast, we drove along the coast to Sidmouth for the day.

We went for a coffee and the minute we'd sat down, a woman with a pile of woofy dogs sat down right next to me. Dog owners are unbelievably selfish and spoil so many joyful occasions. I love animals and quite like dogs but when I am sitting in a café, I don't want three strange dogs sniffing my leg, growling, baring their teeth and barking at me. It isn't the dogs' fault, of course. It's the owners who are thoughtless. Why are people allowed to take dogs into an establishment selling food?

'I hope you don't think I'm rude,' I said to the woman seemingly in charge of the dogs. 'But I'm allergic to dogs.' I picked up my coffee and Antoinette picked up her mint tea and we moved to another table.

'Well you shouldn't go out in public then,' snapped the woman. 'Or just stay out of cafés.'

Goodwill, peace and understanding.

While in Sidmouth, I fell off a pavement.

Antoinette thought it was simply because I am a little wobbly these days. But it wasn't. In the space of a few minutes, I saw two other people fall off the same pavement. One of them fell very heavily and was lucky to avoid breaking a hip or a limb. The trouble is that the folk who designed the pavement and the road surface arranged them in such a way that it is almost impossible to tell where the pavement ends and the roadway starts. The result is that pedestrians simply fall off the kerb. Antoinette did exactly the same thing as we walked back to the car park.

On the way back from Sidmouth, I was horrified to see that half of the Bentley's electrics were not working properly. The main screen in the middle of the dashboard was completely blank.

I suspect the battery is at fault because it's a couple of weeks since we used the car. The boot is also playing up. It has a very sophisticated system which should mean that the boot opens and closes all by itself. But the boot is very easily irritated and since we had a new motor last February, I suspect that the problem is electrical and related to the battery rather than mechanical. (The new motor for the boot lid cost well over £2,500 which is close to obscene. We also had a new battery at the same time. I shudder to think what that cost. I never looked.)

The bizarre thing is that the car is fitted with two car batteries. The second battery is only used to start the car if the first battery has been run down by the car's mass of electrical equipment – much of which continues to function even when the car has stopped. The demand on the first battery is so great that it is well-known that if a Bentley is not used regularly all sorts of strange things will start to happen: the windows will go up and down, the horn will start, the boot will malfunction, display screens will disappear.

We don't use the Bentley enough to keep its batteries properly charged and I am told that I should buy a trickle charger and connect it to the car. There is, I discovered to my astonishment, a special socket in the boot where a special (and inevitably expensive) trickle charger can be connected to the car to ensure that the special (and inevitably expensive) battery is kept satisfied.

The other problem with the Continental is that the doors are vast and when the car is parked in a public parking area, the spaces available are always too small. I hadn't realised this before but when car doors are very wide, the space available for the driver or passenger to get in or out is dramatically reduced. (I had to draw myself a little diagram to prove this to myself. I drew two lines to show the sides of two adjacently parked cars. I then tried opening a very wide door and a narrow door. It was immediately apparent that the wide door made life impossibly difficult. Why didn't the Bentley designers fit the car with sliding doors? That would have made far more sense.)

So, sadly, I am beginning to think that the Bentley has to go.

I've emailed the garage in Cheltenham from which we bought it and asked them if we can sell it and buy a Maserati Ghibli. I've never owned a Maserati and I have a feeling that this is the moment. I did try to buy one a couple of years ago but the garage was in Swindon and our satellite navigation system (which insisted on calling the town 'Swinedon') got us totally lost and we never found the garage.

The AA arrived to look at the Bentley's faulty electrics. Naturally, when I turned on the ignition everything worked perfectly. The AA man did not look pleased.

'Like going to the dentist,' I said, feeling very embarrassed. 'I bet this happens to you all the time.'

'No,' he said rather unpleasantly. 'I've just driven 40 miles for this.'

I apologised profusely, explained that the car had not been working properly and that I had tried it several times before making the call.

The AA man remained unhappy and then told me that even if the car hadn't been working properly he probably wouldn't have been able to do anything about it.

I pay a small fortune every year for specialist Bentley emergency cover which is supposed to be provided by the AA. Heaven knows why. This is yet more evidence supporting our decision to sell the car.

The tree surgeon arrived as planned with a chum. I took them for a walk around the garden. 'Wow,' said one, 'you're higher up than the cliffs!' 'Are you really a pirate?' asked the other, his eyes alight with childish excitement.

He had spotted our Jolly Roger flag.

I hope I haven't made a mistake hiring this pair. I found their advertisement in a local free magazine. But then I do find that millennials seem to be very young and slightly deprived when it comes to having a sense of humour.

They had been at work for no more than half an hour when the local tree officer turned up unexpectedly.

He had, I was later told, been telephoned by a local nosy parker who had complained that we had hired gypsies to cut down our trees.

Why the complainant didn't bother to ask us what was happening is no mystery, of course, because people like this prefer to do their dirty work from afar. As an aside, I couldn't help wondering why the tree officer hadn't reported the caller to the police for what sounds to me to have been racial abuse.

Our tree surgeon (who is rightly proud to be properly trained and licensed) was incensed. He told me that the complainant had said that Antoinette and I were 'new people' who had only just moved in. (This may be because in Devon you are 'new people' if you are first generation residents.) She had apparently also complained that the tree surgeon's truck carried no advertising markings and that this was proof that the owner of the truck was not properly qualified to do things to trees. This seemed to me a trifle unfair. On none of our vehicles does the word 'Author' appear. Does this mean that I am not allowed to write or sell books? Quite probably.

All ended slightly better than moderately well.

Once the tree surgeon had explained that he had been commissioned to remove four dead and dangerous trees (two of which are next to the lane and which are a threat to passing pedestrians, horse riders and motor vehicles) the tree officer was very happy for the cutting to continue.

Then, when the tree surgeon mentioned that a neighbour had asked us to top one or more of the beech trees which impeded his view, the tree officer (who seems to have been not a little aggrieved at having his time wasted by a local busy body) said that we could tell the neighbour that we were not allowed to cut anything off the beech trees. I have therefore written today with these tidings.

I did think it rather odd, in passing, that the tree officer didn't talk to Antoinette or me to make sure that we really had hired the tree surgeons.

The tree surgeon left shortly after 3 p.m. in the afternoon.

Since he arrived at 10 in the morning, and spent some time having lunch and then drinking coffee and eating bars of chocolate which Antoinette provided, it is clear that the millennial's view of a full working day is rather different to mine.

At the rate he is going, he will be with us for a week. He is certainly not going to finish tomorrow unless he does a very shoddy job. And if he does a shoddy job I won't ask him to quote for the other jobs which need doing in the garden.

And he'll still only get paid £700 even if he's here until Christmas.

2

I have ideas for two new laws which I think should be passed immediately. First, all medical research should be done on Liberal Democrats and members of the Green Party. This will mean that these people will be making a useful contribution to society. Second, the police will have to use bicycles instead of motor cars. Even when chasing errant motorists they must use bicycles. This will make the roads much safer for the rest of us.

3

I walked down the driveway to open the gate for the tree surgeons so that they could come in and continue their slow progress. It's an understatement to say that I was disappointed. I shan't be hiring these guys again. They have left an awful mess behind them and it is going to take me days to tidy up the broken plants, abandoned twigs and cut logs. They have trampled bushes and plants and left tree rounds scattered hither and thither. The damned things are so big and heavy I doubt if I will be able to remove them. We already have one tree graveyard elsewhere in the garden where a previous tree surgeon left the segmented slices of arboreal corpses.

By mid-morning, the tree surgeons had already received the first of the day's complaints. A neighbour from around a quarter of a mile away came round demanding to know what they were doing and were they going to cut the beech trees and if so why and would they not, thank you very much because they like looking at the beech trees so leave them where they are.

It seems that it is the fashion these days for people to tell other people's employees what they can and cannot do. It happens to us all the time in the Cotswolds. And now it seems, it is also de rigeur in Devon.

I very much admire our beech trees. And it is good to know that they are, it seems, exceedingly popular with everyone in Devon. So far, we have received four enquiries about their welfare and one visit from the local tree officer. Two enquiries were from people who wanted the trees cut and the other two were from people who didn't want them cut.

No one seems interested in what we want though they are our trees and we're paying the piper.

Next time I see a neighbour having their house painted I will, I think, totter over and tell the painters that I don't like the colour and will they please paint the house a nice shade of lilac.

By the end of the day, Antoinette and I we were both exhausted.

Every ten minutes there was a banging on the door. (The idea of ringing the bell seemed beyond them.)

May I use the toilet? Would you move your truck? Which tree did you say was dead? Which branch do you want removing? Where shall I put the logs? We've finished with these mugs, thank you. Oh, yes, another cup would be very nice. How big would you like the logs to be? There has been another complaint from a neighbour. Would you move the Bentley? Do you have a wheelbarrow we could borrow? What are those knobs for on your Bentley dashboard? May I use the toilet?

I sometimes feel that I am being slowly tortured to death by a constant onslaught of triviality. I object to my own perpetual triviality. But I find it even more difficult to cope when the triviality belongs to someone else.

And from time to time there were screams of anger.

460

Every time I heard a scream, I feared the worst. Had the tree surgeon removed one of his limbs in error? Had he chopped off his head? Were the screams the last sounds from his now disconnected larynx? I hate chainsaws. They terrify me. I gave away the last one I owned when the chain came off and nearly decapitated me. My chainsaw had no 'dead man's handle' and I realised that if or when things went wrong I had no way of defending myself other than by hurling the damned thing away from me with as much force as I could.

Thankfully, it turned out that our tree surgeon's screams were a result of chainsaw malfunctions rather than impromptu and unplanned surgery. On one occasion, the chain broke and became embedded in a tree trunk.

I honestly don't think either of us sat down for more than ten or fifteen minutes. And when we did rest we were jittery with waiting. I lost count of the number of times I went up and down the driveway. I was genuinely worried that the tree surgeon was going to hop up the drive legless. He was at that cocky age when accidents only happen to other people. I found myself wishing that he would have a near miss or a very small accident. Only then, I thought, would he learn enough to avoid a big accident.

I am, I confess, rather disappointed in the number of logs we obtained from our trees. It seems that if you chop up a dead, 35 foot tall silver birch (with many branches) you get nearly enough logs to fill a garden wheelbarrow. It's a pity because silver birch burns well. It isn't a dense wood, and the logs don't last long, but it does burn satisfactorily.

And, to add to the mystery, one of the tree surgeons left twice to take loads of something very heavy and covered in branches-for-burning back to his home.

Why do I find it difficult to escape the thought that we are endlessly ripped off?

When I went round the garden afterwards I discovered that they had successfully destroyed a beautiful pampas grass plant and a huge yucca. How do you destroy a yucca? You chop a branch off a tree and let it fall down without controlling it. Numerous other plants and bushes are destroyed. Hopefully, some of them will grow back.

Actually, I don't much mind the injury to the yucca. I always think they are rather ugly plants which have a tendency to grow too tall and then fall over all by themselves. But heaven knows what I am going to do with the broken plant. It's about ten feet tall and almost as wide. I know from experience that they don't burn terribly well. And you certainly can't compost one.

Still, the good news is that the auction house delivered our bookcase and bronze bull today. And they carried the bookcase upstairs to Antoinette's studio.

We have not heard a word from Paris.

Neither our estate agent (I use the word 'our' with tongue planted firmly in a cheek) nor our notaire (ditto) has been in touch to let us know what is going on. Has our elusive buyer agreed to our sensible requests? Has he vapourised? Has he become President of France?

Nothing.

Antoinette and I had a meeting (over lunch) and decided that we are not going to do anything for the time being. The longer the delay the easier it should surely be for a lawyer to extricate us from this bizarre situation of being forced to sell our apartment to someone who cannot afford to buy it.

I've booked tickets to go to Paris towards the end of the month. While there, I will ask for our keys back from 'our' estate agent. We will then close the shutters, pull the blinds, lock up and leave it until the spring.

Our current plan is that in March we will go over again, see a lawyer (to extricate us from the mess we have been put into), fire our estate agent, find a new estate agent and possibly fire our notaire and ditto. We were very much hoping to finish this business before Christmas but it will clearly not happen this year.

If, perchance, we do hear from our elusive buyers, mere et fils, we will follow their example and be away for a few weeks. We definitely do not want to sell the apartment to them. I have never met these buyers but I neither like them nor trust them. Maybe their plan is to wait until property prices rise in Paris and to then buy our apartment and sell it on to someone else at a higher price. Maybe they are hoping to win the lottery so that they can use the money to buy the apartment. Whatever is going on, these buyers have (with the aid of the French property laws and our estate agent) helped themselves to a free option to buy.

I feel as though we are playing a game for which no one has told us the rules.

Actually, the whole thing is like the Mad Hatter's Tea Party for such rules as do exist seem to mean whatever best suits the buyer and our agent.

The deceit, the lies and the misdirection have all made this far, far more than a property deal which has gone sour. These manipulative, dishonest French bastards have made Antoinette quite ill. They haven't done me a lot of good either.

Never mind, after Christmas we will throw the lawyers at them. This bizarre game is not over yet. Not by a long chalk.

We may not even sell the flat at all. Perhaps all this has happened because the flat doesn't want to be sold.

Antoinette said today that she is going to come back as a seagull, snatch frites from French people and then poop on their heads. 'I shall train myself to be pin point accurate from a height of 30 feet,' she said.

This, I think, is a sound ambition.

I'm going to come back as a flying dog. A Great Dane, I think. I shall fly over Paris in circles and eat only foods which produce copious quantities of diarrhoea.

4

Feeling better after my unpleasant adventure with atrial fibrillation, I had a couple of cheese and onion sandwiches at lunchtime. I ate with my fingers crossed.

Antoinette bought a new Microlife sphygmomanometer from Boots the chemist. It cost around £100 and is grander and more sophisticated than the two we already have. Since we have both experienced some heart peculiarities (Antoinette's far more serious and long-term than mine) it seems a wise investment.

For fun, Antoinette wrapped the cuff around a teddy bear. To her, and my, astonishment the machine showed that the teddy bear has a pulse. There, on the little screen, was the flashing icon showing that its heart was beating.

We've been watching the Netflix series entitled Narcos about Pablo Escobar. I remember being fascinated by Escobar's activities at the time of his notoriety.

The Netflix series is a true story except that people, places, events have been changed to make a better television series.

I do sometimes think that if you're making a television series about something that really happened (or writing a book about a historical event) then you have a responsibility not to mess with the truth. But that is clearly a very old-fashioned viewpoint so I'll stuff the idea right at the back of my mind and forget about it.

If we assume that Netflix have captured the essence of the man then I confess to finding myself increasingly sympathetic towards Escobar who is portrayed as a rather kindly family man who had very loyal henchmen who would shoot his enemies when they really annoyed him. How many of us could honestly say that we would not rather like the idea of having our own personal hit squad to deal with life's irritations and annoyances.

Escobar's pursuers (particularly the police and the DEA from the US) seem downright wicked in comparison. From this showing, it seems to me that Escobar was far less of a psychopath than, say, former British Prime Minister Tony Blair. If I needed someone to feed my pet cat, I'd have chosen Escobar over Blair. Escobar would have fed it. Blair would have probably sold it to vivisectors and then sworn blind that it had run away.

The thing about Escobar is that he sold cocaine (a traditional Columbian commodity) to Americans. It was only when the American Government put pressure on the Colombian Government (as part of the ill-conceived, ill-designed and ill-fated drugs war) that attempts were made to catch and punish drug smugglers. For internal political reasons, the Colombian Government was not content to try to capture Escobar. Instead, they decided to assassinate him. And on the way to that objective, they murdered all sorts of innocent people – including children – and used Escobar's own family as pawns in their game.

When you look at the context then you realise that it is possible to argue that in some ways Escobar was justified in defending his business, his employees and his home. After all, cocaine is far less harmful and far less addictive than tobacco. The number of deaths caused by cocaine is minute when compared to the number of

464

deaths caused by tobacco. And yet no tobacco company bosses have been pursued. And governments around the world have actually defended and subsidised the growing of tobacco. Moreover, cocaine has been used in South America for aeons.

By bed-time, I was beginning to suffer for my stupidity in eating those cheese and onion sandwiches. My IBS had returned with a vengeance. Hey-ho.

5

Antoinette has been getting increasingly worried about our firework extravaganza.

And, to be honest, I have too.

The warnings are everywhere on the box and on the individual fireworks.

Tesco say that spectators should be kept 25 metres away from the action but the makers of the fireworks say that 8 metres is fine. There's rather a difference between the two. I have to dig holes all over the garden so that the fireworks can be safely positioned in such a way that they cannot fall over. I must light each fuse and then retire to the safe distance. In the case of Tesco's warnings this means that after lighting each fuse I must spring 25 metres in the dark in order to position myself in the safe zone.

While Antoinette was busy preparing dinner, I spent an hour, in the cold, preparing the garden for the onslaught.

I dug holes, filled buckets and watering cans with water and made sure that there was plenty of room for me to move away from the danger zone. The bright spot was that a double ended rainbow appeared over the bay. Magnificent.

We had dinner and then it was time for the show.

I had been advised that as the person in charge of lighting the fireworks, I should wear protective goggles and a hat. So I put on a pair of protective goggles and a hat. But I also needed to wear my reading spectacles so that I could read the instructions. And I couldn't manage to wear both my reading spectacles and the protective goggles. So I had to leave off the protective goggles and hope that no one with a telescope spotted me and reported me to the authorities. I also had to leave off the hat because I needed to wear one of those silly looking head torches so that I would have both hands free for lighting the fuses. So in the end I wore just the head torch and my reading spectacles. I couldn't wear the thick gardening gauntlets either. Have you ever tried lighting a fuse while wearing gardening gauntlets?

In the end, our fears were entirely unjustified and so were the warnings.

The fireworks were feeble. We paid approximately £5 per firework and most were so disappointing and feeble that I think we could have safely fired them in the kitchen. There were supposed to be a number of sparklers in the box but there was only one and that one didn't work. Two of the fireworks fell apart in the box and I will have to throw them into the incinerator tomorrow. The rockets were pathetic. No flashes, no bangs, just a bit of a whizz and that was that. The fuses were too short and difficult to light and time and time again I found myself struggling in vain to transfer the flame from my lighter to the fuse. If I had been trying to blow something up, the police would have picked me up long before anything dramatic happened.

We found ourselves watching a firework display taking place over 40 miles away along the coast. We couldn't hear the fireworks but we could see them surprisingly well. I bet they couldn't see ours.

And I missed most of our display because by the time I had retreated my statutory eight metres (there was no way I was going to make the 25 metre mark) the firework I had just lit would be finished. In trying to light the fuses I used up half a dozen disposable lighters and a box of three inch long kitchen matches. This was partly because of the wind but mainly because even when there was a flame licking at them for ten or fifteen seconds the fuses would not ignite. I actually found this rather scary.

An hour after we'd gone indoors to warm up, I felt a little weak and checked my pulse. The damned atrial fibrillation had come back. My blood pressure was 150 over 60 and my pulse was around 100 but definitely fibrillating. Once again I was convinced the problem was caused by my irritable bowel syndrome and the wind pressing on my vagus nerve.

I'm still not keen on going to see a doctor to have my heart checked.

Generally, doctors find it impossible to do nothing. This is partly because doing nothing suggests knowing nothing and partly because the best, easiest and quickest way to end a consultation is to hand over a prescription for something. Doctors also have a terrible (and frequently fatal) tendency to treat symptoms, or consequences, rather than causes.

If I see a doctor, I am confident that I will end up being given a whole range of drugs which will probably do more harm than good. There will, of course, be statins to start with. And an anticoagulant to prevent a stroke developing as a result of the fibrillation. And probably something to prevent the fibrillations. And since my systolic blood pressure reading is often a little higher than the standard acceptable for a 20-year-old (especially when I have a lot of wind) there will probably be an anti-hypertensive drug too. The odds are high that the resulting confusion of drugs would cause far more problems than they would solve. Once you start taking the drugs commonly prescribed for heart arrhythmias you usually end up taking the damned things for ever – and in ever increasing doses – because the original symptoms simply get worse rather than better.

And, I wouldn't bet against invasive investigations such as angiography – which would stand a good chance of killing me.

I very much doubt if anyone will take my IBS theory seriously. And if they do they won't be able to do anything about it.

My first task is to get rid of the wind by avoiding any foods that can cause it. I think it's more important to treat the cause of the atrial fibrillation instead of treating the fibrillation as an isolated problem. I'll start taking acidophilus again. And I'll compromise a little by taking a 75 mg dispersible aspirin tablet every day to act as a modest anticoagulant.

6

This morning I noticed that another piece of fancy wood carving has fallen off our conservatory roof. The dear old thing is falling apart. I rather know how it feels. We will have to find a carpenter in the New Year. There is a good deal for him to do. There are bits of rotten wood everywhere. We have soffits you could put your finger into if you were so inclined.

Our attention for the last six months has been distracted by the Affair of the Apartment. The bewildering confusion caused by our evil buyer and his supporting cast has wasted far too much effort.

There are surprisingly few Christmas decorations in the shops. And I have yet to see a town centre with any decorations. I don't like seeing decorations up too early – it takes the fun out of the festive season. But the High Street in most towns would, in the past, have usually started to show signs of streamers and coloured lights by now.

After discussing this with a few shop keepers, I came to the conclusion that there are three reasons.

First, it is considered politically incorrect to celebrate Christmas because hand-wringing Christians suspect that non-Christians might be upset.

Second, councils are desperate to save money. They spend such a high proportion of their income on salaries for executives, and pensions for former executives, that there is very little cash left for community projects.

Third, health and safety rules mean that it is no longer possible for a shop keeper to pop up a ladder and put some coloured lights up around his shop front and dangling from the branches of a nearby tree. These days there are a zillion forms to fill in, permissions to be obtained and snotty teenagers with clipboards to satisfy. Then, once all the legal stuff has been done a cherry picker must be hired (at enormous expense) to do anything that would otherwise involve standing on a chair or a stepladder.

Life sometimes seems very tiring.

Still, this afternoon Antoinette and I watched a fascinating natural history programme being played out on our lawn.

Every morning I throw two apples out onto the grass for the rabbits and the squirrels to enjoy. Our resident pheasant enjoys an apple too – so much so that when a seagull swooped down to try to take his place (and steal his apple) the pheasant stayed put and saw the seagull off. (Pheasants will repeatedly see off seagulls, even much larger ones, simply by pecking at them until they fly away.) Amazingly, our pheasant can eat a whole apple though he usually eats for a few minutes, walks about for a while, returns and resumes eating, walks about a bit, returns and resumes eating. The whole process can take quite a while.

Today, a rabbit and a crow were both interested in the same apple. As the crow pecked and pecked, the rabbit stayed a few feet distant; watching rather unhappily as pieces of 'his' apple disappeared down the crow's throat. Every time the rabbit approached, the crow would frighten him away.

When the crow had finally had enough, he flew off. The rabbit then picked up the apple and carried it to a safe position underneath the large wooden swing seat which we have. He then munched away happily, comfortable in the knowledge that even if the crow returned, he wouldn't want to go under the swing seat to get at the apple.

I never fail to be amazed at the intelligence shown by animals.

I was reminded of the time when I had a ride on lawnmower and a large croquet lawn which needed cutting regularly from March to October. I always emptied the grass cuttings onto a compost heap in a three acre field I owned and the four pet sheep who lived in the field would happily munch away at the freshly cut grass. One March morning I started up the ride-on mower ready to do the first cut of the year. The mower hadn't been driven since the previous October. As I fired up the engine and drove the mower out of a barn, I watched in astonishment as the sheep, standing in the nearby field, pricked up their ears, recognised the sound and, as one, ran towards the spot where they knew I would be dumping the grass cuttings when the box was full. That was quite a complicated series of thought processes. If anyone ever tells you that sheep are stupid, you can safely tell them that they are wrong. Sheep are extremely intelligent animals.

Going back to our apple eating rabbits, I have noticed, by the way, that if an apple has a decent stalk the rabbits will pick it by the stalk and carry it off, presumably back to their burrow.

We started off by putting out two apples a day. We have now progressed to three a day and I suspect it will soon be four or more. Our weekly apple order is becoming notable.

Later in the day, Antoinette asked me if I thought there was a risk that the plague would return. Irresponsible news media have made this their favourite scare story of the week (alongside the one that threatens deep snow over Britain within weeks). You don't necessarily need rats and fleas to spread the plague. The disease (like tuberculosis) can be spread through the breath. If it comes to

469

Britain, it will be because a traveller on a plane brought it here. And the odds will be that the traveller will be a nurse who had decided to save the world by spending six weeks in one of the African countries where the disease is now reappearing. (Spending six weeks helping the natives is one of the most selfish, pointless, expensive, patronising and reckless things I can think of anyone doing. Did I mention selfish?)

Looking at the papers today, I noticed that when the boss of American Express retires next year, he will have earned nearly $400 million during his 17 years at the company. That is simply obscene.

I don't think anyone objects when someone makes a fortune after starting and developing a company. But the current boss didn't start American Express. He simply worked there as the chief executive. Unless egregious greed like this is stamped out there will be discontent. Nothing feeds socialism more than this sort of obscenity.

The Bank of England put up interest rates a day or two ago. It was the first interest rate rise since the banking disaster of 2007/8 and within microseconds the banks and building societies were raising their interest rates for mortgage holders.

Oddly enough, however, there has been no word of interest rates being raised for depositors. Interest rates are far behind inflation and anyone who has put money into a savings account will still be losing a big chunk of their money to inflation.

Bank bosses are, of course, continuing to pay themselves million pound salaries and huge multi-million pound bonuses. They excuse these over-generous payments on the grounds that it is impossible to find other people able or prepared to manage the work they do. Since a half-witted donkey would be able to manage any of their businesses more reliably and more profitably I think we can safely dismiss this excuse for their greed.

This evening, working on my new novel about Mrs Caldicot, I gave one of the characters a Zimmer frame – assuming, incorrectly, that this was the generic word for a walking frame. On checking, I discovered that the Zimmer frame is far less well-known in other countries than it is in Britain. So I've had to change Zimmer frame to walking frame.

7

I am tired of all the crap which has been wasting our lives this year.

Antoinette suggested (very tactfully and with great gentleness) that I have been allowing the crap to take centre stage in my head when it should be tucked away in a dark corner.

She is absolutely right. And since she's been dealing with the same stresses and understands how irritating and complicated things have been, she has a valid point.

And the reason for this is undoubtedly the fact that I have not had enough to keep me busy. I need to be writing more books, involved in more campaigns and doing more stuff that will blot out the awfulness of things like Barclays Bank and the estate agents who appear to be mishandling the sale of our apartment.

The jolliest news of the day is that Snapchat, the woefully unsuccessful and over-hyped social media idiocy (which also attempts to flog intrusive daft spectacles which secretly take pictures of unknowing innocents) is so desperate that it is now trying to recruit older folk as users.

The company has announced that next year it will target the acquisition of more users – including those from a wider demographic range. As one wag put it this is like a struggling football club announcing that it intends to target the scoring of more goals.

The definition of 'older' is those who are over 30-years-old. So, many millennials such as Lily Allen (who seem to think of themselves as the inheritors of the earth) are now 'older citizens'.

Wonderful, simply wonderful.

I poured myself a malt whisky to celebrate this excellent revelation. Incidentally, I have noticed recently that on many of the better bottles of malt there is printed the name and signature of the distiller. This is a good and simple way of taking responsibility. It's a pity more companies don't encourage this. I would like to see all household items of a certain size and cost bearing the signature of the individual responsibility for their manufacture.

8

We sold our Ford Ranger to a garage in Stroud which specialises in trucks and vans. Having looked up a few similar trucks on the internet I said I thought £6,000 would be reasonable since although the mileage is low there were some dings on the back panel. The truck is seven-years-old and shows scars from where trees have leapt out and hit it. It has, however, done only 36,000 miles which is exceptionally low.

A woman at the garage said she could not possibly go above £5,500, cash or cheque. She said that the 'book price' (whatever that is) was £5,000 but that she could pay a little more because of the low mileage. Believing her, I accepted and took the cheque.

We were really sad to say goodbye to the truck. It has been a good and faithful servant and has carried much stuff for us.

Still, three cars are one too many. If cars aren't used regularly the batteries go flat and one less car will need one less annual service, one less tax to renew, one less MOT to organise and one less insurance to haggle over.

After the deal was concluded, the woman from the garage drove us back to our home in Gloucestershire. En route we passed a Romanian hand car wash place. I don't know whether this is true or not but she told us that the Romanians who work there are paid £50 a day for a ten hour day (9 a.m. until 7 p.m.) and that they work six days a week. On Sundays they only work from 9 a.m. until 2 p.m.). She said they live in a sort of hostel like students.

Driving back it occurred to me that we would all be safer if the street lights were turned off completely. They have been turned down so much that candles would provide more light. The problem is that there is a small pool of weak light under each street lamp and complete darkness between the lamps. It is a very dangerous system, though presumably the eurocrats at the European Union are happy that we are saving the appropriate amounts of energy. They don't give a damn that we are making our streets infinitely more dangerous.

When I rang Churchill to cancel the insurance on the truck I was told that I would have to pay a cancellation fee of £53.76.

I am afraid I laughed.

Big companies find ways to rip off their customers at every opportunity.

(I recently changed the insurance policy on our house in the Cotswolds. The new insurance seems much the same as the old one and costs about a quarter of what SAGA were charging.)

And where on earth did Churchill get the figure of £53.76? It's the sort of precise figure that rip off merchants always prefer because it suggests that they have done much research to find the value of whatever it is they are selling. (Not, of course, that I am suggesting that Churchill is a rip off merchant.) A precise figure is difficult to argue with simply because its very precision suggests that someone has sat down with a calculator and worked out the precise cost of pressing a button on a computer keyboard and cancelling a policy. In the case of Churchill, the button pressing event has clearly been costed at £53.76.

I did have the presence of mind to check out my no claims bonuses. Apparently, I had nine year no claims bonus on the Ford which I was told I could transfer either to the Bentley or to Mitsubishi. I transferred it to the Mitsubishi because that one has a very short no claims bonus for some reason.

This evening I was amused to read today that £12.6 million of the fund which manages money for MP's pensions is invested offshore with half of it invested in companies accused of tax avoidance. Another £5.6 million of the MP's money is invested in a tobacco company.

It is nice to know that Jeremy Corbyn, and the other MPs who so vociferously attack taxpayers who have funds offshore, are themselves in the tax avoidance business. The odd thing is that if Corbyn ever becomes Prime Minister then there is an excellent chance that his government will reintroduce capital controls severely limiting the flow of money into and out of the country. And if he does that then Comrade Corbyn may have difficulty accessing his pension. (Of course, *The Guardian* and the BBC, both of whom are also sanctimonious attackers of anything offshore, also have very murky finances. Stones and glass houses.)

Corbyn was recently reputed to have demanded an apology from the Queen when it was found that she had a very modest investment offshore.

Maybe the nasty little King of the Corbynistas will now demand an apology from himself.

If he doesn't then he is a hypocrite in the Bono bracket.

And gosh wouldn't that be a surprise.

(Talking of Bono I see that the world's most sanctimonious hypocrite has once again been shamed as a tax avoider. Wherever there is a tax avoidance scheme there, it seems, is Bono. We know about his latest shenanigans through the theft of something called the Paradise Papers. Over 13 million records were stolen from a law company and handed to a German newspaper which printed the contents and shared what they found with the media everywhere. Who was the thief? No one seems to know. A hacker? An unhappy employee? A mad socialist? One thing we can guess is that the police will make no effort to find out. It is now perfectly acceptable to steal private banking information and put it into the public domain. I doubt if any bank, onshore or offshore, is now safe from this sort of leaking.)

9

We went to Cheltenham to look at a Maserati Ghibli at H.R.Owen's branch. The company specialises in second-hand performance cars – Bentley, Aston Martin and so on. I had exchanged a few emails with the fellow who sold us our Bentley Continental and he had offered me a choice of four Maseratis to look at. To make life easier for him, I emailed back selecting just one of the cars and giving him plenty of time to prepare the car for us to look at.

When we got there, the salesman didn't have the car in the garage at all. In fact he didn't have any Maserati Ghibli cars for us to look at. Antoinette and I were far too polite to say anything other than appearing surprised, but the truth was that we were very angry since we had travelled quite a distance to look at the darned car. Maybe, just maybe, the salesman knew that he could make more money out of selling us another Bentley. (They don't service Maserati cars.)

This is the second time I have tried to buy a Maserati. Fate has obviously decided that it is not to be. In fact it is probably a good thing since the Maserati we were going to look at is rear wheel drive and I rather suspect that we would not be able to get to either of our homes in it.

The salesman did, however, tell us a good story. He told us that he had been to a James Brown concert and found himself standing next to someone who seemed familiar.

'Do I know you?' he asked the stranger at the end of the concert. The stranger had been bopping merrily to the music.

'You may do,' said the stranger.

'Where do I know you from? What do you do?'

'I'm a singer.'

'Oh. Who with?'

'Led Zeppelin.'

While we were there, we went for a spin in the new Bentley Bentayga; the biggest, most expensive, most wondrous four wheel drive vehicle in the world. It's amazingly comfortable and fast and fitted with so many toys that it would take a week to explore them all.

I have to admit that we rather liked it. From the outside it is an ugly looking brute – more bulldog than panther. But I was particularly impressed by the fact that the car was astonishingly easy to manoeuvre and, therefore, surprisingly easy to park. There is, of course, a heads-up gadget (which shows the vehicle's speed in the windscreen in such a way that only the driver can see it) but most impressive is the camera which provides an overhead view of the car. It is as though the car is being watched from a low flying satellite or has a personal drone permanently hovering ahead. I gather that the picture is obtained using the car's other cameras and some very clever computer software. It is truly one of the most remarkable toys I've ever seen on a motor car.

The model they have on sale (which is fitted with a vast array of extras) is £200,000 new but as it is the company's demonstrator it is offered at £140,000. It seems an obscene amount to pay for a car but it is a very good vehicle. It feels like sitting in a club sitting room disguised as a tank which can travel as fast as a Ferrari. I have no idea what the carbon output is but the top speed is around 200 mph and the three tons of car accelerates to 60 mph in just four seconds.

I asked the salesman how much trade-in he would give us on our Continental.

After humming and hawing for a while he offered £30,000.

I was appalled. We paid £58,000 for it just two and a half years ago. Now, I know that new cars lose a vast amount of their value in their first year or two of life. (An expensive Range Rover will set you back £140,000 when new and be worth £40,000 after three years – a loss of over £30,000 a year.) But second-hand cars don't usually lose value at that sort of rate. Indeed, when I put our Continental into the We Buy Any Car website they came up with an immediate offer of £32,500. In a couple of car magazines I saw other cars of the same age and higher mileage were on sale for £45,000 or more.

I know the dealer has to make a profit but in this case, the dealer would already be making a profit on the car we were planning to buy.

I have, over the years, owned a number of Bentleys and have discovered to my cost and disappointment that Bentley (and Rolls Royce) dealers are just as sharp as other car dealers. In this case, the dealer was going to pay me £30,000. He could then sell it straight to WeBuyAnyCar and make a couple of grand profit. WeBuyAnyCar would then sell the car onto a specialist garage and make a couple of grand profit. And the specialist garage would sell the car onto a punter for £45,000.

In this case, it is a case not of caveat emptor but of caveat venditor.

I know it is my place to be aware for these little scams but, damnit, I actually want to trust people. The trouble is that people are so good at pretending to be trustworthy that I constantly get suckered. Maybe I'm just becoming more gullible. Maybe there's a note somewhere on the internet telling people my name and instructing them to 'rip off the old geezer'.

I was, to say the least, annoyed that the garage which knew the car, which had serviced it, which knew that it was kept in the very best condition, should offer considerably less than a company which makes money buying cars cheaply and selling them on to other dealers.

It seems to me that these days everyone wants to go that extra mile to gouge as much money as they can from the deal. No one, it seems, is interested in doing a fair deal which leaves both parties satisfied.

Antoinette and I were both so cross about the way we had been treated that we changed our minds. And when trust goes it really goes. I found myself wondering what was wrong with the Bentayga.

And then, when you start thinking like that, the relationship is over. That's it.

We aren't going to buy the damned Bentayga (which apparently also has the perennial Bentley battery problem) but we are going to keep our Continental and buy a special trickle charger to keep the one or both of the batteries satisfied. (It seems absurd to me that Bentley, one of the most expensive car firms on the planet, sells cars which, even if they have new batteries and are used regularly, still have to have their batteries charged every week or so. But, hey-ho, if we must have a battery charger then a battery charger we will have.)

Maybe, in a year or two, we will buy a slightly older Bentayga at a third of the price. It is possible to purchase an extended manufacturer's warranty on cars which are up to a decade old.

On the other hand, the Bentayga does look a little flash and there is one thing that worries me. The salesman told us that Bentley will provide a solid gold clock for the dashboard for an additional £100,000 or so. The clock looks exactly like the analogue clock with which the car is fitted except that it is made of gold and studded with diamonds. I assumed that most of these specially equipped cars would be going to sandy climes but apparently not. It seems that there are Britons (or, at least, people who are living in Britain) who are crass enough to decorate their cars with these things. The clock worries me because thieves may well target the Bentayga for the clock alone. I can see them smashing the windscreen and destroying the dashboard in order to grab the clock. And then when they find out that they haven't got one of the rare clocks they may trash the car. It seems just too, too flash and, whisper it softly, rather tacky.

Or maybe we will just buy a two-year-old Continental if and when our beautiful vehicle finally decides to give up the ghost.

The GT Continental really is an exquisite car to look at and to drive in. It always seems to attract admiration rather than envy. Inside it is silence itself – thanks in part to the double glazing. With 6 litres and 12 cylinders and well over 600 bhp there is more than enough power. And even at speed the car sticks to the road like nothing else I have ever driven. Inside it is exquisite luxury.

As we left the garage in Cheltenham, Antoinette did wonder if the whole thing had been a set up.

Here's why.

The salesman knew I was vaguely interested in the Bentayga. I had mentioned it when we'd spoken and expressed a vague interest, tempered by a fear that it would be difficult or impossible to park.

Maybe he deliberately didn't have a Maserati for us to look at. Maybe he parked the Bentayga right by the front door so that we would see it. Maybe he knew that I would discover that the car is fairly easy to park. And maybe we would then abandon the Maserati and buy the Bentayga.

Maybe.

I really have no idea.

Still, he's lost a sale.

And he may have also lost the servicing contract for his firm. I stayed loyal even though the company lost its official Bentley servicing arrangement. And I stayed loyal even though the Bentley is now usually parked some distance away from Cheltenham.

The thing is that a deal is a successful deal only if both parties are satisfied. And a loyal customer only remains loyal if he doesn't consider that he is being 'played'.

When our Bentley needs a service it will, I think, go elsewhere.

Am I wrong in thinking that as I get older people try to rip me off more than ever before – often ruthlessly, blatantly, mercilessly and greedily.

Occasionally, as with the ridiculously expensive gardener, I let them get away with it (though I don't recommend their services to others) because it is convenient and I don't have the time or the energy to find someone else.

Sometimes, I just don't know how to complain. My last dentist charged me around £1,416 for a single consultation. She did a few fillings at one sitting and I spent an hour and a half in the chair but £1,416? The thing was that I was presented with the bill when I came out of the surgery. What was I to do? Go back and tell her to take the fillings out? I reckon my big mistake was turning up in the

Bentley. I bet she wouldn't have charged me £1,416 if I'd turned up in the Mitsubishi truck.

But the man at the Bentley garage really pissed me off.

After that little fiasco, we went into Cheltenham to have coffee and wander round the shops.

I visited the 3E store to ask why the two phones I bought from them no longer work. A kindly teenage assistant patiently explained that since I hadn't used the phones for three months the money that I put into them has disappeared. In addition, one of the phones has had its number taken away.

We haven't used the phones because we bought them to use at our house in Gloucestershire. We bought them because 3E insisted that their phones would work in our area.

Naturally, they don't.

When we bought the phones, no one bothered to explain that if we didn't use them the money and the numbers would disappear.

To make the phones work I had to put money into each of them. And for the phone which had lost its number I had to buy a new SIM card.

As I left, a kid in a hoody sneered and said to his mate that I looked decrepit and that old fogeys like me shouldn't be allowed into phone shops.

'You are correct, I am decrepit,' I agreed. 'But you look like shit and you're still young. At least I know that I didn't always look as bad as you do. Just imagine what you're going to look like if you survive to my age.'

I then left before he could think of a suitable response, let alone produce his carpet cutting tool.

I then went to WH Smith to purchase an armful of magazines.

The machines in Smith's are annoying for several reasons. First, there aren't enough of them. Second, they seem to break down with alarming regularity. The other week I put in a ten pound note and the machine swallowed it up without so much as a thank you and then refused to acknowledge what it had eaten. As a result, I had to call for an assistant. I didn't dare leave the till lest some other shopper starts to use it.

These machines are everywhere now. I gather that banks will soon get rid of their counter clerks for the purpose of paying in cheques. We will all have to use machines. The problem is that big companies of all kinds don't give a damn about our time or convenience. They would rather we all wasted twenty minutes of our time than that they install an additional machine.

Later, I was shocked to discover that my favourite pub, The Old Restoration, was closed for refurbishment. I do hope it is not about to become the New Restoration.

I liked the old pub, rather worn out and weary though it looked. It was shabby chic without an overdose of chic.

I went instead to a new coffee shop across the road which turned out to be excellent.

10

The beauty of writing a diary as opposed to articles or a column is that you can give a subject as much, or as little, space as it deserves. Magazines and newspapers allow writers a fixed amount of space. When I wrote my column in *The Sunday People* I had to fill a page and a half of the newspaper every week (around 3,500 words) but all the items had to fit pre-planned spaces which I had designed at the beginning of my contract.

Today, I checked the *Daily Express* website for a weather forecast. This is always amusing. They are forecasting thick snow, blizzards and a temperature of 11 degrees something. Most of the papers now try to scare us with these absurd forecasts. Predictions about blizzards and snow storms have already come thick and fast this autumn. The website forecasters get away with it because when you examine the forecast carefully the snow and blizzards are predicted for the north of Scotland.

These days the Met Office displays the sort of imagination displayed by a columnist in the old *Sportsman* publication, who described the opening day of Canterbury week as 'quite fine on the whole albeit heavy showers fell at frequent intervals and the sky was consistently overcast'.

After breakfast, I looked at the website of the garage to which we sold our Ford Range truck. I was dumbfounded to see that they had it on offer for £10,000. And I was even more dumbfounded to see that they not only had it on sale for £10,000 but that they'd sold it for £10,000.

Wow.

I don't really mind because I was happy with what I received and the truck had done sterling work for seven years but I was really ripped off with that one. People have become horribly greedy these days. They just want to take what they can. They don't seem to want to build up any sort of long-term relationship with their customers.

I am embarrassed to admit that I have always been ripped off when selling cars. I think I have probably been ripped off when buying them too.

'Never mind,' said Antoinette, trying to make me feel better. 'Think of it as a donation to charity.'

I looked at her. 'I sold it to a car dealer,' I pointed out.

'Well, it was a charitable donation to the car dealer,' continued Antoinette, struggling to make me feel that I hadn't been a complete idiot.

'I was a fool,' I said.

She looked at me trying to think of something else to say. But there wasn't anything else to say. So we laughed about it.

Actually, I haven't done too well with property either.

I was skilfully manipulated into selling my old office building in Barnstaple for £80,000. Within a very short time, it was back on the market at £130,000. And it has now been tarted up and resold for about three times as much.

So, all things considered, it's probably a good job I'm not in the business of dealing in cars or property.

Is it all down to naivety?

Innocence?

Or good old-fashioned gullibility?

There's been a lot of whatever it is around recently.

Maybe I'm more senile than I thought.

I paid £2,500 to have some grass cut. I paid £700 to have a few trees taken down. (And I gave the tree surgeon most of the wood so that he could chop it up and sell it.)

Maybe I'm an easy target because I am no longer in the first flush of youth.

Or is it because I am so tired of wasting time and energy on workmen who don't turn up, or who don't do what they promise to do, that I grab at anyone who seems keen to do a little work – even if they demand a high price for their services.

In the evening, we sat down to watch another episode of 'Better Call Saul'.

When I put the DVD into the player, I was told: 'By purchasing this DVD you are supporting the UK film and television industry'.

What rubbish. The film we were about to watch was made in the United States and as far as I can see everyone in front of and behind the camera is American.

And so by purchasing my new DVD I have harmed the UK film and television industry.

So, let's avoid the smarmy hypocrisy, please.

It's a damned good TV series, though.

11

On reflection, I have decided that our tree surgeon did a good job. He did what I wanted him to do. And I've been able to clear up the mess he made.

I have made a policy decision. In future, I will find all workmen through local newspapers or free magazines. (We found our tree surgeon in a free local magazine.)

The internet has, almost without exception, helped find us a series of crooks, cheats and confidence tricksters. Most of the people who advertise their services on the internet are too incompetent to build up a local clientele of people who are pleased with their work and who call upon them regularly.

The truth, I fear, is that old-fashioned Yellow Pages was a much quicker and more reliable source of information about tradesmen and suppliers. If you wanted a tree surgeon or someone to repair a washing machine, you could look through and find one. The internet is useless because the top search results are invariably from companies which have paid to be there and which don't provide what you want, where you want it or when you want it. Dr Johnson (he of the dictionary and dear old Boswell) said that there are two kinds of knowledge – knowing something and knowing where to find out something you don't know. For too many people the internet has become the way to find something. I know this, I preach this, but I still forget that it isn't.

I spent an hour or two investigating solar panels. We want to have solar panels fitted to our garage roof so that when the electricity runs out we will still be able to run our gas fed central heating and see what we're doing as we stumble about the house.

Doing online research is never easy, of course. Not if you do it seriously.

There are many apparently independent advisory bodies online but they all turn out to be companies trying to flog you their product by pretending that they are offering independent advice.

It is the same sort of scam as some insurance companies run with their comparison sites. (The site simply offers prices offered by different companies within the same group. There is no real comparison. For example, how many people know that Expedia owns hotels.com and trivago?)

I eventually picked a website and was answering questions when I was suddenly asked, 'Are you sure you now want to continue?'

Alarm bells rang. Was I now signing up for something by continuing?

I logged out immediately.

My nervousness was triggered by the fact that everywhere you go on the internet these days there are tricksters. Several times a day I receive emails warning me that my PayPal account or my Apple account have been hacked into and so I must do this or do that and send this or that information to the company's address. They usually want my password, my credit card details, my date of birth and my address. It's oh so easy to almost give them what they ask for. I am usually saved only because their English is awful or there is something not quite right about the logo.

And just about every day I receive very convincing fake emails from HMRC and from banks. These are so frequent that if I ever did receive a real email from HMRC et al I have no doubt that I would bin it.

But among the dross today, I found an email from Eddie Biggs, a chum I haven't seen for decades. We used to watch cricket together at Edgbaston. Eddie was an airline steward for British Airways. He was on long haul flights and used to fly to Bermuda rather often.

Eddie wants me to sign a petition demanding that the Government do not include the EU's fishing regulations into UK law when we leave the EU. If we continue with this daft legislation then we will effectively still be signed up to the Common Fisheries Policy and foreigners will be able to fish our waters and take all our fish. It would also mean a continuation of the absurd quota system which results in a huge wastage of fish and which encourages fishermen to cheat.

I have happily signed though I would, of course, go much further. I don't understand why we want automatically to incorporate any EU legislation into UK law. Surely there are enough civil servants and lawyers employed in Whitehall to go through the EU laws and throw out the patently absurd ones?

(In practice we would do as just well to throw out all EU laws and then re-introduce anything we can find which seems to be a good idea.)

And here's another thing: today I discovered that British tourists spend £39 billion a year on travel in other EU countries. If the EU continues to play nasty, we should simply threaten to boycott all travel in other European countries.

Greece, Italy, Spain and France (all financial basket cases) would go under without British holiday makers.

Oh, and I discovered that if they stay at home, Britons spend six times as much on rail tickets as anyone else in Europe. I don't know if it's still the case but Eurostar used to charge the French less for tickets than they charged Britons.

12

We are thinking of getting a dog. This is a big move for us since we are both rather scared of dogs.

The short list of possible breeds now includes: basset hound, King Charles cavalier, bolognaise, havenese, airdale, great dane and bichon frise.

Something like that.

One of those.

Probably.

I spent the late afternoon bringing logs from around the garden and storing them under cover. It has taken me three sessions to collect together all the logs so we clearly have more than I thought we had. I misjudged our tree surgeon.

I found a lazy way to bring logs from the top part of our garden; throwing them thirty feet down a small rocky promontory, so that they landed on a grassy slope and rolled down onto the lawn where they gathered, more or less together, in a group. This saved wheeling them in a barrow down a long flight of stone steps. There are, I'm pleased to say, far more logs than I previously thought. There should be enough to see us through this winter.

On several occasions, while hurling logs down onto the grass I only just missed hitting the bench I bought through the MCC from Lord's cricket ground a few decades ago. The oak and metal bench, which looks slightly worse for wear but is as solid and sturdy as they come, originally lived on the old Mound Stand at Lord's. I remember I paid £50 for the bench and £50 for a removal company to drive to London to fetch it.

Today, the MCC is selling replica benches for £1,500.

So I suppose it wasn't a bad £100.

Except that I would never sell it, so it isn't really worth anything, is it?

In the evening, we watched *The Founder*; the film about McDonalds the purveyors of McCrap burgers.

Michael Keaton was brilliant as Ray Kroc, the evil psycho who pretty well stole the company from the founders, tricked them out of their royalties and then created a monster empire which, in my view, did more damage to the health and welfare of the world's population than any other business ever created (including the ones making bullets and bombs).

'Business is war,' says Kroc in the film. 'If my competitor was drowning, I'd put a hose in his mouth. Would you do that?'

Well no, Ray, most of us wouldn't want to.

And while we're on the subject, why do McDonalds call their places 'restaurants'? McDonalds burger joints are merely the other end of the food chain from public lavatories.

Meanwhile, down to earth and under it, my letter to Severn Trent about their charges for our non-existing drains at our house in Gloucestershire has, inevitably, been ignored. They have simply sent one of those letters with red writing on them.

I do find that most big companies ignore email correspondence or produce useless responses. I wrote to Flying Spares, a Bentley parts supplier, about buying a battery charger. No reply.

13

It seems that charging up a car battery isn't quite as straightforward as it might seem. Having spent some time online trying to decide what exactly I needed, I eventually ordered a battery charger and the various bits and pieces that seemed a necessary part of the operation.

Amazon then sent me the usual collection of emails confirming that my order had been received and that it was on its way.

They then sent me emails telling me that it was no longer on its way and they then sent an email telling me that they were so upset by this that they were refunding my delivery costs. They sent me an email telling me that the delivery costs had been refunded. Finally, they sent me an email to let me know that the charger et al were on their way after all and would arrive this morning between 10.11 a.m. and 11.11 a.m.

I decided that in future I will order items to be delivered on a day when I definitely know we are going to be out, comfortable in the knowledge that will be the one day that the ordered items will not arrive.

To my astonishment, an Amazon delivery driver arrived between 10.11 a.m. and 11.11 a.m. and handed me a parcel containing my battery charger.

All I've got to do is find out how to use it to pour electricity from the mains into the Bentley.

My immediate problem however is much simpler. Amazon cancelled the delivery charges but then delivered the stuff. Do I email them and tell them that they're entitled to reclaim their delivery charges?

But they surely know that don't they?

I eventually decided that I am safe in assuming that if they want their delivery charges they will simply reclaim them.

Would anyone else worry about this sort of thing?

Still, I may not be charging my battery for long.

The UK's last coal power station will close in 2025 so that we can obey silly EU rules on global warming. So, the years after 2025 will be years of cold and premature death.

These days between 40,000 and 60,000 old people die every winter in Britain because they cannot afford to keep warm. (The figure varies according to how cold the winter has been.) That figure will quadruple after 2025 and the rest of us will need to buy warm underwear and acquire an affection for salads. Those who still have fridges which work will put things into them to warm them up.

After 2025, most of the electricity we manage to produce will be required to power electric cars and computers. There will be very little left for cooking and heating.

Investment tip: buy shares in Funeral Directors and sell shares in Nursing Homes.

14

I am proud to say that I have found out how to make my Bentley battery charger work. This is amazing news. The charger is remarkably straightforward and there is a socket in the boot of the car into which the lead from the charger fits. (Bentley is well aware that their cars need battery top ups at regular intervals – though they don't seem to bother potential purchasers with this piece of vital news.)

Moreover, the electric motor which controls the car boot lid now works much better than it did.

15

For reasons which I cannot explain, we decided to spend the afternoon in Stroud. It's a strange town which contains more hippy shops than anywhere outside India.

On our way through Gloucestershire, still some way from Stroud, we stopped off for a coffee. As we passed a cake shop, I pointed out the smeared window full of fly blown buns and unappetising looking cakes. There were dead flies and wasps mixed in with the bakery items, though I don't think they were on sale.

'Look at that and compare it to a French cake shop!' I said, rather sadly.

'Yes, we do it so much better, don't we?' said Antoinette, without a moment's pause.

It made me laugh out loud.

And I realised that her hatred of the French (and all things French) is just as deep as mine. I don't think either of us will either have a kind word to say about the French ever again.

Last week, I cancelled the insurance for the Ford Ranger truck which we sold. So far this week I have received nine letters from the insurance company.

I have also had a letter from Severn Trent, the water company, about our drains. They have sent me a form to fill in and they have asked me to let them know where their drains are situated. I was hoping they would know where their drains are.

16

We travelled to Chippenham, to the printers, to collect 500 copies each of *Climbing Trees at 112! Real Life Inspirations for the Over 65s* and *Kick-Ass A-Z for Over 60s: the Beginner's Guide to Old Age*.

I wrote and published these two books as ebooks a month or two ago and we decided to produce a few paperback copies to send out to literary editors. I don't have much hope that the books will be reviewed anywhere but we have to try. The other reason for having the hard copies is so that I have copies to send to foreign agents. Antoinette has already printed out a pile of labels and has prepared her fingers for jiffy bag stuffing.

17

I am delighted to see that the medical profession has at last (at long last) accepted that elderly people who do not see the same doctor are at greater risk of being admitted to hospital.

The problems are obvious ones. When a patient sees a new doctor, he or she must waste time explaining their medical history. And without continuity of care, doctors are far more likely to miss changes and make mistakes.

Sadly, the medical profession has still not acknowledged why patients usually end up seeing different doctors.

There are two simple explanations.

First, the enthusiasm for large practices means that patients are likely to see a different doctor every time they need help.

Second, and more importantly, the prevalence of female doctors mean that patients are massively disadvantaged. No one dares say this but female doctors tend to work short working weeks and are, therefore, only available for their patients on two or three days a week. This is very nice for the doctors concerned (who therefore pay less top rate tax and can enjoy more free time) but it is terrible for patients.

The garage which bought our Ford Ranger truck for £5,500 and sold it for £10,000 (presumably without doing anything at all to it) has emailed wanting to know where the spare wheel is. I emailed back to tell them that the last I saw it was fastened in the usual spot, underneath the truck at the back.

Could someone have stolen the spare wheel? How utterly bizarre. Who on earth would steal such a thing?

Actually that's a daft question because the answer is pretty obvious.

But if it was stolen I wonder when it was stolen and who did the stealing.

It reminded me that when I was a kid thieves stole the doormat from my parent's porch. Who would steal an old doormat?

That's not such an easy question to answer.

I thought that selling the Ford was the simplest and most straightforward thing I'd done all year. Now even that appears to be complicated.

18

Antoinette has spent the day packing books into Jiffy bags.

Stupidly, I had forgotten how incredibly unhelpful Royal Mail can be. The cost of posting our two books by second-class large letter post is £1.58 each.

You might imagine that Royal Mail would make a stamp worth £1.58. You would, of course, be wrong.

The nearest stamp available is one for £1.57. Naturally, we can't put a £1.57 stamp on by itself because if we do Royal Mail will put a massive surcharge on every packet. And then they will add an extra demand for the missing postage. So we have to order sheets of £1.57 stamps and sheets of 1 penny stamps. And since neither of these stamps has Large Letter printed on them we also have to order sheets of Large Letter labels. And then we have to hope that Royal Mail staff don't put a surcharge label on all our packets because they think they look too thick to travel as large letter mail. (We have measured them through an official Royal Mail measuring device but in my experience that is no guarantee that some malicious bastard at Royal Mail won't make all recipients pay a surcharge.)

I am reminded why we gave up publishing hard copy books.

We're not going to bother selling any of the hard copy books because it is simply too much trouble. And although we have priced one book at £7.99 and the other at £4.99 we would lose money on every sale if we did so. Bookshops and wholesalers demand 50% discount. And we have to pay the postage. And then the bookshops demand the right to return the books if they don't sell them. We can't possibly send books abroad because the postage cost will far exceed the value of the books. We used to have thousands of customers around the world but we had to abandon them all because of Royal Mail's massive and unreasonable charges.

I honestly don't know how small publishers make any money these days.

It is no surprise that so many now only publish eBooks.

As we do.

Another company which doesn't give a damn about its customers is Eurostar. I discovered today that the lift at Ashford International is out of order 'for maintenance'. It has been hors de combat since August and it will be out of order until 18th December. So all passengers will have to drag their luggage up and down long flights of stairs.

How can it possibly take from August until December to do a maintenance job on a bloody lift? You could build a new railway station in that amount of time. In China they would build a new town.

I discovered today that an increasing number of anglers who fish from beaches are now using special fishing drones. The drones they use are fitted with a camera and can carry 3.5kg of bait. They fly out up to a mile and a half from the shore. On a signal from the fisherman the drone drops the baited hook so that fishing can commence. The drones are even fitted with sonar detection so that they can spot where the fish are feeding. The fisherman, who obviously needs an enormous amount of line on his reel, then fishes in the usual way.

It all seems a bit like cheating to me. Why not just get the drone to drop a depth charge and blow up some fish? Another drone, equipped with a scoop net, could then just gather up as many fish as were required.

Alternatively, it would be just as sporting to go online and order a dozen mackerel from Waitrose.

An American reader has sent me details of an article someone has written about the dangers of prescription drugs. There is apparently a new book out on the same subject. The writer points out that prescription drugs kill hundreds of thousands of people a year.

I cannot get excited or thrilled by this.

I have been writing about this very problem since the early 1970s. My first book, *The Medicine Men* was about the way the medical profession has sold out to the pharmaceutical industry. And as a result I've been attacked, vilified, sneered at and banned – really banned not superficially banned.

There's also a new report just out pointing out that the NHS wastes money.

Oh Gawd help us.

Must today's medical writers merely continue reinventing the wheel? Why don't they find new things to expose?

19

Here is a quote from James Agate's Ego diaries: 'Have made an arrangement with a doctor friend whereby every week I send him two of my review books against two of his free samples. This week while he is absorbing two nauseating novels I am imbibing Incretone, a preventive of senile decay, and Agocholine, 'the most active cholagogue available', whose function is drainage of the biliary tract. Next week he gets two dollops of fragrant bilge against cures for gout and gravel.'

Wonderful.

Agate was, of course, a drama critic and how can you not like a professional drama critic who once described one play he reviewed as being the sort of drama which has witty intervals.

I was horrified to see that the Ministry of Defence is considering cutting the £29 per day allowance paid to soldiers serving in Iraq. This will save £6 million a year which the Ministry needs to help pay out £40 million a year in bonuses for chair bound pen pushers. Even worse the Ministry of Defence recently spent £381 million of our money upgrading its Warrior tanks and is now planning to scrap half of them to cut costs.

A thought: maybe I could buy one of the redundant tanks.

I have always rather fancied the idea of driving a tank when popping to the shops.

20

It occurred to me today that our fake wasps' nests seem to have worked. Last year we had several wasps' nests.

But then we put up the fake nests.

And this year we have had none.

We are still watching a wonderful American series called *Better Call Saul*. I bought the first series on DVD and we've now worked our way through the second series and part of the third series. It is very funny and rather wonderful.

The series is apparently related to another American hit series called *Breaking Bad*. We tried that last year and gave it up and donated the disks to charity.

But our delight in *Better Call Saul* has encouraged me to re-order the DVDs for *Breaking Bad* to try again.

The brilliant part about *Better Call Saul* is the existence of a mad brother. This rather reminds me of Frasier (who had a madder brother called, if memory serves, Nils). And the originator of the idea of introducing a superior brother was, of course, Conan Doyle who having created the cleverest man on the planet (Sherlock Holmes) gave him an even cleverer brother (Mycroft Holmes). That was utterly brilliant. Sheer genius.

This afternoon we sat in the conservatory and watched the wild animals lunching on the apples we put out on the lawn. Our resident pheasant was pecking at one apple. One of our resident rabbits was eating a second apple. And the resident squirrel was eating a third. The sight of these three was more delightful than anything else I have read, seen or watched this year.

And this evening we made the mistake of watching a new film called *Churchill*, which stars Brian Cox in the title role, twirling pretty clearly fake cigars. It was terribly disappointing. I knew within minutes that the script had been written by a woman. And indeed it was so; a woman with a German name who turns out to be a *Guardian* columnist who writes (believe it or not) on historical accuracy in films. The film was directed by an Australian.

In the film, Churchill is portrayed as weak, vain, blubbering, selfish, dangerous and foolish. His wife is strong and lets her husband know how weak he is and how strong she is. She is whingeing and constantly moaning that she has sacrificed her own life for his. The film seems like an advertisement for the worst aspects of the women's liberation movement. Could this be the same Clementine who burnt Graham Sutherland's portrait of her husband because she didn't think it portrayed him well?

It is perfectly possible that Clementine may have complained about Winston to a close friend. But I do not believe that she would have talked to Winston as though he were a slightly backward and troublesome child; nor do I believe that the imaginary conversations are remotely realistic. (It has become quite common for screenwriters to produce dialogue for private conversations conducted between two people who have never confirmed the details of those conversations. Worryingly, this is now done for individuals who are still alive. It is probably argued that it is done in the interests of verisimilitude but I rather fear that the result is exactly the opposite of the proclaimed intention.)

In my view, this film is a wicked misrepresentation of the truth and I believe it to be rather inaccurate. Many reviewers have complained that there are even basic inaccuracies in the characters' uniforms and so on. I don't know about that but I wouldn't be surprised.

The only strong male character in the film is the American: General Eisenhower. The rather repugnant and absurdly egotistical Montgomery comes across as stronger and more powerful than Churchill.

It seemed to me that the writer and the director both hated Churchill and England. Why would such people make a film about one of the most important individuals in British history?

Having spent over 100 minutes trying to destroy his reputation, they attempted to assuage their critics by gluing on a frame at the end pointing out that Churchill is believed by many to be the greatest Englishman of all time.

Too little, too late?

I'm afraid I thought that the film was a disgrace to a legend.

I realise that dramatists often alter history to suit their needs (some historians would argue that Shakespeare was particularly unkind to Richard III and that the 'a horse, a horse, my kingdom for a horse' speech was pure fantasy) but I still think it's wrong to do so.

I usually give DVDs which we don't want to keep to charity. But this one is going into the dustbin – the only suitable place for it.

Actually, I think the inaccuracy and politically correct nonsense made it entirely the worst film I've ever seen.

21

We were supposed to go to Paris today. I purchased train tickets (costing well over £600 which would have probably been the cost of hiring a private aeroplane to take us to Charles de Gaulle airport) because I wanted to collect the keys from our wretched estate agent.

And, more importantly, I wanted to fasten the shutters and pull down the blinds to keep in some of the warmth rising from the rest of the building's occupants.

I didn't do the blinds and shutters when we were last in Paris in September because we had been assured that the buyer would be signing the necessary forms in a couple of days' time. That, of course, turned out to be a wildly fantastical exaggeration.

But we didn't go.

Instead, we've written off the money we've spent. It says on the ticket that Eurostar won't do a refund. Has there ever been a greedier company? They will allow me to change the date and time of travel but I have to pay £40 per person per journey so that's a charge of £160. And then there's a £10 service fee per transaction. So that's another £40. And if you add £160 to £40 you get £200. And if the ticket to which you change costs more, you have to pay the difference. I bet it does turn out to cost more, too. (Naturally, if the ticket to which you change is cheaper they don't give you back the difference.)

What a bloody company. They should be selling electricity or cocaine.

I have, in my life, cancelled more foreign trips than I can truly remember. I have booked and cancelled two trips to Australia, one to South Africa, two to the US, one to the Middle East and three to Sri Lanka. I felt bad only about the trips to Sri Lanka. A friend of mine, Lord Pandit Professor Dr Sir Anton Jarasuriya kept inviting me to speak to the major medical conference he organised each year. And I kept letting him down because when it came down to it I couldn't face the prospect of being cooped up in an aeroplane for hours on end.

I am pleased to say that despite my failure to turn up, we stayed friends until his death (and I was able to help him in other ways) but I still feel terribly guilty about not flying to Sri Lanka. It was dear old Anton who arranged for me to be, among many other wonderful things, a Knight Commander of the Knights of Malta. I have enormously ornate certificates hanging in the boiler room.

Pretty impressive stuff, eh?

This time Antoinette and I were travelling by train but there were several reasons for staying at home.

First, when we thought we had sold the flat we cleared out almost all belongings. Most we gave away or dumped in the rubbish. And, of course, we brought back to the UK everything we wanted to keep and could carry. We cannot now remember whether we have any towels, dressing gowns or other basics in the apartment. We certainly gave away or dumped all our clothes. We emptied our fridge and freezer and threw away the contents. We even emptied the food cupboard and gave away everything it contained. I drank or brought back all the malt whisky and

495

champagne though I think I left a few bottles of claret behind. I knew that we would either have to fill a bag with food or as soon as we arrived in Paris I would have to make a beeline for the supermarket to stock up on essentials. Oh how I hate the people who have put us through this. I intend to do everything I can to make sure that none of the people responsible makes any money out of us or our apartment.

Second, we now loathe France and Paris so much that we can't bear the thought of ever going there again.

Third, we both hate the journey. When I say 'hate' I only use that verb because I can't think of anything which really expresses how we feel about it. There are always hold-ups on the M25 (usually made worse by stupid policemen) and even though we allow nearly five hours for a journey of about 100 miles it is always a challenge to arrive in Ebbsfleet on time. I could do without the extra stress, thank you very much. Our nation is failing because it is no longer possible to move around. Long queues, overcrowded roads, absurd traffic calming devices, endless road works and completely unnecessary holdups mean that journeys which used to take an hour or two now take half a day or more. Anyone who dares to mention this will be leapt on by politicians and the media as a racist.

Fourth, and entirely predictably, France in general and Paris in particular are suffering massive strikes as state employees protest at Macron's plan to stop them retiring at the age of 50 on a pension equal to their salary. This was always going to happen because it happens every time a French president tries to do anything sensible. Macron is trying to drag France out of the 18th century and is, as a result, now enormously unpopular. He seems to be pretty widely regarded by his former followers as a power hungry, arrogant bastard who is ripe for the guillotine. I agree with them that he is an arrogant little fascist who wants to rule Europe but he's right to try to control the French unions and as far as France is concerned it is a pity that he, like his predecessors, will fail.

We aren't too worried about the strikes per se but the strikers and demonstrators will probably make our journey even more unpleasant. And once we get to Paris there is a good chance that we won't be able to buy any food or get back out again.

The bastard buyer and his bastard mother have cost us real money and caused us endless inconvenience. It was entirely because of his lies and deception that we had to book these tickets. But bugger it; I really don't want to have my life ruled by this cretin.

It is our aim now to make sure that the bastard does not get to buy our apartment. And if he doesn't buy it then the estate agent won't get his fat commission and the two notaires won't get their fat fees. Our apartment is going to be one of Paris's empty properties. According to the Mayor of Paris, there are 100,000 empty foreign-owned apartments in the city. Well, gosh, guess what: now there are going to be 100,001 empty foreign-owned apartments in the city.

And we won't be renting out our apartment because if we do then the horrendous regulations and the absurdly high taxes will mean that we will lose money. So it will stay cold, empty and unused.

Stuff 'em all.

Bizarre, isn't it?

The Mayor of Paris seems to me to hate foreigners owning property in Paris. Taxes have been raised for foreign apartment owners in an attempt to force them out. The frogs don't want foreigners in their country. They treat other EU citizens more savagely than French citizens. (I thought that was illegal within the EU but the French ignore those EU rules which they don't like.)

The official Frog policy is to get rid of foreign born folk so that they can ensure that only French people inhabit apartments in the city.

(You and I might regard that as racism. But the French think it is perfectly proper. If Britain tried to do the same thing there would be riots.)

And yet, thanks to French law, Paris has yet another empty and bloody useless apartment.

It's not a happy ending. But it's a French ending.

Before we had lunch (at home), I checked the traffic reports for the M25 to see whether there were any holdups that would have interfered with our journey.

And there was a massive hold up as a result of an accident.

We would not have arrived at Ebbsfleet in time to catch our train.

I would have had to telephone Ebbsfleet somehow (if there was any reception for the three mobile phones I now routinely carry since Vodafone coverage has deteriorated noticeably) and change the tickets (at the cost of £200). We would have had to catch a train up to St Pancras and then catch a later train to Paris. It would have been a real mess.

One decision I've made is that if we do have to go to Paris again to deal with the flat I will buy Business Premier tickets. These are the tickets which are bought by EU staff and people working for companies where price is irrelevant. Two return tickets will cost around £1,000 (possibly more when you add in all the extras Eurostar charge for using the telephone, using a credit card, actually having the tickets posted and so on) but we will be able to change them if necessary without any additional cost.

Thus is travel these days.

Yesterday, having decided not to go to France, I ordered several hundred Jiffy bags, £500 worth of stamps and some more vellum paper suitable for press releases. All the companies concerned promised to deliver within 24 hours. So, today, I abandoned any idea of work and did some tidying up while waiting for the promised deliveries.

The stamps came because Royal Mail sent them by their own Special Delivery service.

But by late afternoon there was no sign of the rest of the stuff I'd ordered. I checked on eBay and what do you know: the companies which promised 24-hour deliveries were now promising to deliver tomorrow, the day after or the day after that or possibly the day after that or maybe sometime next week. So I am supposed to stay in every day for the next week in the hope that they will deliver the Jiffy bags and the paper which I have paid for. And then people wonder why the nation's productivity is so low.

And then a small miracle.

The bell on the gate went.

The Jiffy bags had arrived.

Hoorah.

I opened one of the boxes, hoping to be able to help Antoinette pack up some more books.

And the Jiffy bags are the wrong bloody size.

They are a few centimetres bigger than Royal Mail will accept as packets. If we put the books in these bags we will have to pay parcel postage instead of large letter postage. The packets will weigh much the same but they will be a tiny bit wider. All our stamps will be useless and the mailing will cost us several hundred pounds more.

I checked on the website, thinking that perhaps I had made a mistake.

But I hadn't.

The bags I had ordered, with the measurements given, would have been fine.

But the bags we have been sent are useless.

I couldn't face the thought of sending the damned boxes back to the supplier (even though it was their fault). It would mean days of emails and then a wait for a driver to collect the damned boxes. And there would be forms to fill in and so on and so forth. The company will accept returns but I have to pay and make all the arrangements myself.

(I think this is against the law. The last time I looked, a supplier is required to pay the cost of returns in circumstances like these. But I really don't want to spend days of my life arguing about £35.)

I thought about taking them to a charity shop. But I've tried in the past when I had surplus stationery. Charity shops aren't interested in Jiffy bags.

I doubt if the council will take them in the rubbish.

So I took them down the garden and burnt them. What else was there to do with the damned things?

Next time, to save money and energy, I'll just take a bunch of tenners down the garden and burn them to cut out the middle man.

Through no real fault of our own, we are wasting money at a prodigious rate at the moment.

But I can tell you this, in case you are interested, Jiffy bags do burn exceedingly well. A flight of seagulls flew around and round above the incinerator enjoying the rising hot air currents. And, who knows, maybe they enjoyed the unique smell of burning Jiffy bags.

The ream of paper which I have ordered (and which was promised to arrive within 24 hours) has not appeared. On checking the order, I see that the packet is still destined to arrive sometime during the next week. There is no point in complaining because the company concerned will doubtless say that they dealt with the order within 24 hours and so they have fulfilled their promise. (I first came across this trick some years when I telephoned a 24-hour plumber and spoke to an answering machine. The plumber later insisted that providing an answering machine to take messages 24 hours a day fulfilled his advertisement's promise.) In my experience around 50% of the people selling stuff on eBay are crooks, cheats, liars, fraudsters or confidence tricksters.

Tonight we are going to watch *Where Eagles Dare.*

I need to watch something with absurd levels of gratuitous violence. I can imagine that all the krauts who are being killed are really French property buyers, estate agents and notaires.

22

Some days ago, I sent an email to Royal Mail saying: 'I would like to buy 200 second class large letter 500 g stamps at £1.58. Can I buy these through you?'

I received a reply saying: 'The 2nd class large letter stamps are priced at 76p and these cover up to 750 g. To order 200 of these the price would be £153.45 including delivery.'

I wrote back and pointed out that the reply was completely wrong. The 76p stamp only covers a large letter of up to 100g. It is rather worrying that I know more about Royal Mail's pricing structure than they do.

I am re-reading Eric Ambler and working my way through his oeuvre of magnificently atmospheric thrillers. What a joy. I also have the entire works of Donald E.Westlake, Laurence Block, Ross Thomas, Robert B Parker, Robert Littell and, of course, Adam Hall to which to look forward. And in a year or so, I can start Brian Freemantle's Charlie Muffin books again. There aren't many new authors whose work I like but there is much good old stuff on my shelves.

I made a programme about Ambler for the BBC World Service but refused to meet him because I have always avoided meeting my heroes. The BBC asked me to pick a writer I admired, and I picked Ambler. (Incidentally, the BBC World Service used to be known as the Empire Service. We should remind BBC staffers of this fact as often as possible. It will embarrass and shame them enormously.)

I now regret the fact that I didn't meet him.

I first discovered Ambler's books in the 1960s. I then reread most of them in the 1990s. I can now not quite remember them so I can enjoy them fully again. It is sad to realise that I am unlikely to live long enough to read them all again. Still, I'm enjoying them greatly the second or third time around.

Today, I have been reading *Cause for Alarm*, a thriller about a naïve engineer working in Italy in the months prior to the outbreak of World War II. Ambler was a wise and much respected political observer and this is what he wrote when discussing Mussolini's fascist Italy: 'The idea of the state is not rooted in the masses, it is not of the people. It is an abstract, a God-idea, a psychic dung-hill raised to shore up an economic system that is no longer safe. When you're on the top of that sort of dung-hill, it doesn't matter whether the ends are in reality good or bad. The fact that they are your ends makes them good – for you.'

Ambler wrote that in 1938.

He could have written it today about the European Union.

We took a large parcel to the Post Office today. It contained a huge pile of books which we have to send off to the Copyright libraries. Every publisher has to send free copies of new books to six libraries. But the books have to go to a single address.

It cost over £12 to post the books and when the transaction was completed the woman behind the Post Office counter smiled, probably for the first time in a decade, and said: 'If you'd sent the books in two smaller parcels it would have only cost you £5.00.'

'Thank you for pointing that out,' we said.

It would, of course, have been no fun at all for her to have told us this before we'd paid the postage on the one big parcel.

We had to order a new iron. The last one, which wasn't very old, had completely stopped working. Antoinette said it would have been easier to iron a shirt with a hot spoon than with the iron we had. I suppose the damned thing will have to go into the garage in the Cotswolds. We dump all our broken down equipment there. It's a two car garage and it's damned near full. It contains two lawnmowers, several strimmers and a variety of computer screens and shredders. No one will accept computer screens as rubbish so I have no idea what we are going to do with them. In the end, I plan to rent a skip. But the skip hire people won't let me dump a cathode ray screen.

Our Henrietta hoover is due to go into the garage too. The hose came away from the cleaner's body. I have tried gluing it back into place but even the strongest glue I can find doesn't work. What shoddy workmanship.

This evening we watched another new film. This one, made with the support of the Welsh something or other and the BBC, was called *Their Finest*, and to me it appeared to be, like the terrible film *Churchill*, to be nothing much more than a piece of blunt feminist propaganda. The heroine (Welsh, of course, since Welsh money was used in the making of the film) was quite brilliant while the men seemed to be sexist, dumb and weak. Oddly enough, the film was written by women, directed by a woman and produced by a woman. The film was billed as a comedy but I'm afraid I've watched funnier weather forecasts.

23

When I got up this morning, I wandered into the conservatory and our tame pheasant, who was pecking at the lawn, saw me and hurried to the conservatory door. I gave him his morning apple and he started pecking away. To be honest I am happy to give him as many apples as he wants because he has acquired a habit of pecking at the Bentley's tyres. He is taking seeds and insects that are stuck between the treads but I worry (probably needlessly) that he might puncture the tyre. I just don't want to have to explain to people that my puncture was created by a pecking pheasant. I have noted that he never bothers with the tyres of the Mitsubishi truck. He is obviously a pheasant of breeding.

Today I noted with some astonishment how much we are spending each week on apples for our wildlife.

This evening, I received an email from a new estate agent in Paris who is keen to take on the sale of our apartment. He says that he will talk to their lawyers about our problem.

Ten minutes later, I received an email from our notaire (who has been silent for over a month).

She tells me that the buyer's mother has now struck out on her own. She has chosen another notaire and wants to buy the flat by herself and through a civil company. To add another twist to this utterly bizarre story it appears that mother and son may have fallen out.

The notaire points out that mother is not mentioned in the 'offer d'achat' and suggests that she sends a letter by bailiff to the buyer to tell him that if he doesn't buy the flat by himself at the original price within ten days then the 'offer d'achat' will be considered null and void.

'It won't avoid him to sue you if you decide to sell to somebody else,' she says in her wonderful English. 'But it manages the proof that you did everything you could to find an arrangement. If you agree with this plan you will have to pay the bailiff's fees (around 700 euros).'

What a joke.

They now want us to pay 700 euros for absolutely nothing.

I already have proof that I was tricked into signing the Achat by being told that he did not have to borrow the money for the purchase. And I have already been told that he has abandoned the Achat.

Is there some more trickery here?

If I sell to mother then her son, the original buyer will, it seems, be able to sue me.

I intend to write to the notaire to let her know that if mother wants to be considered as an applicant for the purchase then she must first tell her son to sign a document agreeing that he no longer has any claim on the apartment.

24

I visited a bank to try to buy some euro cheques with which I could pay the taxes on our Paris flat.

'Oh no, we don't do those now,' said the two female counter clerks. They seemed to think I was living in a world populated by dinosaurs.

I walked away, wondering how the devil I was going to pay the bills I've received. I would send cash but I owe several thousand euros and I think the Frogs will get excited if they open an envelope and a pile of cash falls out.

One of the women at the bank told me that I would have to open a new French account to replace the Barclays account.

Great.

Ten minutes later, having done a little shopping, I realised that I could arrange a bank transfer. I went back to the bank, queued again and asked if they could do that for me.

They said that oh yes they could do that.

Why the devil didn't the tellers suggest that the first time?

I then went into a branch of The Works.

I love The Works. It appears to be full of stuff that no one else can sell but which people are buying by the armful. The shops are always stuffed with stock and today I managed to knock over a pile of cardboard boxes containing something or other. The boxes were as light as meringue and were sticking out from the table on which they were balanced.

As I picked up the boxes, a member of staff came running over.

'I'm so sorry,' I apologised. 'I think my bag must have caught the corner of this display. Nothing appears to be broken.' I balanced the last box back on the table.

'No, no that's fine,' said the member of staff, unconcerned about the boxes. 'Did anything land on your foot?'

'No, no,' I assured him. A thousand of the damned things could have landed on my foot and I don't think I would have felt them.

'You're all right?'

'Oh yes,' I said. And I certainly realised that as far as he was concerned this was a health and safety/legal situation.

'There's no health and safety issue,' I told him. 'And I'm not going to sue.'

The smile of relief on his face lit up the shop.

As I left, it occurred to me that we now live in an upside down world.

I knocked off the boxes. It was my place to apologise. But the shop employee was concerned only that I might sue or complain.

Exhausted by my adventures, I tottered along the main shopping street.

I watched in horror as a dog, a large Labrador, decided to empty its large bladder along a row of cyclamen plants being offered for sale ('10 for £10') and various boxes full of fruit and vegetables. The owner, a snooty looking woman, pretended to look the other way. When I called out to her, she pulled at the dog's lead but it was too late. She knew exactly what her dog was doing and she simply didn't care. Some dog owners are a different breed.

I popped into a café for a quiet cup of coffee while I waited for Antoinette to finish her shopping.

Quiet it was not.

Well, it was when I sat down.

But within five minutes, a woman came in with a baby in a pram. The baby was bawling. A mother came in with two toddlers. The toddlers were alternately whining and screaming. A man came in with two dogs. The dogs started barking. And so I sat for a minute or two bathed in a cacophony; a veritable symphony for bawling baby, whining children and two barking dogs.

An hour later, back home, I checked out the budget.

It seems that Jeremy Corbyn's passionate après-Budget speech wasn't quite what it appeared to be. I am told that Corbyn's speech was delivered to him in brown envelopes as he spoke.

What a pity the speech wasn't intercepted.

It would have livened up the day to have heard him say (with great passion): 'What this country needs is votes for teddy bears when they reach the age of 16 and free ice cream for all people living in counties south of Lancashire. The Chancellor should have arranged to give full life-time tax refunds to everyone called Coleman.'

This evening I had an email from our French estate agent. My guess is that he emailed me because the notaire didn't get a reply. And I suspect they only got in touch because another Parisian estate agent wants to sell our flat and was doubtless not discouraged by my reply. (How did they all know what was going on? Are we being hacked? Nothing would surprise me.)

Our irritating estate agent (the one who told me that the Achat was not a legally binding document and who told me to sign a document with no closure date on it) has sent this email: 'I tried to have you on the phone. It seems the notaire find out a way to get out of the offer on our flat. Therefore we could put it back on the

505

market at 1,155,000. Can you confirm it to me please. Thanks and sorry for all this delay I would have liked to avoid.'

Nice of him to remember we are still alive. It is five weeks since I last heard from the agency which is supposed to be selling our apartment.

I sent a polite reply to him and to our notaire to tell them that I didn't think much of the idea. The suggestion that we send a bailiff round to the buyer is so lily livered that only a Frog could have thought of it. It's a pretty wimpy response but what do you expect from a nation which regards the white surrender flag as its national emblem?

I pointed out that I had signed the Achat because I was given misleading information and that according to the notaire the buyer had already accepted that the Achat was null and void. I also pointed out that I could not possibly entertain a bid from the buyer's mother unless her son legally accepted the end of the Achat.

'Otherwise,' I said, 'is it not possible that she might buy it making it possible for him to sue?'

I explained that we have not yet started legal proceedings because Antoinette has been made ill by stress created by these buyers.

But, I went on to say, we will sue the buyer for everything possible, including costs, opportunity loss, currency loss, stress and the exacerbation of my wife's condition. 'We will,' I wrote, 'investigate whether there was any serious intention to buy and look at the buyer's history. We will sue in the European Court of Justice if the French courts do not find in our favour. I already have articles and press releases ready and I intend to draw this fiasco to the attention of Anne Hidalgo (the Mayor of Paris) who might be embarrassed to know of a foreigner being prevented from selling a flat by absurd French laws.' (Ms Hidalgo is keen to get rid of foreign property owners and is punishing foreigners by making them pay especially high taxes.)

I finished by saying that I intend to advise foreign buyers never to sign an Achat. 'To be honest,' I concluded, 'I cannot see any foreigners ever buying in Paris when this horror story has been aired.'

'We are now resigned to the fact that the apartment may not be sold for some years until the court case has been concluded. These things take time and there is no longer any hurry. I accept that I cannot sell until the buyer has gone away. But the longer he persists the greater the damages will be.'

I asked the notaire to destroy the proxies I had signed giving her authority to sign important documents on my behalf.

In a PS I pointed out that if the buyer signed the Achat knowing that he didn't have the money he had agreed to pay then would that not be more serious?

This evening Antoinette and I tried to work out how much money we could make if we could buy a daily newspaper a day ahead.

It probably wouldn't be as much as you might imagine. I doubt if you could win more than five million pounds even if you knew the result of all of tomorrow's sporting results and had, say, access to a million with which to place your bets. And there is, of course, a real danger that the bookies would refuse to pay up.

You could put money on lots of horses and football games but bookies have strict limits on the amount that could be won. You could put money on the stock market and currency market but you would be limited in what you could borrow and the total value of the investments would be pretty much limited by the amount of money you already had.

So, the total winnings would be rather disappointing.

25

I posted off some parcels today. I shoved them into a box at our nearest Main Post Office on Saturday lunchtime. The next collection is due at 5.45 p.m. on Monday. And that is surely reason number 8,475,674 out of an unending series explaining why productivity in Britain is lower than almost anywhere else in the world except Equatorial New Guinea.

26

Computer nerds are forever claiming that their latest app is totally disruptive. These things never are, of course. Most of their silly inventions are usually more annoying than disruptive. Here (in no particular order) is my list of the truly important and disruptive inventions: the wheel; the cog; engines turning energy into power (from water mill to internal combustion engine); sewage pipes; the water closet; the chimney; the compass; the wireless; shoe laces; the washing machine; the pencil and the pen; double entry bookkeeping; the printing press; the plough; parliamentary democracy; the sail; antiseptics; anaesthesia; antibiotics; the tablet (creating tablets meant that drugs could be prescribed in defined quality and quantity); electricity; the hammer , aeroplanes, the camera, and the penknife. The world wide web struggles into the lower reaches of the list, though only as a disruptive influence which has done more harm than good.

Reading James Agate's diary for 1932, I see that he bought a second hand Riley nine drop head coupe for £285 and drove 206 miles from Harrogate to London in six hours. He managed 32 mpg on the journey. That's an average of 34 miles per hour – before trunk roads or dual carriageways, let alone motorways. The Riley Nine which was partly made out of wood had a 1.1 litre engine and a top speed of 60 mph. On another occasion, a friend drove 200 miles from Yorkshire to central London and completed the journey in less than four hours – averaging 50 miles per hour.

You'd have a job to average that sort of speed today in a car twice as powerful. Our last trip from Cirencester to Ebbsfleet (a journey of 114 miles, most of which was on motorways) took just under four hours (an average of 28 miles an hour). The return journey took just three and a half hours (an average of 32 miles an hour) and was a record for us. We were travelling in a vehicle with a six litre engine and a top speed of 200 mph. It is quite customary for the journey to take five hours (an average of 22 miles per hour). They call it progress, don't they?

Possibly the most important thing I learned from Agate's diaries was that people then did so much more with their lives. Productivity, in every respect, was much higher. No time was wasted watching television or reading and responding to emails or on social media but, most important of all, it was possible to move about the country much more easily and speedily than is possible today. Travel by road or train was infinitely faster in the 1930s than it is now. For example, you could get in or out of London, or across London, in a fraction of the time it takes today.

I read today that the average person now spends eight and a half hours a day using some form of electronic device to do stuff on the internet. That means that the average citizen now spends more than half their waking hours using an electronic device instead of reading, talking or finding the time to enjoy the simple things in life.

How many people spend part of their day actually looking at the world around them and obtaining pleasure from the simple things? Isn't that what the revived delight of 'mindfulness' is supposed to mean?

27

I have received a reply from someone at Royal Mail insisting that a 76p stamp will cover a packet weighing up to 750 g. If she is correct then all the Royal Mail literature is wrong and their website is wrong and I have just wasted several hundred pounds on stamps I didn't need to buy. I found this rather worrying. I wrote back, again, querying the advice.

About a week ago, I received a request from a television company asking me to film an insert for a programme about benzodiazepine tranquillisers. (Actually, they referred to them as antidepressants which wasn't a terribly good start since there is, of course, a notable difference between tranquillisers and antidepressants.) I don't do television these days but since the topic is close to my heart I offered two dates this week and suggested places where we could record.

Since then we have exchanged endless emails but they have still not succeeded in confirming a date, time and place.

So, today, I cancelled the whole thing.

I was making television programmes half a century ago and since then I have filmed more programmes than I can even begin to remember. I made three series based on my book *Bodypower*, worked for two years as the BBC's first agony aunt and made numerous programmes as the TV AM doctor. Never, ever have I had to put up with such inability to make a decision about something so simple.

I am honestly surprised that TV companies these days manage to make any programmes at all.

Or is the apparent lack of respect simply a sign of my age and the fact that I am now 'out of the loop' as they say?

Either way I shall, in future, not even bother to respond to requests to make television programmes.

My problem about how to pay the taxes on our Paris apartment continues to puzzle me. I cannot pay by credit card or PayPal because they won't take credit cards or PayPal. I cannot pay by cheque because British banks won't sell me a euro cheque. I can't pay with cash because the bill comes to just under 4,000 euros and it is illegal to pay a bill with that much cash. I cannot pay by bank transfer because I don't have a French bank account and their website (none of which is in English, by the way, which seems fair enough but in England we make stuff available in a zillion languages) doesn't seem able to cope with a transfer from a British bank. Moreover, none of the bills I have received contains the IBAN or Swift details. I can't pay online because to do this they now want a special number which is only given to people who pay tax in France and since I don't pay tax in France I don't have one of these special numbers and cannot obtain one. I cannot pay by direct debit or standing order for the same reason. I cannot send a sterling cheque because they wouldn't accept sterling.

So, to use a banking term, I am completely buggered. I have written to the Mayor of Paris and the Mayor of our arrondissement asking if they can think of a way for me to pay my Parisian taxes. I have suggested that they tell me the city's IBAN and Swift details so that I can send the money by international transfer. I very much doubt if I will ever receive a reply. But at least I will be able to prove that I have tried to pay the damned bills.

It is now over 21 years since my book *How to Stop Your Doctor Killing You* was first published. I have not had to change anything in the book since I wrote it. The chapter entitled *Lowering blood cholesterol* is particularly pertinent since millions of healthy individuals now take statins. The book has been a global bestseller for years (I've lost count of the number of translations but the book has been a huge bestseller in Germany, Japan and China and in America there have been a number of pirated and rip-off versions) but I'm afraid it hasn't had much effect on the sales of statins.

The statins are now the biggest selling group of drugs of all time with sales exceeding $22 billion.

I paid extra delivery charges to have four parcels delivered today – all from separate companies. I thought that this would save me having to sit and wait for parcels over a period of days or weeks. In the end, one parcel came last Friday, two came on Saturday and one never arrived at all though I did receive a card saying that the carrier (Parcel Force inevitably) had been kind enough to leave it at a nearby Post Office so that it would be available for me to collect at my convenience. I do understand that it is difficult to move stuff around the country and then deliver it on a specific date but companies really shouldn't offer such a service (and then charge for it). Nor should they promise delivery within 24 hours when what they really mean is delivery within 24 days. I suppose I should simply stop trusting and give up ordering online. The problem is: where do I buy music or DVDs or books? Thanks to the internet there aren't any shops any more.

There is one delivery company which offers a service which is, in my experience, unique. Yodel provides a constant tracking update of where its driver is and how many drops he or she has to do before bringing your parcel. Theoretically, this is a splendid idea. In practice, I find myself sitting watching the tracker and trying to estimate how long it will take the driver to deal with 39, 24, 17, 12 or 7 other customers.

28

Here is part of the entry from James Agate's diary for June 8th 1932: 'Invited by two somebodies I don't know to attend a welcome lunch to somebody I have never heard of returning from Australia, country I am not interested in. Refused.'

And an entry for July 10th of that year: 'Abominable attack of wind, plus panic, plus heart, which went at 140 to the minute and wouldn't calm down…After getting rid of several balloons full of gas went to bed and slept.'

And an entry from the entry for March 14th of the following year: 'Last week my new-cut latch-key would not go into the lock. Last month I had my study measured for a carpet which on arrival swarmed up the walls. I have just ordered some summer vests and I feel it in my bones that pants will arrive.'

It is our wedding anniversary next Sunday. I asked Antoinette if she wanted to go to Paris for the weekend.

She raised a meaningful and querulous eyebrow but said nothing.

29

My attempts to pay our French bills are still proving ineffective.

So today, I telephoned the customer service line for Lloyds and spoke to a bloke who told me that they could do euro cheques. He was shocked when I told him that the bank clerks had said they couldn't.

Still nervous I then checked out the Lloyds online details. And there it is! They will do an international draft in euros.

The daft biddies in the bank were wrong. And because of them I've wasted hours on this problem.

This evening two rabbits were fighting over an apple so I threw out a second apple, the same variety and size as the first one. They ignored the new apple and continued to fight over the original.

How very, very human.

Later this evening I had an email from our estate agent to say that our buyer has, at last, pulled out of buying a flat he could never afford. He says that he has pulled out of the purchase because of the plan of the apartment, the Carrez measurements and the price. None of these things has changed one jot since last May or since last June when he signed the Achat agreeing to purchase the place. The miserable wretch apologised to the estate agent but not to us. I am told by someone else that he was always relying on his mother's money but that she refused to help him and no bank would lend him the necessary funds. Oddly enough he withdrew a couple of days after I wrote to the estate agent and notaire expressing my intention to sue him for a gazillion euros in damages.

I am furious with our buyer, clearly a fantasist, and his curious mother, but even more furious with the estate agents. My guess is that they knew all along that the buyer did not have the money. I suspect our agent was being disingenuous when, in replying to my question about whether the buyer had the cash, he replied that he was buying without a loan. I suspect that he has been having a good laugh at my expense.

Thanks to our absurd buyers, our estate agent and our notaire we wasted much of the year. None of those responsible for our predicament, our wasted time or our continual expenses has apologised or even hinted at an apology.

We got into a position where we could not sell the apartment and we could not rent it out either though we had to continue to pay inflated local taxes.

Another estate agent told us that the new laws seem especially designed to give buyers all the rights – and to ensure that sellers have no rights whatsoever.

Our plan is to put the apartment back on the market at the full price of 1.1 million euros. We don't really care if we sell it or not before Christmas. If we do have a buyer then the flat will be sold via English rules rather than French rules. I have prepared a list of very specific regulations governing the sale and if the agent and notaire don't like them then they can do the other thing. It seems odd to celebrate a buyer pulling out but believe me we are celebrating.

In the New Year we will hire a new estate agent.

At least, we now know not to trust anyone in France.

30

I received another email from Royal Mail apologising for the confusion caused by the previous advice and telling me that I was right about their pricing schedules. Days of worry caused, yet again, by employees who don't know their company's own rules.

The same thing happened with staff in one branch of Lloyds Bank, of course. They told me that Lloyds would not issue me with a euro cheque. I spent many hours trying to find another way to pay the French bills. And then eventually I found that Lloyds do issue euro cheques.

I visited another branch of the bank, filled in some forms with the help of a very knowledgeable manager, and received the eurocheques within two days.

To let her know that she didn't need to worry any more about the stamp problem, I sent the latest email from Royal Mail along to Antoinette together with a note saying 'A moron writes…'

Unfortunately, instead of sending the email to Antoinette I sent it back, by accident, to Royal Mail. Oh dear.

Back in the 1980s I had to have an insurance medical. It was the usual, routine sort of thing but when performing a standard, simple screening test on my urine, the doctor performing the medical found a trace of blood. I'd also been getting pains in my back and so the doctor referred me to the local hospital for investigations.

The hospital took X-rays and ultrasound pictures and two radiologists came to the conclusion that I had cancer of the kidney. If you're going to choose a cancer this isn't one that would be near the top of the list. It tends to be pretty lethal. The radiologists wanted to refer me to a surgeon straight away but I wanted a third opinion. I didn't feel happy with the diagnosis (and not just for the obvious reason) and somehow I just didn't feel that I needed to have a kidney ripped out.

After a scan it became clear that I didn't have cancer of the kidney. I had a slightly deformed kidney but there was nothing wrong with it. The two radiologists had been wrong.

So, what had caused the haematuria (blood in my urine)?

I made the diagnosis myself on a flight to Paris. As the air pressure in the cabin changed, I started to suffer from the pain I'd been getting in my back. And I realised that the pain was caused by air in my intestine. I had irritable bowel syndrome caused largely by stress. The air in my bowel had been pressing on my kidneys and had caused the minute amount of bleeding.

I managed to get the irritable bowel syndrome under control and when I went back to the doctor for a second urine test he found that the haematuria had gone.

That was my first (and only) unhappy experience with a screening test. (I sent a letter detailing my observation to the *British Medical Journal* but they didn't print it. A decade later, IBS was eventually recognised as a possible cause of haematuria. No one has, as far as I know, recognised that it is also a major cause of urinary frequency.)

I was reminded of all this because I received another invitation to have a routine test for bowel cancer. The NHS wanted me to send in a stool sample which would be tested for blood as part of the NHS Bowel Cancer Screening Programme. If blood were found, they would perform a colonoscopy. I had one of these invitations a year or two ago.

(The really odd thing was that the letter which came to me, from the NHS Cancer Screening Programmes, was written in 14 languages: Albanian, Arabic, Bengali, Chinese, English, Farsi, Gujarati, Hindi, Polish, Portuguese, Punjabi, Somali, Turkish and Urdu. If I were Welsh I would be slightly pissed off that it wasn't in my language. And who picked the 13 that aren't English? What happened to French, German and Spanish?)

I said 'no' because I was worried that the screening programme could kill me.

Here's the scenario that filled my mind.

The IBS (which still flares up) results in there being a little blood in my stools. The NHS screening test finds the blood and so I'm called in for a colonoscopy.

Now, one of the hazards with a colonoscopy is that the tube that is pushed up the bowel can puncture the bowel wall. It seemed to me that this is especially likely to happen if the wall is unusual, stretched or weakened. As it would undoubtedly be in someone with irritable bowel syndrome.

So the colonoscopy tube punctures my bowel wall.

Bang.

I need surgery. I need a hospital stay. I develop MRSA. And I die. It is a concatenation of circumstances which is by no means impossible.

I decided that I would prefer to trust myself and that I would simply keep a look out for signs and symptoms of bowel cancer.

It saddens me, incidentally, that irritable bowel syndrome is regarded lightly by so many who should know better. When some years ago I wrote a book about IBS, it was treated by many as a joke. I was shocked that several editors of women's magazines refused to print adverts for the book, insisting that they would not have the word 'bowel' in their magazine.

We had a nice surprise today.

Tesco have refunded the cost of the whole of last Saturday's shopping which didn't arrive and which we had to collect from the store. Not, I suspect, simply because we had to fetch the groceries

515

which we had paid to have delivered, but also because we weren't told until well after the delivery time that their van had broken down and that our contracted delivery would not be made.

And that is, without a doubt, the way to win customer loyalty.

Tonight Antoinette can start to open the little boxes in her beautiful, hand-made, wooden Advent Calendar. I bought the Calendar from Harrods some years ago and it's large, delicate and beautiful. When you open each one of the 24 small wooden doors, a Santa pops out (rather like a cuckoo), three small roundabouts start turning, music plays and lights come on. It is a solitary work of art. Harrods only had the one and they sent it to us in one of their green vans.

The boxes are quite big by advent calendar standards but they aren't big enough for this year's gifts. I have bought 24 tubes of oil paint because Antoinette has started painting in oils. She is already a brilliant painter, both talented and skilful, and her paintings will, I have no doubt, sell well in fine art galleries (if I can ever bear to see any of them go). The paints I've bought are all different colours and I've put them into a large cloth bag so that Antoinette has to play lucky dip to decide which one she gets. And to ensure that the advent calendar plays a part I have put small toy animals into each of the 24 boxes. I've also put in details of 24 happy memories.

I will tell Antoinette that she has to exchange one of the animals for a selection from the lucky dip bag. By Christmas Day, she should have quite a good addition to her stock of oil paints.

December

1

Antoinette showed me some modern art produced by a minor Scottish television personality who shall remain nameless. The celebrity has apparently written a book about his painting. I hate to say this, I really do, but to me it appears to be appalling stuff: all splodges of colour and pretentious commentary; more occupational therapy than art. Antoinette calls this sort of painting 'lazy art' and she is absolutely right. It is much easier to produce rubbish like this than to work at learning real painting skills.

Our celebrity friend would perhaps do well to read Tom Wolfe's wonderful 1975 essay on modern art entitled, *The Painted Word*. Wolfe attacks modern artists and critics and describes modern art as having 'disappeared up its own fundamental aperture'. It's Emperor's New Clothes time and I fear this celebrity is just another one of a long line of pseuds who can't see that the Emperor is stark naked.

Would the magazines which printed his stuff on art have touched it if he had not been a minor television celebrity? I suspect not.

As I read, I suddenly shivered. I reached out and touched a radiator. It was cold. As cold as only an iron radiator can become. I had forgotten to pump more water into the central heating system.

I retreated to the boiler room, opened the valves and heard the welcoming sound of water rushing through the pipes and more air being pushed out of the valves in the loft. It is nearly eighteen months since our new boiler was installed but still the system contains vast amounts of air. Occasionally, we can hear the gurgles as another vast bubble makes its way along the labyrinth of our heating system. As Antoinette pointed out, it seems as though the house suffers from irritable bowel syndrome.

The boiler, relieved, started to hum again and within minutes, the radiators were warm. These days we leave the heating on for

24 hours a day. We turn it down a few degrees at night but if you turn it down completely the thick walls get cold and then have to be reheated. It seems more efficient and cheaper to keep the house at a constant temperature.

Comforting.

I can remember the days before central heating; the days when the inside of my bedroom window was covered with Jack Frost patterns; the days when the bathroom taps were routinely frozen on cold winter days; the winters, before climate change, when even in the English Midlands we had storms and snow a foot deep.

2

I have noticed that, by and large, people become what they do, in the same way that people are said to grow to look like their dogs.

In other words, people grow to fit their image; they behave in the way that is expected of them and in some strange way they look as they should look or as they think they should look.

So, policemen end up looking and behaving like policemen. School teachers look and behave like school teachers. Bank managers look and behave like bank managers.

Heaven knows what writers look and behave like.

Nothing on earth is my guess.

The flowers which I bought Antoinette for our anniversary are already dead. Every single rose is completely defunct. I bought them two days ago and they were not cheap. I don't know whether to be upset or angry. I think I'll probably have to settle for both.

I received an email from the second estate agent in Paris; the one who has heard that our apartment is for sale. He is desperate to take over as the agent offering the apartment and he tells us that he has buyers who are keen. When I read this, my bullshit antenna started to twitch like crazy. The bottom line is that I don't believe a word of it.

This agent also told me that his mother lives in the same building and my fear is that he wants to make sure that the new owner of the flat satisfies her requirements. (What is it about French men, property and their mothers?)

It would be remarkably easy for the agent's mother to put prospective buyers off the property. If she thinks someone might

518

be noisy, for example, she could tell them that the building is not a good one in which to live and that the neighbours are not very nice people.

She has apparently already talked to the buyer's mother.

And if she is going to muddy the waters I rather doubt if we will ever manage to sell the damned place.

Of course, anyone living in a block of flats would be stupid to do this because the seller might be forced to lower their price and if that happened then the value of all the other apartments in the building would, inevitably, also fall.

But, hey, you don't have to have brains if you're French!

I have sent the new estate agent an email telling him that if we do not sell quickly next year we will rent out the apartment to one of the universities who will put eight students in there. That should make sure that no relatives of his waste any time trying to discourage prospective buyers.

The French are, without a doubt, the most manipulative, selfish and deceitful nation I have ever met. I have learned that in order to survive you need to be pretty manipulative in return.

After dinner this evening, I spent half an hour replacing bulbs in our chandeliers. In Devon, we have four large chandeliers (each with over a dozen bulbs) and several smaller chandeliers. (It's a big house and anything smaller would look silly and leave us stumbling about in the dark.)

We don't replace bulbs as they go because if we did we would never have time to do anything else but today I noticed that between a third and a half of the bulbs in the larger chandeliers were not alight. Fortunately, all four are on dimmer switches so we could merely turn up the brightness.

We have good supplies of old-fashioned bulbs because when the EU announced its lunatic plan to bring its daft mercury packed light-bulbs (the ones that take forever to become bright) I bought up every damned light bulb I could find. I am pleased to say that we still have a cupboard full of replacement bulbs.

3

It is our wedding anniversary. I poured myself a decent dram of an excellent Kentucky Straight Bourbon Whiskey called 'Elijah

Craig'. It tastes and smells of Christmas and is very reminiscent of some of my favourite Scottish malt whiskies; a real Christmas pudding, toffee and home-made thick-cut marmalade smell and taste. I don't remember ever drinking bourbon whiskey before. If this is typical then I am a convert. Truly this is, as they say, a 'sipping whiskey'.

I watched a raven pick an apple up off the lawn and try to fly away with it. Unfortunately, either the stalk broke off the apple or the weight of the fruit proved too heavy for him. Either way the result was that he dropped the apple. He flew off and didn't return. Ravens are very proud birds. I suspect he was too embarrassed to come back for it.

In the evening, we lit the candles on our wooden carousel. There is still something wonderfully reckless about lighting candles on a wooden carousel. After messing around with the vanes for some time, we managed to get it to go round properly. It should be fine for Christmas. At the age of 71, I feel that I want Christmas to be just right. I hope there are many more. But though one hopes for the best it is wise to plan for the worst.

4

The Mayor of Paris (or her accountants and lawyers) have fined me for failing to pay one of next year's local taxes on time (even though we are still a month away from next year). I wrote back returning the demand, explaining the circumstances and pointing out that I could not have paid more speedily.

The Brexit negotiations took a large step backwards today when Ireland stuck its fingers into the process. The interesting thing is that when it was clear that the negotiations with the EU had faltered, and a deal was unlikely, the pound rose noticeably. It is clear that currency traders recognised that Britain will be better off without any sort of deal than with the deal currently being negotiated by the EU's rogues and the hapless and woefully inept Theresa May. We must have the weakest Government in history. There is no sense of loyalty to the nation, no patriotism, no courage and no integrity.

No commentators seemed to notice the attitude of the currency markets although this was probably the most significant support yet for 'no deal'.

There was a time young women (and older ones too) went to Italy and if they didn't get their bottoms pinched they would have complained bitterly. These days, young, English women are the slags of Europe. Most seem to have sex every night with ten complete strangers and think nothing of it. But they complain to the police if their bum gets pinched. It sometimes seems to me to be a very strange world.

Quentin Letts has written an excellent book entitled *Patronising Bastards* – about the Britons, all members of the establishment elite, who seem to believe they have a right to tell the rest of us what to do, how to vote and what we should think. If we ignore their advice, they tend to get very cross and abusive. Here is my personal list of the 12 most supercilious, hypocritical, arrogant bastards in the country:

1) Bono
2) Gary Lineker
3) Richard Branson
4) Lily Allen
5) Nick Clegg
6) Tony Blair
7) Vince Cable
8) Emma Thomson
9) Emily Thornberry
10) Ed Milliband
11) Caroline Lucas
12) Benedict Cumberbatch

It was actually quite difficult to keep the list down to a dozen. I could have easily made a list of 500 supercilious, patronising bastards – most of them luvvies from the world of acting and many of them receiving huge salaries from the taxpayer and EU funded BBC. How, for example, did the highly obnoxious hop-skip-and-jumper Jonathan Edwards not make the list?

5

Driving down the M5 this evening, Antoinette suddenly said that she thought she either had glaucoma or a brain tumour. When I asked her why she thought this, she replied that all the lights she could see (whether belonging to traffic ahead of us, traffic approaching us or motorway lighting gantries) were strangely elongated.

This was odd because for some miles I had been suffering from exactly the same problem.

'Could it be the windscreen?' asked Antoinette.

I squirted soapy water onto the windscreen and let the wipers do their job. A second later we were both cured of our visual problems.

There must have been a lot of diesel fuel on the glass.

The quickest double cure in history.

6

Our entirely useless French estate agent (the one whom I am convinced spends more time tying his scarf than flogging property) now tells us that his firm 'has a long experience of similar cases'.

I wrote back asking why, if they had a long history of similar cases, they did not do something to prevent them. I suggested that all they needed to do was to make sure that potential buyers really had the money they needed. In my experience, this is fairly routine among the more astute British estate agents.

I cannot make my mind up whether he has treated us especially badly because I am English or old or both or if he treats all his customers with the same offensive mixture of patronising superiority and dismissive disdain.

(Actually, come to think of it, it may simply be because Britain voted to leave the EU. I have noticed that the staff in shops in France are considerably ruder now than they were before we chose to turn our backs on the EU. Who knows what lies the French have been told by their EU complaint media.)

I am so looking forward to firing our estate agent after Christmas. I intend to prepare a lengthy speech, in French, in which I draw attention to all his shortcomings.

On second thoughts, maybe I will confine myself to a précis of his shortcomings.

I don't want to have to stand there for six hours reciting his faults.

7

I see that there is an exhibition celebrating ABBA, the Swedish pop group, at the Southbank Centre over Christmas and through until the end of the winter. Fair enough; they were enormously successful. But the exhibition is supported with taxpayers' funds by the Arts Council of England. Why the hell is the Arts Council using public money to celebrate a foreign pop group? And if there really isn't enough public support for an ABBA exhibition should we be paying for one? I sometimes despair at the way public money is thrown around. Every penny that is spent should be analysed and discussed seriously by grown-ups.

8

The weather forecasters said that we would have snow today. It is supposed to be the third huge storm of the season. But in reality it is a calm, sunny day. There is no snow, nor is there likely to be.

The weather forecasters over-sell their scary scenarios for two reasons.

First, they need to drive eyes to their websites so that they can charge more for the advertising which accompanies their absurd, attention seeking prognostications.

Second, they are an integral part of the global warming change myth and so feel they have to persuade us that the climate is truly changing. They have to terrify us with the constant prospect of stormy winters, flooded coastal regions and arid summers when in reality our weather has changed not at all. A careful study of history shows clearly enough that we have no more storms, cold winters and hot summers now than we had a century ago.

Theresa May has now betrayed us completely. The deal she has made with the EU means, in my view, that we are now worse off than we were before the Referendum. We will be constrained by all the worst aspects of the EU and we will be ruled by thugs like

Juncker. We will have no vote and no control over our destiny. I have opposed the EU since the 1970s and have actively fought against it for two decades. I now fear that all our efforts have been in vain. May's deal is pathetic and humiliating. I am today, for the first time in my life, ashamed to be English and ashamed to be British. The Second World War was a complete waste of blood. This is, without a doubt, the most awful day of modern history.

9

There was a funeral service for Johnny Hallyday today. Hallyday, died two days ago at the age of 74, and the centre of Paris came to a halt as the funeral procession, accompanied by the rock star's band playing live, and followed by a lengthy line of black leathered motorcyclists , drove from the Arc de Triomphe down the Champs-Elysee to the Place de la Concorde and finally to the church of La Madeleine. A million people lined the route, French presidents from Macron backwards all attended as did a galaxy of movie and music stars. (It was rather thoughtless of ex-President Hollande to attend since it was his absurdly greedy tax policies which drove Hallyday and other celebrities out of France. Hallyday attacked Hollande in his autobiography. Still, politicians have thick skins and invariably put themselves first. Opportunistic? Self-serving?)

Hallyday, whose real name was Jean-Philippe LeoSmet, sold more than 110 million records and made over 30 films and there was as big an outpouring of national emotion in France at the death of the nearest thing they had to royalty as happened in England when princess Diana died. Every French generation loved Hallyday who was truly one of the most charismatic performers of all time. He was an inveterate smoker of filterless French cigarettes and died of lung cancer.

It will, I suspect, take the French a long time to realise that their Elvis has finally gone to the Great Concert Hall in the sky. For as long as I can remember it has been impossible to visit Paris without seeing his name and face on posters for films, records, television shows, books or magazine features.

10

We have prepared our television viewing for the Christmas season. We will, as usual, declare independence from the schedulers and television companies.

People used to go on TV because they had something to say and share with the viewing public. There were also some fairly basic requirements as to the individual's ability to articulate their thoughts and then present them in an intelligible way. In the 1970s, it was commonplace for television producers to send a researcher to interview a potential 'performer' and to check that they were not likely to startle or confuse the viewers.

Now, going on television is an end in itself. The gawping idiots who stood behind a presenter, waving and pulling faces, have become the programmes.

I no longer watch the stuff broadcast by TV companies. (I no longer watch television.)

The following DVDs are on our list for watching: the *Sherlock Holmes* series (starring Basil Rathbone and Nigel Bruce); *The Third Man* (starring Joseph Cotton, Orson Welles and Trevor Howard); *The Thirty Nine Steps* (starring Robert Donat and Madeleine Carroll); *Uncle Buck* and *Only the Lonely* (both starring John Candy); the first of the *Back to the Future* series and the first of the *Toy Story* series. And *The Quiet Man*. And probably a Bond film. Oh, and the original *Swallows and Amazons* film – quaint, old-fashioned and sweetly English. Alternatives include *The Big Lebowski*, *Mr Wick*, *Stand Up Guys* (the best buddy movie ever made) and *The Equalizer* (the film version starring Denzil Washington rather than the sadly dated television series starring Edward Woodward). I am also looking forward to the latest series of *Elementary*, the excellent American series about a modern day version of Sherlock Holmes starring Johnny lee Miller as Sherlock and Lucy Lu as a surprisingly effective Dr Joan Watson. (The Johnny Lee Miller version is clever, witty, true to the spirit of Conan Doyle and infinitely preferable to the appallingly pretentious and laughable Cumberbatch version.) Other films on the shortlist include: *My Cousin Vinny* (starring Joe Pesci), *Cockneys and Zombies* and *Hopscotch* (starring Walter Matthau). Tons of old Cary Grant movies. *The Thin Man* series starring the immaculate and perfect William Powell and Myrna Loy. (The original *Thin Man*, shot in 1934 in 12 days, is still one of the sharpest, brightest film comedies of all time. The five sequels maintained the standard.) And…oh…the list is endless. We have a huge film library.

Christmas may have to be extended beyond Twelfth Night.

11

It is being suggested by The Idiots who now seem to run everything these days that wild wolves and wild bears should be released into the English countryside in order to keep down the rampaging hordes of wild deer which the rest of us haven't seen but which the Idiots say are now out of control.

And what will the idiots do when the wild wolves and the wild bears get out of control?

Introduce some wild lions and tigers I suppose

You couldn't make this stuff up, could you?

12

Acquaintances of ours recently bought a house on an isthmus. We sent them a house warming greeting. Antoinette created a card which says 'Happy Isthmus.'

We had a series of wrong number telephone calls. Eventually, I got fed up.

'This is the police,' I said sternly, when a woman muttered something incomprehensible.

'Oh dear, I am sorry,' she said, suddenly sober and entirely comprehensible. 'I'm very sorry. I misdialled.'

'Don't do it again!' I said sternly, and put the receiver down sharply.

13

An acquaintance of ours told me that he needs new reading glasses but that he won't go to the optician in case they report him to the authorities and he loses his driving licence. He says his sight is perfectly fine for driving but that he has heard of several people who found that an innocent visit to have their eyes tested resulted in their losing their licences. Our acquaintance lives in the country and points out that without a licence and a car he would be under permanent house arrest.

I have had three unhappy experiences with opticians. One told me I had macular degeneration when I hadn't. One in Devon tried to flog me new spectacles I didn't need. And the other, in Somerset, tried to test my visual fields with a screen which was dirty. If I hadn't wiped the screen with a tissue and insisted on a repeat test I would have been diagnosed as suffering with glaucoma or a brain tumour.

This evening I had an email from Talktalk who told me 'We believe you are now paying more than you have to. That means now may be a good time for a plan review with one of our advisors.'

And so another half an hour of my life will be wasted.

Why do I have to ring all these people every few months? It's not just the phone people. They're all at it. The utility people all write and tell me that I am paying too much and that I must ring them to fix up a better deal.

Why don't these people just give me the better deal and stop wasting my time? Why do they make me ring up to avoid being scalped? Why can't we do it all online? They insist on sending me email bills. They want to do everything online when it suits them.

But when they want me to communicate with them I have to use the bloody telephone, press 1, press 837, press 2737 and then wait a week until Avril has finished painting her bloody nails and can talk to me about the 197 choices which are available and which I know I will never understand.

14

We watched *Let it Ride* – one of my favourite films. Richard Dreyfus is magnificent as the gambler who is having a wonderful day but Robbie Coltrane, as the sympathetic bookmaker's clerk very nearly steals the movie. (In the same sort of way that Sam Elliot, the cowboy, very nearly steals *The Big Lebowski* from Jeff Bridges and John Goldman).

My one claim to fame is that when I was making an awful television series in Scotland, I needed a pair of size 12 wellington boots (don't ask why but I was wearing them indoors and it was Christmas and I also wore a big, white beard) and the only suitable footwear the costume department could find was a pair which had been bought specially for Mr Coltrane.

So I wore Mr Coltrane's wellies.

15

Ronald Reagan, former US President, was and is much derided by the smart bits of the media but he (or his scriptwriters) said the three wisest things ever said by a politician.

1. 'Don't just do something. Stand there.'

2. 'The most terrifying words in the English language are: 'I'm from the Government and I'm here to help you.''

3. 'Government's view of the economy could be summed up in a few short phrases: If it moves, tax it. If it keeps moving, regulate it. And if it stops moving, subsidize it.'

Brilliant.

Those three sayings should be engraved on every politician's heart. And on every civil servant's heart too.

For a very modest fee I'll do the engraving.

16

'I'm a wrapper', he said.

'Oh that's nice. I can never do that properly. I always end up tearing the paper. Do you do those wonderful little bows out of strips of ribbon?'

Him (crossly): 'No, I'm a singer. A rapper.'

'Oh, that's nearly as nice.'

17

Antoinette bought a new steam iron recently. The last one was nearly a year old and well past its sell-by-date. The new one doesn't get rid of wrinkles very well so she now bought a non-steam iron. That does nearly as well as the steam iron. Neither of these expensive irons does the job half as well as an old-fashioned hot iron would do it.

And who can we thank for this deterioration in efficiency?
The EU, of course.
For it was eurocrats who insisted on new regulations which make irons useless.
Here's a quiz for today.
What do David Icke and Jacques Tati have in common.
Answer tomorrow.

18

Publishers have again proudly announced that 'real' book sales are going up after years of losing out to ebook sales.

What they don't say (and what you can easily see if you look at the categories of books being sold) is that 'real' book sales are only rising because those adult colouring-in books and dot-to-dot books are still selling in phenomenal numbers. And they count as 'real' books.

In explaining the supposed increased in sales, publishers say it is because book buyers want to fill their homes with books so that they can show off – and give their pad an old-fashioned 'homely' feel.

And in support of this they point out that loads of people are now taking selfies with their books behind them to show how clever and well-read they are. As I mentioned earlier in this diary, they have borrowed Antoinette's word and call them 'shelfies'.

The answer to yesterday's quiz is that both were professional footballers. And both were goalkeepers.

Facebook has conceded that social media can cause mental illness. Their solution is that sufferers should use social media more not less. This is a commercially brilliant solution and should add a few billion quid to Zuckerberg's wallet – enabling him to promise to leave more of the stuff to good causes at some time in the future. Instead of promising philanthropy, a little more caring just now would go down rather well. Generally speaking, it seems to me that the internet people have a ruthlessness which is quite scary.

(Publicising your philanthropy is common these days. I have, on a number of occasions, seen magazine columns with the words 'The fee for this column has been donated to charity' printed at the bottom. Why do these writers, invariably amateurs, insist on sharing the details of their generosity so publicly?)

The Facebook remedy sounds like one of those utterly insane therapeutic remedies favoured by Sir Roderick Spode, the potty doctor in P.G.Wodehouse's Bertie Wooster stories. Spode recommended that people who drank too much should drink more so that they became bored with the stuff. And he advised people who ate too much to eat and eat and eat on the same rather dubious grounds.

Except that Wodehouse was joking and he was not responsible for the mental health of several billion poor sods around the world.

19

We are in Devon and I woke up to discover that one of our drains is overflowing. What fun. Old houses tend to have peculiar drainage systems which have a mind of their own.

I spent the afternoon on my hands and knees with a bucket. First, you have to get out the water. Then you find the blockage. I looked in the garage for the ubiquitous drain cleaning brushes which are always present in or around properties of a certain size and a certain age but I couldn't find them. They will be there somewhere. We have an insurance policy for the drains (we have individual policies for drains, plumbing, electricity, heating and boiler because our boiler is so large it counts as industrial and cannot be covered on a domestic policy) but I wanted to deal with the problem myself because I hate the process of ringing up, waiting, being rung back, waiting, hoping and being let down.

Eventually, I managed to get the drain working again. Workmen had brushed piles of debris into the drainage system. Once I'd fished out the rubbish they'd deposited down there, the water could flow. The idiots had, believe it or not, swept three bucketfuls of gravel into the drains. Some workmen treat every home like a building site and just don't care how much damage they do. I once watched in horror as an idiot builder poured a can of old diesel into a septic tank.

But I must find the drain brushes. They're bound to be around somewhere; tucked behind old sacks of fertiliser or salt or rock hard cement.

Later, as I had my post prandial coffee, I resumed reading *Print the Legend – the Life and Times of John Ford* by Scott Eyman and it's a brilliant book.

Ford (who won six Oscars and made many of the greatest films of all time) knew everyone from Wyatt Earp to Rudolf Valentino and the stories about his life make gripping reading. He was, without a doubt, a great genius of the cinema. He can't have been an easy man to live with. He could be intensely cruel – as John Wayne, the big bear of a man and the king of the cowboys, could have testified.

I have to confess that my favourite story in the book involves Ford sitting on the lavatory and being told that a journalist has come to interview him.

'That's OK,' said Ford. 'I can deal with two shits at once.'

20

I received a letter from someone who describes herself as a fan. 'I have read all your books,' she says, 'and follow your work with great interest.'

The letter is addressed to Dr Veronica Campbell.

Close, I suppose. The initials were right.

Our drains are blocked again. This is now serious stuff. I had to telephone our drains insurers. They said they will send someone round first thing tomorrow. Knowing our luck there is probably a fully grown seal living in there. Or a walrus. Or some other large beast.

21

At 8.30 a.m. the telephone went. I thought, and hoped, it was the drains man coming to sort out our problem.

It was the insurers ringing to say that the drains man wasn't coming.

I sat down and wept a little. You can survive without electricity, without heat and without a boiler. (We have back up facilities for all of those.) If the water goes off you can buy two dozen bottles and use those for drinking and washing and flushing the loo. But drains are irreplaceable. When the drains aren't working you are stuffed.

Then Antoinette came to the rescue and found a private drains company. They promised to come round this morning. Brilliant! Saved!

And then, a little later, the new drains company telephoned to cancel. They said that they would come late in the afternoon. I told Antoinette to cancel them. It will be dark at 4 p.m. And, besides, one cancellation is enough for me these days.

I drove to the nearest town and bought a new set of drain clearance rods, complete with fancy attachments. (I couldn't find the set I thought we had.) Self-sufficiency rules, OK? I then spent the next three hours messing around with the drains. This involved baling out the blocked drains, with a pudding basin and a bucket, and messing about underground. I managed to clear some stuff but the main drain still wouldn't clear.

And then our insurers came up trumps and found another drains man. He came round at lunchtime, complete with cameras and water jets, and he cleared the problem. It is true that he found a ton of roots growing inside our magnificently complicated drainage system. But that problem can be dealt with next year.

We will have working drains for Christmas. Hoorah! I tipped the drains guy £20 and it was a pleasure to do so.

Astonishingly but not surprisingly 98% of people who buy new homes report defects. These, of course, are houses which were built to satisfy the EU's appallingly low and unsuitable building regulations. And yet the EU wants to knock down solid, well-built old houses or, at the very least, to stop them being sold.

The latest plan is to stop solid, well-made houses being sold if they do not conform to selected insulation standards created by EU eurocrats.

Our best public buildings, bridges, railways and so on, are Victorian but instead of merely updating, mending and revising we knock them down and put up structures made of cardboard which will not last more than a couple of decades. Modern houses might as well be made of paper.

Today, politicians are obsessed with the idea of 'affordable homes'.

An affordable home is, of course, one which satisfies all EU regulations and will be so small that it is claustrophobic and so badly built that it will fall down within a decade or two.

How many of today's affordable homes will still be standing in a century and a half?

I'd guess none.

22

While typing away in Windows, everything suddenly turned red and was underlined. There was also a line on the left of the page that wasn't there moments earlier.

I swear I didn't touch or do anything unusual.

I had to call Antoinette who understands everything.

I hate Windows. It is the most unfriendly, useless, illogical, counterintuitive, over-complicated and appalling piece of software ever invented and Bill Gates should be hung, drawn and quartered before being burnt at the stake. (I am also becoming increasingly annoyed by the fact that Gates is spending a good chunk of his ill-gotten gains on promoting vaccination. It does not seem quite right to me that he, and others like him, should use their money to promote their personal views on public policy and to push vaccination on millions of unsuspecting people.)

I wonder how many people have died of the stress caused by his bloody awful but ubiquitous and unavoidable program

Thankfully, Antoinette did something clever and rescued me.

Today, some Alzheimer researchers have announced that people who eat lots of spinach and kale are less likely to develop dementia.

The only connection I can think of is that both spinach and kale contain lots of iron and lots of vitamins such as vitamins C and K.

Naturally, the media don't seem to have noticed this.

I wonder if the 'Spinach and Kale Farming Cooperative' could be behind the release of this news?

23

I knew that the ravens enjoyed a crisp, morning apple but today, I discovered that the crows also enjoy apples. I watched in astonishment as a crow walked towards an apple, pierced it with a single thrust of his beak and flew off with the apple stuck on his beak as if it were a toffee apple on a stick. I assume he flew somewhere, shook the apple from his beak and ate it at leisure.

24

'Merry Christmas!' called a voice.

I turned around.

'Merry Christmas, Eugene!' said our genial neighbour. He grinned at me. 'I never forget a name,' he said with pride.

'It's a rare and valuable gift,' I told him. I wished him a Happy Christmas.

I know his name but I never use it. It would, I think, take something away from his pride in remembering mine if he knew that I remembered his.

For him, I shall for evermore be Eugene. What's in a name? It is the fact that he makes an effort to remember who I am that really matters.

The funny thing is that neither Antoinette nor I ever gives our correct names to people we meet. I am usually Thomas, Jerome, Pelham or Bertie. Antoinette prefers to be Annabel or Kathy. This may sound silly but we are fed up with people finding me on the web and believing the nonsense they read. I should have used a nom de plume when I started writing but it is a little late now.

This evening we watched *Hercule Poirot's Christmas*. One of our many small traditions.

25

We were not going to have any crackers this year but secretly and privately both Antoinette and I kept looking to see if we could find any worth buying. All I could find were the usual, rubbishy crackers containing metal egg cups, paper dominoes, nail clippers, playing cards too small and thin to be of any use, yoyos which are too light to work properly and the other age-old tat that now appear to be standard fare in all crackers whatever the price. The crackers sold for children have also deteriorated to the point where they are boring.

But Antoinette came up trumps!

She found some marvellous crackers containing decent magic tricks. They weren't cheap but they were well worth the cost.

Not to be entirely outdone, I purchased a variety of small toys for post prandial entertainment over the Christmas period, including: a 100 piece jigsaw, a box of pranks (realistic coffee spill, scary spider, computer screen crack…that sort of thing), a kaleidoscope, a clockwork snowman, a crystal experiment, a balancing game, a packet of bendable glowsticks, a spy camera, a small teddy bear, one of those springs that climbs down steps, a small chemistry set for making magic colour bubbles, magic snow for making an indoor snowman and a couple of gliders in the shape of fairies.

Ho, ho, ho!

Our first snowdrops and primroses are out. The climate change enthusiasts will no doubt blame their favourite disaster theory. But the snowdrops and primroses are always out at this time.

We had a very pleasant bottle of Chateau Gaillard 2006 with our Christmas dinner. Antoinette cooked a magnificent feast. We gave the wildlife extra rations of nuts and apples.

26

We put *The Great Escape* on the DVD player at lunchtime. We always leave it playing while we have lunch.

A wise friend has written to ask what happened to Mad Cow Disease? 'Has it disappeared?' he wants to know. 'Or is it possible that some of the people who have been diagnosed with dementia are really suffering from Mad Cow Disease?'

It is, indeed, very possible that many patients do have Mad Cow Disease but have been diagnosed as suffering from Alzheimer's disease because that is now the default explanation for patients who are demented.

No one looks for the other symptoms of Mad Cow Disease.

This afternoon I watched two crows fly past with twigs in their mouths. Next year's nesting season has clearly started a little early.

27

I never planned what might be called my career in any way. Everything (good and bad) has just happened.

But as I grow older so I have decided that it would be imprudent to do some planning and so I have made myself a plan.

It isn't a bucket list. I think they are largely fake and designed to impress (self or others).

The basic premise is to grow old disgracefully, never declining into weary respectability.

It is said that a wise man will maximise personal comfort without exerting himself unduly, or more than is necessary.

If that is true then I have been as far off the scale in the opposite direction as it is possible to go. I intend to redress this.

I will look after Antoinette, write a few books and re-read all my old favourites.

I see that the film of *Mrs Caldicot's Cabbage War* is being shown yet again on television on New Year's Day. The cast includes Pauline Collins, John Alderton and Peter Capaldi. It is, I believe, the only self-published novel ever to have been turned into a major movie. When you consider that literary and film agents spend their lives pushing novels at film producers it is astonishing that Mrs Caldicot was spotted and that the script won through the process which means that only one in a hundred completed script is ever filmed. The film, which won prestigious awards was hated by the critics who didn't like the idea of a film made about a courageous pensioner but when Antoinette and I saw it in a cinema in Exeter, the entire audience stood up quite spontaneously at the end and applauded. I have never seen that in a cinema before or since. Since the film of Mrs Caldicot was made, films about feisty old people have become commonplace. All of which reminds me, I must get back to the third novel about her and her friends.

28

Here's a thing.

The body ages and the mind ages but the spirit does not age.

Seventy, eighty and ninety-year-olds will tell you to a man or woman that although they may have difficulty climbing the stairs, or may not be able to remember the names of people they know, they still feel the same inside as they did when they were young and just setting out on life's great adventure.

It is strange, is it not, that although we age, and acquire a million experiences, and, hopefully, some wisdom, we still see ourselves in the same way that we did when we were able to run and jump, remember vast amounts of useless stuff and worry endlessly about our acne spots.

Today, I noticed that some of my ebooks are available on a curious website which promises readers free books. I asked Amazon how this could be. They explained that the website doesn't actually provide the books free of charge. It doesn't provide anything. It is, not surprisingly perhaps, a phishing site which collects names and personal data.

29

A British shop assistant reached over and took change out of my hand while I was working out whether I could give her 63 pence in coins or have to put up with being given 37 pence in more change.

And darn me if another one didn't do the same thing ten minutes later.

This is, it seems, another symptom of the way the elderly are treated in Britain.

Shop assistants, most of whom are themselves illiterate and innumerate and unable to add two and two and obtain a result that isn't cabbages unless they have access to something which operates on batteries, automatically assume that because I don't have any visible tattoos I must be potty and suffering from dementia.

Well, bugger them. I am going to buy myself an ear trumpet and carry it everywhere with me. I am not deaf but I will force people to shout into it if they wish to converse with me.

Evelyn Waugh wasn't deaf but he forced people to shout into his ear trumpet because he felt it intimidated and humiliated them. And it also gave the bad-tempered, old bugger a chance to tell them off for shouting.

This is the future for me and for those with whom I come into contact.

Alternatively, I will get one of those large National Health Service hearing aids which are the size of a cigarette packet and which fit into a pocket and connect to the hearing aid by a long wire. The things hiss and make lots of noise.

30

I know that everything I believe could be wrong.

I could be wrong about vaccination, vivisection, global warming and so on.

But knowing that I could be wrong doesn't stop me trying to be right.

If I don't believe that I could be wrong then I am as bigoted, prejudiced and blinkered as 'they' are.

But I do believe that I am right about vaccination, vivisection, global warming and so on. I honestly, passionately believe that I am right. I have studied all the evidence as dispassionately as I can, and with due regard for the quality of the evidence I have examined.

I am, I believe, quite good at analysing scientific papers. I have been doing it for over 50 years so I damned well ought to be pretty good at it by now. When I was in my 20s, writing books such as *The Medicine Men* and *Paper Doctors*, I was lauded by the media for my ability to dissect scientific evidence. (Some of the reviews of both books are on my website www.vernoncoleman.com)

Today, now that I know I am better at that sort of stuff, and have a track record to point to, the establishment sneers or ignores me.

The real problem is that the medical and scientific establishments are owned by the various branches of industry and 'they' do not find it easy to accept that they could be wrong. They won't look at the evidence and they won't debate and they won't allow anyone to publish or broadcast views which are contrary to theirs. And the medical and scientific establishments are as powerful a lobby force as any industry. They control journalists and editors and ensure that nothing too questioning receives any publicity.

I have always regarded my job as making people think a little. Sometimes I have been the grit in the machine.

But now, more than ever, there is no debate and no freedom. This is practical fascism in action. There is no room in the machine for grit.

We live in a world I hardly recognise: overcrowded and overbearing. It is a world which feels uncomfortable; itchy and ill-fitting. The world is full of sneaks and nosy parkers with cameras fixed to their heads; hordes with absolutely no sense of where their business ends and someone else's starts. Privacy is now just a word, rather than an element of morality. Scientific honesty is a distant memory. The bad guys have taken over and we are being manipulated into blind obedience. The fascist hordes are all around us and we have sleep-walked into the hinterlands of oblivion.

I am glad I am no longer a young man.

31

I am going to buy the pipe I have for some time been threatening to purchase. Something rather unusual I think.

I can then point it at people, threaten to light it, puff to avoid questions I don't want to answer, puff thoughtfully, puff to give an impression of wisdom and good sense and enjoy the wonderful associated paraphernalia – silver pokers, and prodders and so on.

And I can pull it out in public places for the fun of watching people complaining even though the damned thing isn't lit. As they grow increasingly hysterical, I will feign ignorance and innocence.

Me a trouble maker?

Don't be silly.

Far too old.

And maybe, after all, I'll buy a boat. I love buying magazines about things which are a mystery to me so I bought another yachting magazine recently.

There is so much choice. We could have a cutter, a ketch, a yawl, a schooner, a motor yacht, a cabin cruiser, a sloops, a MFV, a pinnace or a trawler. Or something unwanted by the navy.

The world is full of nearly new boats for sale. What an excitement that would be. Neither Antoinette nor I has any knowledge of boats so buying one seems a must.

I think I am perhaps reaching an age for adventure.

It will, at least, help me forget and ignore what is going on around us.

I am a year older than I was when I started this diary and nothing has changed to convince me that the world is, generally speaking, a nice place.

Nothing has changed to convince me that common sense, honesty and decency are likely to make a comeback or that hypocrisy and sanctimoniousness are not now the driving forces in human society. I devoutly wish that none of this were true but only a fantasist would believe that it is not. We have had a year in which we have been let down and ripped off mercilessly. (Sometimes both at once). I am, of course, aware that we have much to be grateful for but the letting down and the ripping off can prove tiresome.

(We are all driven by different forces. I am certain that I once wrote a book detailing the many and varied forces which drive our actions. I remember being fascinated by it at the time. But I cannot for the life of me remember what it was called. I do hope this isn't a sign that my brain is turning into porridge.)

Maybe things will change next year.

And that, surely, is as good a definition of optimism as you are likely to find.

What have I learned this year? Well, I have learned that you can never trust the French; cheating, lying and deceiving are the default condition for the frogs.

I have also learned that the elderly are considered fair game for everyone.

And I have learned that the millennials are members of an entirely different species.

Finally, it is now time to put on our DVD of Sherlock Holmes; the episode where Jeremy Brett apparently falls over the Reichenbach Falls. We watch this at the end of every year. And we follow it, immediately after midnight, with the episode when Holmes delights Watson by reappearing as an elderly bookseller. An end of one life and the beginning of a new life. How appropriate.

My resolution for 2018 is a rather sad one.

In view of the number of bad reviews my first diary (*Diary of a Disgruntled Man*) has received in many parts of the world (particularly the UK and the US) I feel there is no point in continuing to write these diaries for publication. Even one really bad review can permanently damage a book's sales. But the real problem is that as a result of a few bad reviews, *Diary of a Disgruntled Man* has a low overall rating, and in the ebook world that is deadly.

New readers see the poor reviews the first diary has been given and so don't bother reading that or any of the other diaries. If no one is going to read them there isn't a lot of point in publishing them. This is not a complaint – merely an observation.

The diaries took up much of my writing life (they are very long and very heartfelt and each diary takes well over 1,000 hours of work) but I am sad that the series has come to an end. It had been my intention to continue with them until the Great Editor in the sky swept down with his Blue Pencil. But I do understand that people either love or hate my style of diary writing.

And I recognise that some readers find them too honest.

I realise, of course, that many readers disagree with some of my views. Of course they do. What a strange world it would be if we all agreed with one another. But, sadly, there are too many people around the world who will these days hammer a book with a damning review solely because they disagree with one or more of the author's opinions or sometimes without even bothering to assess the author's opinions. I have no problem at all with thoughtful reviews but one reviewer (not, I think, in either the UK or the US) admitted that he or she had made his judgement, and given the book one star, after reading just one kindle page of my first diary – a 200,000 word book. I've been writing book reviews for half a century and I would find it impossible to make an assessment after reading less than a thousandth of a book. Another reader from somewhere in the world, who admitted that he or she had read a similar amount of the book, dismissed my book and life as 'boring'. It does hurt when thousands of hours of work are dismissed so lightly. And it is, of course, impossible not to take it personally. A book, especially a diary, is a very personal thing. I stress that this isn't a whinge – it's merely an explanation for a decision I haven't taken lightly, and which I find rather sad.

The (to me) rather awful truth is that most people who are prepared to read diaries want to find out what the author said to

541

Isabella Clingfilm over luncheon, what Simon Nitfellow had to eat and drink at the Twatfart's party, why Douglas Potbelly is leaving the soap opera on which he has been a star for nearly three weeks and why reality television star Johnnie Knucklehead is selling his Mayfair mansion to pop sensation Quentin Lacklustre.

My diaries would have doubtless been more commercial if I had written them when I was working in Fleet Street constantly popping in and out of TV and radio studios. Then I could have filled each day's entry with tittle tattle and gossip. For example, I could have written about the famous diet book author, now sadly deceased, who promoted healthy eating with enormous vigour, but who lived on a diet of chips eaten out of paper bags and plastic take away trays. Or I could have explained how I had frequently been commissioned by national newspapers to write major features to fit television advertising campaigns which had already been filmed and booked.

I understand too that a lot of readers prefer their diaries to be remorselessly upbeat, without going into any of those annoying disappointments and distractions which tend to affect real life and bop you on the neck when you aren't looking. And some readers would have doubtlessly been happier if I had edited out repeated references to things I care about.

In short, I should, perhaps, have edited my life and been more gruntled.

So the end of the diaries is a result of two fundamental errors. First, I have been too honest. I should have kept my opinions to myself – or stuck to the official party lines. Second, I shouldn't have shared my ups and downs. The diaries would then have been more commercial and they would have certainly attracted less vitriol.

Actually, come to think of it I have miscounted.

There were three fundamental errors.

The third error was to refuse to accept that humour in general and irony in particular are only acceptable when the object is an acceptable target. It is permissible to make fun of the elderly, of heterosexual males and of the English. But you must not, under any circumstances, make jokes about foreigners, the European Union or the Corbynistas. My word, no, you must not do that. Too many people only approve of jokes when the targets are acceptably unapproved.

Mea culpa. But no apologies.

And so, without regret and with no further ado, this is the last diary which I shall publish. My diaries are three times as long as most books. They take me a long time to write and they take Antoinette a huge amount of time to edit and to turn into ebooks. The process is surprisingly complicated and removing literals and the worst grammatical howlers from a daily diary can be time consuming. There are only the two of us and I invariably insist that Antoinette stops and moves onto the next project before she has finished a second or third reading of the text. (It is, therefore, entirely my fault if the diaries contain literals which we missed. However, this doesn't stop Antoinette (without whom I would have never published any ebooks at all) from getting terribly upset every time she reads an Amazon review pointing out that a particular book contains grammatical errors or literals (which we simply missed when editing a 200,000 word book). She blames herself because she cares. Antoinette's upset is made far worse, of course, by the fact that the reviews are there forever even if the books have been updated since the reviews were written.). To answer the question which I asked myself at the start of this diary: 'Yes, I probably will continue to keep a diary. But it will not be tidied up for publication.'

I shall carry on writing other books (it's the only thing I now know how to do).

But Antoinette and I will live our tumultuous, sometimes unusual, rather roller coaster life in silence and privacy, well away from those who think that a book which does not mention Gloucester Cathedral must inevitably be damned with a one star review.

I would like to thank very much indeed those readers who have been kind enough to say that they have enjoyed parts, some or all of the diaries. A special thanks to those who have read all six. Bless you! May those who would harm you be overcome by confusion and numb with bewilderment. And may you and those whom you love be blessed with never ending kindness and eternal tranquillity.

I hope you will visit us in future stories about Bilbury; you will be most welcome.

Thank you for your courtesy, your patience and your company.

Finally, I would be enormously grateful if readers who have found this book, in part or in whole, stimulating or entertaining, or even both, would find the time to give it a decent rating. Otherwise the book will doubtless die and my variety of freedom of speech will take another kicking. Thank you.

Vernon Coleman

Author! Author!

A short, unedited biography of the author contributed without charge by his friend 'Patchy' Fogg
('Patchy' Fogg is a long-term resident of the village of Bilbury. He is an antiques dealer and Vernon Coleman's brother-in-law.)

Vernon Coleman is tall and now has less hair than would be considered appropriate for a television presenter or politician. He does, however, have most of his own teeth and nails which is pretty good for an old bloke. He is a qualified doctor and long-term iconoclast who seems intelligent enough but who is stupid enough to write what he believes, with the aim of making people think. This was definitely not a particularly wise career choice for he has attracted a good deal of spiteful criticism from those parts of the medical establishment (such as the drug industry) which have been annoyed by his books and articles.

He was a successful self-published author long before self-publishing became fashionable and this annoyed the publishing establishment. To make things worse he has been quite good at it and has sold a lot of books. The only thing that annoys the publishing establishment more than an author who self publishes is an author who self publishes and turns out to be moderately good at it. Every time someone buys one of his books, you can hear editors and literary agents gnashing their teeth at their lost commissions.

(If you have already spotted a pattern here then you're spot on. The silly bugger has spent much of his life annoying people with power. Pretty stupid but there you go, someone's got to do it otherwise the people in power would get too complacent.)

Vernon's early books were published by many leading London publishers but he chose to self-publish when no one would publish a book called *Alice's Diary*.

Just about every publisher in London turned this one down on the twin grounds that it wasn't the sort of thing he usually wrote and that in any case there was no market for a book purporting to be a diary written by a cat. Silly buggers.

After he had sold more than 60,000 hardback copies, Vernon decided that posh publishers and agents didn't know more about publishing than he did so he'd publish more of his books himself.

Within a few years, Vernon and his missus (whom you will have doubtless met in the Bilbury books) were running a large self-publishing operation from Publishing House, a specially converted building in Barnstaple where he employed over a dozen members of staff. Always a free spirit he said that he enjoyed publishing his own books because he did not have to deal with editors or marketing people and could write whatever he chose to write.

'You mean to tell me that you write whatever you want to write, publish it and then make money?' said one snotty broadsheet journalist from the *Sunday Telegraph*, who was appalled by Vernon's way of working. I was there when she said it and I couldn't believe it, to be honest. In Britain, any sort of success is regarded as embarrassing and rather shameful. (My own experiences as a decently successful antiques dealer based in Bilbury in North Devon confirm this!). His success as a self-publisher attracted a whole new collection of enemies among journalists. (You'd think the idiot would have learned, wouldn't you?)

The Advertising Standards Authority (which is a private body, funded by large advertisers, but which has taken pomposity to a new level and which I suspect likes to give the impression that it is an arbiter of public taste as far as ads are concerned) frequently complained noisily about adverts which upset large corporate interests but VC delighted in continuing to use the same 'banned' adverts for years after the ASA had stuck its stick in his spokes. I remember he was particularly delighted when *The Guardian* newspaper, which most of us in Bilbury have always considered to be a disgustingly sanctimonious and hypocritical rag, agreed to publish (in return for a 'bribe' of something north of £60,000) a series of full page adverts which had been 'banned' by the fact-averse Advertising Standards Authority. Vernon didn't sell any books through the ads (he didn't expect to) but regarded the

546

£60,000 as well spent since it proved beyond doubt that the supercilious *The Guardian* is full of hypocrisy and that when it comes down to a straight fight with money, the Advertising Standards Authority is as toothless as gummy old Archibald Burroughs who does a bit of furniture restoration for me sometimes.

So that was the ASA to add to the growing list of enemies.

Vernon's many books include *Mrs Caldicot's Cabbage War* (which is believed to be the only self-published novel to be turned into a full-length feature film) and the books about the village of Bilbury in North Devon which sell all around the world and which have been bestsellers in some pretty funny places. We get Japanese readers coming to the village quite frequently and as long as they keep buying William Shakespeare's battered old writing desk, I don't mind a bit. They're a nice bunch, to be honest. Actually, Shakespeare's old beds are doing better than his writing desk these days. (Contact me c/o the Duck and Puddle if you want an original bed as slept in by the great dramatist himself.)

Born in Walsall in 1946, Vernon went to the local grammar school, Queen Mary's Grammar School. I've never been there but I'm told that Walsall used to be in Staffordshire until some blokes in cheap suits with dandruff on the collar and lapels moved the whole place into somewhere called the West Midlands. It's probably in Wales by now.

After leaving school, our young hero spent a year working in a place called Kirkby, which is just outside Liverpool, as a Community Service Volunteer. In Liverpool, Vernon organised a small army of volunteers and arranged for them to perform chores such as decorating the homes of the elderly and the poor. This activity proved surprisingly popular with the elderly and the poor and the young people who did the work who regarded it as rather jolly, but it was understandably very unpopular with bureaucrats and trade unions who, predictably, all did a good deal of whingeing and complaining. More enemies for young Coleman.

While in Liverpool, VC began writing for newspapers and was appointed drama critic for a number of local newspapers including the *Kirkby Reporter*, which may have had a circulation of only three but by all accounts they were a pretty feisty three.

After that, Vernon Coleman went to Birmingham University to study medicine. While supposed to be studying bones and rashes, he ran a rather wild youth club called The Gallows in the centre of the city. This was designed to attract teenagers who had nowhere to go in the evenings. The place was popular with a pretty rough crowd and VC kept order by carrying a Victorian swordstick and waving it around whenever anyone pulled a knife or started fighting. If you're a tearaway with a flick knife you tend to have respect for someone who pulls a three foot long blade out of his walking stick. These days, the Old Bill would have had him locked up but in those days they didn't bother about stuff like that unless you actually stuck the blade through someone important. He's still got the swordstick. I've seen it. Impressive. I want him to sell it to me but he won't part with it.

While supposed to be reading big, thick books on neurology and ophthalmology et al, young Master Coleman also reviewed books and plays for the *Birmingham Post, The Times Educational Supplement* and a variety of other publications. Heaven knows how he found the time.

After hospital posts in Leamington Spa in the English Midlands and Shoreham on the South Coast he became a General Practitioner and if you've read the Bilbury books you'll know all about that. In those days, GPs had no specific training and Coleman insists that on the morning when he started work as a GP, he had no idea how to write a prescription or a sick note. ('I hadn't been in a GP's surgery since boyhood when I had visited as a patient,' he told me.)

He resigned from the health service in protest at being required to write diagnoses on sick notes which were, by law, made available to a patient's employer. He quite reasonably argued that this was a breach of the confidentiality aspect of the Hippocratic Oath. Shortly after his resignation, the law was changed which probably proves something or other.

In 1975, his first book *The Medicine Men* was published and both this and the sequel, *Paper Doctors*, received extensive, largely laudatory review coverage in the national press and on television. The papers quickly realised that this was a mistake since it really pissed off some very important people in the Establishment and so this was the last time this would happen.

The Medicine Men, which was serialised in *The Guardian* newspaper (which now probably prefers to keep quiet about the association) was a powerful critique both of the pharmaceutical industry's marketing practices and of the medical profession's close links with the pharmaceutical industry. Coleman was stupid enough to be the first author to draw attention to this dangerous relationship. It has done him no good at all. But it did collect some more enemies. And since collecting enemies is his favourite hobby you have to count it a success.

In the sequel, called *Paper Doctors*, Coleman made things even worse for himself by arguing that much medical research was a waste of money and effort and that doctors would do better to spend time taking advantage of the useful research which had already been done and ignored.

Pretty daft, eh?

Not surprisingly, Coleman immediately made enemies of those parts of the medical establishment which had not been annoyed by the first book. He has been pilloried by doctors, drug companies and everyone else owning a white coat ever since.

These two books were quickly followed by a series of a number of other titles: a mixture of polemics and popular health books. In 1978, Coleman wrote a book called *Stress Control*, which was the first popular medical book on the subject of stress. This one sold van loads and actually made him a bit of money.

Under the pen name, Edward Vernon, he wrote three 'funny doctor' novels for Pan/Macmillan in the UK and for St Martin's Press in the US. For some reason or other, these books have been reported to be autobiographical. I can tell you for a fact that they are not. The stories in the books were, as he says, 'made up'.

His literary agent (at a posh London agency called Curtis Brown) at the time suggested that he use the pen name because he was busy writing non-fiction medical books under his own name and she apparently thought that writing two types of book under one name would prove too confusing for publishers, bookshops and reviewers. She was probably right. There are some pretty stupid people working in publishing.

His book *Bodypower*, published in 1983, explained how the human body can protect and repair itself. This was his first major bestseller – appearing in the *Sunday Times* top ten and becoming a huge success when serialised in the *Sunday Mirror* newspaper. It was subsequently serialised in newspapers around the world.

Other notable health titles included *Life without Tranquillisers* (also a *Sunday Times* top ten bestseller) and *Aspirin or Ambulance*, published in 1980. The latter title was turned into the world's first medical software for home computers and subsequently sold in 26 countries. Coleman now gets slightly peeved when he is described as a Luddite simply because he has not embraced social media. He has never had a Facebook page or a Twitter account – regarding both as being more suitable for small children and the Entitlement Generation. I agree with him. My five-year-old tweets and plays on his Facebook page. And so does his Granny. It's no way for a grown up to spend their time. Today, everyone demands to be heard whether or not they have anything worth saying. Good sense is drowned in stormy seas of dross.

Over the years, Vernon's numerous books were published by many of Britain's leading hardback and paperback publishers and foreign language versions were published by over a score of overseas publishers. His books were regularly published in large print and audio versions.

In 1980, Robert Hale published his novel *Tunnel* under the name Marc Charbonnier. (Over the years Coleman has, like many other prolific authors, written books under a number of other pen names. I did know what the others were but I wrote them down and lost the bit of paper.)

From the early 1980s onwards, Coleman was a regular presenter and guest on a number of television and radio programmes including the Afternoon Show which was broadcast from Glasgow. He was television's first agony uncle on this programme, which was, despite the name, broadcast in the afternoons. (Amazing, where these television people get their ideas isn't it?) I saw one or two of the programmes and to be perfectly honest with you, they were pretty dire. He was the regular doctor on TV AM, which was the first of those breakfast telly shows. (Why do people watch television at that time in the morning?) He made several series of programmes based on his book *Bodypower*. In the 1980s and 1990s, whenever a new book was published, he toured the country for several weeks – often doing 30 to 40 radio and television interviews in each promotional campaign. I expect he found that fun because it gave him a chance to go around the country making new enemies.

He was the first doctor to record a series of recordings which could be accessed through premium rate telephone numbers and his service, known as The Telephone Doctor, was hugely popular and was used by several million people in the 1980s. (I bet it made the old bugger a mint.) He also invented the phrase *People Watching* for a book of the same name.

While still a student at university, Vernon contributed to a wide range of newspapers and including *The Guardian* and the *Daily Telegraph* and magazines such as *The Spectator*, *The Lady* and *Punch*. He wrote columns for several medical magazines. Although still a medical student, he also wrote a weekly 'doctor' column which was syndicated to 40 to 50 local and regional newspapers in the UK and to a number of newspapers in various parts of the Commonwealth. Bit cheeky that was.

After qualifying he was the original editor of the *British Clinical Journal* and continued to write columns and regular pieces for most national newspapers and a wide variety of magazines in the UK and abroad.

In the 1980s, Coleman became a columnist for both the *Daily Star* newspaper and *The Sun*, both sequentially and simultaneously. He was *The Sun* doctor for about a decade and that helped him speed up the rate at which he was collecting enemies.

His *Daily Star* campaign about benzodiazepine drugs led directly to a change in government policy. He also wrote a column under a pen name (Dr Duncan Scott) for *The People* newspaper and for a year or so had the curious distinction of writing columns for three major tabloid newspapers at the same time – two of them under his own name. More or less at the same time he also wrote weekly columns for the *Sunday Independent*, the *Sunday Scot* and the *Sunday Correspondent* and was still writing the weekly column which was syndicated to between 40 and 50 local newspapers. Many of the columns were also syndicated to newspapers in Australia, South Africa and Asia. He even wrote a column for a newspaper in China for a while. He left when the Chinese publisher refused to print an article on vaccination. As a result of that indiscretion, his Chinese book publishers were told that they could not print any more of his previously very successful books.

So he even made enemies in China, which is pretty impressive going.

In 1993, Coleman moved to *The Sunday People* newspaper to write a column under his own name. He continued to write this until 2003, resigning when the paper's editor refused to publish a piece criticising the Iraq War. At the time, Coleman was one of Britain's highest paid columnists.

In addition to all these columns, Vernon also wrote over 5,000 articles and columns for major newspapers and magazines. Honest. I've seen the filing cabinets.

Throughout the 1980s and 1990s, Coleman was a keen campaigner on animal rights issues, regularly speaking at large rallies in the UK and abroad. He founded and funded an organisation called Plan 2000, aimed at eradicating animal experiments, which received considerable celebrity and popular support, including support from many MPs. Coleman gave evidence about the pointlessness of animal experimentation to committees at the House of Commons and the House of Lords. He also campaigned vigorously against vaccination, which he considered far more dangerous than was widely appreciated and, long before it became popular to do so, for the legalisation of recreational drugs.

In support of his campaigns, he has distributed thousands of his books free of charge and provided numerous columns without charge. He has also spoken widely at many events (including rallies in Trafalgar Square.)

These, and other campaigns, succeeded in annoying the people who had failed to be annoyed by his books and resulted in many attacks from and inspired by the drug industry, the medical establishment and others. Coleman was, inevitably, the victim of many libellous and widely inaccurate articles both in print and on the internet. Personally, I'd have sued the bastards but Vernon preferred to just disappear off the scene and spend more time with his good lady and the animals.

After they had lost a number of high profile television debates on animal experimentation, opponents refused to appear with him and even a planned debate at the Oxford Union had to be cancelled after the Union found it impossible to find anyone prepared to speak against him. Instead of debating with him, his opponents chose to organise a massive campaign of abuse and misinformation.

Distressed by the many attacks, which were matched in their inaccuracy only by their venom, Vernon chose to become a recluse; disappearing almost entirely from view and speaking only through his books.

What have I forgotten? Oh, back in the 1980s, he established a number of websites, including www.vernoncoleman.com.

Vernon Coleman's books have always sold well outside the UK, where the attacks from the establishment have been more muted. I gather that his books have been particularly successful in Portugal and Germany though heaven knows why.

Throughout the 1990s and the early part of the 21st century, Coleman continued to write a number of books on health, books on animal issues, and books on politics. Many of these, books such as *England our England* and *Gordon is a Moron* were hugely successful. (I liked that one called *Gordon is a Moron*. Frank, the landlord of our local pub, put it in the window until the cover faded.) For several years, Coleman also wrote a monthly Health Letter which was distributed to several thousand readers in the UK and around the world. He also wrote a number of successful novels including *The Village Cricket Tour* and *The Man Who Inherited a Golf Course*. Many of his novels sold over 30,000 copies each in the UK in hardback but because they were self-published, did not count for the official bestseller lists. *Mrs Caldicot's Cabbage War* was, of course, turned into a popular full-length feature film starring Pauline Collins as Mrs Caldicot and John Alderton as a nursing home owner. We watch it every time it's on the telly.

His non-fiction books included a successful and very personal guide to Paris called *Secrets of Paris*. For a couple of decades, Vernon and his wife had spent several months a year in a large, top floor flat just a two minute walk away from the Eiffel Tower in Paris.

The publishing business became successful because Coleman had acquired a large and loyal readership. Nearly every one of his books sold out and was reprinted many times and Coleman wrote a number of successful books together with his missus. During the most successful years of the self-publishing business, annual sales exceeded those of many well-known small publishing houses. So that meant a few more enemies in the book trade.

(I tried to make a list of the people he's pissed off. Here's a short list of the ones he's pissed off most: the entire medical establishment; the drugs industry; the meat trade; the BBC; the tobacco industry; the arms industry; the ASA; all politicians; the European Union; everyone who is politically correct; social workers; alternative medicine practitioners and – oh, you get the idea.)

When the publishing business was threatened by the soaring cost of postage and the advent of ebooks, he closed Publishing House, intending to retire. However, his wife persuaded him to publish his books as ebooks. Thanks to Patsy/Antoinette's skill and determination in converting the books and Coleman's experience in self-publishing this proved to be an enormous success and the series of books about Bilbury (retitled *The Young Country Doctor*) became bestsellers on Amazon in the US. (In those books, Antoinette is called Patsy but I'm still 'Patchy' Fogg. I've never worked that out but one of these days I'm going to demand royalties.)

Over 60 of his old titles, including the now out of print Edward Vernon novels, were republished as ebooks and Coleman wrote a number of new novels and non-fiction books especially for the ebook market. Coleman happily admitted that without his wife's support, encouragement and knowledge he would not have published any of his books in the electronic format. (Bloody right too!) So I suppose we can blame her for that. (Just kidding Patsy/Antoinette!)

There seems to be some confusion about whether his Bilbury books are entirely factual, entirely fictional or a judicious mixture of both. All I can say is that if the books aren't true then how come I'm writing this? And how do you explain the fact that our friend 'Thumper' Robinson took some cover pictures for the few hardback editions that were published?

Coleman has also published a series of diaries (starting with the *Diary of a Disgruntled Man*), which divided readers: some loved them and some loathed the freedom with which he expressed politically incorrect opinions. As with many of his books, the reviews from readers tended to be either glowing or condemnatory.

I think his diaries are a bit like fish stew and rice pudding. If you like them that's fine, if you don't like them then you don't like them and that's that.

In the first part of his life, Coleman, who is a member of the MCC and a number of other clubs, was a keen cricket spectator. He says he gave up watching cricket when 'they started painting adverts on the pitch'. I don't blame him one bit for that. He is an inveterate bibliophile, with a huge collection of first editions, and has owned a number of classic Bentley motor cars and one Rolls Royce. Not my cup of tea. Big cars are comfortable but you couldn't get a bookcase in the back of any of them and if you're an antiques dealer you need to be able to get a bookcase in the back.

Vernon and Antoinette Coleman moved from Devon to Gloucestershire in 2010, where they bought an isolated house in the country. Eventually, they decided that the house was not isolated enough and in 2016 they moved back to Devon and to Bilbury which was probably the most sensible thing they'd ever done. They purchased a large Arts and Crafts house perched on the cliffs. The house has views often described as the best in England. It's good to have them back where they belong.

So, to sum up, Vernon Coleman is an iconoclast who writes his non-fiction with the aim of making people think and his fiction with the aim of making people smile.

Will that do, Vernon? Chop out anything you don't like and correct anything that's terribly inaccurate.

You owe me a drink. I'll drop this off at your house and see you in the Duck and Puddle later.

Patchy

Printed in Great Britain
by Amazon